ESSAYS ON SCANDINAVIAN HISTORY

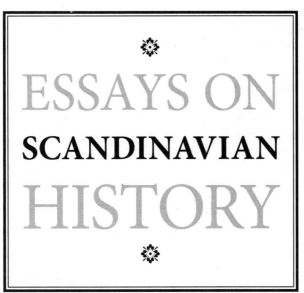

ESSAYS ON SCANDINAVIAN HISTORY

H. Arnold Barton

Southern Illinois University Press
Carbondale

12 11 10 09   4 3 2 1

Publication of this book was subsidized by the
Nordic Cultural Fund, Copenhagen, and by the
Royal Patriotic Society and Letterstedtska Society,
Stockholm.

Nordisk Kulturfond

Library of Congress Cataloging-in-Publication Data
Barton, H. Arnold (Hildor Arnold), 1929–
   Essays on Scandinavian history / H. Arnold Barton.
      p. cm.
   Includes bibliographical references and index.
   ISBN-13: 978-0-8093-2886-4 (pbk. : alk. paper)
   ISBN-10: 0-8093-2886-0 (pbk. : alk. paper)
   1. Scandinavia—History. I. Title.
   DL78.B36 2009
   948—dc22   2008022430

Printed on recycled paper. ♻
The paper used in this publication meets the minimum
requirements of American National Standard for Information Sciences—Permanence of Paper for Printed
Library Materials, ANSI Z39.48-1992. ♾

Contents

Illustrations

Preface

Why should someone born and raised by the shore of the Pacific Ocean in southern California devote his scholarly career to the Scandinavian North and to its offspring in North America? But then, why indeed should anyone take up the history and culture of any part of the world other than one's own?

All history, it is said, is contemporary. It all has something significant to tell us about the human condition. We do not think it strange that outsiders become experts in the histories of, say, Britain, France, or Germany. To the study of other lands, the outsider, unencumbered by entrenched national traditions, may bring new and different perspectives. Scandinavia, too, has its own particular excitement, fascination, and relevance. Moreover, the eminent British historian of Sweden Michael Roberts once said, as I recall, that in the cold, clear air of the North, the essential issues of history emerge in sharper focus than in larger and more heterogeneous lands.

My first exposure to Scandinavia came during the winter of 1948–49 when fresh out of high school I had the opportunity to spend a couple of months in Sweden, both in Stockholm and in rural Hälsingland. It was then that I began to learn the language, together with a good deal about Swedish life and traditions. I was also able to visit, more briefly, both Norway and Denmark.

That experience would prove pivotal for my future. It powerfully reinforced the fascination I had always felt with my father's ancestral Sweden and it Nordic neighbors. Eventually, while at Princeton graduate school in the later 1950s, my professors, in particular my revered mentor R. R. Palmer, encouraged me to take up Scandinavian topics because of my rather unusual language qualification. It was through my dissertation research that I met in New York Aina Margareta Bergman from Solna, Sweden, whom I married in her medieval parish church, in 1960. The direction of my life and work was set. More times than I can recall now we have commuted to Sweden for longer or shorter periods, and there I have done much of my research.

This collection of my selected essays on Nordic, especially Swedish, history is intended as a companion volume to my earlier *The Old Country and the New: Essays on Swedes and America* (2007), a similar selection of my shorter writings on the Swedish emigration and Swedes in North America. From around 1970, much of my research has been in Swedish-American history. Yet I was active as a scholar of the history of Sweden itself for a decade before taking up its transatlantic aspect, and so I have always remained. Many of my readers and even some of my colleagues have been familiar with only the one side or the other of my work as a historian. This volume is therefore meant to redress that imbalance.

Several of the essays selected here came about in connection with books I was writing or had written on Nordic history. The first of these was *Count Hans Axel von Fersen: Aristocrat in an Age of Revolution* (Boston, 1975). As the illustrious count's life and career were closely intertwined with the American and French Revolutions and the Napoleonic Wars, my biography of him led in due course to my *Scandinavia in the Revolutionary Era, 1760–1815* (Minneapolis, 1986). In my research, I meanwhile frequently cited the writings of outside visitors to the Nordic countries, resulting in my *Northern Arcadia: Foreign Travelers in Scandinavia, 1765–1815* (Carbondale, Illinois, 1998). My book *A Folk Divided: Homeland Swedes and Swedish Americans, 1840–1940* (Carbondale, Illinois, 1994) had meanwhile led me on into new areas of Swedish history during the nineteenth and twentieth centuries as they related in various ways to the emigration and emigrants. My most recent book on Nordic history, *Sweden and Visions of Norway: Politics and Culture, 1814–1905* (Carbondale, Illinois, 2003), about strong Norwegian influences in Sweden during the Swedish-Norwegian dynastic union, built in part upon the foundation in this later period that *A Folk Divided* provided.

These essays, in the order they are presented here, reveal gradual changes of focus in my work in Nordic history over time. The earlier ones dealt almost entirely with Sweden, in particular those devoted to the "Gustavian" era: the reigns of Gustav III (1771–92) and Gustav IV Adolf (1792–1809). As time passed my interests came increasingly to encompass the Nordic region as a whole and broadened from politics, war, and diplomacy to deal increasingly with social, economic, and cultural questions. In this book I include an inclusive, chronological bibliography of my writings in Nordic history. (For my work in Swedish-American history, see the bibliography in *The Old Country and the New*.)

In preparing the essays given here, I have made some alterations, following the same principles as in *The Old Country and the New*. I condensed certain passages to avoid undue repetition between the articles and occasionally added words or phrases to provide necessary background for persons who lacked much knowledge about Scandinavian history. I also deleted some comments that were purely topical at the time they were written. A few minor changes or additions have been based on later research, by myself or by others. Citations are made to certain works that have come out since these essays first appeared, as evident from their dates of publication. My aim is once again to present research that is appropriately current. The original articles can, of course, be found in the periodicals or collaborative volumes in which they first appeared.

Going over these essays I am again reminded of all my many debts to colleagues, friends, and students on both sides of the Atlantic. They are far too many to list here, and I realize all too well that some of my ideas and leads I owe to persons or their writings I can no longer even recall. To all, my sincere thanks. I am grateful to Wayne Larsen for his sharp-eyed editing of my manuscript. Aina, my devoted wife for nearly five decades, deserves special recognition for bearing up with and loyally supporting me during all the times I have dwelt obliviously in the distant realms of the past.

Finally, this book is dedicated to the memory of the late Professor Sten Carlsson of Uppsala University, my steadfast friend, source of inspiration, and in the early days my informal mentor in Swedish history on both sides of the Atlantic.

ESSAYS ON SCANDINAVIAN HISTORY

The Swedes and Their Eighteenth Century

For an at least partial outsider like myself, the intriguing question must naturally occur: why are the Swedes so particularly enamored with the eighteenth century? Further, what is it that makes one feel its ambiance as somehow more intense and alive in Sweden than perhaps anywhere else?

The question becomes more fascinating yet because of the apparent paradox it poses. Sweden, during the eighteenth century, was a remote, rugged, thinly populated northern outpost, far from the European heartland and a latecomer to the world of European higher culture. It still contains today much of the continent's last remaining undisturbed nature. Sweden's now mainly urban inhabitants, while they may picture themselves as a nation of cool-headed, hypermodern technocrats and engineers, at the same time pride themselves on being hardy nature lovers and characteristically escape at every opportunity to their primitive *stugor*, or cabins, in the woods, out onto the storm-blown Baltic, or up to Lapland's tundra.

The same conditions apply in varying degree to the other Nordic lands. Yet in none of them is fascination with the eighteenth century so strong. It strikingly reveals the Swedes' characteristic search for an ideal balance between *natur och kultur*—nature and culture—which appropriately is the name of one of Stockholm's leading publishing houses. Fit-looking blond culture enthusiasts on their way out to a baroque chamber music

1

concert at Sturehov manor on the Stockholm subway, clad in their sturdy Fjällräv parkas, may give something of the picture. It seems an attraction of opposites.

The Swedes' special preoccupation with the eighteenth century cannot be a question of the overall number of preserved buildings, furnishings, works of art, and literary and musical accomplishments from that period. In this regard Sweden is easily surpassed by several other European countries. Perhaps Sweden's relative poverty in population and capital long delayed its economic development while protecting a rigid, traditional social structure, which contributed significantly to the preservation of the nation's older cultural milieus in both countryside and town, until the time came when their conservation became a matter of priority. Sweden meanwhile never underwent a violent, iconoclastic break with its entire ancien régime, unlike France and other parts of the Western world. Still, the question remains: why is just the *eighteenth century* such an enduring presence in the Swedish cultural landscape?

The reason seems, up to a point, to have been quite prosaic. In comparison with the numerous palaces and manor houses, churches, parsonages and other official residences, inns, farm buildings, burghers' homes, garden pavilions, and even entire town quarters from the eighteenth century that have been lovingly preserved, architectural relics from earlier periods in Sweden—except for the purely ecclesiastical—are surprisingly few. Stockholm's Old City and, above all, medieval Visby are of course notable exceptions in this regard. Anyone who browses in Stockholm's many antique shops will find them crammed with furniture, painting, silver, porcelain, crystal, and other objects from the eighteenth century, or later replicas and imitations thereof.

Fascination with the eighteenth century is certainly not unique to Sweden. It is widely shared throughout the Western world. But most western and southern European lands have much longer recorded histories that offer a wider variety of memorable periods in their past to glorify—classical antiquity, the Middle Ages, the Renaissance—as well as many more venerable remnants in stone and brick.

In a region rich in forests, most building in Scandinavia was in wood, which was constantly decimated by decay or, more often, by fire. Furthermore, parts of Sweden's oldest and most developed cultural regions along the Baltic coast were systematically ravaged by Peter the Great's Russian galley fleet in 1719–20, toward the end of the Great Northern War. Reconstruction following the restoration of peace in 1721 has bequeathed to posterity many of Sweden's most characteristic and best preserved cultural monuments. After the long war there was much new construction and economic development throughout the kingdom. Older structures were meanwhile remodeled along new lines.

The English visitor Edward Daniel Clarke, who traveled through much of Sweden and Finland—then also part of the realm—was impressed in 1799 by the "unvaried uniformity" of the town architecture, as well as much else, that he saw.[1] Surely the total impression the Swedish eighteenth-century ambiance creates today is in large part due to its remarkably integral character. This integrity was, of course, no accident. It was the result not only of habit or social convention but also of public authority. Sweden was, since the seventeenth century, a bureaucratized and disciplined state.

The royal architect Niccodemus Tessin, the younger, was appointed in 1697 royal overintendant (*överintendent*), on the model of Louis XIV's *surintendent des bâtiments* in France, and was followed in this position by his son, Carl Gustaf Tessin, Carl Hårleman, Carl Johan Cronstedt, and Carl Fredrik Adelcrantz, all of them strong creative personalities. Not only the rebuilding of Stockholm's royal palace, the century's crowning edifice, but town planning and construction of public buildings throughout the country, from town halls and tollhouses to parsonages, churches, rural officers' residences, and simple soldiers' cottages, came during the earlier eighteenth century under these architects' centralized control and were built according to their guidelines. Similar control over construction and appearance was exercised in the larger towns by municipal architects like Johan Eberhard Carlberg, who directed the rebuilding of parts of Stockholm's Söder after devastating fires in 1723 and 1759.[2] The examples they set were widely followed in private construction, for instance the many manor houses planned or inspired by Carl Hårleman. Strict, uniform building codes are obviously nothing new in Sweden.

In this setting, one feels even now a strong sense of the new spirit that began to make itself felt after the Great Northern War: relief following the strain of long decades of warfare and the end of the stern, authoritarian Caroline regime, combined with a growing confidence in the future and in the individual's potential for free self-realization. Sweden experienced the same liberation from compulsion and sacrifice as France following Louis XIV's death in 1715. And France was already then and would remain throughout the century the model, above all others, for fashionable Europe, by no means least for Sweden.

The Finland-Swedish art historian Göran Schildt has offered the "heretical" view that Carl XII's defeat at Poltava in 1709 was indeed a blessing in disguise:

There is something overly ambitious, tyrannical, and unfeeling about the palaces of the Swedish "Era of Greatness," a lack of adaptability and of realism that makes the air in their chambers heavy to breathe. Only after Peter the Great freed the Swedes from their illusions did the nation discover itself. . . . Sweden's true Era of Greatness was the eighteenth century.[3]

The relationship between the pleasure-seeking rococo, on the aesthetic level, and the serious, socially oriented Enlightenment, on the intellectual, is complex. Still, both signified conversion from a somber and resigned medieval theology to a new worldview that confidently asserted the individual's right to "life, liberty, and the pursuit of happiness," in the words of the American Declaration of Independence in 1776, one of the key documents of the century. And "happiness"—*la bonté*—the French revolutionary Antoine de St. Just declared, was a new concept in this world. This is a spirit that people in later times have been able to comprehend and appreciate more fully than all that came before.

Throughout the Western world, including Sweden, the eighteenth century brought a rising level of material welfare. Conditions of life generally improved. They were nevertheless hard enough for the great majority. Poverty and misery all too often lay just outside gilded gates and enclosed, carefully landscaped nature. It is against this dark background that Watteau's *fêtes galantes,* Mozart's *divertimenti,* or Carl Michael Bellman's tavern and Djurgården idylls emerge in such a lovely, yet pensive glow, in the tension between bright ideal and somber reality.

Speaking of Bellman, what has he not meant for the Swedes' vision of the eighteenth century! In the eyes of most, Gustaf III appears nowadays as the king who reigned "in Bellman's time." In no other land has a single poet set his stamp so strongly upon posterity's whole conception of a historic epoch.[4] The Swedish artists of the period, such as Niklas Lafrensen, the younger, Elias Martin, Per Hilleström, Carl August Ehrensvärd, and Johan Tobias Sergel—the last more through his lively pen sketches than his polished marble statuary—have also richly contributed to the picture, as has the composer Johan Helmich Roman.

The same is true of the great architects and royal overintendants Niccodemus Tessin, the younger, Carl Hårleman, Carl Fredrik Adelcrantz, and others, who, as seen, set their distinctive stamp upon the cultural landscape. A number of other architects, designers, and skilled craftsmen, such as Jean Eric Rehn, Louis Masreliez, Louis Jean Desprez, Olof Tempelman, and Georg Haupt played their own indispensable parts. Meanwhile, the well-preserved and carefully restored court theaters at Drottningholm and Ulriksdal bear witness to the period's flourishing theatrical and operatic life under Queen Lovisa Ulrika and especially her son, Gustaf III.

It was in this period, too, that Carl von Linné and his widely traveled disciples, together with such luminaries as Anders Celsius, Carl Wilhelm

Gustaf III Receives the Antique Statues from Italy (1896), by Carl Larsson. The mural, in the grand staircase of the National Museum of Art in Stockholm, epitomizes the Swedes' idealized view of aristocratic refinement and aesthetic grace in their land during the eighteenth century. (Courtesy of Nationalmuseum, Stockholm.)

Scheele, Emanuel Swedenborg, and Christopher Polhem achieved distinction in the natural sciences, mathematics, and practical technology. Much from their time is still preserved today in the old university towns of Åbo (Turku), Lund, and above all Uppsala, to which foreign travelers still made pious pilgrimages up to the end of the eighteenth century.[5]

These well-known figures illuminate a still broader development. It was precisely during the eighteenth century that Sweden and the other Nordic lands first began actively to contribute to Europe's cultural life. Before then, they had relied almost entirely on the work of artists, architects, musicians, and scientists from abroad. In contrast, the eighteenth century became at once one of the most creative periods in the entire cultural history of the North, rich in native talent and creativity. It stands forth as at once cosmopolitan and national.[6]

Gustaf III was a shrewd propagandist and a lavish patron who won the devotion of Sweden's literary and artistic elite. They, in turn, created an idealized vision of his reign as the golden age of Swedish culture that has survived the often bitter criticism of hostile contemporary memoirists. A particular cult figure from the Gustavian era is meanwhile Count Axel von Fersen, the younger, allegedly Queen Marie Antoinette's lover and unquestionably her devoted defender. Although widely despised by the Swedish radicals who lay behind his brutal assassination by a Stockholm mob in 1810, he is fondly envisioned today as Sweden's aristocratic representative par excellence on the brilliant cosmopolitan eighteenth-century scene.[7]

Swedish cultural life during the eighteenth century meanwhile necessarily reflected sparse conditions in the remote and still underdeveloped North in a restrained and human scale more appealing to present taste than the overwhelming magnificence that prevailed in much of Europe's richer and more densely populated heartland.

Protected down to the present by nearly two centuries of undisturbed peace, Sweden has moreover preserved cottages as well as palaces, homespun along with satin, surprisingly much of an integral eighteenth-century material and cultural milieu in both its festive and everyday guises. The well-tended central Swedish countryside, in Göran Schildt's description, evokes "a landscape wallpaper from the eighteenth century," above all through its buildings, whether they be magnificent manor houses or idyllic cottages.[8]

With all due respect to the splendors of Schönbrunn, Amalienburg, and Tsarskoe Selo, where can one feel the immediate presence of the eighteenth century more strongly than in archaic Vissböle village on its rocky ridge or on Pataholm's little cobbled square in Småland, at the Tobo iron works with its water-driven trip hammers and tidy workers' cottages in Uppland, or in places amid weathered, red timbered houses with steep tiled roofs and tall black chimney pots on Söder's heights in Stockholm?

The vision of the eighteenth century as a golden age was set in relief by what would follow Gustaf III's dramatic assassination in 1792: Gustaf IV Adolf's cultural "iron age," the Napoleonic Wars, the loss of Finland, the Revolution of 1809, the Fersen murder, the long, gray years of economic stagnation during the first half of the nineteenth century. To be sure, the young Romantics professed to rebel against the superficial elegance of the rococo and the allegedly dry and sterile "snuff-rationalism" (*snusförnuft*) of the Enlightenment. But it was Esaias Tegnér himself who in 1836 nostalgically recalled the "shimmer" that lay over "*Gustaf's* days."[9]

Architecture, both public and private, interior decor, furnishings, and applied arts during the nineteenth century long continued to follow essentially eighteenth-century patterns, giving in retrospect an exaggerated visual impression of the sheer duration of the period. By the middle of the nineteenth century, they began to express a variety of historicizing trends of mainly foreign inspiration. Yet already by the later decades of the century there flourished a neo-rococo revival, followed around the turn of the century by a neoclassicism in the late Gustavian spirit.

On the literary scene, Oscar Levertin in particular idealized Gustaf III's and Bellman's rococo world during the 1890s, and numerous, now largely forgotten writers of popular fiction and history, such as Sara Pfeiffer ("Silvia"), Sophie Elkan, Wilhelm Granath, and Nils Erdmann, followed his example.[10] Together with major scholarly studies of the Age of Freedom and of Gustaf III's reign by C. G. Malmström and C. T. Odhner, respectively, the later nineteenth century also saw the publication of numerous memoirs and letters from that era.[11] Artists such as Julius Kronberg and Carl Larsson, together with a host of book and periodical illustrators, lovingly portrayed an idyllic rococo world. As conflict escalated within the Swedish-Norwegian union, Swedish National Romanticists, striving to assert their nation's unique heritage, evoked a brilliant eighteenth-century scene unmatched elsewhere in Scandinavia—least of all in Norway![12]

The eighteenth century has not been uncontested as a Swedish ideal. Both the Viking Age and the seventeenth-century age of imperial and military glory have served as other, opposed visions of Sweden's historic and cultural significance. Each has reflected the historical circumstances of changing times.[13] Even Gustaf III himself at times held forth a more Spartan—or Old Nordic—ideal, as did, even more pointedly, his opponents. The dour contemporary diarist Rutger Fredrik Hochschild was by no means alone in blaming the court for encouraging arts and sciences a poor land could better do without.[14]

After the humiliations of the Napoleonic era, the Romantic generation looked back to the ancient North for inspiration to revive the nation, and the Scandinavianists of the mid-nineteenth century found in it confirmation of the fundamental unity of the Nordic peoples. National-Romantic ultranationalists around the turn of the century idealized Sweden's militant seventeenth-century Age of Greatness. But the appeal of the eighteenth century has survived all challenges.[15]

Historians often speak of the "Long Nineteenth Century." The classical eighteenth century of historical imagination was in contrast a relatively short period, in Sweden essentially spanning the six decades between the end of the Great Northern War in 1721 and the assassination of Gustaf III in 1792. During this period there were to be sure notable differences in aesthetic values, between the light and playful rococo of Lovisa Ulrika's day and the cooler, more serious Gustavian neoclassicism that succeeded it. In retrospect, the Era of Liberty (Frihetstiden), between 1721 and 1772, swarms with colorful individuality, in contrast to the more formal, disciplined, and conformist reign of Gustaf III. Both nonetheless merge in popular memory into a timeless vision of grace and elegance. After Gustaf III's death, Oscar Levertin wrote nostalgically in 1896 that "our gray, bourgeois nineteenth century's work day broke its way in."[16]

The sweetness of life during the period, as fondly imagined today, was, moreover, enjoyed only by a tiny privileged minority: the court, the aristocracy, the wealthier bourgeoisie. Some idea of the relative size of this privileged elite is suggested by the Saxon diplomat Johann Georg Canzler's estimate in 1778 that the entire market for luxury goods in Sweden—then including Finland—amounted to no more than some seventy-two thousand persons (out of a total population of around two and a half million).[17] Almost no one today, of course, imagines him- or herself as an eighteenth-century peasant, laborer, or pauper. I well recall a golden late summer day some years ago when I happened upon a group of elegant ladies and gentlemen in resplendent eighteenth-century court dress sauntering through Drottningholm's formal gardens—members of a private coterie—deliberately oblivious of the bemused plebeian visitors around them.

As imagined today, the common folk are only occasionally glimpsed in the background as quaint, pastoral figures, disporting themselves in picturesque holiday dress on stage or in contemporary genre paintings by Per Hilleström or Per Hörberg, or as the colorful nymphs and derelicts of Bellman's Stockholm.[18]

Övedkloster Manor. Regarded by Gustaf III as too palatial for a subject of the crown, the stately residence of the baronial Ramel family, seen from the stable, combines the magnificence with the everyday side of eighteenth-century life in Sweden. (From *Svenska Turistföreningens Årsbok 1943*, courtesy of Nordiska Museets Arkiv, Stockholm.)

Cosmopolitan influences have been a matter of perennial concern in Sweden among those who fear that they have corrupted the native culture and traditions, from well before Hochschild's time to that of August Strindberg, Verner von Heidenstam, and Gustav Sundbärg.[19] Indeed, such concerns are by no means over today. Oscar Levertin, however, found in the Swedes' very openness toward outside impulses a *positive* national trait, combined with their remarkable capacity to naturalize them and make them truly their own. The eighteenth century was, in his view, the most cosmopolitan, yet at the same time the most quintessentially Swedish of centuries.[20]

It is apparent that the nostalgia of later times for that period has above all expressed a reaction against a new Iron Age of industrialization, urbanization, materialism, class conflict, popular mass culture, and devastating wars. It is surely no coincidence that the Swedish Tourist Society (Svenska Turistföreningen), brought out its paean to the eighteenth century in 1943, during the darkest days of World War II. Indeed, the eighteenth-century rococo was itself a flight from hard realities into a world of playful fantasy.

The rococo era was, however, at the same time that of the cosmopolitan Enlightenment. Voltaire's Candide urged that his contemporaries cultivate their "garden." Later times have often tended to picture the garden as a sheltered retreat, rather than as a useful field of activity in the world. But the Swedish eighteenth-century ideal implies—as it did for Voltaire himself—more than escapism and a refined way of life. It embodies the core of the humanistic ethos, as it has evolved in the Western world since antiquity, which combines the individual's right to enjoy life's pleasures with his or her moral obligation to work with others to bring about a better world for all. *"Nytta och nöje"* (utility and pleasure): this was the slogan Olof von Dalin gave his journal *Then Swenska Argus* in 1732 and one wonders what could be more Swedish?

In an era that has undergone more than its share of war and brutality in the wider world, the eighteenth century with its humane and civilized ideals has manifestly held a wider appeal for peaceful and rational Swedes than either fierce Vikings or hard-bitten Caroline warriors.[21] For nearly two centuries, the Swedes have directly experienced neither war nor serious domestic violence. Even their Nordic neighbors have been less fortunate in this regard. Surely this circumstance has been of inestimable importance in sustaining both the cultivated epicureanism of the rococo and the humane idealism of the Enlightenment. As for the Vikings, they seem nowadays to have considerably greater symbolic value for Swedish Americans, for whom the genteel eighteenth century has little apparent relevance, than for homeland Swedes—aside from soccer fans or skinheads.[22]

In a comparison between his own Finnish countrymen and their Swedish neighbors, Göran Schildt was particularly impressed by the Swedes' manifest tendency toward an aristocratic upward cultural leveling, owing, in his view, to Sweden's lack of a long-established and solidly self-confident bourgeois tradition, as in Denmark or elsewhere in western Europe.[23] This recalls, to my mind, an article in the Swedish gastronomic magazine, *Allt om mat,* several years ago about "a Gustavian named Nilsson"—a gentleman, that is, of impeccable taste and polished manner, despite his recognizably plebeian surname.[24] Well into the twentieth century even working-class homes have featured modest versions of "Gustavian" mirrors, console tables, and chandeliers, while workingmen's choruses still lustily sing Bellman's tributes in song to bacchic Fredman and winsome Ulla.

Manufacture of furnishings modeled on eighteenth-century patterns still continues today, with Ikea's recent "Gustavian Line" as perhaps its latest manifestation. The "Swedish Modern" style of decor, from Carl Larsson's Sundborn and Ellen Key's Sund down at least through the mid-twentieth century, meanwhile shows repeated allusions to the late Gustavian style in particular.[25] Traditional Swedish social decorum, or *höviskhet,* remains distinctly reminiscent of the rococo world.

The eighteenth century remains a living cultural heritage for all who share its spirit and values, a tradition that for so many reasons and with particular force appeals to the Swedes and to those in the world beyond who truly appreciate Swedish culture.

Notes

1. Edward Daniel Clarke, *Travels in Various Countries of Europe, Asia, and Africa,* 6 vols. (London, 1810–23), 6:96–97.

2. See Sten Åke Nilsson, *Det sköna 1700-talet* (Stockholm, 1993), esp. 15–16, 24–27, 78–79.

3. Göran Schildt, *Upptäcktsfärd i Sverige* (Stockholm, 1962), 55.

4. The literature on Bellman, both scholarly and popular, is of course immense. See, for ex., Paul Britten Austin, *The Life and Songs of Carl Michael Bellman, Genius of the Swedish Rococo* (London, 1967); in Swedish, *Carl Michael Bellman. Hans liv, hans miljö, hans verk* (Malmö, 1970).

5. See my *Northern Arcadia: Foreign Travelers in Scandinavia, 1765–1815* (Carbondale, Ill., 1998), 7, 35, 36–38.

6. On this characteristic Swedish combination, see Oscar Levertin's celebrated essay, "Bellmans hemlighet," in *Från Gustaf III:s dagar,* 3rd. ed. (Stockholm, 1896), 4–42, esp. 6–9.

7. See my *Count Hans Axel von Fersen: Aristocrat in an Age of Revolution* (Boston, 1975).

8. Schildt, *Upptäcktsfärd i Sverige*, 28, 40.

9. Esaias Tegnér, "Sång, den 5 april 1836," in Esaias Tegnér, *Samlade skrifter*, ed. Ewert Wrangel and Fredrik Böök, 10 vols. (Stockholm, 1918–1925), 8:9.

10. See Levertin, *Från Gustaf III:s dagar* and *Rococonoveller* (Stockholm, 1899). More recently, Jan Mårtenson, for ex., in his *Guldmakaren* (Stockholm, 1984) has presented a vivid picture of Gustaf III's court and Stockholm.

11. C. G. Malmström, *Sveriges politiska historia från konung Carl XII:s död till statshvälfningen 1772*, 6 vols. (Stockholm, 1855–77; new ed., 1893–1901); C. T. Odhner, *Sveriges politiska historia under konung Gustaf III:s regering*, 3 vols. (Stockholm, 1885–1905). See also, for ex., Oscar Levertin and Henrik Schück, eds., *Svenska memoarer och bref*, 11 vols. (Stockholm, 1900–1918).

12. See my *Sweden and Visions of Norway: Politics and Culture, 1814–1905* (Carbondale, Ill., 2003), esp. chapt. 5.

13. Ibid., esp. chapts. 4 and 5, gives considerable attention to these three Swedish historical ideals.

14. Rutger Fredrik Hochschild, *Memoarer*, ed. H. Schück, 3 vols. (Stockholm, 1908–9), 1:51. Cf. Anton Blanck, *Den nordiska renässansen i sjuttonhundratalets litteratur* (Stockholm, 1911); Tore Frängsmyr, *Svensk idéhistoria*, 2 vols. (Stockholm, 2000), 1:382–86.

15. See, for ex., Georg Landberg, *Gustaf III inför eftervärlden* (Stockholm, 1968); Bo Grandien, *Rönndruvans glöd. Nygöticistiskt i tanke, konst och miljö under 1800-talet* (Stockholm, 1987); Staffan Björck, *Heidenstam och sekelskiftets Sverige* (Stockholm, 1946).

16. Levertin, *Från Gustaf III:s dagar*, 6.

17. Johann Georg Canzler, *Nachrichten zur genauern Kentniss der Geschichte, Statsverwaltung und ökonomischen Verfassung des Königreichs Schweden*, 2 vols. (Dresden, 1778), 2:282–83.

18. Per Anders Fogelström, in *Vävernas barn* (Stockholm, 1981) and *Krigens barn* (Stockholm, 1985), provides a sobering antidote to an overly romanticized view of the century in his grimly realistic depiction of life among Stockholm's poorer classes. Cf. Axel Strindberg, *Arbetare och radikaler i 1700-talets Sverige* (Stockholm, 1935), esp. chapt. 1.

19. For this self-criticism, see Hochschild, *Memoarer*, esp. 1:29, 51–52, 56, 61, 66–70; Beth Hennings, *Gustav III* (Stockholm, 1957), 75, 254–55; my *Sweden and Visions of Norway*, 150–58.

20. Levertin, *Från Gustaf III:s dagar*, esp. "Gustaf III" and "Bellmans hemlighet," 4–42, 6–9, 43–88, esp. 74–81.

21. *Svenska Turistföreningens årsskrift 1943. 1700-talet*. For a more recent idealization, see Jan Mårtenson and Gunnar Brusewitz, *Drottningholm, slottet vid vattnet* (Stockholm, 1985), a celebration of what Mårtenson calls "the heart of my Sweden" (*hjärtpunkten i mitt Sverige*, 177).

22. See my article, "Swedish Americans and the Viking Discovery of America," in *Interpreting the Promise of America: Essays in Honor of Odd Sverre Lovoll,* ed. Todd W. Nichol (Northfield, MN, 2002): 61–78.

23. Schildt, *Upptäcktsfärd i Sverige,* 114–15. Cf. Thorkild Vogel-Jörgensen's earlier, *Svenskt väsen och danskt* (Stockholm, 1943).

24. "En gustavian som heter Nilsson," *Allt om mat,* no. 14 (1980), 28–31.

25. See, for ex., Lars Sjöberg, Ursula Sjöberg, and Ingalill Snitt, *Det svenska rummet* (Stockholm, 1994), in English, *The Swedish Room* (London, 1994).

Gustaf III of Sweden and the Enlightenment

Y ou might have thought you were looking at a minuet," wrote Paul Hazard. "The Princes bow to the Philosophers, the Philosophers return
the bow."[1] The relationship is nonetheless a complex and ambiguous one,
as a consideration of Gustaf III of Sweden (reigned 1771–92), traditionally
included among eighteenth-century enlightened despots, will show.

Gustaf was born in 1746, when the monarch in Sweden was a crowned
figurehead under the constitution of 1720 and the all-powerful Estates were
bedeviled by the rivalry of Hats and Caps. His father, King Adolf Fredrik,
was a man of modest pretensions. His mother, the intelligent and ambitious
Lovisa Ulrika, sister of Frederick the Great of Prussia, was keenly interested
in the scientific, philosophical, and aesthetic trends of the day and was in
particular an admirer of Voltaire, whom she had known in Potsdam.[2]

In his fourth year, Gustaf had appointed to him as governor Count Carl
Gustaf Tessin, who employed an informal, relaxed pedagogy, deriving
largely from Locke. The queen, much concerned with the education of her
first-born, wrote her mother in Berlin in 1752 that he was making great
progress through instruction that stressed "reasoning" rather than "me-
chanical" memorization. Tessin had been at the Versailles of Louis XIV
and had later served as ambassador to Paris. He imbued his pupil with the
classical ideals of seventeenth-century France and the precepts of Fénelon's
Télémaque.[3] Gustaf's inspiring tutor in history was meanwhile Olof von

Dalin, known somewhat extravagantly at the time as the "Voltaire of the North," a skeptical *esprit-fort* who subtly undermined much of the effect of Tessin's conventional piety.[4]

In 1756, the Estates, suspecting Tessin's and Dalin's political principles, following an abortive royalist coup, replaced them. The prince's new governor was Count Carl Fredrik Scheffer, likewise a former envoy to Paris, where he was well known in philosophic circles. His instruction drew extensively upon contemporary political theory and stressed the works of Locke, Wolff, and Burlamaqui.[5]

In 1762, the prince's education was declared completed. It had been prevailingly French in tone; French was Gustaf's only foreign language, but he mastered it well and continued to use it by preference."[6] He retained a strong interest in history, literature, and the theater, regarding them all, in the fashion of the time, as effective vehicles for the conveying of ethical and civic ideals.[7] He was meanwhile observed to incline toward grandiose ideas, theatricality, at times a certain indolence, while the difficult political circumstances of his childhood, reflected in the arbitrary change of his tutors, had produced in him tendencies toward secretiveness and dissimulation, which caution the historian against always taking him too literally at his own word.[8]

In 1766, Gustaf married the Danish princess Sophia Magdalena, established his own court, and began to play a role in politics. That system, he had written Scheffer in 1760, "which says the behavior of men depends upon the good or bad examples they receive from their sovereigns appears to me the best of those doctrines you have reported to me." A rough constitutional draft he prepared in 1766 shows a good knowledge of Sweden's existing constitution, together with a clear preference for strong kingship.[9] This is hardly surprising considering the humiliating limitations on royal power at the time. Lovisa Ulrika despised the existing regime, envying her brother Frederick's Prussian autocracy, while Tessin and especially Dalin had idealized the model of the heroic and magnanimous prince.[10]

A powerful influence in this direction were meanwhile Count Scheffer, who had become progressively disillusioned with things as they were, and through him the French Physiocrats. In 1767, Scheffer introduced Gustaf to P. F. J. H. Le Mercier de la Rivière's *L'Ordre naturel et essentiel des sociétés politiques,* published that year, which deeply impressed him. This work, he wrote his mother, contained new ideas that should cause a "revolution in thinking" and could save Sweden from her "present ruin"; for days he could think of nothing but the "principles essential to the social order." The following year, thus inspired, he applied himself for a time to the uncongenial study of financial and economic matters.[11]

As Le Mercier de la Rivière has since been so largely forgotten it is worth recalling that the onetime governor of Martinique, who caused a sensation with his *L'Ordre naturel,* the fullest summary of physiocratic doctrine, at the time largely overshadowed both Montesquieu and Rousseau and aroused the lively interest of such monarchs as Catherine II, Leopold of Tuscany, and Charles Frederick of Baden. He was hailed as a veritable Newton of the social order, which he held to be based upon "physical necessity" rather than voluntary social contract, hence upon "simple, evident, immutable," natural laws. Property, the basis of self-preservation, was the precondition from which all other "natural and essential principles" of society derived, though it was necessarily distributed unequally due to men's differing capabilities, thereby creating social classes.

While all stood to gain from increasing national prosperity, competing particular interests prevented just and efficient government by *"la nation en corps."* Only a hereditary sovereign with unlimited, combined "tutelary" and executive power could uphold the common good while protecting and balancing the legitimate rights of each class for the "reciprocal utility" of all. As "co-proprietor," his own interests would be inseparable from those of the nation. It was the task of this "Legislator," surrounded by a "concourse of *lumières,*" to discover and apply the "evident" underlying principles of society and, through public education, freedom of expression (*"liberté d'examen et de contradiction"*) and an independent judiciary, to demonstrate to his subjects that herein lay their true felicity. Thus basing his regime upon the willing assent of his subjects, rather than upon force, and maintaining "liberty, property, security," he would exercise a "true" or "legal" despotism, like that of the "veritable despot," Euclid, who revealed the natural laws of geometry, and in contrast to the "arbitrary" despotisms of the past or those necessarily resulting from "aristocratic" or "democratic" rule. The latter half of Le Mercier's work consists of a detailed exposition of physiocratic political economy."[12]

In March 1768, encouraged by the Duc de Choiseul to hope for French aid in forcing a change of regime, Gustaf drafted a second constitutional project. Its stated detestation of autocracy must be considered a political stratagem, for its details nonetheless provide for an effective royal absolutism.[13] A coup at this stage, however, required the cooperation of the Hats—then out of office and lusting for revenge against the Caps—and to win them required further concessions. By the end of 1768, Gustaf therefore speculated over a constitution now ostensibly based more upon Montes-quieu's separation of powers than upon the physiocratic ideal of "legal despotism," but which still provided for a greatly strengthened monarchy.[14] These projects for a change of constitution continued into 1769, when they collapsed at the Riksdag of that year.

The court of the crown prince became a center for the cultivation of literary and philosophical interests, drawing to it that kind of select circle of cultivated minds to which it would always remain Gustaf's habit to escape from the cares of office. Contemporaries speak of the reading sessions in the evenings from the latest French works. We thus see Gustaf and his friends in 1762, discussing Helvétius' *De l'esprit* or, twenty years later, Rousseau's *Confessions*. "The prince has read an incredible amount," exclaimed the historian Anders Schönberg in 1768. Catalogs in the Royal Library in Stockholm show how voluminous was his personal library and how quickly he acquired the latest works of the Enlightenment.[15]

Gustaf's preserved correspondence contains few letters to or from the *philosophes,* and most of these contain little more than polite compliments. This is misleading, for he could and did maintain contacts with them through others. The dowager queen's influential lector, the Swiss Jean-François Beylon, apparently played such a role, and Scheffer corresponded diligently with his Parisian friends, especially among the Physiocrats.[16] The Swedish ambassador to Paris after 1766, Count Gustaf Filip Creutz, was well received in philosophic circles and on excellent terms with Voltaire in Ferney. He kept Gustaf informed and sent him new books, including the successive volumes of the *Encyclopédie.*[17] It was Creutz who already in 1763, having visited Ferney, wrote that the patriarch had wept tears of joy on hearing Gustaf had learned his *Henriade* by heart, moving him to prophesy that in fifty years "prejudice" would have disappeared in Europe. Voltaire continued to follow the prince's career with interest.[18]

For Marmontel, Gustaf felt a particular sympathy; when the former's *Bélisaire* was banned by the Sorbonne in 1767, Gustaf wrote him of his admiration for "the great lessons you give to kings" while condemning clerical obscurantism in terms that caused him some embarrassment with the French government when his letter promptly appeared in print in Paris.[19]

Gustaf's correspondence with his mother is filled with literary and philosophical commentary, often showing keen critical insight. She invites him in 1768, for instance, to spend an evening sharing a fresh stock of "bonbons" from the "factory at Ferney." Voltaire is clearly their favorite. Not that Gustaf was an uncritical admirer. To Scheffer he criticized him in 1767 for confusing religious fanaticism with true piety and even admitted that Voltaire sometimes "scandalized"—while delighting—him. Nor could he welcome the philosopher's fulsome praise for Catherine II's intervention in Poland, where the situation perilously resembled Sweden's, or his *L'Homme aux quarante écus* (1768), which ridiculed Le Mercier de la Rivière's "natural order."

Yet Gustaf found Voltaire's style irresistible and warmly admired his struggle for reason and justice. "It is Voltaire," he wrote in 1770, "who first had the courage to rise up against fanaticism. He has thereby perhaps done more good in a few years than sovereigns in the course of the longest reigns." Later that year he contributed to the fund for Pigalle's statue of Voltaire, to honor, in his words, "the defender of Calas, the protector of the unhappy Sirven family, the opponent of fanaticism and superstition, the defender of humanity."[20]

At last, in the winter of 1771, Gustaf himself visited Paris. He was much impressed by Versailles but preferred to stay in the city, where he consorted with the elite of birth and talent. Scheffer, Creutz, and the *homme de lettres* Claude Carloman de Rulhière were his cicerones in the literary world. Within a few days he could write his mother than he had met "almost all the philosophers": these included Helvétius, Marmontel, Grimm, Morellet, Quesnay, Chastellux, d'Alembert, the elder Mirabeau, even the misanthropic Rousseau. "Never has a prince received a finer education and better profited from it," observed Bachaumont's *Mémoires secrètes,* adding that Gustaf was constantly surrounded by the "philosopher-encyclopedists," who saw in him their "protector," the "zealous sectary of their doctrines," and that he showed particular favor to d'Alembert.

Marmontel dedicated his *Les Incas* to Gustaf, and d'Alembert delivered flattering orations at the French Academy and the Royal Academy of Sciences, speaking on the latter occasion of the triumphant advance of philosophy in the face of persecution and praising those monarchs who gave it their protection. Diderot, however, seems to have been relieved to escape the princely visitor, perhaps with a thought to the reaction of his patroness, the Russian Empress Catherine II. Gustaf meanwhile reveled in the conversation of the great salons.

In the midst of this whirl he learned of his father's death. To Marmontel, he confided his grief at being called to the throne so soon, leaving Paris before learning all he had come to learn, and the fear that he must now bid farewell forever to "friendship and truth." "Truth flees only those kings who reject it," replied the philosopher. Regretfully too, Gustaf now had to forgo his pilgrimage to Ferney.[21]

Gustaf's visits with Rousseau, arranged by Rulhière, unfortunately remain rather a mystery. Rousseau owned himself well impressed but evidently declined a flattering offer, probably asylum under royal protection in Sweden. Already in 1760, Gustaf had strongly reacted against Rousseau's critique of "letters and sciences," which would "plunge us . . . back into our original barbarism," and he can have felt scant sympathy for the ideals of the *Contrat social.* Moreover, too close an association with Rousseau could cause unwelcome complications with Voltaire. Most likely, Gustaf expected and hoped Rousseau would decline, after he had won the philosopher's influential goodwill through a magnanimous gesture.[22]

The interest and enthusiasm with which Gustaf was received in Paris reflected a long-standing French interest in Sweden, dating at least from the Thirty Years' War. This enthusiasm had been stimulated by the exploits of Carl XII, especially Voltaire's account of them. Pre-Romantic sensibilities were attracted to ancient Scandinavia through the writings of Paul Henri Mallet. Linnaeus and Swedenborg were internationally renowned figures. Conflicts between the crown and the *parlements* meanwhile encouraged interest not only in the English but in the Swedish constitution of 1720, which was widely admired among the philosophic party.

Montesquieu, invoking Jordanes and Olof Rudbeck, praised Scandinavia in *L'Esprit des lois* (1748) as the home of European liberties, the "factory of those instruments which break the shackles forged in the South," while Voltaire's *Essai sur les mœurs* (1756) called Sweden "the freest kingdom on earth." The chevalier de Jaucourt paid tribute to her *"belle constitution"* in the *Encyclopédie,* noting particularly the political representation of the Peasant Estate, while Rousseau was reputed to have refused to show his model constitution for Poland to a Swede, claiming he had nothing to learn from it. Most enthusiastic of all was the Abbé de Mably, whose works often discuss Sweden. Though he profoundly misunderstood Swedish history and conditions, he considered the Swedish constitution of 1720 "the masterpiece of modern legislation" in its provisions for "the rights of humanity and equality." His *De la législation* is a book-length debate between a Swede and an Englishman, in which the former proves the superiority of his constitution.[23] To the *philosophes,* disillusioned with the France of Louis XV, Gustaf III held out the prospect of a philosophic prince ruling over an enlightened people.

Those with whom Gustaf formed the closest bonds in Paris were meanwhile the *grandes dames* at whose salons the philosophic world forgathered. These friendships were largely for political reasons, for the dismissal of

Choiseul and the suppression of the *parlements* by Chancellor Maupeou at the turn of the year had created a highly fluid situation and Gustaf, heavily dependent upon French goodwill, was eager to have sources of information and influence in each faction. His closest Paris friends—the Countesses de La Marck, d'Egmont, and de Boufflers—were nonetheless avid supporters of the *parlements* and admirers of British institutions.[24] During his stay in Paris and by correspondence afterward they urged upon him, in Mme d'Egmont's words, a "monarchy limited by laws."[25]

How did Gustaf react to his direct encounter with the *philosophes?* Not altogether favorably. "They are more amiable to read than to see," he wrote his mother, adding that she was the only person to whom he dared say such a "frightful blasphemy." He was taken aback by their immodest pretensions. His reaction to the advice of his lady admirers in Paris shows him less sanguine than they regarding the blessings of constitutional liberty. The Swedish Diet, he wrote Mme de Boufflers in the fall of 1771, was "no pleasant spectacle for any but cosmopolitan philosophers."[26]

Yet it would appear that Gustaf returned from Paris not unaffected by libertarian and anglophile influences. He was, to be sure, warned against any violent attempt to change Sweden's constitution by both the French foreign minister and by his uncle, Frederick II, whom he visited in Berlin on the way home. There nonetheless seems to be more than mere propaganda in the assurance he wrote to Mme de La Marck while crossing the Baltic: that he considered "despotism" as harmful for the master as for his subjects and that he would in time prove that he respected "liberty, properly understood, founded on reason and humanity" as much as he despised "anarchy and dissolution." Still more noteworthy seems his condemnation, in a letter to his mother, of Carl XI, the founder of royal absolutism in Sweden in 1680, who, Gustaf claimed, "rent the veil that separates the rights of the people from those of the king," thereby inspiring the nation with fear and suspicion toward the monarch.[27]

Gustaf appears impressed at this point with the importance of the willing obedience of subjects and of Montesquieu's axiom that a true monarchy must rest upon a social hierarchy headed by a healthy aristocracy. George III in Great Britain seemed to exemplify the ideal of the "patriot king," who held the balance between the various interest groups within Parliament. It was this which Gustaf at first tried to realize through his policy of "composition" between the feuding Hats and Caps at the Riksdag of 1771–72. The works of Bolingbroke and his followers were well known in Sweden; Count Tessin had in particular been a strong advocate of their views, which again came to the fore in political discussion at the time of

Gustaf's accession. Already in July 1771, he was hailed by a pamphleteer as a "patriot king," and Gustaf, in opening the Riksdag, claimed it his "greatest glory" to be "the first citizen of a free people."[28]

The experiment in mediation soon broke down, as social conflict began to overshadow the political struggle. The three lower estates attacked noble privileges, both in the Riksdag and through a rash of pamphleteering. To Gustaf, the situation was alarming, yet it offered new opportunities. He wrote Mme de Boufflers in June 1772 of the "onslaught of Democracy against the expiring Aristocracy, the latter preferring to submit to Democracy rather than be protected by the Monarchy, which opens its arms to it." Sweden was rapidly approaching "anarchy, . . . the spectacle Poland affords"; to avoid this, "anything" was "permissible." "They did not want a well-regulated liberty in 1769; they shall have it in 1772," he wrote his mother.[29]

On 19 August 1772, Gustaf carried off an audacious yet bloodless coup d'état and two days later gained consent from the assembled Estates for a new constitution. This greatly strengthened royal power, though it did not establish royal autocracy, and the king in its preamble expressly proclaimed "abhorrence" for "despotic power." The document is nonetheless ambiguous on important points, which cannot have been due to oversight; while it could in time allow the development of a truly constitutional regime, it left ample scope for an ambitious monarch further to extend his authority.[30]

Why did Gustaf not establish a complete autocracy? If this was his desire, he still needed the support of powerful elements that would not accept an absolute monarch, while to go that far would invite foreign, especially Russian intervention.[31] Yet it is not altogether clear that an autocracy was what Gustaf wanted. Scheffer and others evidently urged him to utilize the social conflict by backing the commoners against the nobility; he might thus have won far more absolute powers, as indeed he later did by this very means in 1789.[32] Such a move, however, would imply following the path of Carl XI. He wrote his mother on 22 August:

> I had absolute power in my hands through the voluntary submission, separately, of each of the Estates, but I considered it nobler, grander, more conformable to all I had said previously, and certainly surer for my future government, myself to limit the royal authority, leaving to the nation the essential rights of liberty and keeping for myself only what is necessary to prevent license.

His own intention, he repeatedly claimed, was to reestablish the constitution of Gustaf II Adolf, which provided in his view for the rallying of all the Estates, headed by the nobility, around the throne. While he inveighed against a licentious and corrupt "aristocracy" that had threatened the nation with ruin under the former regime, the actual social significance of Gustaf's revolution was that it rescued the nobility from the attack of the other orders, thereby gaining, initially at least, its enthusiastic support.[33] Clearly, however, he intended for the crown to play the leading role.

These ideas accorded well with certain Swedish traditions, with the emphasis of Le Mercier de la Rivière and the Physiocrats on the natural existence of social classes based on property, with Bolingbroke's ideal of the "patriot king," with Gustaf's exalted conceptions of Henry IV and Louis XIV, all of which has been duly noted by Swedish historians. It would seem however that Montesquieu's influence has not been given sufficient emphasis. To be sure, Gustaf's discovery of his ideas was not sudden or dramatic, as with Le Mercier. Yet one of his earliest childhood essays is his unfinished "Réflexions sur l'Esprit des lois de Montesquieu." He criticized Montesquieu's climatic theory to Scheffer in 1760, arguing instead that "example and education" were decisive to the behavior of nations. Yet Montesquieu's influence upon his constitutional speculations in late 1768 has already been seen. In 1770, Gustaf noted, "I have nourished myself on David Hume's, Cardinal de Retz', and Montesquieu's writings."[34]

Neither political circumstances nor the young king's ambition were altogether conducive to Montesquieu's theoretical, clear-cut division and equal balance of powers, yet Gustaf's constitution of 1772 came closer in both respects to Montesquieu's ideal monarchy than the preceding regime had done. More influential still, however, were Montesquieu's ideas concerning the social bases of the state, which remained fundamental to Gustaf's thinking, as shown, for instance, by a letter to Mme de Boufflers some years later, at the time of the 1778 Riksdag:

> [Not] knowing your customs, your principles, it is so difficult to judge properly each country's internal arrangements: climate, fundamental principles differ so greatly from one nation to the next that what suits the one is harmful to the other. There are certain parties which seek to gain too great an ascendancy over the others and which must be repressed; it is the true science of sovereigns to balance them, and to hold this balance in just equilibrium. If this equilibrium is ever lost, harmful consequences follow. With us it is democracy which seeks to gain the upper hand and all my efforts are aimed at reestablishing the old high nobility. With you, perhaps the people are too oppressed and count for too little, the nobility too favored.[35]

Privately, he noted to himself at the same time:

> Indifference toward birth or those distinctions our forefathers es-
> tablished to separate the most distinguished from the people is at-
> tractive only as speculation, in practice almost always impossible.
> This equality can only exist in a democracy or under a despotism,
> where there is only one master and slaves!

Among Gustaf's most immediate concerns in 1772 was obtaining the
favor of enlightened opinion in Europe for his change of regime. He wrote
without delay to his ladies in Paris, claiming that he had saved the state
from imminent collapse but that far from seeking absolute power, he had
retained only enough to "do good and prevent licence." His new constitution, he claimed to Mme de Boufflers, was based on the true principles of
liberty and distinguished between the rights of the king and of his subjects
"with the equity necessary for the common good."[36]

Gustaf immediately sent an account of his revolution to Voltaire, who
returned enthusiastic congratulations and a poem hailing the "Young and
worthy heir to the name of Gustaf." The event came at a fortunate moment for Voltaire. In his play, Les lois de Minos, which had just come out, a
mythical king of Crete, who had travelled to the "Land of the Velches" and
there become enlightened, returned to his kingdom to overthrow a corrupt aristocratic regime. Voltaire first claimed to have in mind King Stanislaus Poniatowski of Poland, but Paris detected allusions to the struggle
between Chancellor Maupeou and the parlements, causing delays in the
play's production. Voltaire now opportunistically added the explanation
that it referred to Gustaf III and the "just and moderate authority" he had
reestablished in Sweden.[37] D'Alembert and Marmontel were likewise much
impressed, as was the elder Mirabeau who praised the "first revolution
that belonged to reason."[38]

Others were, however, more reserved. Mme d'Egmont congratulated
the "hero" of her heart, adding pointedly that he surely would not abuse
"this power which an elated people has confided to you without limits."
Mme de Boufflers was more direct. Having studied the new constitution,
she wrote Gustaf that she could not at present regard him as other than
an "absolute king," warning that autocracy was "incontestably" a "mortal
malady . . . which ends by destroying states" and urging that he further
limit, when possible, a power others might abuse. An analysis she made,
at about the same time, of the constitution's first sixteen articles, which
she showed Gustaf only in 1780, proves how well she comprehended both
its stipulations and its omissions.[39]

There were meanwhile those who reacted strongly against Gustaf's actions. Catherine II's feelings may well be imagined; to Voltaire she predicted a regime "as despotic as France's." When Mme du Deffand praised Gustaf's revolution to the duchesse de Choiseul, the latter responded contemptuously that she could not understand "this liberty which the king of Sweden has given his nation, in reserving for himself the right to propose anything, to do anything, to prevent anything!"

The Abbé Raynal, who unlike many of the *philosophes* had criticized the former regime in Sweden for its corruption in the first edition (1770) of his *Histoire des deux Indes,* urging the nation itself to restore sufficient powers to its "phantom king," was nonetheless strongly critical of Gustaf's revolution in the second edition of this work in 1774. He condemned the Swedes for throwing themselves abjectly at their monarch's feet and accepting from him, rather than imposing upon him, the conditions of his rule, which was now more absolute than any Sweden had known. Jean Louis De Lolme, discounting fears of a similar royalist coup in Britain, likewise regarded the former Swedish government as "an aristocratical yoke" but considered Gustaf now "as absolute as any monarch in Europe." The Abbé de Mably, then on the point of publishing his *De la législation,* stoutly maintained that the king of Sweden might "change his country" but not his own book, which based its social ideas upon an idealization of the older Swedish constitution.[40]

Gustaf did not take kindly to criticism. His correspondence with Mme de Boufflers languished for over a year, and he thereafter no longer asked her views on Swedish affairs, though occasionally she offered them unsolicited. Continued discussion of French politics in his letters nonetheless shows the direction of his political thinking. He consistently takes the part of the French king and his ministers against the *parlements,* which he saw as analogous with the Swedish Estates, and which Mme d'Egmont until her death in 1773, her companion, Mme Feydeau des Mesmes, and Mme de Boufflers until the eve of the Revolution itself, warmly defended. Maupeou, he told his mother, had "rendered to royal authority a greater service than Richelieu." He favored Turgot, while somewhat suspecting him of being "rather the people's man than the king's"; for a time Necker, whom he facetiously called Mme de Boufflers' "heretical friend"; and even Calonne. He meanwhile discreetly deplored Louis XVI's weakness and indecision, thereby subtly inviting flattering comparison with himself.[41]

Having changed the regime in 1772, Gustaf dissolved the Riksdag and embarked upon an ambitious program of reforms.[42] Reorganizations and the purge of corrupt and inefficient officials improved the civil administration, the judiciary, and military establishments. Councilor Johan Liljencrantz reestablished Sweden's currency on a stable footing. Inspired largely by physiocratic ideas, Gustaf and Liljencrantz increased consolidation of peasant landholdings, reclamation and settlement of uncultivated lands, and free trade in grain, and suppressed guild restrictions on commerce and manufacture. To encourage merit in agriculture, commerce, mining, and the arts, Gustaf established the Order of Vasa. An aspect of economic reform was Gustaf's introduction of a new "Swedish dress" in 1778, to restrain luxury and the caprice of fashion, thereby reducing expensive imports while stimulating national pride.[43]

For a self-avowed disciple of Voltaire, as deeply affected by the Calas affair as by the witchcraft trials in Åls parish in 1757, reform of penal laws and freedom of religion receive high priority. Torture was immediately abolished and penalties for various offenses made more humane. Gustaf himself played an important role in these reforms, which reveal Beccaria's influence while going beyond him in their emphasis upon the social rehabilitation of the wrongdoer.[44] Despite clerical protests, he proclaimed limited toleration for foreign non-Lutheran Christians, including Roman Catholics, in 1781. Lovisa Ulrika, much impressed by Moses Mendelsohn while in Berlin in 1771–72, urged toleration of Jews. Gustaf, who saw the advantage of having such "industrious people" in Sweden, allowed them to settle in certain towns in 1782.[45]

His actions regarding freedom of the press were more ambivalent. Since 1766, Sweden had been notably free in this respect. Gustaf's edict of 1774 invoked the ideals of the Enlightenment, especially of the Physiocrats, but actually permitted a tighter censorship, particularly of criticism directed against the crown itself.[46] Finally, Gustaf warmly encouraged all facets of the nation's cultural life.

These reforms were undertaken with an eye to the effect upon enlightened opinion abroad. D'Alembert was impressed by Gustaf's judicial reforms. One of the first recipients of the Vasa Order was the elder Mirabeau, the self-styled "Friend of Man," to whom Gustaf described himself in 1772 as a disciple of the Physiocrats. In 1776, Mirabeau dedicated his *Supplément à la théorie de l'impôt* to the king in adulatory terms, while S. Dupont de Nemours anonymously refuted De Lolme's critique of the new Swedish government in 1773. Both sent lengthy memoranda, filled with advice, to Stockholm, and their journal, the *Nouvelles éphémérides économiques*, publicized the Swedish reforms and printed Scheffer's justification of the new regime through physiocratic theory. Le Mercier de la Rivière was commissioned by Gustaf to write his *De l'instruction publique*

Gustaf III, by Lorenz Pasch, the younger. The monarch is best remembered today for his important contributions to Swedish culture. Yet, confident in his destiny, he sought to gain martial glory like his illustrious forebears and pursued a highly adventurous foreign policy up to his assassination by aristocratic opponents in 1792. (Courtesy of Svenskt Porträttarkiv, Stockholm.)

(1775), which praised the king for granting "true liberty" and painted a glowing picture of the advance of human progress. Meanwhile, Mirabeau, Dupont, and others of their circle did not fail to importune the king for honors and pecuniary favors.[47]

Gustaf lost no time in sending his edict on freedom of the press to Voltaire, as "the homage reason renders to humanity," asserting that Sweden now enjoyed greater liberty in this respect than any other country. In March 1778, he sought through Creutz Voltaire's public approval of his "Swedish dress." To the enthusiastic Marmontel, Gustaf wrote, "May my reign be that of true philosophy," that which serves "to enlighten sovereigns regarding their duties and peoples on their true happiness."[48]

There were, however, limits. Dupont de Nemours had considered the Swedish ordinance on press freedom of 1766 superior even to Britain's; the silence of the *philosophes* on this point after 1774 shows that they were not misled by Gustaf's edict.[49]

Beginning in 1778, Gustaf underwent a deep personal crisis. Since his coup, he had placed great hopes in the popularity of his reform program. His first Riksdag under the new regime, he wrote Mme de Boufflers, should "be of great importance for my reputation and for posterity," since it would give "a final sanction to all that was established in 1772, a free sanction and without any remonstrance."[50] The Riksdag of 1778–79, however, proved disillusioning, revealing criticism of Gustaf's regime and opposition to proposed religious and penal reforms. Symptoms of discontent among various elements of society thereafter continued to mount. The American Revolution provided an issue with which the more radical opposition belabored the government, and Gustaf's feelings toward his opponents at home are reflected in his personal distaste for the American rebels.[51]

No less distressing was the bitter conflict between Gustaf and his mother, which, long submerged, came to the surface in 1778, when Lovisa Ulrika accepted and spread the rumor that Crown Prince Gustaf Adolf, born that year, was not Gustaf's son. This led to a break that never really mended until the dowager's death in 1782.[52]

These disillusionments manifested themselves in tense, nervous behavior, and surely affected Gustaf's attitude toward the *philosophes* and their doctrines. His criticisms did not begin suddenly. He had experienced some disenchantment with the philosophers already in Paris in 1772, as seen. Of Chastellux's *De la félicité publique* (1772), he wrote his mother in 1773 that "one cannot agree that the execution would be as easy as the ideas are honorable for mankind and useful to its happiness," while the same year, though he read Helvétius' *De l'homme* (1772) with "much pleasure," he found in it "dangerous and destructive maxims, tending to the overthrow of all those barriers which up to the present have been raised to restrain men's desires." Other criticisms follow, while Lovisa Ulrika complained increasingly of the "dearth" of good literature.[53]

But it is above all from 1778 on that Gustaf reveals a growing disillusionment with the Parisian philosophic world. "I envy you the pleasure of being with Mme de Boufflers," he wrote that year to a Swedish officer in Paris. "It is only she and a few friends whom I believe myself to have in France which make me wish to see Paris again; all I have been told otherwise gives me infinite disgust. No more decency, no more politeness. Those amiable French, have they forgotten that they formerly were the models in these things?"

To Mme de Boufflers, he finds fault with Turgot, in retrospect, and with Necker. He complains in 1778 that the principles of the "Economists" are "too general"; that they wished to measure all by the same yardstick, which was possible in small states but in larger ones was "as impossible to put into practice as harmful to try." Philosophy that "generalizes everything," he writes in 1782, "has diminished enthusiasm, and it is meanwhile only through enthusiasm that one can rouse oneself to great deeds," an idea evidently deriving largely from Helvétius and Pietro Verri that thereafter would increasingly captivate him. He expresses growing resentment toward the philosophers' influence over public opinion and in 1784 complains bitterly of the "philosophic-democratic spirit that prevails and which is so incompatible with my principles and interests." Mme de Boufflers meanwhile shows similar reactions, blaming "modern philosophy" for the present lack of religion, morals, discipline, and social distinctions in France.[54]

Gustaf III's time was one not only of sense but of sensibility. Around 1779–80, the king went through a phase during which he was much drawn to the mysticisms of Swedenborgianism and Freemasonry.[55] In 1780, he visited Spa in the Austrian Netherlands, where he associated with cosmopolitan high society, including Mmes de Boufflers and de La Marck, but sought no contact with the philosophers. The following spring, a Swedish informant in Paris warned him that "the interest previously taken in your person and your country in general has visibly diminished" since the Spa sojourn and that various influential ladies were now distinctly hostile.

It was evidently during this journey, too, that Gustaf allegedly sought out a German Freemason named Zinnendorf, to whom he repented having shared the doctrines of the "Encyclopedists" and expressed hopes of finding the "light" through the "new science." His emissaries contacted other reputed seers, including Cagliostro in Paris.[56] From 1780 on, however, Gustaf began to drift away from his passing absorption in religion and spiritualism, apparently under the eminently rationalistic influence of his new favorite, Baron Gustaf Mauritz Armfelt, though he retained a certain interest in the prophecies of the clairvoyant Ulrika Arfwidsson until his death.[57]

From the fall of 1783 until the following summer, Gustaf, accompanied by a suite of courtiers and scholars, made an extended incognito visit to Italy and France, involving both culture and diplomacy.[58] The king visited the Italian capitals, admired the monuments of art and architecture, met Leopold of Tuscany and his brother, Emperor Joseph II, who himself was himself traveling incognito in Italy. He somewhat ostentatiously called upon Pope Pius VI and attended a Christmas mass at St. Peter's basilica to publicize his toleration of foreign Catholics in Sweden, though privately he commented on this situation with his accustomed Voltairian irony toward the Catholic faith.[59]

In Italy, the king noted receiving a book from a "M. Maistre," whom he duly rewarded; probably the *Discours prononcé par les gens du roi à la rentrée du sénat de Savoie* (1784), in which Joseph de Maistre already denounced the "destructive spirit" of the century.[60] As the time approached to continue to Paris, Gustaf showed increasing uneasiness regarding the *philosophes*. Already in 1781 he had complained to Mme de Boufflers that "these learned gentlemen have taken possession of Fame's trumpet" and went on to deplore, like his mother not long before, the lack of recent good books from France. He now wrote that if he could avoid the philosophers, he would do so "with all my heart," for one always risked being looked at askance in their company.

> These gentlemen want to dominate everything. They have pretensions of governing the whole world and cannot govern themselves; they speak of intolerance and are more intolerant than the entire College of Cardinals, and still it is their opinion that determines reputations and transmits them to posterity.[61]

Still, being in France again felt like returning home, Gustaf wrote Creutz. He reveled in the Paris theater and the court spectacles at Versailles, watched the ascent of a Mongolfier balloon, visited the French Academy and a Mesmerist séance. At the *Parlement,* Advocate General Séguier pointedly praised Sweden's "wise and pacific government, distant equally from anarchy and despotism." Gustaf negotiated a renewed French alliance and hobnobbed with Mme de Boufflers.[62] Creutz had meanwhile urged the king to show due regard for the *gens de lettres,* yet it did not escape notice that he showed a studied indifference toward them and the younger salon society in general. To Scheffer, the elder Mirabeau wrote plaintively of his cold reception by the king.[63]

Once back in Sweden, Gustaf learned of the criticisms against him in Paris. His "strong passion" for pleasure, his new ambassador there, Erik Magnus Staël von Holstein, forthrightly reported, was considered hard to reconcile with the burdens of conscientious government.[64] Gustaf's relations with the philosophic party were clearly in decline.

There was nonetheless no definitive break, as shown by his favor toward Beaumarchais. Gustaf had known his work since his first play in 1767, but it was in Paris in 1784 that he first met Beaumarchais, who wrote a Swedish friend that the king fulfilled his ideal of "those Fate has chosen to rule over others." The playwright was then in need of an influential protector. His *Mariage de Figaro* was banned from the stage, and he was thereafter briefly imprisoned. From Sweden, Gustaf gave discreet encouragement and in May 1785 allowed the play's successful performance in Swedish in Stockholm. The same year, Beaumarchais sent Gustaf the magnificent Kehl edition of Voltaire's works, of which he was coeditor.[65] Figaro's impertinences were perhaps not out of harmony with the king's growing exasperation with high aristocratic opponents in Sweden.

It is worth noting too that in 1784 Gustaf appointed Nils Rosén von Rosenstein, an outspoken defender of the Enlightenment, preceptor to his son, Crown Prince Gustaf Adolf, a position he held until after the king's death.

On his way home from Paris that year, Gustaf visited Rousseau's tomb at Ermenonville; the influence of *Emile* seems evident in his description soon after to Mme de Boufflers of his son's education. This differed from that of other children, "who are made into small pedants to do honor to their teachers," in that he was taught only to read and write, and "all he says and does comes from himself," resulting in his great "naturalness." Mme de Boufflers had once been Rousseau's protectress but had become disillusioned with him, especially after the publication of his *Confessions* in 1782. She hoped the prince would learn Latin, for "Latin and Greek are the key to all knowledge and the source of all original ideas as well as of great sentiments." Gustaf replied that the boy would not fail to study Latin, which he constantly regretted not knowing himself. The exchange shows well how both turned increasingly to the past for the inspiration they could no longer find in the new philosophy.[66]

To foreign visitors, such as William Coxe and Francisco de Miranda, Gustaf continued to point out the enlightened benefits of his reign: hospitals, prisons, dockyards, and canals. But his cultural preferences were now more than ever aesthetic.[67] The Swedish Academy, which he founded in 1786, with Rosenstein as its permanent secretary, was dedicated to cultivation of the Swedish language and the memory of great compatriots. His own dramatic authorship, in collaboration with Johan Henrik Kellgren and Carl Gustaf af Leopold—themselves leading representatives of the Swedish Enlightenment—was animated by the same Plutarchian ethos of stimulating patriotism and great deeds in emulation of past heroes.[68] It is incidentally of interest that, from 1787 to 1792, the task of reporting on the Paris social and literary scene fell mainly to his ambassador's wife, Mme de Staël.[69]

"If kings met more often," Gustaf had written his uncle, Frederick II, in 1771, "this would perhaps be both to their own and to their subjects' benefit." Perhaps. But Gustaf III's own relations with contemporary enlightened despots may be instructive here. Though he surely admired Frederick, the latter's close relations with Russia and support for Lovisa Ulrika in her quarrel with Gustaf prevented cordial relations. Yet the similarity between himself and the Prussian monarch is in many ways striking, as Gustaf himself and others were aware in his later, disillusioned years.[70]

Though he claimed good relations with the Habsburgs, toward whom he privately affected amused condescension, his hauteur and pretentiousness repelled Leopold of Tuscany and Joseph II who passed their distaste on to Marie Antoinette. To Joseph, the king of Sweden was a "*fanfaron et petit-maître manqué.*"[71] With his cousin, Catherine II, whom Gustaf visited in 1777 and 1783, his relationship passed through various phases, from sentimental amiability to scornful enmity, depending upon political circumstances.[72] He early became disillusioned with the seemingly spineless Stanislaus Poniatowski of Poland and felt only contempt for the unstable autocrat Christian VII of Denmark-Norway, who in his day had drawn praise from the Paris philosophers but whom Gustaf considered a slave in his own court. Johann Friedrich Struensee, Denmark's enlightened "vizier" in 1770–72, he despised for his "insolence" and "despotism."[73] Gustaf appears to have given his most unreserved praise to Pope Clement XIV, for suppressing the Jesuits, restraining the Inquisition, and rising, for the "general good," above the "ancient dogmas of fanaticism" of his vocation.[74]

Gustaf III meanwhile became increasingly autocratic as he sought ways of bypassing the constitution and established procedure. After 1779 he progressively circumscribed freedom of the press.[75] The Riksdag of 1786 thus revealed an intensity of opposition for which he was not prepared. He thereafter busied himself with plans for an attack on Russia. For this there were plausible strategic reasons. Yet more was involved. To J. A. Ehrenström, the king complained in the fall of 1787 that he had been young and inexperienced when he adopted the constitution of 1772, which now caused "embarrassments." Duchess Hedvig Elisabeth Charlotta reported him to say, about the same time, "The Swedes seem to have tired of a mild and peaceful regime and to long for stricter treatment. If we had a war, they might become more tractable. And who knows whether they may not someday have their way?"[76]

Opposition to the king involved a number of factors. Among the clergy, bourgeoisie, and peasantry, it was based mainly upon various concrete grievances, which Gustaf prudently sought to rectify following the Riksdag of 1786. Throughout society there was also much dissatisfaction of a bluntly philistine kind. "You will find no Voltaire and no bright spirits along your way," Lovisa Ulrika had warned Prince Gustaf when he toured the provinces in 1763, so "hide from them the distaste their manners and conversation will cause you . . . we will laugh at them together when you return." Her ill will was repaid in full to her son. It was she, the diarist Rutger Fredrik Hochschild complained at her death in 1782, who had introduced into Sweden "foreign tastes and luxury," who had "encouraged arts and sciences a poor land could better do without," as well as "theism and Voltaire's doctrine"; such were the principles her son continued to follow. Many agreed with such criticisms.[77]

More serious was opposition on ideological grounds, especially among the nobility. This certainly stemmed mainly from old Swedish constitutional traditions.[78] Ideas deriving from the Enlightenment were nevertheless influential. Locke's social contract, Voltaire's condemnation of Carl XII's irresponsible tyranny, Montesquieu's checks and balances, all were well known in Sweden before Gustaf's accession. After 1772, the growing opposition drew further sustenance from the attacks of Rousseau, Mably, Raynal, and Paine upon all forms of despotism. The American Revolution, not least in retrospect, stirred their hopes, which were infused with the *Sturm-und-Drang* emotionalism of the rising pre-Romantic tide.[79]

The explosion came in 1788 when Gustaf attacked Russia, then embroiled in a war with Turkey. His attempts to prove Russian provocation deceived no one; it was evident he had violated his own constitution, which forbade offensive war without the consent of the Estates. This provoked open mutiny among the officers of his Finnish army corps, widely supported by the aristocracy as a whole. Their Anjala Confederation, charging breach of social contract, appealed to Catherine II herself and drafted constitutional projects aimed at curbing royal power."[80] In despair, Gustaf considered abdicating and settling in France. To J. J. Oxenstierna, he grieved that all his reforms for the public good had gone for naught.[81]

Denmark now declared war in accordance with its Russian alliance; yet what should have been the final blow proved Gustaf's salvation. He could turn to rallying the defense in Sweden, where with spectacular success he played upon both the danophobic and the anti-aristocratic passions of the mass of his subjects. The Danes were repelled, the nobility isolated, branded with treason.

In the winter of 1789, Gustaf called a Riksdag at which, supported by the three lower Estates, and by patently unconstitutional means, he forced through an Act of Union and Security that amended the constitution, giving the crown widely increased powers in return for the abolition of most noble privileges. The Act created a high degree of social mobility and free circulation of property some weeks before the Estates-General convened in France; it was epoch-making in the evolution of modern Swedish society.[82]

Thereafter, Gustaf devoted as much effort as the war with Russia allowed to rationalizing the central administration."[83] It appears that from the beginning he considered the Act of Union a temporary expedient. He told P. O. von Asp in 1789 that Sweden's present situation allowed no solution except "full power to the king" yet admitted that if the country should not have a "king"—one equal to his task—he could conceive its eventually becoming a "republic."

He was already thinking of reorganizing the Noble Estate or even the entire Diet, and during the next three years continued to speculate over constitutional changes. "I have renounced the French and France since she became oligarchic, republican," he wrote in October 1789. "For a republican [system], I prefer the English." At the end of 1791, he immersed himself in the study of British institutions, particularly through De Lolme's *Constitution de l'Angleterre* (Geneva edition, 1790).[84]

When financial pressures compelled him to convene a Riksdag at Gävle in January 1792, he planned another coup to establish a new constitution, based on the English. This, it appears, would have created a bicameral legislature, with an upper house of 24 "*jarls*," elected by the nobility, and a lower house of 240, elected by the "people," with substantial property qualifications for both. The king would "communicate" with this legislature through ministers heading specialized government departments. The plan was farsighted and ambitious, anticipating the basic administrative and representational reforms of the nineteenth century in Sweden. The atmosphere at the Riksdag, however, persuaded Gustaf to defer the idea.[85]

By mid-1790, Gustaf managed to end the Russian war without loss. He had meanwhile long been deeply concerned over the situation in France. He was disturbed by the Assembly of Notables of 1787, for, as he wrote Mme de Boufflers, he knew by experience the ways of "such assemblies," where "they used big words but generally are moved only by personal feelings." His determined action against the aristocratic mutineers of 1788 was fortified by his reaction to the contemporary noble revolt in France, and he thereafter repeatedly compared his own firm behavior with Louis XVI's fatal weakness and irresolution."[86]

Gustaf was quick to see the disturbances as part of a larger pattern of insurrection throughout Europe. "The end of this century is the time of revolutions," he observed in December 1789. He feared a constitution in France like that of Sweden in 1720, which would weaken his traditional ally; worse, though he had stemmed insurrection in 1788, he feared its return to Sweden under the influence of French ideas. He thus ordered Ambassador Staël in Paris to make every effort to oppose the *constitionnel* faction there, to prevent the establishment of a "metaphysical," mixed form of monarchy. No sooner did he make peace with Catherine II than he sought her support in a great monarchical crusade under his own leadership to crush the "epidemic of popular disturbances" that had "spread from the soil of America to France" and that threatened all thrones.[87]

The connection between the Revolution and the Enlightenment seemed clear. The present unrest, he had written Mme de Boufflers in August 1787,

is a consequence of this system of innovation that our modern philosophers have introduced. It would be most strange if their speculations, which they consider intended for mankind's greatest good, should simply lead to the opposite result and end, in the last analysis, by turning sovereigns—into tyrants, and peoples—into rebels.

Gustaf complained in 1788 of the "Anglicizing" of France and the following year of the ruinous counsels of "a minister with democratic ideas"—Necker—"who is a citizen of a small republic and believes the French state can be governed by the same principles as the city of Geneva, principles which moreover have brought even that city to grief." "It is your philosophers," he told G. G. Adlerbeth in December 1789, "a Franklin, a Bailly, a Necker, and the Duc d'Orléans with his intrigues, who have overturned everything." The "real interests" of the French nation, he cautioned Ambassador Staël in Paris in July 1791—stable tranquility, security of person and property—were "absolutely incompatible" with "the new [French] constitution, and in general with the principles upon which it is based," which were "impractical" and "chimerical."[88]

Gustaf III's projects were cut short by his assassination on 16 March 1792. Though opposition had gone largely underground, the nobility as a whole had never forgiven him his Act of Union of 1789. Since then, handwritten pamphlets had circulated, claiming that since the king had failed in his obligations to the nation, the civil authorities were justified in acting against him.

A group of officials conspired to change the regime if circumstances should permit. Jacob von Engeström, who had opposed the coup of 1772, drafted the outlines of a constitution featuring a strong council, dependent upon the Diet, and a securely tenured bureaucracy, to limit royal power. He evidently envisioned a unicameral legislature elected by classes based on property ownership, and the opening of all state employments and categories of land to all citizens. The plan reflects much in the political thinking of the Enlightenment and the earlier French Revolution, as well as older Swedish traditions. That its apparent physiocratic emphasis upon property rather than status recalls Gustaf III's own last constitutional plans and the Act of Union itself is more than coincidental: principles aside, the aristocratic conspirators realized they must win over the other Estates from the king. The crux of the matter was the power of the crown. As the nobility had already lost most of their privileges, von Engeström and his friends were evidently prepared to consider further sacrifices to restore constitutional freedom."[89]

Though this circle was disinclined to appeal to force, von Engeström could at least theoretically justify tyrannicide in extreme circumstances."[90] Separately, meanwhile, another conspiracy formed which, more violent in its hatred, was prepared to take the ultimate step. Gustaf's actual assassin, Captain Johan Jacob ("Jean-Jacques") Anckarström, a man of strong passions and personal grievances, ably defended himself at his trial—as did von Engeström—by accusing the king in Lockean terms of having violated his social contract with the nation.[91]

His younger associates, especially Counts Adolf Ribbing and Claës Horn, and C. A. Ehrensvärd, went farther: they were passionate admirers of the radical Enlightenment and of the American and French Revolutions, and romantic votaries of a cult of genius and antique virtue. Their ideals, nebulous though they might be, were complete social equality and popular sovereignty, and they despised Gustaf as much for his designs against the Revolution in France as for his despotism in Sweden. The king was in their eyes a modern Tiberius or Nero, their "tyrannicide" a high-minded sacrifice on the altar of liberty."[92]

The king's death came as a profound shock to the Swedish people, including the great majority of the old aristocratic opposition. If Gustaf himself had already grown weary of much that the Enlightenment contained, his death—seen against the backdrop of mounting excesses in France—struck a grievous blow to its bright faith in Sweden.[93] A few stout souls sought to revindicate the *philosophes* by disassociating them from fanaticism and revolution.[94] But Gustaf III's passing cleared the way for the "Iron Age" of Gustaf IV Adolf that followed.

Gustaf III's relationship to the Enlightenment may perhaps best be evaluated in terms of the degree to which he may be regarded as an "enlightened despot." Certainly few of his contemporaries on Europe's thrones were as familiar as he with the thought of their times nor, initially at least, so impressed by it. Still, if he was "enlightened," was he an "enlightened despot"?

His enemies accused him of creating the greatest despotism Sweden had ever known. Yet, much as he strengthened royal authority in 1772 and 1789, Gustaf was never a complete autocrat in the juridical sense. His weakness, Sten Carlsson pointed out, lay in his having to contend with more vigorous constitutional traditions and more dynamic social developments in Sweden than, for instance, Frederick II or Joseph II had to face.[95] A stronger case may be made for Gustaf's "enlightened despotism" on the basis of practical reforms carried through in the face of widespread apathy or hostility; for example, religious toleration, the reform of penal laws, above all the leveling of privileges in 1789. Perhaps "enlightened despotism" was no less obstructed in Russia, Austria, or even Prussia by problems of size, heterogeneity, and social backwardness. Thus Gustaf's practical record remains impressive. No eighteenth-century monarch or minister entirely fulfills the ideal of the "enlightened despot," yet the ideal was a potent one at the time. Was it Gustaf III's?

Considering his ever-exalted conception of royal authority, it would be easy to conclude that it was. Yet the picture is more complex. It could be argued, for instance, that Gustaf became less "enlightened" as he became more "despotic." His progressive disenchantment with the philosophic party is evident from an early date. Beth Hennings has indeed asserted that he was not basically "philosophically inclined," that he was by nature more romantic than rationalist.[96] Certainly to understand him one must seek to unravel a shifting complex of ideas and sentiments deriving from the medieval chivalric ethic, from the epicureanism, stoicism, and lust for glory of Antiquity as variously transmitted through the Renaissance and Baroque traditions and the neoclassicism of his own day, from the pre-Romantic awakening, from changing conjunctures, and from his own enigmatic personality, as much as—often more than—from the new philosophy.

Both Gustaf's kingly office (*métier du roi*) and his romantic sensibilities always counteracted in part the influence of the Enlightenment. As a monarch, he was convinced of the decisive role, for good or for evil, of the ruling prince in the life of his people, and he exalted national solidarity, loyalty, and social harmony, qualities he perceived in the reigns of his ideal models, Henry IV and Louis XIV in France, Gustaf Vasa and Gustaf II Adolf in Sweden; he was thus naturally mistrustful toward basic social criticism.[97] As a romantic, he saw noble "enthusiasm" as the source of great deeds. He was clearly attracted to various of the *philosophes,* such as Voltaire, Marmontel, and Beaumarchais, largely in their capacities as playwrights or as historians in the heroic manner. Voltaire he praises in 1770 not only as "Corneille's and Racine's equal" but, in the same sentence, as the lifelong apostle of "unity and concord."[98] His undeniable fascination with Rousseau, so unlike him in political and cultural values, surely lies in the latter's revindication of ennobling emotion.

Gustaf's criticisms were, however, directed more toward certain philosophers and their uncritical admirers—or toward "false" or "misguided" philosophy—than toward philosophy as such.[99] Concerning the "Swedish dress," he had proclaimed in 1778,

> It is philosophy itself which I call to my aid; not that dangerous philosophy which teaches one to despise everything, to deliver up good sense to ridicule, which creates sects, and which, to dominate alone, overturns all that is respectable. I call upon that benevolent philosophy which clears away all harmful prejudices, all those petty considerations which are opposed to the execution of the most important projects, [which] delights in conceiving or encouraging every bold enterprise that tends to the general good.[100]

Such was the "true philosophy" he had written Marmontel in 1774 he hoped his regime would exemplify. Considering the growing radicalism of the Enlightenment during the 1780s, Gustaf's position does not seem so inconsistent. In fundamental ways he remains throughout a man of the Enlightenment, showing above all the lasting influences of Voltaire, Le Mercier de la Rivière, and Montesquieu.[101]

True to Voltaire, Gustaf remains at once rational and empirical, free from the "prejudices" of the past and the "spirit of system," while his humane concern for suffering and deprivation is not diminished by his obvious political opportunism.[102] He never falls back on divine or supernatural sanctions. His justifications for his regime are always those of utility, with underlying implications of a de facto social contract, as shown by his constant, intense concern with public opinion, at home and abroad. Not that he could condone the deposition of kings, as his reactions to the American and French Revolutions make clear, but he is unsparing in his criticisms of weak, ineffectual monarchs such as Stanislaus Poniatowski, Christian VII, and Louis XVI.

Throughout his reign he meanwhile wavers between Le Mercier de la Rivière's "legal despotism" and Montesquieu's conception of "monarchy."[103] He is early drawn to Le Mercier, deriving from him his lasting formula for the "true interests" of peoples—"liberty, security, property"—which he repeats in his edict on freedom of the press in 1774 and expresses as "the true freedom of peoples, which is the security of persons and property," in a letter to Staël in December 1791.[104]

Gustaf is, however, also attracted for both sentimental and practical reasons to Montesquieu's ordered, hierarchical monarchy, both at the beginning of his reign and at its end—then largely as restated by De Lolme— ultimately perceiving therein a surer means to effective royal authority than theoretical absolutism. He was thus deeply disturbed by the alienation of his nobility in 1788–89, to the point of claiming to Armfelt that he envied Louis XVI, since the Revolution had restored to him the loyalty of the French *noblesse*. "The nobility do not understand me nor do they understand their own interest," he stated early in 1792. "I am the nobles' friend and I cannot be king without a nobility. The king of England has more power than I do under the Act of Security."[105] The leitmotif is ever the search for effective power, surely in Gustaf's mind "to do good and prevent licence," as he explained to Mme d'Egmont in 1772, whether under the guise of the "enlightened despot" or that of the "patriot king."[106]

Gustaf III's reign finally serves to recall that the Enlightenment was complex and many-sided, and that it could inspire not only monarchs but their political opponents as well. In Sweden, powerful weapons were likewise drawn from this great arsenal of ideas, with which to strengthen and defend an ancient tradition of political freedom and to champion newer, more universal conceptions of man's rightful heritage.

Notes

1. Paul Hazard, *European Thought in the Eighteenth Century* (New York, 1963), 328.

2. On Lovisa Ulrika, see Olof Jägerskiöld, *Lovisa Ulrika* (Stockholm, 1945). Cf. Auguste Geoffroy, *Gustave III et la cour de France*, 2 vols. (Paris, 1867), 1:60–61.

3. Beth Hennings, *Gustav III som kronprins* (Stockholm, 1935), 20–49; see also Marie-Christine Skuncke, *Det offentliga barnet. En prins retoriska oh patriotiska fostran* (Stockholm, 1993); Erik Lönnroth, *Den stora rollen. Gustaf III spelad av honom själv* (Stockholm, 1986); *Ögonvittnen om Gustav III*, ed. Beth Hennings (Stockholm, 1960), 16–17 (hereafter cited as *Ögonvittnen*). Cf. *En gammal mans bref till en ung prins*, 2

vols. (Stockholm, 1756 ed.), which was widely translated into other languages, and Gustaf's replies in *En ung herres svar på en gammal mans bref år 1753* (Stockholm, 1753). Geoffroy, *Gustave III*, 1:76–94, gives excerpts from Tessin's letters.

4. On Dalin, see Alrik Gustafson, *A History of Swedish Literature* (Minneapolis, 1961), 113–17. On his skepticism, see Hennings, *Gustav III som kronprins*, 30, 35, 47, 61, 88; Bernhard von Schinkel and C. W. Bergman, *Minnen ur Sveriges nyare historia*, 12 vols. (Stockholm, 1852–93), 1:244–45.

5. Hennings, *Gustav III som kronprins*, 71–98; [C. F. Scheffer], *Pièces concernant l'éducation du Prince Royal à present Roi de Suède* (Stockholm, 1773); [C. F. Scheffer], *Commerce épistolaire entre un jeune prince et son gouverneur* (Stockholm, 1771); Geoffroy, *Gustave III*, 1:94–97. Geoffroy is unjustifiably critical of Tessin and Scheffer (cf. ibid., 99–100).

6. See Gunnar von Proschwitz, *Gustave III de Suède et la langue française* (Gothenburg, 1962).

7. *Gustaf III:s och Lovisa Ulrikas Brevväxling*, ed. Henrik Schück, 2 vols. (Stockholm, 1919), 1:1–2 (hereafter, *Brevväxling*); Scheffer, *Commerce*, 288; *Ögonvittnen*, 20–24, 35, 375; Beth Hennings, *Gustav III*, 2d ed. (Stockholm, 1967), 35–36; Sven Delblanc, *Ära och minne. Studier kring ett motivkomplex i 1700-talets litteratur* (Stockholm, 1965), esp. 136–43; Georg Landberg, *Gustav III i eftervärldens dom*, 2d ed. (Stockholm, 1968), 122–24.

8. *Ögonvittnen*, 24–25; *Hedvig Elisabeth Charlottas dagbok*, C. C. Bonde and C. af Klercker, eds., 9 vols. (Stockholm, 1902–42), 1:167–69. Cf. Landberg, *Gustav III i eftervärldens dom*, 108. Cf. Gustaf's own justification of dissimulation, under certain circumstances, to Scheffer in 1759, in *Collection des écrits politiques, littéraires et dramatiques de Gustave III, roi de Suède, suivie de sa correspondance*, ed. J.-B. Dechaux, 5 vols. (Stockholm, 1803–5), 4:3 (hereafter, *Ecrits*).

9. Scheffer, *Commerce*, 282, 284; Beth Hennings, "Gustaf III och författningen," in her *Fyra Gustafianska studier* (Stockholm, 1967), 10–11.

10. *Brevväxling*, 1:1–3, 6, 16–17, 114; 2:38; Hennings, *Gustav III som kronprins*, 35, 41, 43–44, 54.

11. *Brevväxling*, 1:111, 116–17. Gustaf's letters do not speak of this work by name; it is identified by Hennings in *Gustav III som kronprins*, 299–300. On Gustaf's economic studies, see *Brevväxling*, 1:141, 145–46, 149, 152–53. For discussion of physiocratic influences on Gustaf and Scheffer, see Eli F. Heckscher, "Fysiokratismens ekonomiska inflytande i Sverige," *Lychnos* (1943): 1–18; Oswald Sirén, "Kina och den kinesiska tanken i Sverige på 1700-talet," *Lychnos* (1948): 1–82; Per Nyström, "Thorhilds lära om harmonien och dess idéhistoriska bakgrund. En linje i den Gustavianska tidens politiska ideologibildningar," *Scandia*, 12 (1939): 1–31; Folke Almén, *Gustaf III och hans rådgivare 1772–89* (Uppsala, 1940), 8–10, 42–43.

12. P. F. J. H. Le Mercier de la Rivière, *L'Ordre naturel et essentiel des sociétés politiques* (London, 1767), passim. Cf. Hennings, *Gustaf III som kronprins*, 302; Nyström, "Thorilds lära," 8–12; Henry Higgs, *The Physiocrats* (London, 1896), 68–74, 88–89.

13. Hennings, "Gustaf III och författningen," 13–15.

14. Ibid., 16–17; Hennings, *Gustav III som kronprins*, 338–40; Almén, *Gustav III och hans rådgivare*, 12–22; *Konung Gustaf III:s efterlemnade och femtio år efter hans död öppnade papper*, ed. Eric Gustaf Geijer, 2d ed. (Stockholm, 1876), 58, 60–61 (hereafter *Efterlemnade papper*).

15. Johan Ehrensvärd, *Dagboksanteckningar förda vid Gustaf III:s hof*, ed. E. V. Montan, 2 vols. (Stockholm, 1877–78), 1:17; *Ögonvittnen*, 33–35, 44–46, 85, 112, 171; Sven Delblanc, "Le manuscrit suédois de la Correspondance Littéraire de Grimm. Une découverte complémentaire," *Samlaren* (1957): 77–79; Handskriftssamlingen U.210–214, Kungliga biblioteket, Stockholm.

16. *Gustavianska samlingen*, Uppsala universitetsbibliotek, catalog; W. Swahn, *Beylon, Sveriges store okände* (Stockholm, 1925); Hyppolite Buffenoir, "Lettres inédites du XVIIIe siècle. Le comte suédois Charles–Frederic Scheffer et ses amis de France," *Feuilles d'Histoire du XVIIe au XXe siècle* (1909), 2:485–514. Cf. "Lettres inédites de Madame Du Deffand, du président Henault et du comte de Bulkeley au baron Carl Fredrik Scheffer, 1751–1756," ed.Gunnar von Proschwitz, *Studies on Voltaire and the Eighteenth Century* 10 (1959): 267–412.

17. *Efterlemnade papper*, 77–79; cf. Geoffroy, *Gustave III*, 1:101–6; *Œuvres de Voltaire*, ed. A. J. O. Beuchot, 72 vols. (Paris, 1829–40), 61:438–39.

18. *Efterlemnade papper*, 78; *Œuvres de Voltaire*, 67:91, 282; 68:156. The standard work on Creutz is Gunnar Castrén, *Gustaf Philip Creutz* (Stockholm, 1917). Cf. Gustaf's comments to Scheffer in 1760 on the *Henriade* (Scheffer, *Commerce*, 352–60).

19. Sven Ulrik Palme, "Gustaf III cch Marmontel," *Personhistorisk tidskrift* 53 (1955), esp. 15–19. Cf. Geoffroy, *Gustave III*, 1:103–4; Hennings, *Gustav III som kronprins*, 172.

20. *Brevväxling*, passim. (quotation from ibid., 1:129). Cf. ibid., 1:124; Hennings, *Gustaf III som kronprins*, 170–72; Pierre de Luz, *Gustav III. Ett porträtt* (Stockholm, 1949), 52–54, 107–8; Higgs, *Physiocrats*, 112–16.

21. *Ögonvittnen*, 52–59; *Correspondance littéraire, philosophique et critique par Grimm, Diderot . . . etc.*, ed. Maurice Tourneux, 16 vols. (Paris, 1877–82), 9:275–77, 279–80; 10:21–22; *Mémoires secrètes pour servir à l'histoire de la République des lettres en France*, ed. Louis Petit de Bachaumont, 36 vols. (London, 1784–89), 5:262–63; Denis Diderot, *Correspondance*, ed. Georges Roth and Jean Varloot, 16 vols. to date (Paris, 1955–), 14:226; *Mémoires de Marmontel*, ed. Maurice Tourneux, 3 vols. (Paris, 1891), 2:339–40; *Correspondance inédite de Mme du Deffand*, 2 vols. (Paris, 1859), 1:264, 279–80; *Brevväxling*, 1:262, 2:341; Geoffroy, *Gustave III*, 1:107–19; Hennings, "Gustav III och författningen,"49–50; de Luz, *Gustav III*, 49, 55; Sirén, "Kina," 45. The *Œuvres complètes de d'Alembert*, 5 vols. (Paris, 1821–22) contains his address at the French Academy of 6 March 1771 (4:468–75) but not his address to the Academy of Sciences, which is, however, summarized in a letter of 10 March 1771 from Mme du Deffand to Horace Walpole, given in *Ögonvittnen*, 58.

22. Scheffer, *Commerce*, 282, 286, 288, 300, 302; de Luz, *Gustav III*, 262–65; Hennings, *Gustaf III som kronprins*, 171, 173, 388; Michel Launay, "J.-J. Rousseau et Gustave III de Suède," *Révue de littérature comparée* 32 (1958): 496–509.

23. Voltaire, *Histoire de Charles XII* (1731); *Essai sur les mœurs*, in *Œuvres de Voltaire* 18:397; Montesquieu, *L'Esprit des lois* (1748), bk. 17, chapt. 2; bk. 17, chapt. 5; Paul Henri Mallet, *Monuments de la mythologie et de la poésie des Celtes, et particuliérement des anciens Scandinaves* (1756); Abbé de Mably, *Le droit public de l'Europe*, in *Œuvres complètes de l'abbé de Mably*, 12 vols. (London, 1789), 6:164, 169–70, 180, 188–89, 192–94; 7:41–42, 48–49, 203–4, 234–35; Mably, *De la législation ou principes des loix*, in *Œuvres complètes*, 10, passim; Harald Elovson, "Raynal och Sverige," *Samlaren*, ny följd, 9 (1928): 23–25; Stig Boberg, *Gustaf III och tryckfriheten 1774–1787* (Gothenburg, 1951), 39. On Mably, see also Kingsley Martin, *French Liberal Thought in the Eighteenth Century*, rev. ed. (New York, 1963), esp. 247–49.

24. Geoffroy, *Gustave III*, 1:110–12, 115–16, 204–16, 223–74; du Deffand, *Corréspondance*, 1:260, 262–64, 273, 279–80, 284, 294, 298; *Gustaf III och grevinnan de Boufflers*, ed. Beth Hennings (Stockholm, 1928), 7–32; Hennings, "Gustav III och författningen," 18–20. Cf. Comtesse Marie d'Armaillé, *La comtesse d'Egmont, fille du maréchal de Richelieu, 1740–1775, d'après ses lettres inédites à Gustave III* (Paris, 1890); Beth Hennings, *Grevinnan d'Egmont och Gustav III* (Stockholm, 1920).

25. Geoffroy, *Gustave III*, 1:232–36, 239–42; Hennings, "Gustav III och författningen," 20–21.

26. *Brevväxling*, 1:264; *Lettres de Gustave III à la Comtesse de Boufflers et de la comtesse au ro de 1771 à 1791*, ed. Aurélien Vivie (Bordeaux, 1898; hereafter Vivie, *Lettres*), 39. Hennings, *Gustav III och grevinnan de Boufflers*, contains all Gustaf's letters to Mme de Boufflers and excerpts from hers to him, in Swedish translation.

27. Geoffroy, *Gustave III*, 1:252–53; *Brevväxling*, 1:117. Lovisa Ulrika replied with a spirited defense of Carl XI (*Brevväxling*, 2:153). Cf. *Efterlemnade papper*, 77, 250; Almén, *Gustav III och hans rådgivare*, 45–46.

28. Hennings, "Gustav III och författningen," 20–23; Gunnar Kjellin, "Gustav III, den patriotiske konungen," in *Gottfrid Carlsson 18.12.1952* (Lund, 1952), 323–38; Birger Sallnäs, "England i den svenska författningsdiskussionen 1771–72," *Vetenskapssocieteten i Lunds årsbok 1958–59* (Lund, 1959), 19–31; *Ecrits*, 1:87. On the prevalence of belief in the essential role of the aristocracy as the foundation of monarchical government in the eighteenth century, see R. R. Palmer, *The Age of the Democratic Revolution*, 2 vols. (Princeton, 1959–64), 1:55–67.

29. Vivie, *Lettres*, 51–52; *Brevväxling*, 2:135. For Gustaf's preoccupation over the fate of Poland, cf. *Efterlemnade papper*, 41–43.

30. On the provisions of the constitution, see esp. Hennings, "Gustav III och författningen," 25–27. The constitution is given in full, in English, in William Coxe, *Travels into Poland, Russia, Sweden, and Denmark*, 5 vols. (Dublin, 1802), 4:327–50. Cf. *Ecrits*, 1:101–9.

31. Gustaf's actual intentions in 1772 have been much debated. See, for instance, C. T. Odhner, *Sveriges politiska historia under konung Gustaf III:s regering*, 3 vols. (Stockholm, 1885–1905), 1:112–13, 240–41; Ludvig Stavenow, *Den gustavianska tiden 1772–1809* (Stockholm, 1925), 11–13; Hennings, "Gustav III och författningen," 7–8, 24–30. See also my "Gustaf III of Sweden and the East Baltic, 1771–92," in this volume.

32. Hennings, "Gustav III och författningen," 23.

33. *Brevväxling*, 2:255; Sten Carlsson, *Svensk historia*, 2 (Stockholm, 1961), 251; Odhner, *Gustaf III:s regering*, 1:113, 241: Landberg, *Gustav III i eftervärldens dom*, 94–95; Hennings, *Gustaf som kronprins*, 302–3; *Efterlemnade papper*, 58–59; *Ecrits*, 1:101–9. Cf. S. Boberg's discussion of Gustaf's royalist propaganda using the Gustaf Adolf theme, in *Gustav III och tryckfriheten*, 138–58; also *Fredrik Axel von Fersens historiska skrifter*, ed. R. M. Klinckowström, 8 vols. in 5 (Stockholm, 1867–72), 3:115, on Gustaf's manipulation of the term "aristocracy."

34. *Gustavianska samlingen*, vol. 1 (Folio), no. 9, Uppsala universetetsbibliotek; Scheffer, *Commerce*, 282, 290; *Efterlemnade papper*, 77; Hennings, *Gustav III som kronprins*, 338–40.

35. Vivie, *Lettres*, 115–16; *Efterlemnade papper*, 60, 250. Cf. Nyström's emphasis ("Thorhilds lära," 13–14) on the physiocratic features of the new constitution. Almén, *Gustav III och hans rådgivare*, 19–22, 27–33, 37–45, 51–53, argues the limitations of the influence of Montesquieu and the Physiocrats as applied to the constitution.

36. Geoffroy, *Gustave III*, 1:204–7, 217, 243–44; Vivie, *Lettres*, 58.

37. Geoffroy, *Gustave III*, 1:217–21; *Œuvres de Voltaire*, 9:360 and note.

38. Geoffroy, *Gustave III*, 1:222; Heckscher, "Fysiokratismens ekonomiska inflytande," 10.

39. Vivie, *Lettres*, 61–62, 65–67, 69–74, 160–61.

40. *Efterlemnade papper*, 154, 238–39; de Luz, *Gustav III*, 93; du Deffand, *Correspondance*, 2:120, 124, 128; Elovson, "Raynal och Sverige," 23–31; Abbé Raynal, *Histoire philosophique et politique des établissemens et du commerce des Européens dans les deux Indes* (1st ed., 1770; 2nd ed., 1774); [John Louis Delolme], *A Parallel between the English Constitution and the Former Government of Sweden* (London. 1772), esp. 34, 49; cf. Nyström, "Thorhilds lära," 15; Sallnäs, "England," 30. Coxe, in *Travels*, 4:98–100, 106, denied that Gustaf was a "despot," even after 1789. Geoffroy, *Gustave III*, 1:222–23.

41. Vivie, *Lettres*, 101–2, 107–8, 112, 117–18, 120–22, 127–28, 139, 143–46, 188, 198, 210–11, 215–16, 348, 385–86; Geoffroy, *Gustave III*, 1:232–39, 276–77, 305–6; *Brevväxling*, 2:410–14, 418, 421, 455; *Efterlemnade papper*, 239.

42. *Ecrits*, 1:210–23; *Efterlemnade papper*, 234–37.

43. Geoffroy, *Gustave III*, 1:316–17. Cf. Ehrensvärd, *Dagboksanteckningar*, 1:337–52; Fersen, *Historiska skrifter*, 4:5–23.

44. On Gustaf's penal reforms, see Erik Anners, *Humanitet och rationalism* (Stockholm, 1965). Cf. Hennings, "Gustav III och författningen," 8–9; *Brevväxling*, 1:122, 124; de Luz, *Gustav III*, 52–54, 97–98.

45. *Brevväxling*, 2:84, 132, 135.

46. *Ecrits*, 1:234–40; Boberg, *Gustaf III och tryckfriheten*, passim, esp. 17, 39–42, 65–70, 75–76, 343; de Luz, *Gustav III*, 102–3.

47. d'Alembert, *Œuvres complètes*, 5:447–78; Boberg, *Gustav III och tryckfriheten*, 37–40; Heckscher, "Fysiokratismens," 10–11; Nyström, "Thorhilds lära," 14–15; Sirén, "Kina," 44, 54–65; Geoffroy, *Gustave III*, 1:312–16; P. F. J. H. Le Mercier de la Rivière, *De l'instruction publique* ("Stockholm" [actually Paris], 1775), esp. 10–13; [P.-S. Dupont

de Nemours], *Lettre à M. le comte Charles de Scheffer* (Paris, 1773). Cf. C. F. Scheffer, "Discours économique au Roi de Suède et a son Académie des sciences, sur le Bonheur des Peuples et sur les Loix fondamentales des Etats," *Nouvelles éphémérides économiques* (1774), 18–53.

48. Geoffroy, *Gustave III*, 1:221–22, 309–12; Palme, "Gustaf III och Marmontel," 20–21; Boberg, *Gustav III och tryckfriheten*, 42; *Efterlemnade papper*, 237.

49. Boberg, *Gustav III och tryckfriheten*, 39, 60–61.

50. Vivie, *Lettres*, 120–21.

51. See my "Sweden and the War of American Independence," in this volume.

52. See Jägerskiöld, *Lovisa Ulrika*, 262–78. Cf. *Ecrits*, 4:111–14.

53. *Brevväxling*, 2:307–8, 413–14, 472, 534.

54. *Ecrits*, 4:266–67; Vivie, *Lettres*, 107–12, 115–18, 139, 145, 198–201, 206, 210–11, 215–16, 221, 245, 254, 320. On Gustaf's preoccupation with the role of the passions, see *Ögonvittnen*, 220; Delblanc, *Ära och minne*, 191–94, 224–34; Lars Gustafsson, review of Delblanc, *Ära och minne*, in *Samlaren* (1965): 184–94.

55. *Ögonvittnen*, 139–40, 153–54; Elis Schröderheim, *Skrifter till konung Gustaf III:s historia*, ed. Elof Tegnér, 2nd. ed. (Stockholm, 1892), 78–98, 181–205 passim; Fersen, *Historiska skrifter*, 3:255–56; 4:206–10; Geoffroy, *Gustave III*, 2:253–60. On these pietistic and secular mysticisms, see Martin Lamm, *Upplysningstidens romantik*, 2 vols. (Stockholm, 1918–20).

56. Geoffroy, *Gustave III*, 2:2–4; Vivie, *Lettres*, 153, 160–61; Hennings, *Gustav III och grevinnan de Boufflers*, 147–55; U. Lilljehorn to Gustaf, 19 April 1781, U. Lilljehorns arkiv, Riksarkivet, Stockholm.

57. Hennings, *Gustav III*, 176.

58. On this voyage, see Henning Stålhane, *Gustav III:s resa till Italien och Frankrike* (Stockholm, 1953); Elof Tegnér, *Gustaf Mauritz Armfelt*, 3 vols., 2nd ed. (Stockholm, 1892–94), 1:74–132; Stig Ramel, *Gustaf Mauritz Armfelt* (Stockholm, 1997); Axel von Fersen the younger's letters to his father in Fersen, *Historiska skrifter*, 5:302–17; Geoffroy, *Gustave III*, 2:6–50; G. G. Adlerbeth, *Gustaf III:s resa i Italien*, ed. Henrik Schück (Stockholm, 1902). Adlerbeth's account is filled with "philosophical" reflections on the grandeur that was Rome, popish superstition, etc. Cf. also Vivie, *Lettres*, 297–98, 303–6.

59. Geoffroy, *Gustave III*, 2:16–18, 20, 417–18; Fersen, *Historiska skrifter*, 5:304; Tegnér, *Armfelt*, 1:96; Stålhane, *Gustav III:s resa*, 105. On Gustaf's private attitude toward Catholicism, see *Brevväxling*, 2:425.

60. Geoffroy, *Gustave III*, 2:413–14.

61. Vivie, *Lettres*, 198–201, 320.

62. *Efterlemnade papper*, 411–12; Fersen, *Historiska skrifter*, 5:217–18, 226–30, 317; Bachaumont, *Mémoires secrètes*, 26:31–113, passim; Tourneux, *Correspondance littéraire*, 13:537–59, passim; Geoffroy, *Gustave III*, 2:21–50; Tegnér, *Armfelt*, 1:121–31.

63. Fersen, *Historiska skrifter*, 5:226–27; *Efterlemnade papper*, 403n.; Sirén, "Kina," 45–46.

64. Vivie, *Lettres*, 338–39; *Ögonvittnen*, 229–30.

65. *Brevväxling*, 1:109; *Ögonvittnen*, 229; Vivie, *Lettres*, 353, 359–60, 384; Geoffroy, *Gustave III*, 2:420.

66. Vivie, *Lettres*, 115, 254, 341, 357, 359. On Rosenstein, see Alma Söderhjelm, *Sverige och den franska revolutionen*, 2 vols. (Stockholm, 1920–24), 1:166, 239–41; 2:265–68.

67. Coxe, *Travels*, 4:67; [Francisco de Miranda], *Miranda i Sverige och Norge 1787* (Stockholm, 1950), 136–37. Cf. William Coxe, *Account of the Prisons and Hospitals in Russia, Sweden and Denmark* (London, 1781), 31–45. Coxe visited Sweden a second time in 1787. That Gustaf continued to make propaganda abroad in justification of his regime is shown by Olof von Feilitzen in "Carl Fredrik Nordenskiölds teckning av berömda svenskar 1784. Ett kapitel ur den svenska utlandspropagandans historia," *Personhistorisk tidskrift* 44 (1946): 25–39.

68. *Ögonvittnen*, 257–61; *Ecrits*, 1:1–14. Cf. Gustafson, *History*, 136–42; Delblanc, *Ära och minne*, 191–94, 224–34, 244–45; Gustafsson, review of Delblanc, 190–92; Olle Holmberg, *Leopold och Gustav III 1786–1792* (Stockholm, 1954).

69. Geoffroy, *Gustave III*, 1:385; 2:430–61, passim; Söderhjelm, *Sverige och den franska revolutionen*, 1:87–88; Vivie, *Lettres*, 368–69, 372.

70. de Luz, *Gustav III*, 49. See Lovisa Ulrika's correspondence with Frederick II and Prince Henry of Prussia in Fersen, *Historiska skrifter*, vols. 3 and 4, appendices, passim. Note also Gustaf's comments to Miranda in October 1787 (Miranda, *Miranda i Sverige*, 137); cf. *Ögonvittnen*, 317.

71. *Efterlemnade papper*, 370, 373, 390–91, 394; Vivie, *Lettres*, 285, 304–6, 317–18; *Ecrits*, 4:367; *Joseph II und Leopold von Toscana. Ihr Briefwechsel*, 2 vols. ed. Alfred, Ritter von Arneth (Vienna, 1872), 1:177–79, 191–92; Fersen, *Historiska skrifter*, 5:229–30.

72. Ya. K. Grot, *Yekaterina II i Gustav III* (St. Petersburg, 1877); *Catherine II et Gustave III: une correspondence retrouvée*, ed. and trans. Gunnar von Proschwitz (Stockholm, 1998; abridged Swedish version, *Katarina II och Gustav III: en återfunnen brevväxling*, Stockholm, 1998); *Joseph II und Katarina von Russland. Ihr Briefwechsel*, 2 vols., ed. Alfred, Ritter von Arneth (Vienna, 1869), 2:315–17; Catherine's letters to Grimm, in *Sbornik imperatorskago russkago istoricheskago obshchestva*, 148 vols. (St. Petersburg, 1867–1916), vol. 23; Vivie, *Lettres*, 112–13. Cf. my "Gustaf III of Sweden and the French Revolution," in this volume, 96–97, 106–7.

73. *Brevväxling*, 1:223, 225, 238; 2:328; Vivie, *Lettres*, 116, 178–79; *Efterlemnade papper*, 41–43, 409.

74. *Brevväxling*, 2:425. Gustaf meanwhile predicted in 1784 the disappearance of the papacy (*Ecrits*, 4:203).

75. Boberg, *Gustav III och tryckfriheten*, 247–49, 344; Elovson, "Raynal och Sverige," 33, 42–43, 54–57, 83–84; *Efterlemnade papper*, 385; *Ecrits*, 4:190–91; my "Sweden and the War of American Independence," 56. Cf. the justification of Gustaf's press policy in de Luz, *Gustav III*, 102–3.

76. *Ögonvittnen*, 183; *Hedvig Elisabeth Charlottas dagbok*, 2:182–83. Cf. my "Gustaf III of Sweden and the East Baltic, 1771–92," in this volume.

77. *Brevväxling*, 1:8; Rutger Fredrik Hochschild, *Memoarer*, ed. Henrik Schück, 3 vols. (Stockholm, 1908–9), 1:29, 51–52, 56, 61, 66–70; Fersen, *Historiska skrifter*, 5:230–31, 242. Cf. Hennings, *Gustav III*, 75, 254–55.

78. See Michael Roberts, "On Aristocratic Constitutionalism in Swedish History, 1520–1720," and "The Swedish Aristocracy in the Eighteenth Century," in his *Essays in Swedish History* (Minneapolis, 1967).

79. See Lolo Krusius-Ahrenberg, *Tyrannmördaren C. F. Ehrensvärd* (Helsingfors and Stockholm, 1947), chapts.1 and 2; Olof Dixelius, *Den unge Järta* (Uppsala, 1953), chapt. 1; Stig Jägerskiöld, "Tyrannmord och motståndsrätt 1792–1809," *Scandia* 25 (1962): 113–66; Elovson, "Raynal och Sverige,"; Hennings, "Gustav III och författningen," 47–50; Göran Gudmund Adlerbeth, *Historiska anteckningar*, ed. Elof Tegnér, 2 vols. (Stockholm, 1892–93), 1:192; J. A. Ehrenström, *Statsrådet Johan Albert Ehrenströms efterlämnade Historiska anteckningar*, ed. S. J. Boëthius, 2 vols. (Stockholm, 1883), 1:29–31; Boberg, *Gustav III och tryckfriheten*, 179. For the opposition in Finland, see esp. Bruno Lesch, *Jan Anders Jägerhorn* (Helsingfors, 1941), chapts. 3 and 4. On the relationship between the Enlightenment and pre-Romantic emotionalism, see Lamm, *Upplysningstidens romantik*.

80. See my "Gustaf III of Sweden and the East Baltic, 1771–92," in this volume, 74. The various manifestos of the Anjala Confederation are given in the original Swedish, French, and German in A. R. Cederberg, *Anjalan liiton historialliset lähteet* (Helsinki, 1931). See also Adlerbeth, *Historiska anteckningar*, 1:43–44; *Bihang till Minnen ur Sveriges nyare historia*, ed. S. J. Boëthius, 3 vols. (Stockholm, 1880–83), 1:38–41; S. Jägerskiöld, "Tyrannmord," 132; Lesch, *Jägerhorn*, chapt. 4.

81. *Ögonvittnen*, 273–76.

82. See esp. Sten Carlsson, *Ståndssamhälle och ståndspersoner 1700–1865* (Lund, 1949), 254–57; Landberg, *Gustav III i eftervärldens dom*, 35–36; *Ecrits*, 1:139–62.

83. Hennings, "Gustav III och författningen," 73–78. In this, the Prussian minister, A. von Borcke, was an influential advisor (ibid.).

84. Ibid., 56–57, 69, 79–85; *DeLaGardiska arkivet*, ed. Wieselgren, 20 vols. (Lund, 1843), 18:105–7; Adlerbeth, *Historiska anteckningar*, 1:166–67; Ehrenström, *Historiska anteckningar*, 1:249; C. D. Hamilton, *Anteckningar af en gammal gustavian* (Linköping, 1855), 51.

85. Hennings, "Gustav III och författningen," 85–94; Hamilton, *Anteckningar*, 52–53; Adlerbeth, *Historiska anteckningar*, 1:229; *Ögonvittnen*, 349. The details of Gustaf's constitutional project of 1791–92 are known only through an anonymous memoir from 1833 (*Ögonvittnen*, 349); "A. B—z" [Axel Brusewitz,] "Till frågan om Gustaf III:s sista författningsplaner," *Historisk tidskrift* (1912): 210–16.

86. Vivie, *Lettres*, 386, 398; Geoffroy, *Gustave III*, 2:186–87; Söderhjelm, *Sverige och den franska revolutionen*, 1:142–43; Hennings, *Gustav III*, 234; Adlerbeth, *Historiska anteckningar*, 1:236. Cf. Erland Hjärne, "Gustav III och franska revolutionen," *Svensk tidskrift* 19 (1929): 502–22; Nils Åkeson, *Gustaf III:s förhållande till den franska revolutionen* (Lund, 1887); my "Gustaf III of Sweden and the French Revolution," in this volume.

87. Vivie, *Lettres*, 386–87, 390, 397; Fersen, *Historiska skrifter*, 7:189; Geoffroy, *Gustave III*, 2:112, 168–69, 174–75; Söderhjelm, *Sverige och den franska revolutionen*, 1:258–59.

88. Vivie, *Lettres*, 386, 408; Adlerbeth, *Historiska anteckningar*, 1:191, 236, 241; *Mémoires posthumes du feldmaréchal comte de Stedingk*, ed. Comte de Biörnstierna,

2 vols. (Paris, 1844–47), 1:137; Söderhjelm, *Sverige och den franska revolutionen*, 1:142, 258–59; Holmberg, *Leopold*, 185, 320.

89. Beth Hennings, "Det gustavianska enväldet," in *Svenska folket genom tiderna* 7, ed. Ewert Wrangel (Malmö, 1938): 27; Krusius-Ahrenberg, *Tyrannmördaren*, 141–43, 179-81, 187–94; Lolo Krusius-Ahrenberg, "Jacob von Engeström," *Svenskt biografiskt lexikon* 23 (1950): 615–26; Ludvig Stavenow, "Till diskussionen om Jacob von Engeströms författningsprogram och dess beroende av franska revolutionsidéer," *Uppsala universitets årsskrift* (1923), Program 4, 17 pp. (unnumbered); Ludvig Stavenow, "Jacob von Engeströms förslag till regeringsform och kungamördarnes författningsprogram," in *Studier tillägnade Harald Hjärne* (Stockholm, 1908), 443–76; Fredrik Lagerroth, "Var det von Engeströmska författningsförslaget reaktionärt?" *Statsvetenskaplig tidskrift* (1936): 303–39, 403–35; Carlsson, *Ståndssamhälle*, 259; Geoffroy, *Gustave III*, 2:277; Dixelius, *Den unge Järta*, 43n. Note also the similarity of Gustaf's ideas from 1789 to those of the radical journalist, Josias Cederhjelm, in 1780 (Knut Hagberg, "Missnöjets skiftningar," in *Svenska folket genom tiderna* 7:379–80).

90. Jägerskiöld, "Tyrannmord," 135.

91. Ibid., passim, esp. 117, 137–56; Krusius-Ahrenberg, *Tyrannmördaren*, 20; Ludvig Stavenow, "Johan Jacob Anckarström," *Svenskt biografiskt lexikon* 1 (1918): 610–14.

92. Krusius-Ahrenberg, *Tyrannmördaren*, chapts. 1 and 2, passim; Dixelius, *Den unge Järta*, 58–66; Stavenow, "Jacob von Engeströms förslag," 446–47.

93. See, for instance, *Hedvig Elisabeth Charlottas dagbok*, 3:228–29, 333–34, 376–77, 439.

94. Söderhjelm, *Sverige och den franska revolutionen*, 1:239–41; Elovson, "Raynal och Sverige," 77–78.

95. Carlsson, *Svensk historia*, 2:216.

96. Hennings, *Gustav III som kronprins*, 170; Hennings, *Gustav III*, 141.

97. Cf. Almén, *Gustav III och hans rådgivare*, 43–45, 51–53.

98. de Luz, *Gustav III*, 53.

99. See, for instance, Adlerbeth, *Historiska anteckningar*, 1:191, 236. Even during the French Revolution his criticisms remain moderate compared, say, with Catherine II's. Cf. her letters to Grimm in *Sbornik*, vol. 23. Gustaf's pronouncements against "philosophy" after 1788–89 may well have been intended largely for the consumption of certain politically influential clerics; persons such as Rosenstein meanwhile continued freely to defend the *philosophes* at the court itself. See Holmberg, *Leopold*, 185, 320.

100. *Ecrits*, 1:222.

101. The great syntheses, by Odhner (1885–1905), Stavenow (1925), and Hennings (1957; rev. 1967), have all sought to explain the apparent contradictions of Gustaf's life and reign by stressing a break in his attitudes and behavior during the crisis years, 1778–82. Recently, Sten Carlsson, in *Ståndssamhälle*, Boberg, in *Gustav III och tryckfriheten*, and Lönnroth, in *Den stora rollen*, have, in more specialized studies and in different respects, perceived underlying consistencies, as I do here in this connection.

102. The view, represented by F. Lagerroth, S. Boberg, S. Delblanc, and others, that Gustaf's enlightened stance was only a hypocritical pose, a "salon liberalism," in

Lagerroth's words, for the sake of effect, is unduly simplistic. Cf. Fredrik Lagerroth, *Konung och adel* (Stockholm, 1917), 16; Boberg, *Gustav III och tryckfriheten*, 34–35, 76; Delblanc, *Ära och minne*, 144–48; S. U. Palme, "Filosofen på tronen," in his *Vår tids hjältar* (Stockholm, 1953), 86–89; Landberg, *Gustav III i eftervärldens dom*, 121–24. This idea builds upon the same logical weakness as much recent historiography on enlightened despotism: a kind of moral Gresham's Law, whereby more mundane motives ipso facto invalidate more ideal ones. Surely mixed motives were the rule rather than the exception for eighteenth-century monarchs, no less than for ordinary mortals.

103. Cf. Odhner, *Gustaf III:s regering*, 1:239–40.

104. *Ecrits*, 1:236; Boberg, *Gustav III och tryckfriheten*, 41; Åkeson, *Gustaf III förhållande till den Franska revolutionen*, 30. Cf. Le Mercier de la Rivière, *L'Ordre naturel*, 445–46. Note also Montesquieu on liberty and security (*L'Esprit des lois*, bk. 11, chapt. 3; bk. 12, chapt. 1).

105. *Gustaf III:s bref till friherre Gustaf Mauritz Armfelt*, ed. Elof Tegnér (Stockholm, 1883), 196; Adlerbeth, *Historiska anteckningar*, 1:191–92, 228–29; Hennings, "Gustaf III och författningen," 90, 92, 95; Landberg, *Gustav III i eftervärldens dom*, 96–97.

106. C. F. Sheridan wrote in the second edition of his *History of the Late Revolution in Sweden* (Dublin, 1778) that if Gustaf continued to reign as heretofore "we shall see the wish of my lord Bolingbroke accomplished . . . a patriot King" (Kjellin, "Gustav III, den patriotiske konungen," 338n); Gustaf's addresses to the Gävle Riksdag of 1792 seem once again to point to this conception (*Ecrits*, 1:173–74, 176). On Gustaf's flexibility regarding political forms, see his comment from 1787 on the dangers of holding "one-sidedly to a set plan of government" (*Hedvig Elisabeth Charlottas dagbok*, 2:180).

Sweden and the War of American Independence

A great deal has been written about the encouragement and support, direct and indirect, given the Americans during the Revolution by various European governments and individuals. This writing has been of varying quality, particularly as it is in the nature of the subject to have attracted the attention of many Europeans and Americans of immigrant background who have seen it as a way to foster goodwill between the United States and the countries of their origins. Taken as a whole, the literature on this topic has therefore tended to present a rather overidealized picture of the nature, extent, and motivation of the European contribution to American independence.

The relationship of Sweden to the American Revolution is a case in point, for it has received its share of attention from authors who, among other things, sought to demonstrate a natural affinity and wide support in that country for the American cause. Of particular relevance are Adolph B. Benson and Amandus Johnson, whose work in this field, the result of long and devoted labors, has been of fundamental importance. There is no need at this point to undertake once again the tasks accomplished in Benson's pioneering study or in Johnson's magisterial volumes, which in particular provide an indispensable mine of information. In view of their basic assumptions, however, there is a need to reconsider certain points of interpretation and to introduce some additional evidence in the hope of raising questions applicable to the wider study of the European reaction to the American revolt and of European assistance to it.[1]

The revolution in America quickly became a leading topic in the Swedish press, received comment on the popular stage, and gave rise to endless discussion in taverns and coffeehouses. It was in one such establishment that the poet and balladeer Carl Michael Bellman described his friends of the Society *Pro Vino*, "as usual . . . sitting with long Holland pipes and wise perukes by their glittering pear-glasses, constantly arguing about the good of the city, about the English colonies, Washington, the price of hay, the scarcity of money and similar subjects."[2]

The attention aroused by the Abbé Raynal's *Histoire des Deux Indes* from 1774 onward, particularly with regard to the American colonies, and the publication in Stockholm in 1781 of the chapters devoted to them in the third edition under the title *La Revolution de l'Amérique* is also symptomatic of widespread interest in the American revolt. The king himself, Gustaf III, confided an interest in the Americans in a letter to Mme de Boufflers in October 1776, predicting that perhaps America, like a new Rome, might someday "put Europe under tribute." The Swedes, it should be said, during their "Era of Freedom," between the death of Carl XII in 1718 and Gustaf III's *coup d'état* in 1772, had become accustomed to very much the same kind of political vocabulary as was now in use across the Atlantic.[3]

Indications such as these may lead to an impression of unbounded enthusiasm in Sweden for the American cause, but the fact is that reactions to the events in the colonies were mixed. The king's apparent interest in the Americans quickly turned to a marked aversion. The newspapers, while filled with news from America and discussions of developments there, were by no means in agreement in their attitudes toward the revolution. Some, such as Johan Pfeiffer's *Dagligt Allehanda*, were clearly hostile, drawing for their material upon such sources as the writings of the anti-American publicist August Ludwig Schlözer of Göttingen. Others, like the various journals published by Carl Christofer Gjörwell, while not showing any attachment to Britain or much interest in her colonies, regarded the Revolution with disapproval as the usurpation of legitimate authority.

Stockholms-Posten, the organ of Johan Henrik Kellgren, the foremost representative of the Enlightenment in Sweden, expressed in the philosophical language of the day a general approval of the American Revolution as a warning to "tyrants" and a promising portent to all true friends of liberty and truth, but always in the most general terms and without application, expressed or implied, to actual conditions in Sweden. Finally, certain small journals, published toward the end of the war by relatively obscure opponents of royal policy such as Josias Carl Cederhjelm and Major Pehr af Lund, enthusiastically backed the American cause; these journals borrowed from Raynal as liberally as the *Dagligt Allehanda* made use of Schlözer.[4]

Much of what apparent enthusiasm for the American cause did exist in Sweden can be explained on nonideological grounds. Of great importance was Sweden's traditional pro-French alliance in international affairs, strengthened by periodic French subsidy conventions. Together with this relationship went the general resentment in continental countries—Sweden included—of British high-handedness in matters of trade and maritime rights.

At the same time, the Swedish commercial community responded enthusiastically to the opportunities the war offered for trade with the belligerents, especially with the anti-British powers that were largely dependent on neutral shipping. The war also offered opportunities to initiate trade with the former British colonies in North America, which heretofore had been closed to foreign commerce. By September 1775, the British government had taken note of the loading of a large Irish ship in Gothenburg with munitions, presumably for the American rebels. American vessels are known to have called at Gothenburg and the free port of Marstrand as early as mid-1777 and may have done so earlier. Thereafter, the reports of the British consul in Gothenburg, Thomas Erskine, to his government are filled with information on the arrivals, departures, and cargos of American ships.[5] The overall rise in Swedish trade during the war years is reflected in statistics that show the volume of exports increasing from a value of 3.9 million *riksdaler* in 1774 to 5.8 million by 1782, resulting in a favorable balance of trade and considerable accumulation of silver.[6]

A detailed study of Swedish trade with the United States during the American Revolution has not yet been undertaken, but sufficient evidence exists to show that it was not negligible. The official statistics of the Swedish Commerce College (*Kommerskollegium*) show that between 1777 and 1783, total exports to the "West Indies," which is to say to the whole of the New World, increased from 6,107 to 153,005 *riksdaler.* This commerce, it seems clear, was not limited to noncontraband goods.[7] How much of it was with the United States can only be approximated, but certainly the Swedish government was not insensible to the advantages to be gained through trade with the new nation.

From 1780 onward, "West Indian" trade was encouraged by the granting of both reductions on import duties for products from that part of the world and favorable bonding privileges for imports destined for eventual re-export. Even before the war was over, the Swedish ambassador in Paris, Count Gustaf Philip Creutz, began to discuss with Benjamin Franklin the possibility of a commercial treaty, and Baron Samuel Gustaf Hermelin was sent to the United States to investigate trade prospects.

Shortly after the signing of preliminary terms of peace between Great Britain and the United States on 30 November 1782, Creutz and Franklin prepared a Swedish-American treaty of friendship and commerce, which was signed on 3 April 1783. The agreement provided for trade on the basis of the most favored nation, which had been stipulated for the first time in the Franco-American Commercial Treaty of 1778, and itself served as the model for American trade negotiations soon thereafter with Denmark and Portugal. Count Creutz hoped that Sweden might be remembered as the first power to offer unsolicited friendship to the United States. In sum, Sweden's interest in the American Revolution was not, to say the least, solely ideological.

That a considerable number of Swedes served against Great Britain in the War of American Independence might seem the most convincing argument for widespread enthusiasm in Sweden for the cause of the American patriots. Such is the implication drawn by Benson and Johnson, even though the evidence they give suggests that the Swedes who did serve in the war were among those least likely to be ideologically inspired.[8]

Writing at the end of the nineteenth century, the great historian of the Gustavian period, C. T. Odhner, estimated that some seventy Swedes had participated in the war; he was able to name twenty-six. During the 1920s, Benson, through the careful study of the incomplete French and Swedish records, identified sixty-four Swedish officers who had served in the French forces. To this list, Harald Elovson added twenty-five names. Thereafter, Amandus Johnson, establishing somewhat more generous criteria in his use of evidence, produced a list of more than one hundred Swedes in French service, including some rank and file as well as officers. He also gives the names of thirty-two Swedes who served in the Continental navy or on American privateers (including a number on John Paul Jones's *Ranger*), 116 in the Dutch forces, as well as various lists of Swedes or suspected Swedes who, for various reasons, Johnson believes might have served in the Allied ranks. Both Benson and Johnson provide pertinent biographical data in every possible case.[9]

Among these Swedish volunteers, there was no Swedish Kosciuszko or Lafayette, and while a few apparently did serve in the American forces, we hear practically nothing about them. Most of the Swedish participants served with the French, and it was only after France entered the war against Great Britain that any considerable number of Swedes showed interest in taking part. From 1778 onward, however, Swedish officers turned up in Paris in such numbers that Count Creutz complained that he hardly knew what to do with them. Of those seeking employment in the French army, most were turned away, although a few of them seem thereafter to have found their way to the Continental army.[10] Volunteers for the navy were, on the other hand, much in demand, for while only a small part of the French army was employed in the war, almost the whole of the navy saw action in all parts of the world.

The great majority of the Swedish officers were members of the nobility, and almost all were officers when the war began, holding commissions in the Swedish service and, in some cases, in the French. With few exceptions, all volunteered after France entered the war. So far as can be determined, virtually none remained in America after the peace or later returned there. As a group, the veterans of the American war distinguished themselves later in life in loyal service to their king in the military or civil establishments of the Swedish state.

The Swedish officers who volunteered for service in the war seemingly did so primarily out of practical considerations, particularly the desire for professional military employment and experience during a period of peace at home. This was Odhner's contention and was the point of view effectively upheld by Elovson in his vigorous critique of Benson's study.[11] Service abroad was very much in keeping with long-established Swedish practice. For generations, Swedish officers, with the encouragement of their government, had sought employment in the forces of foreign powers, particularly of France, Sweden's traditional ally. This practice, incidentally, survived at least as late as the American Civil War, when a number of Swedish officers obtained leave to serve in the Union forces.[12]

As for the Swedes below officer rank, most—except for a number of warrant and noncommissioned officers of the regular Swedish forces who also obtained leave to participate—were seamen who shipped onto American, Dutch, or French privateers in Swedish or foreign ports, or who were otherwise caught up in the uncertainties of life at sea at that time. Generally speaking, we need not look for ideological motives to explain their presence.

What probably makes it clearest of all why only a very few of the Swedes taking part in the war did so for idealistic reasons is that at least fifty Swedish officers served in the British navy as well, the majority of whom sought employment there after the beginning of the revolt in the colonies. After France's entry into the war, Gustaf III for diplomatic reasons discouraged service in the British forces, and some Swedish officers resigned their British commissions. Still, a number stayed on and several others obtained appointments after 1778 and even as late as 1782. In at least two cases there were brothers who served simultaneously in the British and French navies. More than 370 Swedish seamen either enlisted or were impressed into the Royal Navy during the war.[13]

Although more Swedish officers served in the French navy than in the British, the largest single group served in the navy of the United Netherlands, despite the short duration of Dutch involvement in the hostilities. As it happens, and hardly coincidentally, the Dutch offered greater opportunities to foreign naval officers than did the French, who, in turn, offered more than the British. In the British navy, it was standard practice for foreign officers to serve as midshipmen, regardless of the rank they held in their own countries, and for the Admiralty to withhold promotion to lieutenant from any who would not become British subjects. Foreign officers were frequently assigned to routine duties of little educational value. It was also British practice to distribute prize money to foreign midshipmen at the same rate as to common seamen.

The French navy made foreigners more welcome, and a number of the Swedes who left the British navy after 1778 to join the French fleet probably did so because the French service provided the opportunity to attain the rank of *lieutenant de vaisseau*, somewhat higher than a British lieutenant, and to receive prize money commensurate with this status. The Dutch, however, imposed hardly any limitations on appointment or promotion based on nationality or social origin.[14]

Virtually all of the Swedish officers, as well as most of the other foreign officers who sought service in the war, were in straitened circumstances. During the summer of 1781, Baron Curt von Stedingk, who had already seen action in America, wrote sourly from Paris to a friend at home in Sweden: "Our ambassador in Paris is almost nothing but an agent for the requests and affairs of individuals, which often are harmful to the interests of the king, and many times these requests are nothing more than disguised begging. In order to restore our prestige there ought to be a careful choice made of those to whom permission is granted to serve in France."[15]

War was the principal employment of the European aristocracy, and the War of American Independence came after a relatively long period of peace. In Sweden, the aristocracy was to an unusual degree a service nobility, a large part of it deriving from the ennoblement of commoners who obtained officer rank during the wars of Carl XII. In times of peace, much of the Swedish aristocracy was hard pressed economically; competition for civil and military positions was always keen and became increasingly so as growing numbers of ambitious commoners vied for appointment.[16]

In the 1920s, Elovson strongly criticized as mainly the result of wishful thinking the view implied by Benson and Johnson that the Swedish officers who participated in the War of American Independence did so primarily out of enthusiasm for the American cause. He considered that they were above all motivated by their ambition and love of adventure, and denied that they considered themselves in any way champions of the American Revolution or the principles for which it stood, or that they introduced any revolutionary or democratic spirit into Sweden.[17]

More recent works dealing with the antiroyalist opposition in the later years of Gustaf III's reign, while not disputing Elovson's thesis with regard to the majority of Swedish participants, hold that Elovson fails to do justice to a minority of the volunteers who, enthusiastic over the humanitarian ideals of the Enlightenment, were genuinely inspired by the revolution in America and were later involved in the opposition to Gustaf III.[18] Among these were the three brothers of Hans Järta, the principal author of the Swedish constitution of 1809; Adolf Ludvig Ribbing, who in 1792 took part in the assassination of Gustaf III; and Göran Magnus Sprengtporten, leader of the movement for Finnish autonomy in the later 1780s, who held a temporary commission in the French army, without pay, for a few months in 1780–81.[19]

None of the Swedes in foreign service who actually fought in America published accounts of their experiences, but some described in private letters their impressions of that land, its inhabitants, and its political situation. Two of them, Baron Curt von Stedingk (1746–1836) and Count Hans Axel von Fersen (1755–1810), are of particular interest because of their observations and of the important parts they played in later Swedish and European history.[20]

Claims have been made that both men were seized by the general enthusiasm that prevailed among the young noblemen of the French court for the cause of republican liberty. Their letters, however, make it clear that such considerations were, in fact, far from their minds. Both desired active military service, while Fersen, whose name was already linked romantically to that of the French Queen Marie Antoinette, considered it prudent to seek a temporary change of scene. Stedingk, for his part, wrote from Paris in March 1779 to his friend, Carl Sparre, in Sweden, that the "desire to go to America has become so great and fashionable since Lafayette received such a favorable reception from the whole [French] nation, that it can be compared with nothing less than what the Crusaders of old experienced when they made their way to the Holy Land." However, he concluded, "As far as I am concerned, who sadly enough cannot be reckoned among their number, it is reason and calculation that have determined the matter." It might be added that his precarious financial circumstances and need for active employment were well known to his correspondent.[21]

Though keenly enthusiastic at the prospect of French success in the war against Britain, Stedingk and Fersen regarded their British adversaries with professional admiration and had little but contempt for the ragged American forces. They noted the existence of large and influential loyalist elements. Though at first well impressed with America, Fersen soon became greatly disillusioned over what seemed to him the exceptionally mercenary nature of the Americans, who he felt in this respect resembled the Dutch more than the English.

Both he and Stedingk for a time considered it likely that Britain would partition America, keeping the more desirable southern colonies. Fersen, later noting that the Virginians possessed "all the aristocratic principles," expressed surprise that they should have been able to "enter into the general confederation and to accept a government based upon a perfect equality of condition." Indeed, he expected that "the same spirit which has brought them to free themselves from the English yoke" would lead the Virginians to detach themselves from the other states and that the American government itself might in time degenerate into "a perfect aristocracy," presumably on the same disjointed and licentious model as Poland or Sweden before Gustaf III's coup of 1772.[22]

Elovson maintains that the attitudes toward the Americans and the conflict expressed by Stedingk and Fersen may be taken as representative of the Swedish volunteers as a whole. It must be remembered that relatively few of the Swedish participants ever set foot in the United States, and among those who did, none can be readily identified as taking part in the later opposition to Gustaf III. Those who did see something of America and who left some record of their impressions, while showing great concern about the progress of the war and some curiosity about the country and its inhabitants, reveal little or no interest in the political or social revolution.

Pehr Ulrik Lilljehorn, who was informally attached to Rochambeau's headquarters for some three months in the fall of 1782 and was, according to his letters to Gustaf III, moderately well disposed toward the Americans, noted with satisfaction that Sweden enjoyed a certain popularity in leading American circles. Carl Gustaf Tornquist visited America with de Grasse's fleet but betrayed in his account no interest in political matters, nor do the two anonymous letters written by Swedish officers in French service and published in *Stockholms-Posten* in 1781 and 1782. Otto Henrik Nordenskiöld, who served in both the British and French fleets, made little reference to any but military affairs. Carl Olof Cronstedt, who served in the British navy and was a prisoner of the Americans on parole for two months in 1776, likewise revealed no political views, while the journal of his two compatriots Hans Fredrik Wachtmeister and Fredrik Herman von Walden expressed the same contempt and indignation toward the rebels as they heard from their British messmates. Wilhelm Odelberg considers such indifference to the political issues involved as characteristic of the young Swedish officers who fought in the war [23]

The key to Sweden's position vis-à-vis the American Revolution was the king himself. Gustaf III very quickly overcame any romantic admiration he might have had for the colonists in the early stages of their revolt. In April 1779, the French ambassador to Stockholm wrote to the foreign minister Vergennes in Paris, "In general, the cause of the Americans is not that of sovereigns; Gustaf III has not, as of the present moment, shown himself favorable to them." When in 1780, the king revised his ordinance of 1774 on freedom of the press, one of the first victims was Abbé Raynal's *Histoire des Deux Indes*, which he banned in July 1781.[24] Once the involvement of his ally, France, and the events of the war called for some sort of commitment on his own part, Gustaf III's sentiments turned steadily against the Americans. His letter of August 19, 1778, to Creutz in Paris foreshadows that fear of revolution which he was to show so strongly for the rest of his life:

> The action of the French ministry [in recognizing American independence], it seems to me, has deviated from the principles of justice and practical interests, and from state principles of nations that have been in force for centuries. I cannot admit that it is right to support rebels against their king. The example will find only too many imitators in an age when it is the fashion to overthrow every bulwark of authority.

In the same letter to Creutz, Gustaf went on to reveal the first of those imaginative and adventurous schemes in the field of foreign affairs that were to occupy his mind increasingly until the end of his reign. By intervening in the faraway quarrel between Great Britain and its colonies, he wrote, France was neglecting the more favorable opportunities offered by the conflict in Germany between Prussia and Austria over the Bavarian succession. He suggested a far-reaching French intervention in the Holy Roman Empire, which, among other things, would restore to Sweden the lost territories of Bremen and Verden.[25] When the Germanic powers composed their differences in the Treaty of Teschen in May 1779, Gustaf adapted himself to the changed situation. His personal feelings about the revolution in America, however, were now more hostile than ever. In December 1782 he wrote Creutz concerning a plan for mediation between France and Britain but urged the greatest discretion upon his ambassador,

> so that the King of Great Britain cannot reproach me for siding with his *rebellious subjects*. For such is the point of view from which I have always regarded them. This is the cause of the kings. I have always considered it so; either this is a prejudice belonging to my position, or it derives from the relationship in which at the beginning of my reign, I stood with regard to my own subjects, the impression of which is hard to efface. However that may be, it offends my sense of discretion to deal with people who are not independent. For I cannot regard them as such before the King of England has *released them from the oath of allegiance which they have sworn to him and declared them free and independent.* I command you expressly never to lose this from your sight.[26]

But despite Gustaf's personal misgivings about the American rebels, he allowed Creutz to proceed with his mission; at this very time, moreover, Creutz was negotiating with Franklin in Paris the treaty of friendship and commerce with the United States.

Gustaf III's foreign policy was necessarily determined by Sweden's position in Europe, which was precarious throughout the eighteenth century and especially so after his "revolution" of 1772. He was always aware of his country's dependence on the larger powers. In particular, he was apprehensive about Catherine II's Russia on his Finnish frontier, while looking for support above all from Sweden's traditional ally, France, whose foreign minister, Vergennes, had played a vital role, as French ambassador to Stockholm, in bringing about Gustaf III's successful coup in 1772. The American war offered opportunities to build up Sweden's strength and prestige among European nations. Gustaf thus encouraged and aided his officers in seeking employment in the French forces to increase goodwill at Versailles, to train his officers in case of a future war in the North, and to restore a healthy respect for Swedish arms in Europe. The king must have felt considerable satisfaction when Creutz wrote from Paris on April 27, 1783, about the Swedish naval officers in the French service:

> I can declare without exaggeration that they have done great honor to the Swedish nation and served to revive and establish the current opinion about this nation's bravery and skill in war operations . . . the good opinion about the Swedes—which has been not a little strengthened by their good behavior—has procured for them a confidence which has exceeded that enjoyed by other nations.[27]

Despite the portrayal of Count Creutz by Benson and Johnson as an enthusiastic supporter of the American cause, his enthusiasm was little greater than that of his royal master. He was, to be sure, persona grata in enlightened circles in the French capital and was the friend of Voltaire, Franklin, d'Alembert, Marmontel, and others. But politically, Creutz was a proponent of enlightened despotism. While he was certainly Francophile and resented British "despotism on the sea," there is little reason to believe that he held any real sympathy for American principles of government. Creutz's correspondence with Gustaf III, especially his private *apostilles*, reveal him as an unusually astute practitioner of eighteenth-century *politique d'aventure*.[28]

While urging French intervention in the German crisis in 1778, Gustaf III was apparently considering the possibility of an attack on Denmark for the purpose of annexing Norway, if European conjunctures should prove favorable. Creutz enthusiastically urged such a course in a long memorandum submitted on November 24, 1779. By 1783, the conquest of Norway had become Gustaf's dominating interest and Creutz was called home to become foreign minister, in which capacity he served until his death two years later.[29]

The desire for some sort of territorial compensation was unquestionably a part of Gustaf III's attempts to offer his mediation in the conflict between France and Britain in 1778, in 1780, and again in 1782.[30] In April 1779, the Marquis de Lafayette, home from America, wrote the Comte de Vergennes suggesting that France lease four Swedish ships of the line together with half their crews for service with the Continental navy. The Swedish ambassador, he added, appeared to favor this project.

Such a plan, however, would have dangerously compromised Swedish neutrality, and no more is heard about it.[31] But Lafayette had apparently held out the possibility of Sweden's obtaining in return one of the West Indian islands taken from Britain during the war, thereby touching upon

Gustaf III's long-standing desire to obtain a New World colony and doubt-less accounting for Creutz's initial interest in the proposal. The ambassador soon thereafter instructed Count Fersen to "explore quietly, and under pretense of personal curiosity, the possibility of obtaining from the United States some district on the Continent of North America, or some island in the vicinity," which might serve as an entrepôt for Swedish commerce in that part of the world. Nothing apparently came of this project, however, for Gustaf III's colonial ambitions drop out of view until 1784, when, as part of a new subsidy convention with France, he received the island of St. Barthélemy in the Leeward Islands.[32]

Gustaf had meanwhile come to play a role in the events leading up to the establishment of the League of Armed Neutrality of 1780.[33] The entrance of France into the War of American Independence raised once again, and in acute form, the old problem of neutral maritime rights. Britain's enemies were dependent on the naval stores—ship's timber, masts, sailcloth, pitch, tar, hemp, cordage—that played so vital a role in the commerce of the Baltic neutrals, particularly Sweden, while the British government, backed by the might of the Royal Navy, held that such goods constituted contraband and were thus subject to seizure. It was under such circumstances that the first tentative proposals for a common defense of maritime rights were made by the Danish and Russian courts, both dated 25 August 1778.[34]

During the following month, Vergennes made strong representations through his envoys in Stockholm and Copenhagen in favor of Scandinavian cooperation to this end. The Swedish government gave an evasive reply, which the French ambassador attributed partly to traditional suspicion of Denmark and, more important, to apprehensions about the position of Russia vis-à-vis Great Britain. When France threatened the neutrals with a stricter maritime policy and Russia seemed to respond, Gustaf III invited the two other northern courts, in October and November, to undertake joint measures.[35]

By March 1779, no less than thirty-two cases involving Swedish merchant ships had been tried by British admiralty courts and decided to the disadvantage of their owners. With the apparent support of Russia, and hence of Denmark, Gustaf III in February outfitted a squadron to escort Swedish merchantmen through the English Channel and as far as the Mediterranean. The squadron was to resist visit and search by belligerents and to guarantee Swedish subjects free trade in all goods except contraband, which was not understood to include naval stores.

Sweden was the first of the neutrals to take active measures to defend its shipping. In March, however, the Russian government unexpectedly proposed a joint declaration on neutral maritime rights to both Paris and London, which, given the existing situation in the northern seas, could only favor British interests. Gustaf III, having committed himself to the active defense of Swedish shipping upon expectation of Russian and Danish support, had no choice but to accept. In the belief that Catherine tended toward Britain, Gustaf during the latter half of 1779 closed all Swedish ports, except the free port of Marstrand, to French and American but not to British privateers. Denmark meanwhile abstained from any commitments but sent out a separate squadron of its own.[36]

By the beginning of 1780, however, it was apparent to Gustaf III that the Russian empress was becoming decidedly anti-British in attitude, and Swedish policy veered once again in the direction of France. In March, Catherine II issued a proclamation on the rights of neutrals, based on the provisions of the Danish proposal of August 1778, and invited the adherence of other powers. Denmark joined in July and Sweden in September, to be followed in due course by Prussia, Austria, Portugal, and the Kingdom of the Two Sicilies.[37]

When the Swedish ambassador informed Lord North of his government's decision in the winter of 1779 to convoy its merchant vessels, the latter is supposed to have asked, "Who then is to escort the Swedish war vessels?" The British nevertheless treated Swedish shipping with greater respect, while the League of Armed Neutrality of the following year was a considerable success from the Swedish point of view. Although refusing any commitment to the League's interpretation of neutral rights, and while declaring war on the principal neutral carrier, the United Netherlands, the British government in fact curtailed the activities of privateers against the remaining neutrals, with the result that commerce raiding declined markedly by the end of the war.

For Sweden, this protection meant rapidly expanding trade, and at the same time the government was able to attain a rapprochement with Russia without weakening its ties with France or breaking openly with Great Britain. Escort operations provided valuable experience for officers and seamen and greatly strengthened the Swedish navy. The principles of the League, though abandoned by Russia by the end of the war, were incorporated into the Swedish-American Treaty of Friendship and Commerce of April 1783.[38] Nevertheless, Vergennes wrote to the new French ambassador to Stockholm in June of that year:

> The conduct of the King of Sweden toward England during the war that has just ended was not always as firm as we would have expected.

This prince has even appeared not to be aware of the power which the association of neutrals, of which he was one of the principal supports, gave him. If he had dared to make his flag more respected, it would appear that the empress of Russia would not have cooled as much as she did last year toward a project that brought her glory.

Gustaf III's role in the defense of neutral rights seems less steadfast and principled than those who have dealt specifically with the subject generally believed. Nor was the king of Sweden successful in profiting from the diplomatic credit he hoped to derive from the situation. His counterproposals for the neutrality convention with Russia in the summer of 1780 were rejected out of hand by Catherine, whose own final draft was almost identical. It was clear that the empress brooked no rival in prestige. When Gustaf in August 1782 proposed a congress to discuss an international maritime code, taking into account the demands of both belligerents and neutrals, Catherine evaded the issue while at the same time considering a similar project with Austria. None of Gustaf's attempts between 1778 and 1782 to mediate in the Anglo-French conflict evoked any response. In sum, Sweden's dependence upon the greater European powers becomes evident upon closer examination.[39]

That Gustaf III's personal animus toward the Americans continued to harden even after the end of the war is demonstrated by his reaction to the award of membership in the Society of the Cincinnati, in the winter of 1784, to Count Fersen and Baron Stedingk, the only two Swedes with the rank of colonel in the French forces during the war and thus eligible. The king categorically forbade them to accept the order, explaining to Stedingk in March:

I do not despise the nomination . . . but . . . it is not in my interest, nor is it wise for me, to permit my subjects, and especially those distinguished by their positions and by my personal sentiments toward them, to wear and to consider themselves honored by a public mark of the success of a revolt of subjects against their legitimate sovereign, and especially a revolt, the cause and motives of which were so unjust and so unfounded. I know very well that today America is regarded as independent and even as my ally, but the success which legalized this enterprise cannot however justify it. Too recently having ourselves escaped from our troubles that there should not still exist, no doubt, some germs of our former divisions, it is my duty to avert anything which could reawaken such ideas. These are my reasons for which I have forbidden you, as I have already forbidden Count Fersen, to receive and to wear this decoration and this order of the American Army, and it was in these terms that I have already advised the King of France ... of my intentions in this matter.[40]

George Washington came close to the truth when he wrote to General Rochambeau on August 20, 1784, "Considering how recently the King of Sweden has changed the form of the Constitution of that Country, it is not much to be wondered at that his *fears* should get the better of his *liberality* at anything which might have the semblance of republicanism."[41]

During the period of the American Revolution, an important political transformation occurred in Sweden. In 1772, most Swedes of all classes had welcomed Gustaf III's coup d'état, which greatly increased the royal prerogative, as the necessary antidote to factiousness and corruption, indeed to the sad fate that was just then overtaking Poland at the hands of its more powerful neighbors. When the American Revolution first began, it aroused, as has been noted, much interest, a good deal of incipient anglophobia, but relatively little political response among a people who were still basically satisfied with their regime and strongly attached to their king. The Riksdag of 1778, however, began to reveal signs of discontent, stemming largely from the king's autocratic propensities and his tendency to disregard his own constitution of 1772, a fatal rift that was to lead ultimately to the constitutional crisis of 1788–89 and to Gustaf III's assassination by an aristocratic conspiracy in 1792.

The growing popularity of the later editions of Raynal's *Histoire des Deux Indes* and the king's ban on the work in 1781 are indicative of a changing atmosphere, as was the appearance about 1780 of certain small journals expressing opposition to royal policy, such as Josias Carl Cederhjelm's *Sanning och Nöje* and the publications of Major Pehr af Lund, which enthusiastically espoused the American cause as a means of belaboring the government in Sweden. Lund for instance wrote in his *Tryck-Friheten den Wälsignade* of April 28, 1783, that the knowledge that "there is one place on earth where man can be free from his chains" should "frighten the despots and hold them in rein."

Similarly, events in America had a strong influence upon the thinking of the small autonomist movement in Finland, whose leader, Göran Magnus Sprengtporten, had sought service in the French army during the war. The heart of the Finnish noble opposition was the secret Valhalla Order at Sveaborg Fortress with its cult of antique civic virtue, which characteristically at first had been enthusiastically royalist but whose members gradually turned against the king in disillusionment. To these young idealists, Sprengtporten appeared in the guise of a Finnish Washington.[42]

As opposition to Gustaf III increased during the years following the war, important segments of Swedish opinion tended to idealize the American Revolution in retrospect. This trend is apparent in literature, especially in poetry. In his *Året 1783* (written in 1784), Bengt Lidner sang the praises of a "Brutian Washington" who "snatches a bloody scepter from the tyrant's hand," and several years later, Bishop Johan Olof Wallin lauded "the first American" in his *George Washington*. In 1797, in celebrating the friendship of Count Creutz and Benjamin Franklin in Paris, Frans Mikael Franzén in Finland paid a warm tribute to the American "philosopher."[43] Writing in 1790, the editor of the radical journal, *Medborgaren*—"The Citizen"—Karl Fredrik Nordenskiöld, looking back on the events in America, proclaimed that the independence of that country

> for all time shall cause wise rulers to govern their subjects under the banner of freedom, for America has taught Nations to know their rights and the equal protection which a benevolent nature affords to all. *All men are born free and equal;* this was the first meaning of the actions of the American states. These words were made the fundament of their form of government. The virtuous Americans will soon teach all nationalities the meaning of the Majesty of Nations: the Majesty of Man! Already in the fields of Mexico and the mountains of Chile they have heard a cherished echo of the enchanting voice of Liberty; already a small principality in the Netherlands has shaken the shackles of force; already the Brabançons have awakened in their absolutistic monarch a just concern; already the Spaniards recall the oath of free subjects: *"We, who are as good as you, swear to you, who are no better than we, to accept you as our king and sovereign lord, provided you observe all our statutes and laws; and if not, no."* Soon the Hungarians will show their own pride and the ignominy with which they are treated; soon Florence and Milan will be justly wroth against their internal spies and their Duke's fiscal inquisitions . . . Philosophers, Friends of Mankind, Citizens, what a magnificent prospect for you![44]

Even when in later years, members of the old radical opposition in Sweden became disillusioned with the excesses of the French Revolution, they tended to retain their admiration for America.[45]

In 1779, the American Francis Dana wrote from St. Petersburg, "Britain has not a single friend among all the powers of Europe."[46] The case of Sweden is a reminder that to be anti-British or pro-French in the American conflict did not necessarily imply either understanding or sympathy for American ideals or dissatisfaction at home. It further gives some indication of how Europeans, whether sympathetic, antipathetic, or indifferent, tended to conceive—or misconceive—the American situation in traditional European terms.

The Swedish example demonstrates the extent to which aid in material and even in military manpower could accrue to the American cause by virtue of essentially practical motives, such as commercial profit or the desire for military experience and reputation, from persons basically unconcerned with the deeper issues at stake. The actions of Gustaf III show how a European monarch could follow a course at least indirectly favorable to the Americans for reasons of policy, while at the same time holding the greatest aversion for American principles.

Finally, we are once again reminded of the manner in which reactions in Europe to the events in America were conditioned by changing circumstances at home. The American Revolution and War of Independence lasted for more than eight years. These were eventful years in Europe, not least of all in Sweden, where important political developments took place that tended to polarize opinion, in part at least, around the American cause.

Notes

This was my first published article.

1. Adolph B. Benson, *Sweden and the American Revolution* (New Haven, 1926), esp. 12, 15, 66; Amandus Johnson, *Swedish Contributions to American Freedom, 1776–1783* (Philadelphia, 1953–57), esp. 1:33–34, 37, 44–45, 147–53, 203–4, 207, 211–13, 460. See also Johnson's "Swedish Officers in the American Revolution," *American Swedish Historical Foundation Yearbook, 1957*, 33–39. A brief but essentially sound account is in Eric W. Fleisher and Jörgen Weibull, *Viking Times to Modern* (Minneapolis and Stockholm, 1953), 20–28.

2. Johnson, *Swedish Contributions*, 1:58, 110–11; quotation is from Bellman's *Fredmans testamente* No. 1, *ibid.*, 148.

3. Harald Elovson, "Raynal och Sverige," *Samlaren*, ny följd 9 (1928): 35; *Lettres de Gustave III à la Comtesse de Boufflers et de la comtesse au roi de 1771 à1791*, ed. A. Vivie (Bordeaux, 1898), 101–2. Cf. Johnson, *Swedish Contributions*, 1:151. Much less is known about reactions to the American Revolution in the neighboring Danish-Norwegian kingdom, due to stricter censorship. See, however, Thorkild Kjærgaard, *Denmark Gets the News of '76* (Copenhagen, 1975).

4. For the best analysis of Swedish editorial reactions to the American Revolution, though limited to the Stockholm journals, see Harald Elovson, *Amerika i svensk*

litteratur 1750–1820 (Lund, 1930), 98–125; Elovson, "Raynal och Sverige," 57–62; and Johnson, *Swedish Contributions,*1:147–48, 151, 189–90. On Lund, see Stig Boberg, *Gustaf III och tryckfriheten, 1774–1787* (Gothenburg, 1951), 178–98. On Schlözer, see Herbert P. Gallinger, *Die Haltung der deutschen Publizistik zu dem amerikanischen Unabhäng-igkeitskriege, 1775–1783* (Leipzig, 1900), 25–32, 38–46. Gallinger's work on German editorial opinion on the American Revolution provides an interesting comparison with Sweden.

5. *British Diplomatic Instructions, 1689–1789,* vol. 5, Sweden, 1727–1789, ed. James Frederick Chance, (London, 1928), 232. This work contains many references to Swed-ish trade with the Americans, 231–55. Cf. Johnson, *Swedish Contributions,* 1:542–52. Johnson makes extensive use, for the first time, of Erskine's reports and gives in brief the best account of Swedish trade with America during the Revolution. See also Baron Samuel Gustaf Hermelin, *Berättelse om Nordamerikas Förenta stater 1784. Bref till Kanslipresidenten* (Stockholm, 1894), which gives the views of a contemporary Swedish traveler to America on trade possibilities with that country.

6. See Olof Jägerskiöld, *Den Svenska utrikespolitikens historia,* vol. 2, part 2: *1721–1792* (Stockholm, 1957), 285, for the above figures. C. T. Odhner, *Sveriges politiska historia under konung Gustaf III:s regering,* 3 vols. (Stockholm, 1885–1905), 2:121 (tables), gives slightly higher figures, respectively 4.1 and 6.0 million *riksdaler.* See also Olle Gasslander, "The Convoy Affair of 1798," *Scandinavian Economic History Review* 2 (1954): 27.

7. Ingegerd Hildebrand, *Den svenska kolonin S:t Barthelemy och Västindiska kompaniet fram till 1796* (Lund, 1951), 41–43, 315 (Table 1), gives the Commerce College statistics for "West Indian" trade, 1777–85. Johnson, *Swedish Contributions,* 1:546, 551–52, 564–65, makes some criticism of these figures. See Wilhelm Odelberg, *Viceamiral Carl Olof Cronstedt* (Helsingfors, 1954), 47. Riksarkivet in Stockholm contains much material on volume of trade, commercial policy, privateering by belligerents, etc., during the American war, which invites further archival study.

8. Johnson, *Swedish Contributions,* 1:572–81; Benson, *Sweden and the American Revolution,* 48–55; Jägerskiöld, *Svenska utrikespolitikens historia,* vol. 2, part 2, 286; Hildebrand, *Svenska kolonin S:t Barthelemy,* 44–47.

9. Odhner, *Gustaf III:s regering,* 2:103–5; Benson, *Sweden and the American Revo-lution,* 87–128; Harald Elovson, "De Svenska officerarna i nordamerikanska frihet-skriget," *Scandia* 2 (1929): 321–26; Johnson, *Swedish Contributions,* 2:5–225.

10. Odhner, *Gustaf III:s regering,* 2:104. Axel von Fersen, serving in Rochambeau's army, wrote to his father from Newport, on 7 Dec. 1780, of the arrival there of "several Swedish officers who have come to the American army," *Lettres d'Axel de Fersen à son père pendant la Guerre d'Amérique,* ed. F. U. Wrangel (Paris, 1929), 94. This calls into question Elovson's assertion that no Swedish officers served in the American army. ("De svenska officerarna," 316–17.)

11. Odhner, *Gustaf III:s regering,* 2:105; Elovson, *Amerika i svensk litteratur,* 86–87; and Elovson, "De svenska officerarna," 316–20.

12. Cf. Odelberg, *Carl Olof Cronstedt,* 18–20, 22.

13. Johnson, *Swedish Contributions*, 2:225–82. For details on the service of Swedish naval officers with the British fleet, see Odelberg, *Carl Olof Cronstedt*, 18–48; and Wilhelm Odelberg et al., "Two Swedes under the Union Jack; A Manuscript Journal from the American War of Independence by Hans Frederick Wachtmeister and Frederick Herman von Walden," *Swedish Pioneer Historical Quarterly* 7 (1956): 83–120.

14. Johnson, *Swedish Contributions*, 2: xiii; Odelberg, *Carl Olof Cronstedt*, 20–23; Joannes Tramond, *Manuel d'histoire maritime de la France des origines à 1815*, 2nd ed. (Paris, 1927), 441–64.

15. Stedingk to Carl Sparre, 27 June 1781, in H. L. von Dardel, *Fältmarskalken von Stedingks tidigare levnadsöden skildrade efter brev till överståthållaren Carl Sparre* (Örebro, 1922), 93. Cf. Pehr Ulrik Lilljehorn, letters to Gustaf III, 19 Apr., 5 May 1781, MSS F-503, Uppsala Universitetsbibliotek, Uppsala, Sweden.

16. See Michael Roberts on Sweden in *The European Nobility in the Eighteenth Century*, ed. A. Goodwin (London, 1953), esp. 138–42; and Sten Carlsson, *Ståndsamhälle och ståndspersoner 1700–1865* (Lund, 1949), 136–37.

17. Elovson, *Amerika i svensk litteratur*, 86–87; Elovson, "De svenska officerarna," 316–17. The work by Johnson here criticized is his earlier *Swedish Contributions to American National Life, 1638–1921* (New York, 1921). See ibid., 50–51.

18. Lolo Krusius-Ahrenberg, *Tyrannmördaren C. F. Ehrensvärd* (Helsingfors and Stockholm, 1947), 41–54; Olof Dixelius, *Den unge Järta; en studie över en litterär politiker* (Uppsala, 1953), 18; Stig Jägerskiöld, "Tyrannmord och motståndsrätt, 1792–1809," *Scandia* 25 (1962): 132.

19. Dixelius, *Den unge Järta*, 17–19; Johnson, *Swedish Contributions*, 2:105; Elovson, *Svensk litteratur*; Bruno Lesch, *Jan Anders Jägerhorn* (Helsingfors, 1941), 144–45; Theodor Westrin, "Om G.M. Sprengtportens tillämnade deltagande i Nordamerikanska frihetskriget," in *Skrifter utgivna av svenska litteratursällskapet i Finland*, 9 (Helsingfors, 1887–88), 34–41.

20. M. F. F. Biörnstierna in [Curt von Stedingk,] *Mémoires posthumes du feldmaréchal comte de Stedingk*, ed. M. F. F. Biörnstierna, 2 vols. (Paris, 1844–47), 1:19, 28; Stedingk to Carl Sparre, 27 Mar. 1779, in Dardel, *Stedingks tidigare levnadsöden*, 75.

21. Wrangel, ed., *Lettres de Fersen*, 18–20; *Diary and Correspondence of Count Axel Fersen*, trans. Katherine Prescott Wormeley (Boston, 1902), 19–20. Although Miss Wormeley's collection contains much of the same material as Wrangel, ed., *Lettres de Fersen*, and Baron R. M. Klinckowström's *Le Comte de Fersen at la Cour de France* (Paris, 1877), her translations are poor, as are those of a collection of Fersen's letters to his father during the American war, edited by Georgina Holmes, which appeared in *Magazine of American History* 25 (1891): 55–70, 156–73. Cf. Franklin D. Scott, who writes in *The United States and Scandinavia* (Cambridge, Mass., 1950), 65, that "Axel von Fersen was one of the adventurous and liberty-loving Swedish noblemen who played his dashing role in the American Revolution. . . ." On Fersen and the French Queen, see Alma Söderhjelm, *Fersen et Marie-Antoinette* (Paris, 1930), esp. 67–69; my *Count Hans Axel von Fersen: Aristocrat in an Age of Revolution* (Boston, 1975), esp. 61–74. For the views and attitudes of French participants in the war, see Durand

Echeverria, *Mirage in the West: A History of the French Image of American Society to 1815* (Princeton, 1957).

22. Quotations from Wrangel, ed., *Lettres de Fersen*, 133–34. Cf. Ladislaus Konopczynski, "Polen och Sverige i det 18:de århundradet; ett historiskt parallel," *Historisk tidskrift* (1925): 101–31.

23. Elovson, *Amerika i svensk litteratur*, 87; Lilljehorn to Gustaf III, 26 Sept., 12 Oct., and 20 Dec. 1782, MSS. The nature of Lilljehorn's motives has been the subject of some dispute. Benson, *Sweden and the American Revolution*, 302, calls him "a real volunteer for the American revolutionary cause." This was denied by Elovson in "De svenska officerarna" (318–19, 321n.), which in turn drew a somewhat heated rejoinder from Johnson, *Swedish Contributions*, 2:86. Examination of the correspondence inclines me toward Elovson's conclusion. Benson (123) likewise claimed that the later famous general, Georg Carl von Döbeln, who served with the French army in India, was inspired by the American cause, which is denied both by Elovson and by Döbeln's latest biographer, Sture M. Waller, in *Georg Carl von Döbel* (Lund, 1947), 564–66. Carl Gustaf Tornquist, *The Naval Campaigns of Count de Grasse during the American Revolution*, ed. and trans. Amandus Johnson (Philadelphia, 1942); *Stockholms-Posten*, 27 Dec. 1781, and 15 May 1782; Odelberg, *Carl Olof Cronstedt*, 22, 47; Odelberg et al., "Two Swedes under the Union Jack." Johnson gives extensive excerpts from the official reports of Swedish officers in foreign service. *Swedish Contributions*, 2:300–419, include much interesting information on the war but naturally nothing on political opinions. For a listing and description of known documents left by Swedish participants in the war in America, see Esther Elisabeth Larson, *Swedish Commentators on America, 1638–1865: An Annotated List of Selected Manuscript and Printed Materials* (New York and Chicago, 1963).

24. See Boberg, *Gustav III och tryckfriheten*, 162–73. Boberg demonstrates that despite his early show of attachment to the enlightened ideal of press freedom, Gustaf III was from the start opposed to it and sought through various expedients to limit it. Ibid., 65–70, 75–76, 343. See also Elovson, "Raynal och Sverige," 22–23, 35–43; and Paul Fauchille, *La diplomatie française et la Ligue des neutres de 1780 (1776–1783)* (Paris, 1893), 17.

25. Gustaf III to Creutz, 19 Aug. 1778, in Bernhard von Beskow, *Om Gustaf den tredje såsom konung och menniska* (Stockholm, 1860–69), 3:131–35; Odhner, *Gustaf iii:s regering*, 1:529–30; Elovson, *Amerika i svensk litteratur*, 97–98.

26. Gustaf III to Creutz Dec. (?) 1782, Beskow, *Om Gustaf den tredje*, 3:160–61. Cf. Elovson, *Amerika i svensk litteratur*, 91–96.

27. Quoted in Benson, *Sweden and the American Revolution*, 93; Odhner, *Gustaf III:s regering*, 2:105. On Vergennes's earlier activities in Sweden, see L. Bonneville de Marsigny, *Le comte de Vergennes; son Ambassade en Suède, 1771–1774* (Paris, 1898). For Vergennes's misgivings about Gustaf III's reliability as a French ally, see Commission des archives diplomatiques, *Recueil des instructions données aux ambassadeurs et ministres de France* (Paris 1884–1929), vol. 2 (*Suède*), 453–56.

28. Benson, *Sweden and the American Revolution*, 13, 56, 61–63, 65. Cf. Johnson, *Swedish Contributions*, 1:44. The standard biography of Creutz is Gunnar Castrén,

Gustaf Philip Creutz (Stockholm, 1917); see especially 272. For an account of Creutz's diplomacy in action see Hildebrand, *Svenska kolonin S:t Barthélemy,* 3–47.

29. Odhner, *Gustaf III:s regering,* 1:528–29, 2:96–97; Jägerskiöld, *Svenska utrikespolitikens historia,* vol. 2, part 2, 273–72, 278–80; Johnson, *Swedish Contributions,* 1:93–95; Castrén, *Creutz,* 283–85.

30. Odhner, *Gustaf III:s regering,* 2:78–79, 91, 94–95, 107–8, 110–11, 113–16; Jägerskiöld, *Svenska utrikespolitikens historia,* vol. 2, part 2, 281, 286; Chance, ed., *British Diplomatic Instructions,* 5:254; Elovson, *Amerika i svensklitteratur,* 91–92.

31. Lafayette to Vergennes, 26 Apr. 1779, in Charlemagne Power, *The Marquis de Lafayette in the American Revolution* (Philadelphia, 1894), 2:68–69.

32. Odhner, *Gustaf III:s regering,* 2:79–80; Hildebrand, *Svenska kolonin S:t Barthélemy,* 2–5, 12n; Johnson, *Swedish Contributions,* 1:570–75. Cf. Harald Elovson, "Kolonialintresset i Sverige under slutet av 5700-talet," *Samlaren,* ny följd, 9 (1928): 207–55.

33. There is a considerable literature on the Armed Neutrality. See esp. Isobel de Madariaga, *Britain, Russia, and the Armed Neutrality of 1780* (New Haven, 1962), which gives little information on the Scandinavian kingdoms and uses no Swedish sources. See also Bemis, *Diplomacy of the American Revolution,* chaps. 9–12, and Raymond E. Lindgren, "The League of Armed Neutrality," in *Scandinavian Studies,* ed. Carl F. Bayerschmidt and Erik J. Friis (Seattle, 1965), 396–409. For Sweden specifically, see first of all the relevant sections of Fauchille, *La diplomatie française et la Ligue des neutres de 1780,* based upon a thorough study of the French *Corréspondance politique;* Odhner, *Gustaf III:s regering,* 1:531–35, 2:65–93; Johnson, *Swedish Contributions,* vol. 1 chapt. 9; Jägerskiöld, *Svenska utrikespolitikens historia,* vol. 2, part 2, 285–86; and the old but still useful C. A. Zachrisson, *Sveriges underhandlingar om beväpnad neutralitet åren 1778–80* (Uppsala, 1863).

34. Odhner, *Gustaf III:s regering,* 1:532, 2:64–65, 88, 96, 519–520; Zachrisson, *Sveriges underhandlingar,* i–viii, 7–8, 61–62; Jägerskiöld, *Svenska utrikespolitikens historia,* vol. 2, part 2, 281–82; Johnson, *Swedish Contributions,* 1:557–59; Bemis, *Diplomacy of the American Revolution,* 130–35, 150–55; Madariaga, *Armed Neutrality,* 57–64.

35. Fauchille, *Diplomatie française,* 210–29.

36. Ibid., 229–73, 453, 482–84.

37. Zachrisson, *Sveriges underhandlingar,* 25–45, 76–85.

38. Odhner, *Gustaf III:s regering,* 2:76–77, 93, 119; Jägerskiöld, *Svenska utrikespolitikens historia,* vol. 2, part 2, 285–86; Johnson, *Swedish Contributions,* 1:542; Bemis, *Diplomacy of the American Revolution,* 130–35, 150–55; Madariaga, *Armed Neutrality,* 405, 409, 435, 435, 445.

39. Fauchille, *Diplomatie française,* 474–81, 584–85; *Recueil des Instructions,* 2 *(Suède),* 468; Odhner, *Gustaf III:s regering,* 2:108–55, 119–20. Cf. George Bancroft, *History of the United States from the Discovery of the American Continent,* rev. ed. (Boston, 1896), 5:346–47; H. Doniol, *Histoire de la participation de la France à l'établissement des Etats-Unis d'Amérique* (Paris, 1886–92), 3:712–16; Knute Emil Carlson, *Relations of the United States with Sweden* (Allentown, Pa., 1925), 9–10, 19–20; Benson, *Sweden and the American Revolution,* 20–38; Johnson, *Swedish Contributions,* 1:539.

40. Stedingk, *Mémoires posthumes*, 1:72–73. Cf. Beskow, *Gustaf den tredje*, 3:162–64.

41. *Writings of George Washington*, 27, ed. John C. Fitzpatrick (Washington, 1937), 458. For Fersen's and Stedingk's reactions, see Fersen to his father, 17 Feb., 27 Apr. 1784, in *Riksrådet och fältmarskalken m. m. Grefve Fredrik Axel von Fersens Historiska skrifter*, ed. R. M. Klinckowström (Stockholm, 1867–72), 5:Appendix, 309–50, 312–13; Stedingk to Gustaf III, 2 Mar. 1784, in Stedingk, *Mémoires posthumes*, 1:67–70; Stedingk to Carl Sparre, 22 Mar. 1784, in Dardel, *Stedingks tidigare levnadsöden*, 109. Cf. Benson, *Sweden and the American Revolution*, 160n. On the Society of the Cincinnati, see Hermelin, *Berättelse*, 36–39; and Baron Ludovic de Contensen, *La Société des Cincinnati en France et la Guerre d'Amérique, 1778–1783* (Paris, 1934).

42. Elovson, *Amerika i svensk litteratur*, 93–95, 121; Elovson, "Raynal och Sverige," 65–62; Lesch, *Jan Anders Jägerhorn*, chapt. 3, also 50–94; Stig Ramel, *Göran Magnus Sprengtporten, förrädaren och patrioten* (Stockholm, 2003).

43. Parts of Lidner's poem are translated into English in Johnson, *Swedish Contributions*, 1:149–50; part of Franzén's in Benson, *Sweden and the American Revolution*, 63; *Skaldestycken af Frans M. Franzén*, ny upplaga, 1 (Örebro, 1824), 88; Elovson, *Amerika i svensk litteratur*, 135–35.

44. Elovson, *Amerika i svensk litteratur*, 152. Italics and Spanish oath in the original Spanish in the text.

45. Ibid., 175–90.

46. Johnson, *Swedish Contributions*, 1:144.

Gustaf III of Sweden and the East Baltic, 1771–92

Sweden's contacts with the east Baltic region predate its recorded history, beginning with the settlement of Swedes in the Baltic lands and leading subsequently to the incorporation of Finland into the Swedish kingdom from the twelfth century on. A new era began, however, in the latter part of the sixteenth century when the collapse of the Teutonic Knights led to Erik XIV's annexation of northern Estonia and thus to rivalry with Poland, as well as with Muscovy and Denmark, over domination of the entire region. In 1562, meanwhile, Erik's brother, the future Johan III, seeking to develop his own policy of rapprochement with Poland, married Katarina Jagellonica, sister of the Polish king. Their Catholic son was elected King Sigismund III of Poland in 1587 and succeeded his father on the Swedish throne in 1592. The short-lived Swedish-Polish dynastic union was ended in 1595 by a Swedish revolt led by the young king's uncle, Duke Karl, who in 1604 himself assumed the crown. The claim of the Polish Vasas to the Swedish throne was not renounced, however, until the Peace of Oliva in 1660.

During the 1620s Sigismund's cousin Gustaf II Adolf wrested the greater part of Livonia from Poland, and in 1654 Karl X Gustaf made a bold but unsuccessful bid to extend Sweden's control of the Baltic coastline to Kurland and East Prussia in the crisis that soon after led to Poland's first actual partition by Brandenburg and Russia between 1657 and 1667. Karl XII had greater success in temporarily deposing Augustus II and securing the election of Stanislaus Lesczynski to the Polish throne in 1704, as the first step in attempting to put together a great Swedish-Polish-Turkish alliance against Russia. Though never fully realized, this power bloc was to remain one of the leitmotifs in eighteenth-century diplomatic thinking.

Neither Karl XII's Russian war—which ultimately led to the loss of Sweden's Baltic provinces and a part of Finland to Russia in 1721—nor the War of Polish Succession of 1733–35, nor the Russo-Turkish War of 1736–39, nor Sweden's rash attempt to recover the Baltic provinces from Russia in the war of 1741–43, however, ever quite succeeded in marshaling the three powers into a common front. In 1788 Russia nonetheless became embroiled in war with both Sweden and Turkey, giving rise once more to the prospects that Sweden might recover the lost Baltic lands and that the long-awaited Swedish-Polish-Turkish system might at last be brought to bear against the common enemy.[1]

Gustaf III, who led Sweden into this last great Baltic venture, had previously shown little interest in the lost provinces. Since coming to the throne in 1771 he had indeed concentrated on winning the support of his cousin Catherine II of Russia in order to seize Norway from Denmark, for which purpose he had journeyed to meet her in St. Petersburg in 1777 and in Fredrikshamn in Russian Finland in 1783, though without success. Only when relations between them began to cool after their second meeting did Gustaf shift his attention eastward.

Visiting Italy later in 1783, he sought to ingratiate himself with Prince Charles Edward Stuart in Florence, believing the aging pretender to the British throne to be the secret leader of international Freemasonry, thus successor to the grand masters of the ancient chivalric orders. The Swedish king speculated, once Frederick II and Catherine II should die, that he might thereby be put in a position to reassert the former rights of the Teutonic Order over Livonia on behalf of his brother, Duke Karl of Södermanland.[2]

As a showdown with Russia approached, Gustaf observed the Baltic provinces with growing interest. In 1783 Catherine's government had extended to the region the standard Russian administrative and judicial systems and in 1785–86 the new ordinances affecting the nobility and towns, thereby overriding local privileges guaranteed in the Peace of Nystad of 1721 and arousing much disaffection.[3]

Gustaf, in October 1786, instructed his minister in St. Petersburg, C. E. von Carisien, to travel through Livonia and Kurland, taking careful note of anti-Russian sentiment. Carisien reported unrest among all classes of society in Livonia, which, though of no immediate danger to the Russian government, could cause trouble in time of future war.[4]

A year later, in November 1787, after the outbreak of war between Russia and Turkey, the new Swedish minister to St. Petersburg, Fredrik von Nolcken, who knew the Baltic provinces well, was to watch for any signs of revolt. He found, however, that the Baltic nobles were too fearful for their remaining privileges and too dependent on imperial service to rise in rebellion, while any such attempt would threaten to turn their oppressed serfs, "more harshly treated than those of Russia," against themselves. From Warsaw, Gustaf's unofficial agent, Lars von Engeström, provided what information he could about Livonia from late 1787 on.[5]

In the late fall of 1787 Gustaf sent J. A. Ehrenström on an ostensibly private journey to Livonia and Estonia, not only to sound opinion but to seek to organize a rebellion. Though Ehrenström reported much anti-Russian and pro-Swedish sentiment, "boldness in words does not prove courage in the heart." He found the Baltic nobles demoralized by despotism, to which they had grown accustomed, dependent on the favors of the imperial court, divided among themselves. They believed Gustaf could seize the provinces with a relatively light force but feared he would never do so, since to hold them, they claimed, he would have to restore the lost privileges of the nobility, thereby reducing his income from the provinces below that needed to support an army large enough to defend them against Russia's inevitable counterattack after the Turkish war.

Ehrenström wished the Baltic nobles could somehow be infused with "that enthusiasm for freedom that seems to be awakening among the Polish nobility." Above all, he found the Baltic nobles "completely neutralized" by the fear of their own peasantry, who were "devoted heart and soul to Sweden" and whose soothsayers were already predicting a war with the Swedes. At the appearance of the first Swedish troops, Ehrenström reported, they would rise in rebellion, as much against their masters as against Russian overlordship, in expectation of their freedom.[6]

After Ehrenström's return to Stockholm in May 1788, Gustaf sought through other sources as well to inform himself of the situation across the Baltic. Swedes returning from the Baltic provinces were closely questioned. A former officer named Wolff and a Dutch merchant, Wilhelm Witte, both of whom had somehow been mixed up in the Dutch revolution of 1787, were sent off to the region via Memel and Danzig in August. Before departing, Wolff submitted to Gustaf in May a highly sanguine project for raising a rebellion against Russian rule among the Baltic nobility, based on the strict guarantee of their ancient privileges, to be followed by Sweden's reannexation of her lost territories.[7]

In mid-July 1788 Gustaf declared war on Russia, arousing serious fears in St. Petersburg. Only some eighteen thousand troops covered both the exposed capital and the Baltic provinces, while the bulk of the Russian army was heavily engaged against the Turks far to the south. From Livonia, General J. J. Sievers wrote the empress that although the Baltic nobility remained loyal, seven or eight thousand Swedes would suffice to overrun both Estonia and Livonia within three weeks with the help of a mass peasant insurrection, which would be assured if the Swedes promised the serfs their freedom. The governor-general of the Baltic provinces, Count George Browne, was likewise fearful of the behavior of the peasantry. Their views thus accord closely with those of the Swedish observers, Nolcken and Ehrenström. As a precaution, some six or seven hundred Swedish subjects in the Baltic provinces were deported to the interior of Russia during the summer.[8]

At the outbreak of the war, the Livonian and Estonian *Ritterschaften* in their *Landtage* proclaimed their staunch loyalty to their empress, and there seems little reason to question it thereafter.[9] The behavior of the peasants, meanwhile, showed considerable unrest, particularly during the first year of the war. In August 1788 Count Browne in St. Petersburg dispatched troops to the Estonian villages of Waiwara and Fockenhof upon rumors of an intended uprising, which thereafter failed to develop.

Disaffection meanwhile manifested itself mainly in the widespread flight of peasants from the coastal districts of Wirland, Harrien, and Wiek in Estonia to Swedish naval vessels offshore or across the Finnish Gulf to Swedish Finland. It was reported in the winter of 1788–89 certain Finns were observed in the Estonian countryside urging serfs to flee with the assurance that in Sweden every peasant was a free man. The island of Tytärsaari, in the middle of the Finnish Gulf, although belonging to Russian Finland, served as a way station for many fleeing Estonians who were helped and protected by its Finnish inhabitants. By the spring of 1789 cavalry detachments were quartered in the affected districts to prevent further flights. The degree to which such unrest signified a real danger of mass insurrection remains open to conjecture.

There appear to have been few documented expressions of fear over such an uprising among the Baltic nobles themselves after the war began, and as the Swedes did not invade the provinces, the situation was not put to the test. Yet under the tense circumstances of the first year of the war, such apprehensions may well have seemed to the nobles almost too horrible to articulate, and the assertion of the Baltic-German historian Friedrich Bienemann, made over a century ago with the approval of official censorship, that no such danger from the Estonians and Latvians really existed cannot simply be accepted at face value. Later studies show the 1780s and 1790s to have been particularly troubled in the relations between serfs and landlords in the Baltic provinces. Only six years after the war began, in 1794, the Latvian peasantry in Kurland supported Kosciusko and the Poles upon the assurance of their freedom.[10]

The Russians meanwhile had other reasons to fear for the Baltic provinces. They had strongly suspected that Gustaf had been secretly encouraged and even subsidized to attack them by Prussia and Great Britain, which in July 1788 concluded a triple alliance with the United Netherlands. The policy of these powers now took a distinctly anti-Russian turn, and in August the Russians feared the imminent invasion of Livonia by sixty thousand Prussians.[11]

Sweden's initial strategy in the war was above all the work of General J. C. Toll, who had carefully considered the possibility of attack directed against St. Petersburg via the Baltic provinces in conjunction with a holding action in Finland, on the basis of similar speculations going back to the early years of the century. The most detailed project of this sort had been prepared between 1749 and 1751 at the behest of Frederick II of Prussia by none other than Field Marshal James Keith, who at the head of a Russian army had occupied Swedish Finland in 1742.

Although some of his associates held out for an attack on the Baltic provinces and Toll himself long remained undecided, he ultimately advised an amphibious attack near Oranienbaum, in the immediate vicinity of St. Petersburg, to seize the Russian capital itself before its defenses could be organized.[12]

Gustaf III failed, however, to gain decisive naval control over the Finnish Gulf in the battle of Hogland in mid-July 1788, and shortly thereafter his army in Finland was temporarily paralyzed by the Anjala mutiny of his Finnish officer corps in August. Nevertheless, in the weeks following Hogland, the Russian naval commander, Admiral Samuel Greigh, feared a landing on the Estonian coast from the Swedish fleet cruising in the Finnish Gulf.[13] The attempt of Denmark-Norway in August to attack Sweden from the west in support of its Russian allies was meanwhile neutralized by the diplomatic intervention of Prussia and Britain.

Following its opening phase, the Russo-Swedish war was less threatening to the Baltic provinces. The campaign of 1789 was fought in desultory fashion by both sides on the north shore of the Finnish Gulf. In March 1790 the Swedes at last made their only descent on the Baltic provinces when a small landing party seized Baltischport in Estonia and, after destroying its defenses and military supplies and raising a tribute of five thousand rubles from its inhabitants, set sail the same day. Though this raid caused much consternation in St. Petersburg, it provided no opportunity for the Swedes to raise a local insurrection.

The repulse of a strong Swedish fleet in April by a smaller Russian force covered by shore batteries in Reval Roads may have averted more serious consequences; certainly it caused apprehension in St. Petersburg, compounded by the renewed fear of Prussian intervention in the war by way of Livonia.[14] Although Sweden's forays against the east Baltic coast were too little and too late, and although the Prussian offensive never materialized, the renewed threat to the region by the early summer of 1790 surely helped induce Catherine to conclude a white peace with Sweden at Värälä in August of that year.

Gustaf III's interest in Poland was of longer standing. Even before coming to the throne in 1771, he followed events there closely and frequently expressed both his apprehensions and his indignation at what he considered King Stanislaus Poniatowski's supine behavior.[15] He saw Poland's weaknesses in the face of powerful and avaricious neighbors as painfully analogous to Sweden's own under the constitution of 1720, with its rubber-stamp king, all-powerful Riksdag, and proconsular foreign envoys.

When he carried out his coup d'état in August 1772, greatly strengthening royal power, he justified it, both publicly and privately, as necessary to avoid the sad fate of Poland, just then undergoing its first partition. It was clear to him that only Catherine II's involvement with her first Turkish war, with Pugachev's rebellion, and not least with Poland itself saved his "revolution" from being nipped in the bud.[16]

Having arrived in Stockholm after the Peace of Nystad in 1721, the new Russian minister, Mikhail Bestuzhev, had described Sweden as a "veritable Poland," and many since that time saw obvious parallels. Gustaf's coup was thus a humiliating reverse for Catherine, who protested indignantly that the king of Sweden made himself "as despotic as the Sultan, my neighbor," thereby revealing her characteristic solicitude for the liberties of her weaker neighbors.[17]

Faced with the first partition, the Poles appealed desperately for help to much of Europe, including Sweden, but the new regime in Stockholm, having once flouted the Russian empress, prudently avoided any involvement. If King Stanislaus envied Gustaf the success of his bold action, he could hardly consider emulating it, despite the urging of, among others, F. X. Branicki, who, ironically enough, would lead the Confederation of

Targowica against a reformed Polish monarchy in 1792. Gustaf's skill and audacity, Stanislaus wrote plaintively in October 1772 to an agent of his in Paris, while admirable, were favored by circumstances and support, while in his own case mere courage could not outweigh his lack of means.

In Paris his agents sought to strengthen their appeals for French support with the argument that Poland's ruin must bring Sweden's in its train. But the French government, seeing in Gustaf III's revivified Sweden "the already developed means to establish its influence in the North," as Stanislaus himself ruefully put it, steered clear of any commitment to the tottering Polish Republic. Wladislaw Konopczynski has suggested that Russia meanwhile had its revenge in Warsaw for its setback in Stockholm, by imposing on Poland after the first partition a "caricature" of the former regime in Sweden, stripping the king of what little power he had left.[18]

Though Sweden had had no regular diplomatic representation in Warsaw since 1770, Swedes occasionally found their way to Poland or had contacts with Poles abroad. In 1779 G. M. Sprengtporten and his younger compatriot, Baron G. M. Armfelt, arrived from Finland. It would be interesting to know what Sprengtporten, the future leader of a small, conspiratorial "independence" movement among the Finnish nobility during the following decade and eventual proponent of Russian annexation of Finland, might have learned in Polish political circles. As for Armfelt, he was absorbed in amorous activity but was evidently sufficiently impressed by the nature of Polish liberty to help make him Gustaf III's right-hand man and the champion of monarchical absolutism in later years.[19]

Already in December 1779 Baron Evert Taube, on the basis of a rumor that King Stanislaus might abdicate his throne, reminded Gustaf III that Poland was an old Vasa inheritance. J. C. Toll, who later planned Sweden's attack on Russia, traveled to the continent in 1782, discussing ambitious plans for revolution with various Polish magnates in Aachen and thereafter visiting Poland itself from whence he sent a detailed report on conditions and future prospects to Gustaf in Stockholm. Marriage between Stanislaus and Gustaf's sister, Sophia Albertina, was even considered informally.[20]

As Gustaf's relations with Catherine II deteriorated, he cast about for possible means to bring pressure to bear against Russia. In the fall of 1786, Pastor C. G. Nordin, by his own account, urged the king that no more effective means could be found than the restoration of Poland's strength.[21]

A year later, after the outbreak of the Russo-Turkish war and at the same time that he sent Ehrenström to the Baltic provinces, Gustaf sent Lars von Engeström to Warsaw, ostensibly on a private visit but in reality to report on the Polish magnates and foreign diplomats, on the possibilities of a

Polish intervention in Sweden's favor in the event of war with Russia, and on signs of discontent in the interior of Russia, the Ukraine, and Livonia.[22] Gustaf meanwhile kept his options open. In seeking an alliance with Prussia in April 1788, he instructed Carisien, now his minister to Berlin, secretly to offer his guarantee of any future Prussian territorial acquisitions in Poland resulting from a war against Russia and its ally Austria.[23]

Engeström arrived in Warsaw at the end of January 1788 and found the situation unpromising. The Russian ambassador, Baron Otto Magnus Stackelberg, reigned as virtual viceroy, while King Stanislaus put his hopes in close cooperation with Catherine II. To this end he had offered her his alliance against Turkey at Kaniow in the spring of 1787, in return for some increase in his royal prerogatives and territorial gains from the Turks in the southeast.

Engeström immediately saw Poland's only salvation in rapprochement with one of the other partitioning powers of 1772; the obvious answer was Prussia, left out of the Austro-Russian alliance against the Ottoman Porte.[24] He would hold staunchly to this position until the end of his mission in 1791.

In reality, Prussia's position was less steadfast and more tortuous than Engeström ever apparently realized. Frederick II's Machiavellian disciple Count E. F. Hertzberg was ready enough to mobilize Polish support but only as one way to induce the imperial courts to accept his "grand plan" for a complicated exchange of territories, of which the main thrust for Poland would be the recovery of Galicia from Austria in return for the cession of Danzig and Thorn to Prussia; an adjunct to this policy seems to have been the cessation of Swedish Pomerania to Prussia in return for the Russian part of Finland.[25]

The outbreak of the Swedish-Russian war in July 1788 placed Engeström, who still lacked any official status, in an uncomfortable position. Through the influence of the Russian ambassador he was widely ostracized in Warsaw society. From Finland Gustaf III wrote that although he did not expect Poland in its present state to provide troops or money, Engeström should make every effort to encourage powerful Polish magnates in the border regions to form confederations and carry out "diversions" against the Russians. Engeström's official diplomatic accreditation arrived soon after.[26]

After the initial reverses on the Finnish front and the Anjala officers' mutiny—whose aristocratic participants formed a "confederation" with interesting parallels to Polish precedents—Gustaf felt briefly compelled to send out peace feelers, including one that Engeström was instructed to make through Count Stackelberg in Warsaw.

However, communications between Finland and Poland were round-about and slow; by the time these instructions arrived the situation had already improved for Sweden and Engeström was relieved of the necessity of a humiliating approach to the Russian ambassador. The delegates of the Polish nobility were now gathering in Warsaw for the opening of the Diet, and their mood encouraged Engeström to hope that something might be undertaken in combination with Prussia.[27]

The Great Diet convened on 6 October 1788 and quickly revealed a strongly anti-Russian temper, despite the promptings of the king and the threats of the Russian ambassador. Catherine II had approved the idea of a Polish alliance but was prepared to concede essentially nothing in return. Rumors of this project had meanwhile aroused the fears of the Berlin cabinet, which, as seen, joined with its new British ally in neutralizing the Danish-Norwegian attack on Sweden in support of Russia. The Prussian minister in Warsaw, von Buchholz, now promptly offered the Poles an alliance with Prussia, with the assurance that while his government had guaranteed the integrity of Poland's remaining territory in 1773, it had not undertaken to prevent internal reform. In the fever of enthusiasm that followed, the Diet declared itself a confederation, to circumvent the liberum veto. As the Swedes had done in 1772, the Poles now sought to profit from Catherine's involvement in war with Turkey to strengthen the state administratively and militarily, and to shake loose from Russian domination.

Engström meanwhile built up his personal contacts, above all with the powerful Potocki clan—or at least that part of it that was Patriot and pro-Prussian—and with the British and Saxon ministers. Together they urged Buchholz to vigorous action. When the Prussian minister seemed too slow-moving and complacent, they brought their combined influence to bear in Berlin to have him replaced by the habile Marquis Jerome Lucchesini, who had been sent to assist Buchholz and who was a great success in Warsaw.[28]

The Poles, however, had good reason to suspect Prussia's ultimate intentions, and Berlin, despite its disclaimers, was chary of tying itself to the cause of reform in Poland. Engeström strove to bring Lucchesini together with the Patriot leaders and to overcome the latter's misgivings toward Prussia. Negotiations for a Prussian-Polish alliance nevertheless dragged, as both sides were reluctant to make major concessions. Prussia would not commit herself to support hereditary monarchy in Poland or to relax the economic stranglehold imposed on the Republic by her Vistula tolls.

Engeström and his British and Saxon colleagues sought to persuade the Poles to cede Danzig and Thorn to Prussia in exchange for an advantageous commercial agreement, but the Poles understandably jibbed at the thought of further territorial losses. The negotiations were further complicated after August 1789 by divided counsels in Berlin, with King Frederick William II (and Lucchesini in Warsaw) favoring war against the imperial courts, while Hertzberg still sought to realize his "grand plan" through diplomatic means. By early 1790 the war party was temporarily in the ascendant and concluded an alliance with Turkey while Sweden did the same, arousing much apprehension in St. Petersburg.

Partly at Engeström's urging, the Poles and Prussians were prepared by March to conclude an alliance first, leaving the commercial settlement, including the troublesome questions of Danzig and Thorn, until later. When Engeström revealed to the Diet Catherine II's latest humiliating peace demands to Sweden the same month, the Poles overcame their last hesitation and concluded an alliance with Prussia on 29 March.[29]

Throughout the war Gustaf III, like his cousin Catherine, engaged in intensive propaganda, both at home and throughout Europe. Gustaf's publicists—the most notable (it has since been learned) being the Swiss, Jacques Mallet du Pan—played heavily on the themes of Russia's threat to the European balance of power, despotism in the Baltic provinces, and dominance in Poland. In Warsaw, Engeström was particularly effective in arranging for the translation, publication, and dissemination of anti-Russian publications.[30]

Gustaf III meanwhile made repeated demands that his minister in Warsaw arrange some immediate relief for Sweden in the form of Polish subsidies, diversions against the Russian rear, or, best of all, some internal insurrection in Russia "like Pugachev's." Here the king's policy stood in clear contrast to his minister's. Engeström sought, conscientiously and consistently, to further Poland's national regeneration as the basis for long-term, mutually beneficial cooperation with Sweden. He argued to his monarch that for the Poles to expose themselves unnecessarily before Prussia was prepared to support them militarily would immediately provoke civil war through the formation of a pro-Russian counter-confederation under the hetman F. X. Branicki, cut Sweden off from a vital source of grain, and bring ultimate Russian retaliation down upon their country. Gustaf replied that by attacking Russia, Poland could drag in Prussia after her. "May they risk all," he wrote in the fall of 1789, "it little concerns me whether they succeed as long as they hold Russia in check."[31]

The Polish-Prussian alliance of March 1790 opened up a prospect more to Engeström's liking: a Swedish-Polish alliance. Engeström began by proposing a preliminary convention, providing for a commercial agreement and mutual aid in the event of future aggression against either by a third power, which was initially well received by the Polish Diet. Sentiments toward Prussia, and consequently toward Sweden, cooled when the Prussian government tempered its warlike ardor by entering into negotiations with Russia's Austrian allies at Reichenbach in June, but they soon after revived. The Poles, by now increasingly enthusiastic for a joint Prussian-Polish attack on Russia, offered their alliance to Turkey and, heartened by the news of Gustaf III's brilliant naval victory over the Russians at Svensksund in June, pursued their negotiations with Engeström.[32]

The Congress of Reichenbach, however, initiated Prussia's rapprochement with Austria, which largely neutralized the Polish-Prussian entente. In August, Gustaf III, still unable to get a firm commitment of support from either Britain or Prussia, capitalized on his recent success to conclude the Peace of Värälä with Russia on the basis of the *status quo ante bellum*. Gustaf had obtained the immediate objective of his war: Russia's formal renunciation of any right, implicit or explicit, to intervene in Sweden's internal affairs. For Catherine, the peace came like a gift of Providence; hard-pressed in her Turkish war and by the death of her ally, Joseph II, whose successor, Leopold II, was now seeking an understanding with Prussia, she was saved from the impending threat of the formation of a Prussian-Swedish-Polish-Ottoman common front against her. The Poles found themselves abandoned at this critical juncture by both Prussia and Sweden to ultimate Russian retribution, which would not be long in coming. Engeström's negotiations languished, and the convention was never concluded.[33]

Gustaf III meanwhile went over to a new Polish policy. The Polish Diet now addressed itself to the question of a successor to King Stanislaus, and the large number of aspirants reflected Poland's renewed importance on the European scene. In October Gustaf revealed to Engeström his own intended candidature. In a series of letters and memoranda he argued that he had proven himself superior, both in the council chamber and on the field of battle, to any of the other contenders and discounted the evident practical arguments against a Swedish-Polish dynastic union. Only such a union, he maintained, could prevent Poland's falling into dependence on Russia, Prussia, or Austria. Gustaf also candidly admitted to Engeström in November that he needed an ally who could replenish his empty treasury and that this was his real reason for seeking the Polish crown, which, he foresaw, would surely force him to drink "a thousand bitter draughts" and would be "a sacrifice for my country." As if to give point to his interest, Gustaf and members of his court appeared in Polish dress by the turn of the year.[34]

Engeström saw nothing but disaster in this scheme; it would unquestionably conciliate "Herod" with "Pilate"—Prussia with Russia—the Poles themselves were hard-pressed financially and needed outside subsidies, geography worked against an effective Swedish-Polish union, since Poland was virtually cut off from the Baltic, and one could no longer count on a few great magnates to determine the votes of their numerous clienteles in the Diet. In sum, it seemed a near miracle when the Diet managed to agree to offer the succession to the Elector of Saxony, and Engeström tactfully urged his king to leave well enough alone.[35]

In the meantime the Peace of Värälä was followed by a surprisingly rapid rapprochement between Stockholm and St. Petersburg; within a month rumors circulated in Warsaw of an impending Swedish-Russian alliance. Soon after these rumors came those of Gustaf III's ambitions regarding the Polish crown together with the insinuation that he might be imposed upon Poland by Russia.[36] It seems altogether probable that such rumors emanated from Russian sources. Although Gustaf informed Engeström in October that his candidature had been suggested by a Count Potocki, it may actually first have been raised by the new Russian minister to Stockholm, who, according to one account, told Baron Armfelt that Catherine would much prefer to see Gustaf, rather than the Elector of Saxony, on Poland's throne, or that if Gustaf wished to betroth his son to her granddaughter she might provide Poland as a dowry.[37] A plausible explanation for such behavior on the part of St. Petersburg may be the worrisome rumor in the fall of 1790 that the king of Prussia was considering a dynastic union with Poland.[38]

Catherine can have had, of course, no real desire to see her erstwhile foe, the Swedish king, on the Polish throne, and rumors linking the Swedish candidature with Russia naturally meant the kiss of death for any prospects Gustaf might conceivably have had. Yet aside from this, the Swedish king was already regarded with mixed feelings by Poland's governing aristocracy. He was widely admired for having restored Sweden's power and prestige in Europe and for his enlightened reforms since 1772. In the winter of 1789, however, Gustaf had convened the Riksdag and, playing on the resentments of the other estates over the aristocratic Anjala officers' mutiny in Finland the previous summer, forced through an Act of Union and Security, which further fortified royal authority in return for the abolition of most noble privileges. The Polish nobility reacted strongly, for a time complicating Engeström's diplomatic efforts in Warsaw. Even Stanislaus Staszik, one of the most advanced ideologues of the reform-minded Patriots, who as recently as 1787 had praised Gustaf III's first coup of 1772, believed the Swedes after 1789 could no longer be considered a free people.[39]

That Gustaf was aware of such sentiments is shown by his argument, in his memorandum of 7 November 1790 to Engeström, that his revolution of 1772 had been directed only against "the foreigner" and that he had then declined the absolute power his subjects, aroused by the contemporary fate of Poland, had freely offered him; that in 1772 and again in 1789 he had saved his nation from "a democratic anarchy, such as that France has recently fallen victim to"; and that insinuations against his devotion to "the freedom, independence, [and] security of his people" emanated from the ministers of "the most autocratic courts of Europe."[40]

In January 1791 Gustaf's ambassador in Paris, Baron E. M. Staël von Holstein, on the king's secret instructions, discussed Gustaf's candidature with Count Jan Potocki. When the count objected that the king had placed himself at the head of the "Third Estate" against the nobility at the Riksdag of 1789, Staël replied, clearly echoing his master's political philosophy, that the king had been forced to act as he did to save both royal power and the nobility itself "from the same revolution as in France," while his lenient treatment of the leaders of the noble opposition proved "the importance he places upon the rights of the nobility and upon the intermediary ranks, without which no monarchy can exist." The count thereupon professed himself convinced.[41]

Certain of the more radical Patriots in Poland meanwhile welcomed Gustaf III's Act of Security of 1789, such as the priest Peter Switkowski, who hailed it as an example to be followed by other governments, above all the Polish: to throw off the aristocratic yoke with the support of the non-noble classes. It may be noted—looking ahead—that the assassination of Gustaf III by his aristocratic enemies in March 1792 caused a sensation in Poland and led to considerable retrospective justification and idealization of his reign, perhaps most notably by Engeström's good friend J. U. Niemcewicz in his *Gazeta Narodowa i Obca*.[42]

Engeström meanwhile found himself in an increasingly untenable position in Warsaw in the fall of 1790. On the one hand he was largely ostracized by his former friends among the Patriot party, who suspected Sweden's relations with Russia, while on the other Gustaf bombarded him with demands for decisive action. Engeström at last raised Gustaf's candidature in February 1791 with the grand marshal of the Diet, Count Ignaz Potocki, who tactfully but firmly rejected the idea, to Engeström's evident relief.[43]

By April 1791, meanwhile, Gustaf gave up his Polish aspirations, at least for the time being, and turned almost exclusively to mounting a great monarchical crusade against revolutionary France. He nonetheless made bitter comments about Poland's folly to Armfelt on receiving news of the new Polish constitution and formal offer of the succession to the Elector of Saxony in May: "There goes Poland, f . . . ! The Poles will pay for this, I hope, and we will have our share."[44]

A few weeks later, Engeström, now married to a Polish wife and naturalized into the Polish nobility, ended his mission to Warsaw. He would not resume his long career in Sweden's diplomatic service until after Gustaf III's death in 1792. If he was left disconsolate at the course of his master's policy, he could take consolation in the encouragement he had given Poland's national revival; on his departure Prince Adam Czartoryski wrote to him with satisfaction that the Poles were now beginning to "speak Swedish."[45]

To inquire into the motives behind Gustaf III's east Baltic policy is to inquire into one of the most enigmatic minds of that period. If nothing else, it illustrates strikingly his remarkably fecund imagination, supple opportunism, and restless energy.

His attitude toward the Baltic provinces seems to show little more than a concern for immediate tactical gains. There was by now little interest left among any of his subjects to recover these lost territories. Gustaf's ultimatum to Catherine in July 1788 was quite evidently intended to provoke a Russian declaration of war and specifically demanded only the return of those parts of Finland ceded to Russia in 1721 and 1743, which were of clear strategic value.[46]

It was meanwhile widely believed in St. Petersburg that Gustaf intended to regain the Baltic provinces.[47] He might well have demanded their return had the opportunity arisen; indeed, in attempting to negotiate an alliance with Prussia, Gustaf instructed Carisien as late as April 1790 to demand Prussia's guarantee of the Swedish frontiers of 1721—which would restore that part of Finland lost to Russia in 1743—and even of Sweden's acquisition of Viborg and Livonia "if you see they are well on their way toward making concessions and promises."[48] It is obvious, meanwhile, that he made no serious effort to create such an opportunity.

In retrospect it may nonetheless be wondered why Gustaf did not attempt a landing in the Baltic provinces when contemporary sources strongly suggest that even a relatively small force in conjunction with an uprising of the Baltic peasantry might have wrought serious havoc upon the enemy. To be sure, logistical considerations played an important part. Sweden disposed of only some thirty thousand effectives for operations across the Baltic, and any diversion against the Baltic provinces would have detracted from the main strategic objectives: the knockout blow against the Russian capital itself and the defense of Finland. Had the main offensive been directed against the Baltic provinces, the Swedes would have lost much of the advantage of surprise by allowing the Russians to rally their forces, while the consequent overland attack against St. Petersburg could have been blocked at Narva in the same way that a march from Finland could have been held up at Fredrikshamn and Viborg, as General Toll was forced to conclude in January 1788.[49]

Perhaps Gustaf did not want to block the natural corridor of attack in the event of a Prussian intervention against Russia; the delusive hopes and fears aroused by Berlin form indeed the red thread running through the speculations of Stockholm, Warsaw, and St. Petersburg throughout the war.[50] Possibly too, the king was sobered by Ehrenström's report that the Baltic nobles believed Sweden could easily seize but not ultimately hold the provinces.

Such practical explanations may suffice. Yet there may have been a social and ideological dimension to Gustaf's thinking as well. Ehrenström in his reports had strongly stressed the potentialities of peasant insurrection and thereafter became increasingly convinced of its effectiveness. Still, in his memoirs he wrote that after his final report to Gustaf in May 1788, the king concluded that "a part of his plans, which were based upon cooperation from the Estonian and Livonian side, were not feasible."[51]

This statement suggests that Gustaf was prepared only to consider utilizing an aristocratic revolt against Russian rule. By 1788 he was already becoming apprehensive over mounting social unrest both in France and in Sweden itself. The following year he believed only his decisive action at the Riksdag had saved Sweden from social dissolution, as he sought to assure the Polish nobles in 1790. Thus he may well have feared the repercussions in his own domains of deliberately provoking a jacquerie across the Baltic. To do so would, moreover, have worked at cross purposes with his attempts to gain support from both autocratic Prussia and the aristocratic Polish Republic. A *pugachevshchina*, such as Gustaf urged Engeström to stir up through Polish intermediaries in Russia's southern provinces, would have been comfortably remote from Sweden and Finland.

Toward Poland Gustaf's policies were similarly opportunistic. Unlike his minister to Warsaw, he sought throughout his Russian war to gain only short-term tactical advantages in Poland. After the war he raised his candidature to the Polish succession in the hope of recouping his financial losses and realizing the old dream of a solid Swedish-Polish-Turkish front against future Russian aggression. Yet the impracticalities of a Swedish-

Polish dynastic union seem manifest, and the whole project may essentially have been a ploy in Gustaf's search for a firm great-power alliance to replace the traditional French entente, either with Prussia and Britain or with Russia itself. The need to find a way out of his dangerous diplomatic isolation and financial weakness may indeed provide a key to Gustaf's unusually tortuous foreign policy after the Peace of Värälä.

Meanwhile, throughout late 1790 and early 1791, the mounting crisis between Russia and the Triple Alliance over the continued Turkish war created unusual opportunities for Gustaf to play the one side off the other to his own advantage.[52] At length, after the immediate eastern crisis had passed, a Swedish-Russian defensive alliance was signed at Drottningholm in October 1791, naturally arousing apprehension in Poland.[53]

Such fears were in fact not without grounds. Already in November 1790, at the very time he was pushing most vigorously for the Polish crown, Gustaf informed Engeström in Warsaw that he had reason to suspect the Prussians of contemplating a further partition of Poland; though he found the idea repugnant, "the force of circumstances could be such that one might be compelled to join in and take part in their iniquity, especially when they take the full odium upon themselves and we reap the harvest."

Over a year later, on 13 March 1792—the very day of his assassination—Gustaf wrote his minister in St. Petersburg, Baron Curt von Stedingk, that he now suspected Catherine of the same intention, in which case Sweden must seize the opportunity to gain such advantages as the situation allowed. What advantages he had in mind he did not specify; Baron Armfelt later noted that this would have been in the "only area for expansion that would be suitable to him." Conceivably this might have referred to Russian Finland. Much more likely, however, Gustaf had returned to his old dream of acquiring Norway from Denmark, presumably against compensation to be provided by Prussia.[54]

Yet there remains an intensity to Gustaf's arguments for his Polish candidature and a sharpness in his reaction when the Polish crown was at length offered to the Elector of Saxony in May 1791 that suggest something deeper than a mere *politique d'aventure*: the old, romantic fascination that Poland had long exercised upon him. The same letter to Engeström of 7 November 1790, in which he hinted at Sweden's possible gains through a new partition of Poland, also reveals with unusual clarity the other side of his character. "We are created," he wrote, "to work, to strain our powers, suffer, fight against success, which spoils us, and against adversity, which oppresses us: that is man's lot, as long as he lives, and that is the duty of kings."[55]

Notes

1. For background see my "Russia and the Problem of Sweden-Finland, 1721–1809," *East European Quarterly* 5 (1972): 431–55; Ludvig Stavenow, "Läget i Europa vid tiden for svensk-ryska kriget 1788–90," in *Femte nordiska historikermötet i Helsingfors,* ed. R. Rosén (Helsingfors, 1933), 30–34. See also the discussion of bibliography on the Oriental-Polish-Baltic crisis of the 1780s in E. L. Birck, *General Tolls krigsplan år 1788,* Skrifter utgivna av Svenska litteratursallskapet i Finland, 296 (Helsingfors, 1944), 411–12n.

2. Elis Schröderheim, *Skrifter till konung Gustaf III:s historia,* ed. Elof. Tegnér, 2nd ed. (Stockholm, 1892), 81–82. See also Auguste Geoffroy, *Gustave III et la cour de France,* 2 vols. (Paris: Didier, 1867), 2:16, 259–60.

3. See Birck, *Tolls krigsplan,* 412–13n.

4. "En rapport till Gustaf III om tillståndet i Livland 1786," *Historisk tidskrift* 25 (1905): 113–16; Evald Uustalu, "Estlands och Livlands del i de svenska krigsforbere-delserna 1786–1788," *Svio-Estonica* (1949): 121–23. In the variable usage of the day, "Livonia" was often understood to include Estonia, as well as Livonia proper.

5. Uustalu, "Estlands och Livlands del," 123–25.

6. J. A. Ehrenström, *Statsrådet Johan Albert Ehrenströms efterlemnade historiska anteckningar,* ed. S. J. Boëthius, 2 vols. (Stockholm, 1883), 1:124–40; A. R. Cederberg, "Johan Albert Ehrenströmin kirjallista jäämistoä vuosilta 1787–1789," *Historiallinen arkisto* 39 (1932): 70–106 (documents in Swedish), 160–65 (German summary); Uustalu, "Estlands och Livlands del," 125–36, 149–50. See also Friedrich Bienemann, "Zur Geschichte des schwedisch-russischen Krieges 1788–1790," *Russische Revue,* ed. Carl Röttger, 5 (1874): 51–56, which gives Ehrenström's reports in German translation. (This latter work was also published separately under the title *Die Ostseeprovinzen, vornehmlich Estland während des schwedisch-russischen Krieges* 1 [St. Petersburg, 1877]; A. R. Cederberg, "John Albert Ehrenströmi poliitiline misioon Eestija Liivimale aastail 1787–1788," *Ajalooline ajakiri* (Tartu, 1924), 41–55.

7. Birck, *Tolls krigsplan,* 38–39, 412n., 455–62; Uustalu, "Estlands och Livlands del," 136–38.

8. K. L. Blum, *Ein russischer Staatsmann. Des Grafen Jacob Johann Sievers Denkwür-digkeiten zur Geschichte Russlands,* 4 vols. (Leipzig & Heidelberg, 1857–58), 2:489–98; Bienemann, "Zur Geschichte," 65–66, 71–72; Alexander Brückner, "Die Ostseeprovin-zen während des schwedisch-russischen Krieges 1788–90," *Baltische Monatsschrift* 18 (1869): 234–37, 245; Uustalu, "Estlands och Livlands del," 138. See also Louis Philippe, comte de Ségur, *Mémoires, ou souvenirs et anecdotes,* in *Œuvres complètes,* 33 vols. (Paris: P. Eymery, 1824–26), 3:372–74; Aleksandr V. Khrapovitskii, *Dnevnik A. V. Khrapovitskago 1782–1793,* ed. N. Varsukov (St. Petersburg, 1901). 63; Karl Stählin, *Geschichte Russlands von den Anfängen bis zur Gegenwart,* 5 vols. (Königsberg & Berlin, 1923–39), 2:658–61; Uustalu, "Estlands och Livlands del," 139–42. On the Russo-Swedish conflict in general, see, besides Stählin, *Geschichte Russlands,* 2, and my "Russia and the Problem of Sweden-Finland," A. Brückner, "Russland und Schweden 1788," *Historische Zeitschrift* 22 (1869): 314–402.

9. Bienemann, "Zur Geschichte," 56–64; Brückner, "Ostseeprovinzen," 234, 236–37.

10. Bienemann ("Zur Geschichte," 64–68), Brückner ("Ostseeprovinzen," 238), Birck (*Tolls krigsplan*, 412–13n.), and evidently Uustalu ("Estlands och Livlands del," 140) take the peasant threat seriously. On the general situation of the Baltic peasantry, see Arnold Soom, "Die Lage der estländischen Bauern um die Wende des 18. zum 19. Jahrhundert," *Zeitschrift für Ostforschung* 12 (1963): 719–23, and Teodor Zeids, "Formen des bäuerlichen Klassenkampfes in Lettland im Zeitalter des Feudalismus," *Johrbuch für Geschichte der UdSSR und der volksdemokratischen Länder Europas* 12 (1968): esp. 268, 270, 285–86. These events in Estonia would suggest the possibility of similar ferment in Russian Finland.

11. Khrapovitskii, *Dnevnik*, 70, 77–78, 80, 105. See also Geoffroy, *Gustave III*, 2:65–66. On Prussia's policy toward Sweden, see Alfons Siegel, *Gustaf III von Schweden und die preussische Politik nach dem Tode Friedrichs des Grossen.* Erlanger Abhandlungen zur mittleren und neueren Geschichte, 18 (Erlangen, 1933); for Britain's, see Signe Carlsson, *Sverige och Storbrittanien 1787–1790* (Lund: Gleerup, 1944).

12. Birck, *Tolls krigsplan*, 3–89, passim.; Uustalu, "Estlands och Livlands del," 15 1–52.

13. Stählin, *Geschichte Russlands*, 2:661; Brückner, "Russland und Schweden," 323. Cf. A. Brückner, "Der Anjalabund in Finnland 1788," *Baltische Monatsschrift* 19 (1870): 309–54; my "Russia and the Problem of Sweden-Finland," 448–49.

14. Khrapovitskii, *Dnevnik*, 191–92, 194; Bienemann, "Zur Geschichte," 74–79; Brückner, "Ostseeprovinzen," 240–44.

15. E. G. Geijer, *Konung Gustaf III:s efterlemnade och femtio år efter hans död öppnade papper*, 2nd ed. (Stockholm, 1876), 41–43; *Gustaf III:s och Lovisa Ulrikas brevvaxling*, ed. Henrik Schück, 2 vols. (Stockholm, 1919), 2:65, 157–58.

16. *Collection des écrits politiques, littéraires, et dramatiques de Gustave III de Suède, suivie de sa correspondance*, ed. J.- B. Dechaux, 5 vols. (Stockholm: C. Delén, 1803–5), 1:103–5; *Lettres de Gustave III à la comtesse de Boufflers*, ed. Aurélien Vivie, Actes de l'Académie nationale des sciences, belles-lettres et arts de Bordeaux, 1898 (Paris: F. Dentin, 1898), 51–52, 59; Brückner, "Russland und Schweden," 339.

17. Sergei M. Solov'ev, *Istoriya Rossii s drevnyeishikh vremen*, 16 vols. (Moscow, 1960–66), 9:433; *Sbornik imperatorskago russkago istoricheskago obshchestva*, 148 vols. (St. Petersburg, 1867–1916), 13:265, 268–69; Geijer, *Efterlemnade papper*, 154; Geoffroy, *Gustave III*, 1:245–46; Stählin, *Geschichte Russlands*, 2:521. On the much-debated parallels between Sweden and Poland in the eighteenth century, see Geoffroy, *Gustave III*, 1:36–38; Ladislaus [Wladislaw] Konopczynski, "Polen och Sverige i det adertonde århundradet. En historisk parallel." *Historisk tidskrift* (1925): 101–31 (translation of the last chapter of his *Polska i Szwecja*, Warsaw, 1924); the same author's "Svensk-polska analogier," *Svio-Polonica*, no. 8/9 (1946–47): 5–17; N. D. Chechulin, *Vnyeshnyaya politika Rossii v nachalye tsarstvovaniya Yekateriny II, 1762–1774* (St. Petersburg, 1896), 160–61; B. H. Sumner, *Peter the Great and the Emergence of Russia* (New York, 1962), 165–66; Erik Amburger, *Russland und Schweden 1762–1772. Katharine II., die schwedische*

Verfassung und die Ruhe des Nordens, Historische Studien, ed. Emil Ebering, 251 (Berlin, 1934), 267–68.

18. "Handlingar angående Sveriges förhållande vid Polens första delning," *Historiska handlingar* 5 (1865): 138–50; [Stanislaus Poniatowski,] *Mémoires du roi Stanislas-Auguste Poniotowski,* ed. S. Goriainov, 2 vols. (Petrograd/Leningrad, 1914–24), 2:11, 268; Eugène Mottaz, *Stanislas Poniatowski et Maurice Glayre. Correspondance relative aux partages de la Pologne* (Paris, 1897), 43–46, 70–7 1, 93, 99, 109; Konopczynski, "Svensk-polska analogier," 15.

19. Elof Tegnér, *Gustaf Mauritz Armfelt,* 3 vols., 2nd ed. (Stockholm, 1892–94), 1:22–26.

20. Bernhard von Schinkel, *Minnen ur Sveriges nyare historia,* ed. C. W. Bergman, 10 vols. (Stockholm, 1852–68), 1:280–81; Axel Raphael, *Bidrag till historien om Gustaf III:s planer på Polen* (Uppsala, 1874), 4–5; Wladislaw Konopczynski, "Lars von Engeströms mission i Polen 1787–1791," *Historisk tidskrift* 44 (1924): 3–5.

21. C. G. Nordin, *Dagboksanteckningar för åren 1786–1792,* Historiska handlingar, 6 (Stockholm 1868): 273; Raphael, *Bidrag,* 4–5.

22. Lars von Engeström, *Minnen och anteckningar,* ed. Elof Tegnér, 2 vols. (Stockholm, 1876), 1:111 (cf. the Polish translation of part of Engestrom's memoirs: *Pamietniki Wawrzynca Engestroma,* trans. J. I. Kraszewski [Poznan, 1875]); Raphael, *Bidrag,* 5–6; Konopczynski, "Engeströms mission," 6–7.

23. Siegel, *Gustaf III und die preussische Politik,* 17.

24. Engeström, *Minnen,* 1:115–49, passim., 284–85; Siegel, *Gustaf III und die preussische Politik,* 6–8; Konopczynski, "Engeströms mission," 7–10, 24. On the proposed Polish-Russian alliance, see Robert Howard Lord, *The Second Partition of Poland* (Cambridge, Mass., 1915), 82–91.

25. Siegel, *Gustaf III und die preussische Politik,* 25; Konopczynski, "Engestroms mission," 24–25, 54. On Hertzberg and his plan, see Lord, *Second Partition,* 75–81.

26. Engeström, *Minnen,* 1:140–41; Siegel, *Gustaf III und die preussische Politik,* 9–10; Konopczynski, "Engeströms mission," 10–12.

27. Siegel, *Gustaf III und die preussische Politik,* 11; Konopczynski, "Engeströms mission," 13.

28. Engeström, *Minnen,* 1:143–44, 286–89; Konopczynski, "Engeströms mission," 17–18.

29. Konopczynski, "Engeströms mission," 18–19, 24–28; Siegel, *Gustaf III und die preussische Politik,* 25–26, 30–32, 36–41; Engeström, *Minnen,* 1:157–59; Lord, *Second Partition,* 112–27. See also Khrapovitskii, *Dnevnik,* 187, 193; *Hedvig Elisabeth Charlottas dagbok,* ed. C. C. Bonde and C. af Klercker, 9 vols. (Stockholm, 1902–42), 3:251–52.

30. Stig Boberg, *Kunglig krigspropaganda,* Studia Historica Gothoburgensia, 8 (Gothenburg, 1967), 65–84, passim., 103–4, 129–32.

31. Siegel, *Gustaf III und die preussische Politik,* 9–10, 24, 27–28, 30, 33–35, 42–46; Konopczynski, "Engeströms mission," 12, 14–16, 28–30; Engeström, *Minnen,* 1:153–54.

32. Siegel, *Gustaf III und die preussische Politik,* 41–51; Konopczynski, "Engeströms mission," 29–33.

33. Siegel, *Gustaf III und die preussische Politik*, 51; Konopczynski, "Engeströms mission," 33–38; Engeström, *Minnen*, 1:159–60; Lord, *Second Partition*, 128–5 2; Khrapovitskii, *Dnevnik*, 204.

34. Siegel, *Gustaf III und die preussische Politik*, 52–59, 62–64; Konopczynski, "Engeströms mission," 38–45; Schinkel, *Minnen*, 2:175, 309–12; Nordin, *Dagboksanteckningar*, 129.

35. Siegel, *Gustaf III und die preussische Politik*, 54, 61–62; Konopczynski, "Engeströms mission," 45–47; Engeström, *Minnen*, 1:169–70, 290–304.

36. Siegel, *Gustaf III und die preussische Politik*, 51, 67–69; Konopczynski, "Engeströms mission," 49; Engeström, *Minnen*, 1:295, 297.

37. Schinkel, *Minnen*, 2:310; *Konung Gustaf III:s bref till friherre G. M. Armfelt*, ed. Elof Tegnér, Historiska handlingar, 12, no. 3 (Stockholm, 1883), 173–75. Siegel (*Gustaf III und die preussische Politik*, 53) assumes Gustaf referred to Count Jerzy Potocki, the Polish minister in Stockholm since August 1789. Engeström (*Minnen*, 1:169) claims the latter's brother, Count Jan Potocki, raised the idea of the candidature of Gustaf's brother, Duke Karl, which suggested to the king his own candidature. For the Russian minister's remarks, see C. T. Odhner, "Gustaf III och Katarina II efter freden I Värälä," special reprint from *Svenska akademiens handlingar från 1886*, 9 (1894), 20, which does not give the date, the original source, or the minister's identity, though it must have been Baron P. A. von der Pahlen. See also Siegel, *Gustaf III und die preussische Politik*, 66–68; Konopczynski, "Engeströms mission," 49; Engeström, *Minnen*, 1:297–98; [C. B. von Stedingk & J. J. F. Jennings,] *Lettres au roi*, ed. A. Papkoff (Petrograd, 1916), 50. It seems that Baron C. B. von Stedingk, Gustaf's minister to St. Petersburg, was not informed of his master's Polish plans.

38. *Sbornik*, 42:121; Engeström, *Minnen*, 1:295–96; Lord, *Second Partition*, 195–96.

39. Engeström, *Minnen*, 1:117–18, 148–51, 299; Siegel, *Gustaf III und die preussische Politik*, 28–29; Konopczynski, "Svensk-polska analogier," 15.

40. Siegel, *Gustaf III und die preussische Politik*, 58–59. See also Engeström, *Minnen*, 1:293.

41. *Correspondance diplomatique du Baron de Staël-Holstein, ambassadeur de Suède en France*, ed. L. Léouzon le Duc (Paris: Hachette, 1881), 190–92. Cf. Siegel, *Gustaf III und die preussische Politik*, 64–66. On Gustaf III's political philosophy, see my "Gustaf III of Sweden and the Enlightenment," in this volume.

42. Konopczynski, "Svensk-polska analogier," 15–16; Bogdan Zakrzewski, "Wierz na smierc Gustawa III króla szwedzkiego," *Svio-Polonica*, no. 8/9 (1946–47): 46–53.

43. Engeström, *Minnen*, 1:298, Siegel, *Gustaf III und die preussische Politik*, 69–75.

44. Siegel, *Gustaf III und die preussische Politik*, 76; Tegnér, *Gustaf III:s bref till Armfelt*, 177, 185. Bernhard von Schinkel in his *Minnen*, 2 (1855), claimed to know on good authority that King Stanislaus, fearing a further partition of Poland, negotiated an agreement with Engeström in 1791, whereby he would relinquish his crown to Gustaf in return for eighty thousand ducats and suitable residences in and near Stockholm. Schinkel held that Gustaf intended to involve a sizable part of the Russian army in an intervention in France, then attack Russia together with the Poles (*ibid.*, 176–77).

Siegel (*Gustaf III und die preussische Politik*, 77) was unable to find any evidence to support these curious allegations. If they seem wildly improbable, they nonetheless show what Gustaf's enemies were prepared to believe of him.

45. Konopczynski, "Engeströms mission," 51–52.

46. *Hedvig Elisabeth Charlottas dagbok*, 2:294–97; Uustalu, "Estlands och Livlands del," 143–49.

47. Khrapovitskii, *Dnevnik*, 10, 12; Brückner, "Ostseeprovinzen," 232–34. Cf. *Hedvig Elisabeth Charlottas dagbok*, 3:118.

48. C. F. I. Wahrenberg, "Bidrag till historien om Konung Gustaf III:s sednaste regeringsår," *Tidskrift för litteratur*, ed. C. F. Bergstedt (1851), 340–41n.

49. Brückner, "Ostseeprovinzen," 239; Uustalu, "Estlands och Livlands del," 142–43.

50. Gen. Toll feared in March 1788 that the Prussians might consider the Swedes more dangerous neighbors in Livonia than the Russians (Uustalu, "Estlands och Livlands del," 149).

51. Ibid., 136; Ehrenström, *Historiska anteckningar*, 1:140.

52. See Odhner, "Gustaf III och Katarina II," 18–19; Signe Carlsson, "Till frågan om Sveriges utrikespolitik efter freden i Värälä," in *Gottfrid Carlsson 18.12.1952* (Lund, 1952), 348–76. Lord's half-facetious remarks (195) about Gustaf III's penchant for "fantastic schemes" and his "chimerical project" regarding the Polish throne fail to do justice to the complexity of the situation.

53. Nordin, *Dagboksanteckningar*, 193, 209.

54. Siegel, *Gustaf III und die preussische Politik*, 62; Konopczynski, "Engeströms mission," 53; Odhner, "Gustaf III och Katarina II," 60–62.

55. Konopczynski, "Engeströms mission," p. 46. On the romantic strain in Gustaf's nature, see Beth Hennings, *Gustaf III*, 2nd ed. (Stockholm, 1967), esp. 141; Sven Delblanc, *Ära och minne* (Stockholm, 1965); and my "Gustaf III and the Enlightenment," esp. 22–23, 31–32.

Gustaf III of Sweden and the French Revolution

The outbreak of revolution in France by the summer of 1789 caught most European rulers and statesmen off guard. It took time and the ongoing course of events before they could properly grasp what was taking place.

To the general confusion there was one noteworthy exception, King Gustaf III of Sweden, who had always followed events in France with the closest attention. The crisis that had begun there more than two years earlier with the convening of the first Assembly of Notables in February 1787 had filled him with mounting apprehension. He immediately took alarm at the earliest reports from Paris during the summer of 1789 and had, from the start, no doubts as to their sinister import. He was the first sovereign ruler to seek to rally monarchical Europe against the rising tide of revolution, until his life was cut short by assassination in March 1792.

The year 1789 found Gustaf heavily engaged in a war with Russia, which began with his attack the summer before to take advantage of the ongoing Russian-Turkish conflict. His letters from his headquarters in Finland, where he himself directed the operations of his forces, especially to his confidants Curt von Stedingk and Baron Gustaf Mauritz Armfelt, reveal his dismay over developments in France. Already on 15 July, before word of the storming of the Bastille had reached him, he wrote to Baron Curt von Stedingk of the "horrible confusion into which France is falling." This threatened, he wrote to Armfelt, "to throw all of European politics into a new chaos." His letter to his close confidant Baron Gustaf Mauritz Armfelt of 19 August meanwhile reflects the emotion behind this reaction:

> The news from France has so horrified me that I could not sleep last night until 4:00 o'clock. The nights of 17 February 1789 and 19 August 1772 [before Gustaf's own decisive political coups] I meanwhile slept very well. . . . And this is charming Paris, where all the nations of Europe came together to seek pleasure and relief from their concerns! There, too, we would have found our asylum, if we had been forced into exile. In truth that would have been to go from Scylla to Carybdis! What a hateful people! They are the orangutangs of Europe! How is it possible to combine so much grace and civility with such deliberate savagery?[1]

There are understandable reasons for Gustaf III's revulsion, over and above his *métier du roi*. He had been raised in a court where French language and culture reigned supreme. France for him was the epitome of courtly and aristocratic taste, refinement, and elegance. In 1771 and 1784 he had visited Paris, where he had widespread contacts in society and the world of the intellect. To Gustaf the outbreak of revolution in France seemed to threaten all those civilized values he held so dear.[2]

The revolution likewise challenged his most deeply held political principles. These represented a balance between the ideal of "legal" or benevolent despotism advocated by the Physiocrats, above all by Le Mercier de la Rivière, and the stable hierarchical society envisioned by Montesquieu, in which—as Gustaf saw it—the nobility should be the pillar of the king's authority. Gustaf's concept of an ideal monarchical order was embodied in what he somewhat vaguely referred to as the "constitution of Gustaf Adolf," that vision of a heroic, magnanimous king ruling over a trusting, loyal, and well-ordered society which is perhaps best conveyed by his dramatic authorship.[3]

For all his fascination with the French *philosophes*, Gustaf had long since become apprehensive of the militant rationalism of the radical High Enlightenment. Already in 1778 he wrote his confidante, the Countess de Boufflers in Paris, that the Physiocrats sought to measure all by the same yardstick, which might be possible in small states but which in larger ones was "as impossible to put into practice as harmful to try." He thereafter expressed growing resentment of the philosophers' influence and in 1784 complained indignantly to Mme de Boufflers of the "philosophic-democratic spirit that prevails and which is so incompatible with my principles and interests." He feared, in 1787, that "this system of innovation that our modern philosophers have introduced" would end "by turning sovereigns—into tyrants, and peoples—into rebels."[4] The outbreak of revolutionary violence in France during the summer of 1789 confirmed the menace he had long seen approaching.

Gustaf III's political experience since even before his accession had also long prepared his reactions to the French Revolution. As crown prince he had been apprehensive of mounting anti-aristocratic fervor in Sweden and already in 1768 had speculated over a coup d'état against the existing constitution of 1720 to replace it with a new one designed to preserve the social hierarchy. These aspirations were at length realized in August 1772, after the Riksdag that convened upon his succession in 1771 revealed even more threatening class antagonisms. Gustaf's "revolution" of 1772—as it is traditionally called—while shielding the noble order, greatly strengthened royal power, permitting the king to carry out numerous enlightened reforms over the next several years. These, in Gustaf's view, reflected true or "benevolent" philosophy.[5]

The king's hostility toward the rebellion of subjects against their rulers clearly surfaced during the American Revolution. Although for political reasons his neutrality favored France, he felt no sympathy toward the Americans, particularly after his Riksdag of 1778 revealed signs of an opposition to his increasingly autocratic regime that tended to idolize the freedom-loving Americans. To Stedingk the king wrote in 1784, following the American war, "Too recently having ourselves escaped from our troubles that there should not still exist, no doubt, some germs of our former divisions, it is my duty to avert anything which could reawaken such ideas."[6]

George Washington was shrewdly perceptive when he wrote that year to his French comrade in arms, General Rochambeau, "Considering how recently the King of Sweden has changed the form of the Constitution of that Country, it is not much to be wondered at that his *fears* should get the better of his *liberality* at anything which might have the appearance of republicanism." In October 1787, Gustaf himself told the French Chevalier de Gaussen, apropos of the troubles in the United Netherlands, "I am happy to have my revolution over with."

In time Gustaf's political opponents in Sweden would make similar accusations. In April 1788, "one of his less enthusiastic admirers" reportedly said that "the king is himself nothing more than a revolutionary, although he was favored by success." The month before his assassination, Gustaf himself wrote to the Marquis de Bouillé in February 1792, "I have been in the position too often of conducting revolutions or of combating them not to know that this cannot succeed unless led by a single person."[7] The intensity of Gustaf III's reaction to the French Revolution can best be compared with that of his *"chère cousine"* and favorite enemy, Catherine II of Russia, whose own rise to power had been highly irregular.

In the summer of 1788, Gustaf faced the greatest crisis of his reign when he launched his thinly disguised offensive war against Russia, then embroiled with the Turks to the south. This act of aggression was a flagrant violation of Gustaf's own constitution of 1772, which prohibited an offensive war without the Riksdag's prior consent. The result was the Anjala Mutiny or "Confederation" of most of his Finnish officer corps, which enjoyed widespread sympathy and support among the Swedish-Finnish nobility as a whole. This aristocratic revolt was aimed at compelling the king to acknowledge constitutional restraints to his authority, but it in turn stirred up latent antinoble passions from the 1760s and early 1770s among the non-noble estates.

Skillfully playing on this powerful popular reaction, Gustaf managed to suppress the revolt during the fall of 1788 and in February 1789 convened a Riksdag at which he forced through his Act of Union and Security with the support of the non-noble orders over the bitter opposition of the Noble Estate. This crucial act greatly increased the king's authority in return for the virtual leveling of privileges between noble and commoner. When Gustaf dismissed this Riksdag scarcely a week before the French Estates-General convened at Versailles, he had indeed become a "crowned revolutionary." He had, in essence, himself carried out a social revolution that in France could be won only at the cost of violence and bloodshed.[8]

Throughout this period, Gustaf III constantly compared France's situation with Sweden's and himself with Louis XVI. He had been uneasy in 1787 over Louis' first Assembly of Notables, for, as he wrote Mme de Boufflers, he knew by experience the ways of such assemblies," where "they use big words but generally are moved only by personal feelings." He complained in 1788 of the "Anglicizing" of France. Learning of Louis XVI's decision that summer to convene the Estates-General the following year, Gustaf reputedly prophesied, "The king of France will lose his crown, perhaps his life." The mutinous French Guards in the summer of 1789 recalled to him his own Anjala mutineers of the year before. "The worst thing, in desperate situations," he wrote to Stedingk in July 1789, "is not to maintain any position at all, and that is what it appears the king of France will do." "There is what they are doing to *la délicieuse France*," he wrote a few days later. "That is the result of weakness and indecision." Louis XVI, he wrote to State Secretary U. G. Franc in early August, was "the best man in the world and the least suited to govern a great state, especially a state like France." To Armfelt he described Louis as "certainly a poor king in every sense of the term."

In contrast he stressed his own resolute qualities of leadership. To Queen Sophia Magdalena he wrote from Finland in November 1789.

> After God and His supreme will, that which prevents the fall of empires is firmness. Where would we be by now if I had not relied upon it, even upon a firmness which you, perhaps, considered severe, but it has saved us from bloodier scenes. All have returned to obedience, which could not have been achieved through feeble means, which would have led to incalculable consequences, such as those revealed to you by France.

Speaking of the French Revolution, Gustaf told his sister-in-law, Duchess Hedvig Elisabeth Charlotta, the following month, "If I had not acted as I did at the last Riksdag, we would certainly have had to experience the same thing ourselves."[9]

It is not our purpose here to undertake a detailed examination of Gustaf III's attempts to organize and lead a monarchical crusade against the French Revolution. This has been done elsewhere and perhaps in sufficient detail, considering that ultimately nothing came of them.[10] A brief summary should suffice.

Involvement in his war with Russia during the first year of the revolution in France restricted Gustaf to observing it from afar. He soon became apprehensive over the enthusiastic dispatches he received from his ambassador in Paris, E. M. Staël von Holstein—Jacques Necker's son-in-law—to say nothing of the unsolicited letters from the literary Mme de Staël. Already in December 1789 he speculated over providing fifteen ships and twelve thousand troops for the king of France, at the latter's expense, once his Russian war was over, should Sweden's French alliance be renewed. The following month, at the urging of his confidant in French affairs, Baron Evert Taube, Gustaf secretly appointed as his special agent in Paris Count Axel von Fersen, who through his close personal attachment to Queen Marie Antoinette had direct access to the French royal family. Fersen, unbeknown to Staël, thereafter sent lengthy secret reports to Taube and Gustaf III, which clearly influenced the latters' view of the situation in France.[11]

In July 1790 the Swedes, under Gustaf's personal command, managed to trap and practically obliterate the Russian galley fleet at Svensksund on the Finnish coast. Catherine II, intent on pursuing her ongoing Turkish war and on the affairs of Poland, quickly concluded the Peace of Värälä with Sweden the following month on the basis of the status quo ante. Gustaf's attention now quickly turned to France.

The ceaseless inquietude and remarkable zeal with which King Gustaf III followed the disturbances in France [Elis Schröderheim later recalled] could not but amaze and almost irritate. At table almost nothing else was ever discussed. All other reading gave way to the *Moniteur*, the *Journal de Paris*, and the newspapers. The womenfolk tried to reason with him over this and in the council this subject interrupted the deliberations.[12]

To Baron Taube, the king wrote in September 1790 that the chaos in France seemed to have reached its peak and that a league, "like that of the Greeks against Troy," should be formed "to restore order and avenge the honor of crowned heads." "I should like," he added, "to be the Agamemnon of that host." Already that same month he discussed with the Prussian minister to Stockholm the idea of a joint Swedish-Prussian intervention to restore royal authority in France.[13]

An opportunity to sound out the possibility of Russian backing arose when France adopted the tricolor. In January 1791 Gustaf proposed to St. Petersburg that Russia, Denmark, and Sweden jointly close their ports to French vessels flying the new flag. Catherine II replied evasively, but fearful by early 1791 that the Swedish king might be tempted to join a possible Anglo-Prussian intervention against Russia in support of the Turks, the empress discreetly encouraged his noble sentiments toward France.

To restore order there, she told Curt von Stedingk, now Swedish ambassador in St. Petersburg, in February 1791, it would surely be necessary that the command be given to "someone" who could "outdo what he has done"—a clear reference to Gustaf's masterly suppression of the disorders in his own kingdom in 1788–89—although she added that the time had not yet come to act hastily. On 10 May Stedingk conveyed the message that "it is Your Majesty's duty to lead the good cause to victory and by breaking the chains of an unfortunate monarch to add to your great glory." If only she had peace, Stedingk was assured, the empress's army and treasury would stand at Gustaf's disposal.[14]

Opportunity appeared to present itself in the spring of 1791 when Gustaf learned of plans afoot in Paris, involving Count Fersen, for the French royal family to flee to the protection of supposedly loyal troops on their eastern frontier. Anticipating Russian support, Gustaf in May promptly offered Louis XVI's secret diplomatic agent, the émigré Baron de Breteuil in Switzerland, a Swedish-Russian military force of at least twenty-four thousand men, two-thirds of them Swedes, under his own command, to be paid for by France or its Bourbon ally Spain against future French repayment, and in return for a renewed French alliance with an increased subsidy. Gustaf thereupon departed for Aachen (Aix-la-Chapelle), close to the French border, to take charge of developments. Meanwhile, on 9 June Breteuil declined Gustaf's offer as long as the French king still remained in the hands of the "factious." On 20 June, Fersen spirited the French royal family in masterly fashion out of the Tuileries Palace and Paris, but their flight attempt was stopped at Varennes and they returned to their gilded captivity.[15]

Only thereafter, on 30 June, did Catherine II's envoy arrive in Aachen with a disappointing counterproposal for a total combined force of only ten thousand men, with no clear assurance of Russian support. Nonetheless his contacts there with French émigrés had redoubled Gustaf's zeal for the cause. That same day he wrote secretly to Louis XVI, urging, as his "oldest ally" and "most faithful friend," to uphold his royal dignity, in which case his fellow monarchs would come to his rescue.

In response to Catherine's minimal offer, encouraged by word of her flattering private statements about him, he set about to organize a European grand coalition with 100,000 to 120,000 troops under his own command, of which 16,000 were to be Swedes and 8,000 to be Russians, to crush the revolution with "steel and cannon," as he wrote to Stedingk. In anticipation, he began drafting a proclamation to the French people, declaring his intention to free the royal family from captivity, "to return to the different Estates within the state their legal rights and privileges, to free the people from anarchy and destruction, as well as to restore order and respect for the law," with the support of the "healthy part of the nation."[16]

The key to such a grand alliance was the Habsburg Emperor Leopold II, brother of the French queen. Gustaf sent Fersen to Vienna to negotiate. Leopold was not, however, unsympathetic toward the reform program in France, which resembled his own earlier enlightened efforts as grand duke of Tuscany. Not wishing to endanger his sister and her family in Paris he preferred negotiation with the National Assembly, backed by an armed congress of powers. To complicate the situation, the emperor was quietly encouraged to favor such a solution by Gustaf's own envoy, Fersen, who for his own reasons was particularly concerned about the safety of the French queen and who had indeed first proposed the idea of an armed congress of powers to Gustaf III as early as August 1790. Taking their cue from Emperor Leopold, the other European powers remained equally recalcitrant toward a direct armed intervention in France led by the king of Sweden.[17]

In September 1791, Louis XVI officially accepted the new French constitution, which most European sovereigns quickly recognized. To Gustaf, this "shameful behavior of the king of France . . . surpassed in cowardice and dishonor anything we could have expected and which the past might show," as he wrote to Fersen. He now turned to the idea of forming a more limited alliance with Russia and Spain, which like Sweden refused to recognize the

Axel von Fersen, the younger, by Peter Druillon (1893). The intimate of both the French royal family and of Gustaf III, Count Fersen played a prominent role in Gustaf's attempts to organize a great European crusade to crush the French Revolution. (Courtesy of Svenskt Porträttarkiv, Stockholm.)

new French constitution, to carry out a landing operation in Normandy. The French émigré general, the Marquis de Bouillé, entered Swedish service and undertook to lead a combined Swedish-Russian force of thirty-six thousand men under Gustaf III's overall command. Already during the summer two Swedish fortifications officers had secretly reconnoitered the ground and prepared a detailed map of the Seine Valley from Le Havre to Paris.

Fersen, now in Brussels, meanwhile continued to urge the convening of an armed congress of powers and even took it upon himself to correspond directly with the Swedish envoys in St. Petersburg, Madrid, and Berlin to promote this idea. "Do not fear any rash undertaking on the part of the king," he wrote secretly to Marie Antoinette on 25 October. "I know how to stop him." How, he did not specify, but he continued to oppose direct military intervention until France itself declared war on Austria and Prussia in April 1792.

On 19 October 1791, Gustaf III concluded the Treaty of Drottningholm with his recent enemy, Russia. While forming a defensive alliance, it made only vague reference to France and provided Sweden with only a small subsidy of three hundred thousand rubles. Spain remained evasive toward any definite commitment. By early December it was becoming evident that this plan, too, seemed destined for failure.[18]

Already that month, Gustaf and Baron Taube wrote to Fersen about the idea of seeking to persuade the French royal family to try once again to flee Paris, this time via Normandy to England, the implication being that they might find protection with their "oldest ally," the king of Sweden, rather than with the "treacherous Florentine," as Taube now called Leopold II. Thus encouraged, Fersen, although now outlawed in France, on his own initiative secretly visited the royal family in the Tuileries Palace itself in February 1792. A few days after receiving word that Fersen had departed on this dangerous mission, Gustaf III was assassinated on 16 March by a group of aristocratic conspirators, a deed which the king, on his deathbed, believed was inspired by French Jacobins.[19]

Gustaf's dying suspicions are altogether understandable in the light of recent developments in the Swedish monarchy. In 1790 and again in 1791 he tightened censorship to prohibit the Swedish press from referring to the unrest in France or the proceedings of the National Assembly. Nonetheless, rumors of his intended intervention in French affairs, which surfaced when he planned his trip to Aachen in the spring of 1791, aroused not only grave apprehensions but also moral outrage, particularly in aristocratic circles. Although Gustaf III had favored and protected the Swedish-Finnish nobility since his coup d'état of 1772, it had progressively reverted to its historic traditions of defending constitutional liberty against royal encroachment. Defeated in its clash with the king in the Anjala Mutiny and the ensuing Riksdag in 1788–89, it was thereafter strongly inclined to welcome the revolution in France—often with intense fervor—as a heroic struggle against royal despotism.

Duchess Hedvig Elisabeth Charlotta noted open rejoicing over the capture of the French royal family at Varennes among "our *enragés*" at the court itself, who all the while made "insinuations aimed at our king." A characteristic mixture of pre-Romantic ardor and the neoclassical cult of civic virtue was conveyed by Malla Montgomery-Silfverstolpe, whose father had been arrested for complicity in the Anjala Mutiny, when she recalled how she regarded Gustaf III as "a tyrant like Tiberius and Christian II" and thrilled to "republican principles" from France while she "dreamed of Sparta and Athens."

Faced with the possibility of having to bear arms against the temple of liberty in France, Gustaf's more vehement high-born adversaries sought, according to J. A. Ehrenström, to arouse disaffection by depicting him as "a despot, prepared to suppress abroad the regained rights of an oppressed nation, so as to be all the more able to suppress them in his own." By early 1792, Swedish aristocratic society "swarmed with men who wished to play the role of Brutus," in the words of Count Adolf Ludvig Ribbing, one of the young conspirators who by then plotted the king's assassination, in their eyes an act of noble tyrannicide. It was hailed in the same terms in France, where one enthusiastic member of the Convention even adopted the name "Brutus-Anckarstroem," after the king's assassin, a few months later.[20]

In retrospect it is hardly surprising that nothing ultimately came of any of Gustaf III's antirevolutionary projects regarding France, considering all the factors that conspired against them: his manifest lack of military, material, and financial resources; the suspicion and ill will of other powers and his failure to gain foreign support; the fears and opposition aroused at home by his suspected designs; as well as his principal agent Count Fersen's quiet but determined efforts to forestall the direct use of force. Ironically, less than a fortnight after Gustaf's death on 29 March 1792, France declared war on Austria and Prussia, thereby precipitating the war to crush the revolution that he had so avidly sought to bring about.

Meanwhile, the very idea that Sweden, a minor power seriously weakened by recent war and internal strife, should presume to take the lead in intervening against a vast revolution in what was then regarded as Europe's greatest realm was "quixotic" in the extreme, a term applied to it both at home and abroad. In Sweden, virtually no one except Baron Taube, Armfelt's rival for the king's favor, seems to have supported the idea.[21] How could Gustaf III possibly contemplate such a course?

In the first place, more promptly than his fellow monarchs he saw the "revolutionary Hydra" as a direct menace to all crowns, including not least his own. Contemplating, in December 1789, the ferment then evident in much of Europe, he described the end of the century as "the time of revolutions." Already in 1785, with regard to his old ambition to acquire Norway from Denmark, he had noted, "To arouse a republican spirit there could easily take place; but who knows whether it might develop as we might wish, and I would then fear its contagion in Sweden, which has so recently *been* cured of it." It seems evident that he refrained from following up the idea of stirring up rebellion against Russian rule among the peasantry of the Baltic Provinces during his war with Russia in 1788–90, again for fear of repercussions in Sweden and Finland. It was only with deep misgivings that he turned, in extremis, to the non-noble orders for support against his rebellious nobility during the Anjala Mutiny in 1788. The popular militias raised in the face of that emergency were quickly disbanded once it passed by 1789.[22]

The Revolution, he wrote in 1791, was an "epidemic" that had "spread from the soil of America to France." It would rage, in his view, until it was decisively stamped out. There could thus be no compromise with it. Gustaf's program for France, as Taube described it to Fersen in May 1791, had as its guiding principle "to make no accommodation with anyone whomsoever, nor to form any mixed government, but to restore royalty in its full powers." "A stable peace and the security of property and persons," he wrote to Staël in July that year, "are incompatible with the [new French] constitution and the principles upon which it is founded"; he thus considered the moderate *constitutionels* in the National Assembly more dangerous than the extremists, who were ultimately bound to discredit themselves.

Growing fear that Louis XVI, with Austrian encouragement, might come to terms with the Assembly caused him to favor the émigré Comte de Provence's claim to serve as regent for his captive brother. In July 1791 Gustaf wrote to Stedingk in St. Petersburg that great as was his interest in the French royal family, that which I take in the public cause, in the private interest of Sweden, and in the cause of all kings is greater yet . . . it may be all the same whether it be Louis XVI or Charles X who occupies the throne, as long as the monster of the Manège is crushed. . . . It may be that at this moment the king and queen are in danger, but this danger is not as great as that to all the crowned heads that are menaced by the Revolution.[23]

Count Fersen well summarized his monarch's view in September 1791 when he urged that the powers should recognize no constitution for France, "not even a good one," which Louis XVI had not freely accepted. It has been seen that Gustaf III was himself amenable to a considerable measure of "revolution"—always providing that it was revolution from above. In February 1790 he could with surprising candor say to P. O. von Asp, "I am myself a democrat." Time would show how true this would prove: Gustaf III, the nobles' friend, left his most lasting mark upon Sweden's history by drastically leveling corporate privilege.[24] In his own view, nonetheless, the crux of the matter was royal authority.

What meanwhile cannot fail to impress, looking back, was the surprisingly small scale of Gustaf's planned operations. Could he seriously have believed that a limited military expedition under his command could have reversed the course of events in France? Quite evidently he both could and did. Like most of the enemies of the Revolution before the fateful Battle of Valmy in the fall of 1792, Gustaf, encouraged by Fersen's reports, considered it the work of a small clique of self-seeking scoundrels possessing neither courage nor idealism. In his view, the disillusioned "sound" majority of the nation only awaited firm leadership and the support of even a small Swedish-Russian force—including bands of Cossacks and Tatars, "whose appearance is bound to excite extreme terror in France"—to rise up against the Revolution and bring it down like a house of cards. The Empress Catherine's expressed attitude toward the revolutionaries was, if anything, even more contemptuous.

Gustaf's initial plan, during the summer of 1791, nonetheless envisioned a coalition army of 100,000 to 120,000 men, which, modest as this might seem compared with the vast forces later arrayed against revolutionary and Napoleonic France, was sizable for its time and with regard to existing circumstances. A year later the duke of Brunswick would invade France with some one hundred thousand Austrian and Prussian troops against a weakened French army. Gustaf's later plan for a more restricted Swedish-Russian operation was clearly predicated upon the idea that it would exert sufficient moral pressure on the other monarchical powers to draw them too into the fray.[25]

Meanwhile, in seeking to understand Gustaf III's motives less tangible factors must also be taken into account. Although he could be remarkably hardheaded and calculating in matters of *grande politique,* this side of Gustaf's character stands in striking contrast to his markedly aesthetic and imaginative qualities of spirit. Beth Hennings described him as ultimately more romantic than rationalist by nature, and Folke Almén wrote of his essentially "heroic" concept of kingship.

Gustaf saw the boldness and determination of princes as the determinant force in history and had a strong sense of his own historic destiny, as borne out by the brilliant success of his desperate gambles in the coup of 1772, during the Anjala Mutiny in 1788, at the Riksdag of 1789, and at the Battle of Svensksund in 1790. "Do not forget the old coffee woman," he wrote to Armfelt in November 1791, referring to the soothsayer Ulrika Arfwidsson, with whom he had had earlier dealings. "It would be interesting to know what that old sorceress will have to tell us." His view of the past, as embodied in his own historical dramas, was highly mythic.[26] In this spirit, the chivalric rescue of the French king and his fair queen from the revolutionary dragon was clearly a fascinating scenario for the royal impresario.

Related to his abhorrence of revolution from below was Gustaf's deep concern over the alienation of most of his own nobility in 1788–89. Not only did this cause much personal grief to a monarch who gloried in the role of first gentleman of the realm; he remained convinced, as before, that the stability of a monarchical regime must rest on the loyal support of its nobility. He insisted that in 1789 he had chastised his nobles only to save them from popular vengeance. "Had I not placed myself at the head of the faction which the nobility had then aroused against itself," he told G. G. Adlerbeth in December that year, "the other Estates would have gone much further," adding that if the Riksdag had occurred after, rather than before, the outbreak in France, "the public's passions" would have been "harder to manage."

Following his return from Aachen in August 1791, Gustaf described to the Swedish Academy how "*philosophe* and aristocrat are identical in Sweden, but represent conflicting concepts in France." To the Marquis de Bouillé, he wrote of the Swedish nobles in February 1792: "We are trying to make them understand that in the eighteenth century it is necessary that this first order of the state be sustained by the stability of the throne and by its protection, and in not seeking to fight against it."[27]

In a letter to Armfelt from Aachen on 14 July 1791, Gustaf meanwhile revealed the interrelationship in his mind between Sweden's internal and external situations. His new finance minister, Anders af Håkanson, had proposed the convening of a Riksdag to restore order to Sweden's state finances, ruined by the recent Russian war. The king reacted powerfully against the "very idea," which caused him to shudder at the thought of fresh disorders at home, in which the old spirit of faction would be stirred up by "Jacobins" to "overthrow everything." Thus only after Louis XVI's restoration to full power in France, "to provide me with a sure and solid support" and "the means to govern the First Estate of the Realm" in Sweden, would Gustaf consider a Riksdag. Among the French émigré princes and their retinue in Aachen, Gustaf could not but envy the hapless Louis XVI for the loyalty of his *noblesse*. Nonetheless, he envisioned that a Swedish campaign against the revolution in France would cure his own nobles of their misguided opposition: "The principles which the officers who would fight there would absorb among the French nobility, overwhelmed with the evils of anarchy and dreaming only of a monarchical government, would achieve much; and then I would have the means to control those spirits that must be bought."[28]

Ever paramount from the viewpoint of Sweden's security was the need for an alliance with a major power capable of providing sizable subsidies as well as military backing. Since the seventeenth century this role had traditionally been filled by France, the European power best served by the strong Swedish state restored by Gustaf III's coup of 1772. Already in August 1789, Gustaf feared that the revolution in France would result there in an ineffectual regime like Sweden's under the crippling constitution of 1720, from which no dependable support could be expected.[29]

The matter of the French alliance in turn raises even more fundamental questions concerning ideal versus practical considerations in Gustaf III's statecraft, as well as the consistency of his determination to take up arms against the French Revolution.

It has generally been argued by those who in the past have devoted the greatest attention to Gustaf's French plans that he remained committed to the end to his antirevolutionary crusade. Nils Åkeson stressed, in 1885–86, the king's message to the French émigré princes, via his envoy in Coblenz, as well as to certain of his other diplomats, not to be misled by his feigned indifference toward French affairs during the Riksdag, held in Gävle in January and February 1792. Alma Söderhjelm invoked in 1920 the reports from Stockholm of the French Chevalier de Gaussen.

Olof Jägerskiöld pointed in 1957 to Gustaf's ongoing exchange of views with Catherine II and his effort to encourage a new escape attempt by the French royal family by the beginning of 1792.[30] Yet none of this evidence can be considered decisive. Certain persons close to the king at the time drew other conclusions, while examination of the alliance problem in particular raises serious questions concerning the consistency of Gustaf's antirevolutionary course.

Gustaf III always had other irons in the fire. From the fall of 1790, after the peace of Värälä, until the spring of 1791, when he departed for Aachen, he unsuccessfully sought election to the Polish throne. There seems evidence that the ultimate purpose of this ploy was mainly to claim compensation in the event of a second partition of Poland: presumably Norway, against Prussian compensation to Denmark. This idea surfaced again around March 1792—three days before Gustaf's assassination—when he received a discreet inquiry from Catherine II regarding his thoughts on the Polish situation, which aroused his lively interest.

Similar suspicions arose by the beginning of 1792, with regard to his French project. In his memoirs, G. G. Adlerbeth wrote:

> In Sweden several of the king's confidants held that His Majesty was not really serious about his armament against France. Some maintained that Denmark was the real enemy against which it was intended; that France served only as a cover, and that a campaign would be mounted against Norway as soon as the season permitted.[31]

Already in December 1789, during his Russian war, Gustaf wrote to Taube that he would have to demand the stiffest conditions, particularly financial, in return for renewing his existing French alliance, in view of "the little assurance which the whole existence of France gives me"; meanwhile he was negotiating with Great Britain.[32]

After 1790, in seeking to organize an effective coalition against revolutionary France, he looked by necessity to his erstwhile enemy, Russia, for the major ally he needed. The Russian alliance would thus be the means to the ultimate end of restoring Sweden's old alliance with France. Yet in his negotiations with Catherine II during the summer of 1791 the outlines of a broader scenario dimly emerge: a future tripartite alliance among Sweden, Russia, and a restored French monarchy, excluding Russia's old ally Denmark, obviously intended to prepare the way for Sweden's acquisition of Norway. Indeed, the Treaty of Drottningholm in October 1791 seemed to presage a diplomatic revolution in the North that did not fail to arouse apprehensions in Copenhagen.[33]

For Sweden simply to participate in an antirevolutionary coalition under other leadership would meanwhile have meant sacrificing Gustaf's own particular internal and external policy goals. Hence his unwavering determination to take and retain the initiative and his apprehensions that Austria and Prussia sought to bypass him. The emperor, he wrote to his ambassador in Madrid on 4 November 1791, hoped to dominate a weakened France, as Russia had formerly dominated both Sweden and Poland.

From this perspective, his idea in early 1792 of urging the French royal family once again to try to flee Paris may be seen as a last, calculated gamble to remain in the lead when all else failed. The impulse would appear to have come from Catherine II's letter to Gustaf of 9/20 November 1791, in which she speculated that Leopold II might seek to encourage such a flight. If Gustaf could not persuade Louis XVI to make the attempt, this could justify recognizing a regency under the latter's brother, the émigré Comte de Provence, with whom the Swedish king had long been on friendly terms. On 20 January 1792, Gustaf wrote to both of Louis XVI's brothers, offering them asylum under his protection in Swedish Pomerania.[34]

By the beginning of December 1791, certain persons close to the king came to believe that his ardor to intervene in France was beginning to cool. On 28 October, Gustaf had sent his detailed plan for a combined Swedish-Russian landing operation in Normandy to Catherine II. By the beginning of December he received her reply, dated 9/20 November, counseling against any precipitous action before gaining the cooperation of the Emperor and other powers, while assuring him of their basic similarity of views. According to the diary of Carl Gustaf Nordin, then part of the king's inner circle, Gustaf was "very satisfied with this letter," as he had "cooled toward the French affair, to which, for political reasons, he had shown much more passion than he actually felt, to produce an effect in France and [to arouse] fear there."

On 30 November, the king had reproached Armfelt for his and his friends' opposition to his French plans. However, again according to Nordin, Gustaf admitted the following day that they were right. "But I have been drawn so far into French affairs: I have promised the [French] princes my support. I have Baron Taube after me. He is difficult for me to escape." He further reflected, "It would be unreasonable for me to try to restore tranquility to the French nation while destroying it in my own." In consequence Håkanson, "as though by his own accord," sought to persuade Taube himself to urge the king to refrain from his French expedition. Taube, somewhat surprisingly, agreed, saying he could not urge such a venture unless the king had in hand the necessary means. This was precisely what Gustaf lacked, and Armfelt, Håkanson, Nordin, and their friends hoped that the Riksdag to deal with the financial problem, to which Gustaf had necessarily though reluctantly agreed on 18 November, would distract him from his French preoccupations.[35]

Gustaf's behavior and private statements during these crucial days give the strong impression that he by now welcomed the chance to maneuver himself out of an untenable situation, consoled by the thought that he had done what he could. Since September at least, Catherine II had been well informed of his plans for a Swedish-Russian attack on Normandy with Spanish financial support, and already by then Stedingk had reported that Catherine gave every indication of opposing it. To her private secretary, A. V. Khrapovitskii, the empress had meanwhile been ridiculing Gustaf's French chimera—"We often follow him in our thoughts with his cannon boats on the Seine!" she wryly remarked in late July—and admitted to making every effort to involve the Swedish king, as well as the Austrian and Prussian monarchs, in French affairs to give her free hands elsewhere.[36] Gustaf may surely have suspected as much. Thus his detailed proposal of 28 October for the Normandy expedition could well have been intended to obtain clear confirmation, allowing him to save face by attributing the failure of the plan to the Russian empress. There had obviously never been any question of Sweden's facing revolutionary France alone.

Through Stedingk, the Spanish minister in St. Petersburg had meanwhile urged Gustaf early in September to let the French Revolution destroy itself through its own excesses and to seek the goodwill of the dominant party in Paris to preserve the French alliance as the bulwark against Sweden's dangerous neighbor, Russia, without weakening France through war and sacrifice.[37]

That such reflections had not escaped Gustaf himself is attested to as early as 8 June 1791 when, on his way to Aachen, he wrote to Armfelt that if he were unable to help the king of France he would at least have "the satisfaction of having made an attempt to fulfill the duty of friendship toward my old ally and will only leave him to his fate on the basis of impossibility," which would then free him to consider other diplomatic opportunities. It is further borne out by a seemingly incongruous passage in a lengthy memorandum he wrote to Catherine II on the French situation on 9 July 1791, in which he proposed their alliance as the core of the European monarchical host. It seemed not unreasonable to state, Gustaf wrote,

> that for the consideration in which this alliance would be held, (however much this might go against the principles of both sovereigns, and even be immoral!) it would be better and more useful to side

with the National Assembly against the [émigré] princes than to remain indifferent and neutral observers of what is going to take place. For in such a case one would at least gain respect. If, contrary to all probability, the National Assembly should gain the upper hand, one might hope for a useful ally, while on the other hand if one were to remain passive, the South would leave the North out of account, which would be too impolitic. . . .

"King Gustaf considers this matter carefully," Nordin wrote in his diary on 31 August: either Louis XVI's restoration to full power would resurrect the French alliance or France under its new constitution would also need to seek Sweden's support. It was, he quoted the king as saying, thus "necessary that order be restored in France in one way or another, and the sooner the better."[38]

From early December, Gustaf was, as Armfelt and his friends had hoped, largely preoccupied with the forthcoming Riksdag, which at length was convened on 28 January 1792 in Gävle, to avoid possible disturbances in the capital. The aristocratic opposition meanwhile played, as seen, upon fears that the king sought funds for a new war against France.

The king's papers include drafts of a curious document in Gustaf's hand, in both Swedish and French versions: a declaration of fraternal greetings to the French people and its representatives from the "Council and Estates of the Swedish realm," evoking two centuries of friendship and alliance, while expressing confidence that the leaders of the new France would reveal themselves to be "new Solons and Lycurguses" by establishing "the most perfect order" out of "the disorder your enemies claim you have created." Appended, likewise in the king's hand, are the names of prominent members of the Council and Estates, some of the latter known for their earlier opposition to Gustaf III and sympathies toward revolutionary France. This draft document bears the date 28 January 1792, during the Gävle Riksdag, although nothing became of it.

It is strongly tempting to see in this nothing more than a flight of fancy on the part of the literary monarch. In view of all he had previously stated regarding not only the revolution in France but revolution in general, one may—with Nils Åkeson, who first discovered these drafts—easily read bitterness and irony between the lines.[39] One wonders, too, at the evocation of the Council (råd), since after the Riksdag of 1789 it had ceased to exist in practice if not entirely in theory, but under the circumstances this might have had propaganda value both at home and abroad; it is known, moreover, that Gustaf was speculating at that very time over further constitutional changes.

Yet considering his situation and behavior through the fall, these per-plexing drafts cannot be dismissed out of hand. If the prevailing spirit at the Riksdag had seemed sufficiently ominous—if it had, in Erland Hjärne's words, held forth the prospect of a "new Anjala"—it might conceivably have been arranged for a suitable member of the Noble Estate to propose such a declaration.[40] If it then gained enthusiastic support, Gustaf might allow himself to be persuaded to accept it, thereby justifying a necessary change of course. This in turn might have opened the way to the conciliation with his nobility which, a half year earlier, he had written Armfelt, he hoped an armed intervention in France would accomplish, while he could attribute the responsibility to others.

In the event, this stratagem was not attempted. Surprisingly little opposi-tion was apparent at the Riksdag. Gustaf could well have concluded that the wounds of the past were beginning to heal and that so drastic and distasteful a measure was unnecessary. On the day the Riksdag ended, 24 February, Gustaf told Armfelt, *"Le mieux, mon ami, est souvent l'ennemi du bien."* [The best, my friend, is often the enemy of the good]. A war against the French could once again bring Sweden to the brink of ruin, "while I only need peace to live happily." He had no money, nor was it likely that anyone would give him any. Still, both his deeply divided feelings and the strongly romantic side of his character were evident when he continued: "So I think and so must I think as a king; as a nobleman and bold knight I would indeed wish to take part in my own person, and perhaps I might go off to seek my fate as a private individual." Armfelt, of course, protested against any such thought, but to the king it could still offer some wistful consolation.

Soon afterward, he again assured Armfelt that his subjects need have no fear of a new war, but added,

I still cannot help speaking heatedly, when the occasion arises, against the criminals who have ruined France and unrestrainedly showing my ill will toward those who have dissolved the bonds of society in that lovely land, as well as calling for the revenge of all sovereigns upon their heads. But the time is past when the wrath of a king was the same as a declaration of war.

When Magdalena Rudenschiöld, a lady of the court who enjoyed his confidence, expressed fears of a war with France, he reassured her, "One often speaks of things which one champions to preserve appearances, but one does not always bring them about."[41]

Already on 13 January 1792, even before the Gävle Riksdag, Gustaf sent Taube certain documents evidently just received from the French king and queen, who *secretly* encouraged by Fersen had opposed the direct use of force.

> Alas, to what a weak prince have I not promised my support! [Gustaf commented]. . . . If I had ever pulled back from such enterprises in my life and were not myself bound by my ties with the Empress, I should be tempted to abandon the whole affair. But it will be necessary to see what the Empress will do. . . ."[42]

On 28 February 1792, Gustaf wrote to Fersen in Brussels, instructing him to make clear to Louis XVI's agent, the Baron de Breteuil, that unless provided with the necessary money, "it is impossible for me to play any active part in this affair."

> If those powers most interested in the reestablishment of France see themselves deprived of the aid of a prince who alone, until now, has been able to take advantage of the irresolution of the others regarding the common good, the fault for this is entirely their own, as well as for the harmful results that may come from it.

To Breteuil himself, Gustaf reiterated the same message in a letter dated 13 March 1792—the same day on which he wrote to Stedingk about opportunities that might arise through a new partition of Poland. Although his sentiments regarding France remained unchanged, he told Breteuil, he could not realize them without a sufficient subsidy, as he had made clear to the latter already in Aachen the preceding summer. However, he added—with an unmistakable, bittersweet irony—he did not doubt that Breteuil, through his influence upon Louis XVI, "would be able to find the means . . . to send me the necessary funds."[43]

Erland Hjärne may have come closest to the truth when he held in 1929 that Gustaf's correspondence during his last three months shows no lessening of concern over the French Revolution but that one need not doubt the evidence of contemporaries that he came to feel strong and well-justified apprehensions over his plans to intervene.[44] Head and heart pulled in opposite directions.

If there is, meanwhile, a red thread running through Gustaf III's reactions to the revolution in France, it must surely be sought in his constant preoccupation with the security of his realm. In 1772 and 1789 he had strengthened the Swedish state by increasing royal authority; internal revolt either in Sweden or in its traditional ally, France, would, conversely, weaken Sweden's position. Alliance with Russia might, in the long run, do the same; in October 1791 Rutger Fredrik Hochschild feared that through the Treaty of

Drottningholm "we have been sold to the Russians," an idea the king since childhood had regarded with "loathing and contempt."[45] Yet in the short run this might conceivably accomplish the opposite, by restoring a strong French monarchy and, it might be hoped, by breaking the old Russian-Danish encirclement, most effectively through Sweden's acquisition of Norway.

What the future might have held, had Gustaf III's life not been cut short at this point, can only remain a matter of conjecture. Armfelt later reflected that had he lived, "we would have seen at Haga the philosopher of Sans Souci," recalling the older and wiser Frederick II of Prussia, Gustaf's uncle, following the trials of the Seven Years' War. In the "affairs of France"—as in much else—Gustaf III had not meanwhile made things easy for the historian, and to Baron Taube he once confided, in January 1790, "My principle is Richelieu's maxim that in Europe's troubles it is always necessary to keep throwing out new ideas, if only to increase the confusion."[46]

Notes

1. *Mémoires posthumes du feld-maréchal comte de Stedingk*, ed. Count M. F. F. Biörnstierna, 2 vols. (Paris, 1844–47), 1:193; *Konung Gustaf III:s bref till friherre G. M. Armfelt*, ed. Elof Tegnér, Historiska handlingar, 12, no. 3 (Stockholm. 1883; hereafter Tegnér, *Bref*), 99, 102–4. Cf. Alma Söderhjelm, *Sverige och den franska revolutionen*, 2 vols. (Stockholm, 1920–24), 1, for general reactions in Sweden to the revolution, including the king's. See also my *Scandinavia in the Revolutionary Era, 1760–1815* (Minneapolis, 1986), chapt. 8.

2. On Gustaf's upbringing, see Beth Hennings, *Gustav III som kronprins* (Stockholm, 1935): also my "Gustaf III of Sweden and the Enlightenment," in this volume.

3. My "Gustaf III and the Enlightenment." On the political idealism of Gustaf's historical dramas, see Erik Lönnroth, *Den stora rollen. Kung Gustaf III spelad av honom själv* (Stockholm, 1986), esp. 75–80.

4. *Lettres de Gustave III à la comtesse de Boufflers et de la comtesse au roi*, ed. Aurelien Vivie (Paris, 1898; hereafter Vivie, *Lettres*), 116, 319, 386.

5. For Gustaf's conception of true or benevolent philosophy, see *Collection des écrits politiques, littéraires et dramatiques de Gustave III, roi de Suède, suivie de sa correspondance*, ed. J.-B. Dechaux, 5 vols. (Stockholm, 1803–5; hereafter *Ecrits*), 1:222. On his reign in general, see C. T. Odhner, *Sveriges politiska historia under konung Gustaf III:s regering*, 3 vols. (Stockholm, 1885–1905), through 1788, Ludvig Stavenow, *Den gustavianska tiden 1771–1809*, Sveriges historia till våra dagar, 10 (Stockholm, 1925), and my *Scandinavia in the Revolutionary Era*.

6. Stedingk, *Mémoires posthumes*, 1:72–73. Cf. my "Sweden and the War of American Independence," in this volume, 49.

7. *The Writings of George Washington*, ed. John C. Fitzpatrick, vol. 27 (Washington, 1937), 458; Lönnroth, *Den stora rollen*, 130. Cf. *Hedvig Elisabeth Charlottas dagbok*,

ed. Carl Carlsson Bonde and Cecilia af Klercker, 9 vols. (Stockholm, 1902–42), 11:221; François-Claude Amour, Marquis de Bouillé, *Mémoires du marquis de Bouillé*, ed. M. F. Barrière, 2 vols. (Paris, 1859), 2:140.

8. See my *Scandinavia*, 156–74. Cf. Claude Nordmann, *Gustave III, un démocrate couronné* (Lille, 1986). For a Marxian view of Gustaf's "anti-feudal reforms" as the antidote to revolution, see Jörg-Peter Findeisen, "Gustaf III, und die 'Epochenschwelle 1789.' Reaktionen des schwedischen Monarchen auf die Französische Revolution," *Zeitschrift für Geschichtswissenschaft* 37 (1989): 812–23.

9. Vivie, *Lettres*, 385–86; Bernhard von Schinkel, *Minnen ur Sveriges nyare historia*, ed. C. W. Bergman, 10 vols. (Stockholm, 1852–68), 2:147; Stedingk, *Mémoires posthumes*, 1:137, 203–4, 206; *Konung Gustaf III:s bref till Riks-Drotsen Grefve Carl Axel Wachtmeister och Stats-Sekreteraren Ulric Gustaf Franc*, ed. Gust. Andersson (Örebro, 1860), 112; Tegnér, *Bref till Armfelt*, 94, 96; Gunnar von Proschwitz, *Gustave III par ses lettres* (Stockholm, 1986), 304, 305, 321; *Hedvig Elisabeth Charlottas dagbok*, 3:216.

10. See Nils Åkeson, *Gustaf III:s förhållande till franska revolutionen*, 2 vols. in 1 (Lund, 1885–86); Erland Hjärne, "Gustaf III och franska revolutionen," *Svensk tidskrift* 19 (1929): 502–22; Olof Jägerskiöld, *Den svenska utrikespolitikens historia*, vol. 2, part 2, *1721–1792* (Stockholm, 1957); my *Count Hans Axel von Fersen: Aristocrat in an Age of Revolution* (Boston, 1975), chapts. 5 and 6, and *Scandinavia*, chapt. 8. Auguste Geoffroy, *Gustave III et la cour de France*, 2 vols. (Paris, 1867), and R. Nisbet Bain, *Gustavus III and His Contemporaries*, 2 vols. (London, 1894), also remain useful.

11. Geoffroy, *Gustave III*, 2:88–93; Söderhjelm, *Sverige och franska revolutionen*, 1:189–204, 212–14; my *Fersen*, 84–93; Proschwitz, *Gustave III par ses lettres*, 325.

12. [Elis Schröderheim,] *Skrifter till konung Gustaf III:s historia jämte urval ur Schröderheims brefväxling*, ed. Elof Tegnér (2nd ed., Stockholm, 1892), 102. Cf. Rutger Fredrik Hochschild, *Memoarer*, ed. H. Schück, 3 vols. (Stockholm, 1908–9), 2:177.

13. Gustaf III to Taube, 3 Sept. 1790, Stafsundssamlingen: Evert Taubes samling, 1; [Elis Schröderheim,] *Skrifter till konung Gustaf III:s historia*. Cf. Rutger Fredrik Hochschild, *Memoarer*, ed. H. Schück, 3 vols. (Stockholm, 1908–9), 2:77. Cf. Proschwitz, *Gustave III par ses lettres*, 338.

14. Stedingk to Gustaf III, 8 Feb. 1791, Diplomatica, Muscovitica, 451, RA; cf. Schinkel, *Minnen*, 2:153–55; Hjärne, "Gustaf III och franska revolutionen," 510. For general diplomatic background, cf. C. T. Odhner, *Gustaf III och Katarina II efter freden i Värälä* (Stockholm, 1886) and Signe Carlsson, "Till frågan om Sveriges utrikespolitik efter freden i Värälä," in *Gottfrid Carlsson 18.12.1952* (Lund, 1952), 348–76.

15. Geoffroy, *Gustave III*, 2:132–33, 135–36. The original French draft of Gustaf's letter of 17 May 1791 to Breteuil, in Kungliga handskriftssamlingen, Gustaf III, Riksarkivet, Stockholm (hereafter RA), says *"ses mil"* Swedish troops (plus hopefully at least half that number of Russians), which Geoffroy and Åkeson (*Gustaf III:s förhållande*, 42) have interpreted as sixteen thousand and which makes sense in view of Gustaf's later correspondence during the summer of 1791. Proschwitz, *Gustave III par ses lettres*, 341, has taken this to be six thousand. On Fersen and the Escape to Varennes, see my *Fersen*, chapt. 5.

16. *Louis XVI, Marie-Antoinette et Madame Elisabeth. Lettres et documents inédits*, ed. F. Feuillet de Conches, 6 vols. (Paris, 1864–73; hereafter Feuillet de Conches, *Louis XVI*), 3:391–402; Geoffroy, *Gustave III*, 2:171–72; *Le comte de Fersen et la cour de France*, ed. R. M. Klinckowström, 2 vols. (Paris, 1877–78), 1:143; Proschwitz, *Gustave III par ses lettres*, 351; Åkeson, *Gustaf III:s förhållande*, 65–69; Söderhjelm, *Sverige och den franska revolutionen*, 1:254–55; Schinkel, *Minnen*, 2:171–72.

17. My *Fersen*, 127–37. Concerning Leopold II and the French Revolution, see esp. Adam Wandruszka, *Leopold II*, 2 vols. (Vienna, 1963–65), 2.

18. My *Fersen*, 137, 140–46; Bouillé, *Mémoires*, 2:99–100; Åkeson, *Gustaf III:s förhållande*, 128, 133–34; Klinckowström, *Fersen et la cour de France*, 1:176–77, 180–83, 202.

19. Klinckowström, *Fersen et la cour de France*, 1:275, 278, 288–91, 296–97, 313; 2:165, 184; my *Fersen*, 145–50, 154; Söderhjelm, *Sverige och den franska revolutionen*, 2:14, 25–29.

20. *Statsrådet Johan Albert Ehrenströms efterlemnade historiska anteckningar*, ed. S. J. Boëthius, 2 vols. (Stockholm, 1883), 1:375–76. On the ideological background to Gustaf III's assassination, see esp. Lolo Krusius-Ahrenberg, *Tyrannmördaren C. F. Ehrensvärd* (Helsingfors, 1947), chapts. 1–4; Stig Jägerskiöld, "Tyrannmord och motståndsrätt 1792–1809," *Scandia* 25 (1962): 113–66; my *Scandinavia*, 164, 171, 175, 191, 201; and Jägerskiöld, *Den svenska utrikespolitikens historia*, 346. For suspicions of Jacobin involvement in the assassination, see Söderhjelm, *Sverige och den franska revolutionen*, 2:14–29. Regarding reactions to it in France, see ibid., 2:14, 19–21, 25–28.

21. See Söderhjelm, *Sverige och den franska revolutionen*, I: 301. Cf. *Hedvig Elisabeth Charlottas dagbok*, 3:348–49, 375–76, 392; Hochschild, *Memoarer*, 2:198, 201.

22. *Riksrådet och Feld-marskalken m. m. Fredrik Axel von Fersens historiska skrifter*, ed. R. M. Klinckowström, 8 vols. (Stockholm, 1867–72), 7:188; Lydia Wahlström, "Gustaf III och norrmännen," *Nordisk tidskrift* (1907): 63; my "Gustaf III of Sweden and the East Baltic, 1771–1792," in this volume, 71; my *Scandinavia*, 134, 155–56, 163–64.

23. Klinckowström, *Fersen et la cour de France*, 1:117; Geoffroy, *Gustave III*, 2:112, 168–69; Proschwitz, *Gustave III par ses lettres*, 352.

24. Feuillet de Conches, *Louis XVI*, 4:113; cf. my *Fersen*, 133; *DeLaGardiska arkivet. Handlingar ur grefliga DeLaGardiska biblioteket på Löberöd*, ed. P. Wieselgren, 20 vols. (Stockholm, 1831–44), 18:111. Cf. Hochschild, *Memoarer*, 2:191–92. See also Söderhjelm, *Sverige och den franska revolutionen*, 1:137–38.

25. See my *Fersen*, 89–90; Proschwitz, *Gustave III par ses lettres*, 351–53; L. Manderström, *Om Gustaf den Tredjes yttre politik under de två senaste åren af dess regering* (Stockholm, 1859), 74–76; Schinkel, *Minnen*, 2:316; Åkeson, *Gustaf III:s förhållande*, 229. Cf. Georges Lefebvre, *La Révolution française* (Paris, 1951), 261–62. For Catherine II's reactions, see, for ex., her letters to Baron Friedrich Melchior Grimm in *Sbornik imperatorskago russkago istoricheskago obshchestva*, 148 vols. (St. Petersburg, 1867–1916), vol. 23; also Aleksandr V. Khrapovitskii, *Dnevnik A. V. Khrapovitskago 1782–1793*, ed. N. Varsukov (St. Petersburg, 1901).

26. Beth Hennings, *Gustav III* (Stockholm, 1957), 141; Folke Almén, *Gustaf III och hans rådgivare 1772–1789* (Uppsala, 1940), 41–46, 51–52; Tegnér, *Bref till Armfelt*,

198. Cf. Sven Delblanc, *Ära och minne* (Stockholm, 1965), esp. 136–43, 191–94, 224–34; Lönnroth, *Den stora rollen.*

27. *Historiska anteckningar af Gudmund Göran Adlerbeth*, ed. Elof Tegnér, 2 vols. (2nd ed., Lund, 1892), 1:191; C. G. Nordin, *Dagboksanteckningar för åren 1786–1792* (Stockholm, 1868), 176; Bouillé, *Mémoires*, 2:141.

28. Tegnér, *Bref till Armfelt*, 193–96. Cf. Lydia Wahlström, "Skrifvelser från Gustaf III ur Anders af Håkansons papper," *Historisk tidskrift* 33 (1913): 235:29.

29. Tegnér, *Bref till Armfelt*, 96; Åkeson, *Gustaf III:s förhållande*, 232.

30. Åkeson, *Gustaf III:s förhållande*, 160–63, 220–21; Söderhjelm, *Sverige och den franska revolutionen*, 1:301–9; Jägerskiöld, *Den svenska utrikespolitikens historia*, 346. Cf. Lönnroth, *Den stora rollen*, 259, for criticism of Gaussen's evidence. Much of Gustaf's correspondence with Catherine II during this period is given in *Catherine II et Gustave III: une correspondence retrouvée*, ed. Gunnar von Proschwitz (Stockholm, 1998).

31. *Hedvig Elisabeth Charlottas dagbok*, 3:328; Hochschild, *Memoarer*, 2:199; Schinkel, *Minnen*, 2:182; Åkeson, *Gustaf III:s förhållande*, 252–53; Jägerskiöld, *Den svenska utrikespolitikens historia*, 346–47; my "Gustaf III and the East Baltic."

32. Proschwitz, *Gustave III par ses lettres*, 325.

33. See Schinkel, *Minnen*, 2:302–9; Wahlström, "Skrifvelser," 235; Manderström, *Gustaf den Tredjes yttre politik*, 67; Jägerskiöld, *Den svenska utrikespolitikens historia*, 344.

34. Manderström, *Gustaf den Tredjes yttre politik*, 78; Åkeson, *Gustaf III:s förhållande*, 152, 244; my *Scandinavia*, 195. For suspicions regarding Austria and Prussia, see Klinckowström, *Fersen et la cour de France*, 1:176–79, 226, 263, 272; 2:165, 200–201; Åkeson, *Gustaf III:s förhållande*, 232; my *Fersen*, 134, 146, 152.

35. Catherine II to Gustaf III, 9 Nov. 1791 (o. s.), Diplomatica, Muscovitica, 625, RA; Schinkel, *Minnen*, 2:313–19; Åkeson, *Gustaf III:s förhållande*, 227–30; Nordin, *Dagboksanteckningar*, 201–9 passim.; Elof Tegnér, *Gustaf Mauritz Armfelt*, 3 vols. (Stockholm, 1883–87), 1:420–26. Cf. Lönnroth, *Den stora rollen*, 256–57.

36. Stedingk to Armfelt, 3/14 July, 3/14 Aug., Stedingk's dispatches, 4/15, 14/25 July, 31 July/11 Aug., 19/30 Sept., Stedingk to Gustav III, 27 Aug./7 [Sept.] 1791, Diplomatica, Muscovitica, 451, RA; Manderström, *Gustaf den Tredjes yttre politik*, 74–76; Hochschild, *Memoarer*, 2:199, 201–6; Khrapovitskii, *Dnevnik*, 368, 369, 375, 386; Åkeson, *Gustaf III:s förhållande*, 134–35; Hjärne, "Gustaf III och franska revolutionen," 514–15; Lönnroth, *Den stora rollen*, 257. Cf. Geoffroy, *Gustave III et la cour de France*, 2:176–81.

37. Stedingk to Gustav III, 27 Aug./7 [Sept.] 1791, Diplomatica, Muscovitica, 451, RA. Lönnroth, *Den stora rollen*, 258.

38. Tegnér, *Bref till Armfelt*, 181; Schinkel, *Minnen*, 2:307; Nordin, *Dagboksanteckningar*, 177–78.

39. Gustavianska samlingen, 415, Uppsala universitetsbibliotek; Åkeson, *Gustaf III:s förhållande*, 163–64n., which includes the text of the Swedish version. Cf. Lönnroth, *Den stora rollen*, 259–61.

40. Cf. Hjärne, "Gustaf III och franska revolutionen," 522.

41. Tegnér, *Armfelt*, 1:426–28.

42. Proschwitz, *Gustave III par ses lettres*, 373. On Fersen and the French king and queen's appeal to Gustaf III, see Klinckowström, *Fersen et la cour de France*, 1:221–22, 233–59, 261, 265–72. Cf. my *Fersen*, 143–44.

43. Åkeson, *Gustaf III:s förhållande*, 247, 251.44

44. Hjärne, "Gustaf III och franska revolutionen," 520–22.

45. Hochschild, *Memoarer*, 2:205.

46. Tegnér, *Armfelt*, 1:429; Gustaf III to Taube, Haga, 5 Jan. 1790, Evert Taubes samling, I, RA. Cf. *Gustaf III. Mannen bakom myten,* ed. Gunnar von Proschwitz (Höganäs, 1992), 381–82. This collection of the king's correspondence in Swedish translation, which appeared after the completion of my article, contains a number of previously unpublished letters—including the one cited here—not found in von Proschwitz's earlier *Gustave III par ses lettres,* none of which, however, modify my findings.

Late Gustavian Autocracy in Sweden: Gustaf IV Adolf and His Opponents, 1792–1809

King Gustaf IV Adolf has had bad press. After seventeen years on the Swedish throne he was deposed by revolution. Between the well-known "shimmer" that "lay over Gustaf [III]'s days," which preceded, and the colorful era of Carl XIV Johan, the former Marshal Bernadotte, which followed, his reign remains in Swedish popular memory as a time of national humiliation and a gray and sterile "Iron Age."[1]

Such is the tradition created by the revolutionaries of 1809, based above all on Gustaf Adolf's later, ruinous foreign policy. Later attempts at reappraisal have focused on this side of his reign. Relatively little attention has meanwhile been given to his internal regime, considered as a whole, which, in line with most contemporary memoirs, has generally been dismissed as reactionary and obscurantist. In some ways this view was true enough. A closer study, however, shows that if the "Men of 1809," who deposed him, were progressive politically, in the context of their time they were socially conservative; that therefore both the revolution and strong popular reactions against it during the following year and a half sharply reflect social and ideological conflicts deeply rooted in Sweden's past; and finally, that Gustaf IV Adolf's internal regime was indeed of fundamental significance for the evolution of modern Swedish society and that it enjoyed the confidence of the greater part of his subjects to the end.

After the assassination of Gustaf III in 1792, when the young prince was thirteen years old, Sweden was at first governed by a regency under Gustaf Adolf's uncle, Duke Carl of Södermanland. Gustaf Adolf commenced his personal reign in 1796, implacably opposed to the French Revolution and the "new philosophy," which he considered the inspiration behind his father's murder; this was henceforward to set the tone of his repressive cultural policy. He was from the start determined to follow his father's policies, using to the full the extensive prerogatives provided by Gustaf III's constitution of 1772 and Act of Union and Security of 1789. It was only with the greatest reluctance that he at last convened the Estates in 1800 to deal with a mounting crisis in the state finances. This Riksdag, held

Gustaf IV Adolf, by Niclas Lafrensen, the younger. Gustaf III's successor largely implemented the reforms begun during his father's reign, but posterity has generally dismissed him as a failure due to his inept foreign policy and military failures, which led to his deposition in 1809. (Courtesy of Svenskt Porträttarkiv, Stockholm.)

in Norrköping, revealed an opposition he considered "Jacobinical," after which he determinedly avoided further diets to the end of his reign. By executive action his autocratic-bureaucratic regime nevertheless implemented a number of practical reforms, as will be seen.

The king's main concern, both by inclination and necessity, was always foreign policy. The Revolutionary and Napoleonic wars posed serious threats to Sweden's security and economy. Gustaf Adolf moreover aspired, as his father had done, to seize Norway from Denmark when circumstances permitted. In 1805 he abandoned his earlier neutrality to join the Third Coalition against Napoleon, for which there were justifiably practical reasons at the time.[2] His role in the ensuing war was, however, both modest and ignominious, in part because of the successive defeats of his allies but largely through his own military and diplomatic ineptitude. By 1807, when the Swedes were driven from northern Germany, his reputation at home and abroad was gravely damaged.

After the Peace of Tilsit of July 1807, Sweden remained Britain's only continental ally and was attacked by Napoleon's new allies, Russia and Denmark-Norway, early in 1808. Again the war was mismanaged, leading ultimately to military insurrection on the Norwegian front under Lieutenant-Colonel Georg Adlersparre and the king's arrest in Stockholm by a group of officers led by General C. J. Adlercreutz, on 13 March 1809.

Duke Carl was once again made regent. In May a Riksdag was convened that, accusing the king of violation of the social contract, deposed him and barred his descendants from the succession. The following month, it made the aging and childless duke King Carl XIII, after his acceptance of a new constitution, and a few weeks later elected as his successor Prince Carl August, as he came to be called in Sweden, of the house of Augustenburg. By September Sweden was forced to accept the humiliating Peace of Fredrikshamn, ceding to Russia all of Finland and the Åland Islands, more than a third of the territory and a quarter of the population of the realm. Gustaf Adolf and his family were deported in December. His eccentric behavior during his last years in exile until his death in St. Gallen in 1837 seemed to confirm the wisdom and foresight of the "Men of 1809," who not surprisingly sought in retrospect to blacken Gustaf Adolf's regime in order to justify its overthrow.[3]

Who were the Men of 1809 and what was their background? The most striking facts about them are their predominantly noble origin and the essentially political, rather than social, nature of their opposition. In these respects it is evident that they represented an ancient tradition of aristocratic constitutionalism in Sweden, aggrieved by Gustaf III's seizure of greater royal power in 1772 and 1789, and fortified by the libertarian doctrines of the Enlightenment.[4] Coming hard on the heels of Gustaf III's conflict with his nobility in 1788–89, the French Revolution at first strongly appealed to the aristocratic opposition in Sweden, which naturally saw in it above all the overthrow of royal despotism.[5] These varied influences all played their part in the aristocratic conspiracies leading to Gustaf III's assassination in 1792.[6]

The regency of 1792–1796 disappointed liberal hopes, and disaffection remained endemic. At Uppsala, radical students, claiming the current world situation laid greater claims to their attention than routine studies, set up a "Convention" in imitation of the French in early 1793, which was soon suppressed by the alarmed authorities. A group at the same university, however, calling itself the "Junta" and including several future revolutionaries of 1809 remained a seedbed of Swedish radicalism through the 1790s.[7]

Many free spirits at first welcomed Gustaf IV Adolf's personal reign in 1796 as a relief from the oppressive regency but soon became disillusioned with the young king's autocracy, anti-Jacobinism and anti-intellectualism.[8] In 1799–1800, when a combination of economic problems caused considerable unrest, pro-French manifestations in Stockholm, Uppsala, and elsewhere sharply reflected the disaffection of Swedish radicals, not least that of the "Junta" and its sympathizers. Members of this circle formed the nucleus of the radical "Mountain" at the Norrköping Riksdag in 1800, which sought to use the government's financial difficulties to compel the convening of frequent and regular diets, thus the surrender of an important royal prerogative. At the height of the conflict, five young radicals dramatically renounced their noble status in protest against the government's maneuvers, among them Hans Järta, traditionally regarded as the principal author of the constitution of 1809, and were joined by several others, including Georg Adlersparre, in withdrawing from further participation in the Riksdag.[9] Adlersparre and Järta hotly denied that they were "Jacobins"; indeed, a recent study of Järta shows them to have been at this time really more "Girondin" in outlook and sympathies.[10] After 1800, little more is heard from the opposition. The conservative Count Axel von Fersen's chancellorship at Uppsala University, increasing censorship, and restrictions on the import of foreign, particularly French, publications stifled public debate until the revolution of 1809 restored freedom of the press, thereby bringing the conflicts within Swedish society back into the light.

The revolution of 1809 was first and foremost the work of members of the nobility, as that Estate pointedly reminded the others at the Riksdag convened in May that year.[11] Georg Adlersparre, marching on Stockholm at the head of his insurgent troops, had issued a manifesto clearly modeled on William III's proclamation to the English in 1688, and others too were quick to point out the parallel with England's Glorious Revolution. Count H. G. Trolle-Wachtmeister exulted in May that "the revolution whereby James II was expelled from the English throne shall now no longer be admired as the only one of its kind."[12] The comparison is indeed an apt one, for the revolution of 1809 tended to consolidate the ascendancy of an oligarchy of birth and wealth not unlike England's before the First Reform Bill. The new Swedish constitution adopted in 1809, like the English Bill of Rights of 1689, has stood the test of time, and the events of that year have provided the basis for a Swedish "Whig" tradition, which in following generations could be applied as much in a conservative as in a liberal sense.[13]

As the Swedish constitution was one of the few framed in the Western world outside the area of French domination during the Revolutionary-Napoleonic era, it is of particular interest, not least because it shows how *political* the radicalism of the noble opposition in Sweden was and how far it had moved away from social radicalism during Gustaf IV Adolf's reign. The idealistic young noblemen who plotted Gustaf III's assassination in 1792 had espoused complete civic equality, and even some of that monarch's less visionary noble opponents had considered an extensive leveling of those corporate privileges that still remained after the Act of Security of 1789.[14] Hans Järta and his four friends renounced their noble status, as noted, at the Norrköping Riksdag of 1800, where some modifications to existing privileges were brought up in the Noble Estate, though without result. In 1809, meanwhile, it was Järta and persons close to him who took the lead in drafting the new constitution, influenced not only by old Swedish traditions but by the doctrines of Locke, Montesquieu, Blackstone, J.-L. Delolme and J. J. Mounier, and thus placed considerable emphasis on an aristocratic "intermediate body" to hold in check the despotism of either the one or the many.[15] Danish, Russian, and British observers, knowing something of Sweden's past, were quick to note the "aristocratic" nature of the new regime in Stockholm.[16] Looking back on the student radicalism of his youth, Count Trolle-Wachtmeister wrote in the 1840s that he and his friends would now be ridiculed as "doctrinaires" and "adherents of the *juste-milieu*," revealing "our present-day reformers' contempt for the constitution of 1809, which is the realization of Uppsala Jacobinism."[17] Järta has since been called "Sweden's Edmund Burke."[18]

Recent research, however, has made it increasingly clear that the aristocratic revolutionaries of 1809 were far from representing the nation as a whole. There remained widespread sympathy for Gustaf IV Adolf and his family within all classes; most markedly, however, among the *non-noble* orders. The clergy and peasantry seem to have remained basically unshaken in their loyalty, and on the whole the burghers too, despite the commercial dislocations of the war.[19]

This cleavage is more than coincidental, for royalism and anti-aristocratic sentiment were traditionally closely associated in Sweden. Michael Roberts speaks in this regard of the "demagogic tradition of Swedish kingship."[20] Gustaf Vasa had first turned to the peasants in 1520 to free Sweden from the Kalmar Union and in 1680 Carl XI, whose memory the nobility abhorred, saved the peasantry from the evident threat of serfdom. The peasants had faithfully shouldered the burdens of Caroline despotism, and during the so-called "Era of Liberty" after 1718—the golden age of aristocratic predominance—they first sought unsuccessfully to strengthen the crown in 1723, then tried in 1743 to secure as successor the crown prince of Denmark, thereby showing their preference for a royal absolutism on the Danish-Norwegian model to Swedish aristocratic, parliamentary liberty.[21] The victories of the Younger Cap party in the later 1760s cleared the way for a strong attack by the three lower Estates against noble privilege, only forestalled by Gustaf III's coup d'état and constitution in 1772.

Though Gustaf III himself had strongly aristocratic sympathies, his growing autocracy brought him into conflict with the nobility by the 1780s, culminating with the mutiny of much of his Finnish officer corps early in his war with Russia in 1788.[22] Gustaf thus turned to the lower orders for support and deliberately stirred up anti-aristocratic passions, partly to rally the defense of the country, partly to force through the Riksdag of 1789 his Act of Union and Security, supplemented by an Edict on the Rights and Liberties of the Peasantry, which greatly strengthened royal authority in return for abolishing most noble privileges.[23]

It has been seen that the young regicides who assassinated Gustaf III in 1792 were romantic enthusiasts for both freedom and equality as they saw these ideals embodied in the French Revolution, but that thereafter aristocratic radicalism became increasingly less social in content. In actuality, what appears to have occurred after 1792 is a growing rift between aristocratic libertarianism on the one hand and anti-aristocratic social radicalism on the other, each inspired by different aspects of the revolution in France.[24] For some time this divergence nonetheless remains unclear, in part because of frictions within the nobility itself between, for example, the three classes of counts, barons, and untitled nobles reestablished by Gustaf III in 1773; nobles of older and more recent title; generations; and bureaucrats and landowners. Thus during the regency certain noblemen could publicly dispute the justification for noble status itself, and their arguments could strongly impress Hans Järta and the others who renounced their nobility in 1800.[25] But, as seen, such enthusiasms soon thereafter faded among the noble opposition.

It is clear, meanwhile, that more powerful currents of social radicalism were stirring *other* levels in Swedish society. "The former royalists," complained R. F. Hochschild in 1793, "miss the king [Gustaf III] and are becoming attached to Jacobinism, going from one extreme to the other." French principles, the Austrian chargé d'affaires reported in 1797, had made great progress among the Swedish "Third Estate" in connection with "that sort of Jacobinism already fomented by the late king against the nobility.[26] The Norrköping Riksdag revealed smoldering discontents. A Stockholm shoemaker campaigned for election by calling for the limitation of all unearned incomes to 1,000 *riksdaler* and the distribution of surpluses to the people. There was talk in the Peasant Estate of eliminating surviving clerical and noble privileges. An observer warned, "There is great danger that lust for revenge [for the assassination of Gustaf III] will break forth and if the nobles commit the least indiscretion, that will do it." Tsar Paul was so alarmed at the prospect of the spread of Jacobinism in the North that he contemplated occupying Finland. Meanwhile, the peasantry and clergy provided almost solid, and the burghers strong royalist majorities at the Riksdag.[27] Thereafter, until 1809, overt criticism was repressed as much in the social as in the political sphere.

The aftermath of the coup d'état of March 1809 illustrates most clearly the cleavage between aristocratic libertarians and plebian social radicals. In the weeks that followed, some isolated attempts were made to raise a counterrevolution, which came to nothing mainly because Gustaf IV Adolf accepted his deposition with remarkable equanimity. He had indeed long toyed with the idea of abdicating, and now hoped only for the succession of his nine-year-old son, Prince Gustaf.[28] There was henceforward little sentiment for restoring the deposed king, though there remained much personal sympathy for him, as shown by the common people along the way when he went into exile.[29] On the other hand, the exclusion of Prince Gustaf, the rightful heir, through procedures of questionable legality by the Riksdag in May 1809, triggered a strong legitimist reaction, both within and beyond the Riksdag.[30]

This response, in turn, was soon reinforced by widespread dissatisfaction with the new constitution of June 1809. Several leading "Gustavian" legitimists and bureaucrats intrigued with Carl XIII to replace it with one restoring greater royal authority, though ultimately without result.[31] Meanwhile, debate over two constitutional questions in particular reveals both the now unmistakable social conservatism of the new oligarchy and popular reactions against it. The first was that of representational reform of the Riksdag, for the existing four estates directly represented only a small part of the population while grossly overrepresenting the old elites. During the past century there had developed considerable "middle-class" elements (*ofrälse ståndspersoner*), commanding much wealth, talent, and education, which did not fit into any of the four traditional estates and hence were excluded from any voice in national affairs. Proposals were made, either to expand the existing estates, to add a fifth estate, or to replace the estate system itself with a more modern type of legislature. The question was referred back to the constitutional committee, which nearly one year later, in April 1810, finally recommended eventual conversion to a bicameral legislature on the English model, the matter to be determined however only by some future riksdag. The committee's rapporteur on this question, Count A. G. Mörner, privately observed that this proposal "has served to distract from much more extensive projects." The oligarchs of 1809 thus managed to sidestep the issue for the present, while proposing an eventual solution in which an aristocratic upper house could hold the balance between the crown and the "democratic spirit."[32] The conservative tide of the following decades ultimately delayed the reform of Sweden's estates system until 1866.

The second question involved noble privileges with respect to ownership and tax exemption of so-called *frälse* or noble land. Gustaf III, with his Act of Security in 1789, had removed class restrictions on the purchase of scattered noble lands. Immediate manorial (*yppersta frälse*) lands—those surrounding noble country seats—had remained the exclusive preserve of the nobility and included much choice land. There was therefore great pressure from the Peasant Estate at the Riksdag of 1809 both to make acquisition of immediate manorial land accessible to all classes and to tax all noble land on an equal basis with all other land.

The Estate refused at first to sign the new constitution in June 1809 until these demands were met. Passions reached the point, according to Count Trolle-Wachtmeister, where the more radical peasant leaders spoke of "turning us into a republic under a president, like in North America," since without the desired property and tax reforms they argued that Sweden could not afford to support the monarchy. This agitation, he added ironically, "has brought some measure of moderation to the more stormy members of the nobility, who want no one but themselves to act as revolutionaries and are more devoted to their manors than to democracy." Many of the latter, he added, now found themselves prepared to "accept any constitution whatsoever" or to resort to any other means necessary to put an end to the wrangling in the Riksdag.

In its relative political naïveté, however, the Peasant Estate was at length browbeaten, cajoled and duped into signing the constitution by the crown and the other estates. As was the case with representation, the settlement of the question of noble land was a compromise, which appears more favorable to the peasantry than it in fact proved to be for generations to come: the nobility relinquished its exclusive right to own immediate manorial land but retained the special tax exemptions attached to all noble lands. By 1809, the peasantry had acquired only some eleven percent of noble land of any type, while at least seventy percent—including theoretically all immediate manorial land—was still in noble hands. Placing this latter category on the open market with its specially favored tax status intact in fact raised its value and, hence, the economic assets of its aristocratic owners. In effect then, the enjoyment of special land taxation privileges remained confined to the few, especially to noblemen, until the abolition of the old land tax in 1892.[33]

Thus the Riksdag of 1809–10 gave rise to much disenchantment, especially among unenfranchised middle-class elements and the peasantry; some peasants even feared the new oligarchy intended to establish serfdom on the Russian model.[34] Such discontents proved grist for the mill of the leaders of the Gustavian faction in the Noble Estate. In January 1810, their leading spokesman, Count Jacob De la Gardie, hurled a bombshell at his rivals by proposing the abolition of *all* corporate privilege, equal taxation of *all* land, and representational reform. The Men of 1809 counterattacked bitterly, both in the Riksdag and through poisonous personal slander. De la Gardie was denounced for his "aristocratic-demagogic" spirit and compared with the "deserter" Count Mathieu de Montmorency, who in 1789 had so lightheartedly renounced for his Estate the privileges of the French *noblesse*.[35]

In the "Whiggish" tradition of 1809, this move by De la Gardie and his associates was long dismissed as mere political opportunism. More recent scholarship, however, is rather inclined to recognize in it a kind of "Tory democracy," at once principled and shrewd, of a type increasingly familiar in nineteenth-century Europe. Despite the efforts of some of its politically sophisticated leaders, the Peasant Estate was now more than ever suspicious of initiatives from the Nobility and fearful of a new tax assessment, while the Clergy and Burghers hesitated to sacrifice their remaining privileges. The proposal was therefore quickly buried, to the relief of most of the Riksdag.[36]

Thus, by the spring of 1810, the Men of 1809 were caught between Gustavian legitimism, with its traditions of strong kingship, and widespread popular radicalism, with dangerous crossovers between the two. The newly elected successor, Prince Carl August of Augustenburg, emerged as the focus for the hopes of the bitterly divided factions. He had been the nominee of the Men of 1809, who saw in him their protector. At the same time, he was popularly considered to be anti-aristocratic in outlook and thus appealed to the broader masses, while it was rightly surmised in Gustavian circles that the bachelor Carl August seriously considered adopting the debarred Prince Gustaf as his own heir.[37]

Carl August's sudden death in May blew apart this unstable balance of forces. The Men of 1809 sought to replace him with his brother, Duke Frederik Christian of Augustenburg. On 20 June 1810, violence broke out in Stockholm in connection with Carl August's funeral. The grand marshal of the court, Count Axel von Fersen, a particularly conspicuous representative of the old high nobility, was set upon and killed by an infuriated mob and several rioters were also killed before the troops could restore order. There is good reason to believe that various of the aristocratic oligarchs of 1809 were themselves involved in a plot at least to humiliate Count Fersen, in order to strike at their Gustavian rivals; this violence may in some respects represent a settling of scores by the lesser "country" nobility against the old high "court" nobility in a way that again recalls seventeenth-century English developments.[38]

Yet the Fersen riot was evidently more directly the work of certain middle-class conspirators who, doubtless unbeknown to the oligarchs, already hoped thereby to secure as successor the Napoleonic Marshal Bernadotte and under his auspices to carry out a genuine social revolution against *all* aristocracy. According to a secret Russian report, this "revolutionary party" desired "to overthrow entirely the whole order that had recently been *reestablished* in the country." Significantly, the crowd that killed Count Fersen unjustly accused him not only of having poisoned Crown Prince Carl August but also of complicity in the assassination of Gustaf III, the deposition of Gustaf IV Adolf, and the exclusion of his heirs from the throne.[39]

Bernadotte's election as heir to the throne, in August 1810, however, turned out to be a profound disappointment to the social radicals, for becoming the real ruler of the country upon his arrival in October, he proved staunchly conservative. One of the Men of 1809 soon thereafter wrote gratefully to the new crown prince, praising him for saving "the sacred hierarchy of the social order."[40] The revolution was over.

Since Gustaf IV Adolf suppressed public discussion, the place of his reign in Sweden's history must be evaluated largely with reference to the conflicts of the year and a half following its downfall. It seems clear, looking back, that the revolution of 1809 was directed as much against the Gustavian regime as a whole, since 1771, as against Gustaf IV Adolf's own failings. If Gustaf III's reign remains bright in Swedish popular memory while his son's does not, it is largely due to personal differences between the two monarchs. Gustaf III himself once feared his son would come to a bad end because of his narrowness and obstinacy. Contemporaries described Gustaf Adolf as proud, remote, and taciturn—a British diplomat claimed he had "more of the Castillian than the Swede" about him—yet honest and conscientious.[41] He was hardly the "charmer king" his father had been, though his sobriety, thrift, and piety were surely more to the national taste than Gustaf III's somewhat exotic ways. Unlike his publicity-minded father, he did nothing to gain for posterity the gratitude and praise of courtiers, artists, and literati.[42] Yet there is more to a reign than the personality of the monarch, and there remains a basic unity to the Gustavian period, particularly with respect to Sweden's social and economic development from 1789 on.

Gustaf IV Adolf was no political theorist, yet on one occasion around 1799 he wrote specifically to deny the allegation that he inclined toward "Russian" despotism, "having been born free in a kingdom where the king governs according to the laws and where each individual enjoys his rights but knows how to obey," thereby avoiding "licentious liberty," which ultimately makes men "slaves under several or under a single despot."[43] Among his faithful servants there were meanwhile those who more frankly espoused autocracy. Count Johan Christopher Toll boastfully called himself "despotism's firstborn son." The government, Count Fersen wrote in 1794, should strive to make itself respected, to be just, to "raise itself above the murmurings of the people," to which it "should not pay the least attention."[44] In sum: *tout pour le peuple; rien par le peuple.*[45]

Though he feared Jacobinism, Gustaf Adolf had no great love for the nobility as such and was widely believed to be distinctly anti-aristocratic. One of the revolutionaries of 1809 contemptuously described him in June of that year as a "friend and member" of the "rabble." His bureaucratic appointments went by preference to men of recent ennoblement or to commoners.[46] According to Count Trolle-Wachtmeister, the king spoke in November 1808 of consulting directly with the Swedish people, thereby bypassing the Estates, over the means to continue the ongoing war. The following month, the count complained—somewhat incongruously—that the "lower classes" had not yet come to experience and thus to comprehend "the general misery" caused by the war. He feared the king wanted nothing better than an outbreak among the "higher classes" to provide "an opportunity to appeal to the people against their *masters [herrarna]*, throw all the blame upon them and seal his power in blood."

A peasant had recently told the king the country still suffered no need, that there were still resources and the only fault was that "the king did not command." If the wealthier classes would not pay new extraparliamentary levies, the king is reported to have claimed in January 1809, he would appeal to the poorer classes against the egotism of the rich. If the officials refused to collect such levies, Trolle-Wachtmeister feared later that month, the king could represent this to the "rabble" as confirmation for their ingrown suspicion of collusion between the "distinguished" classes and the Russians, "under whose dominion the lord is *powerful* but the *peasant a slave.*"[47]

Gustaf Adolf's actions in Swedish Pomerania seem to show what he would probably have liked to do by this time in Sweden itself: when the local aristocracy protested his exceptional war measures in 1806, he abolished by decree the province's special privileges under the Holy Roman Empire (which dissolved later the same year), disbanded the *Landtag,* abolished serfdom, which still existed there, and extended the protection of Swedish law. Extensive agrarian reforms were evidently only prevented by French occupation the following year.[48]

In all of this, Gustaf IV Adolf's regime was the consistent and logical outgrowth of the latter part of Gustaf III's reign, from the Act of Security of 1789. Yet it was more than this and indeed in some of its practical, pragmatic accomplishments went beyond it. The ideal of the regime was the *Rechtsstaat* and is to be sought more in actions than in words. If Gustaf IV Adolf's anti-intellectualism rather disqualifies him as an "enlightened despot," Sweden in his reign was nonetheless ruled by a relatively "enlightened government," staffed by honest, capable, and devoted bureaucrats.[49] The king's personal interest in certain aspects of their work could sometimes be considerable, though sporadic; nonetheless, he alone gave their projects the force of law.

Before the final disasters of the Russian war, there was little friction between the monarch and his bureaucracy, as there had been under Gustaf III. The reforms they carried out were, if more mundane and certainly less publicized than most of those of the preceding reign, no less needful. Through various administrative reorganizations, especially the restructuring of the Chancellery in 1801, the business of government was steered back into established and now largely rationalized channels from which it had frequently been diverted by Gustaf III. Already in 1796, a new finance committee (*statsberedning*) was set up to regularize the annual budget and adjust expenditures to standing revenues. At the same time, Gustaf III's inflated court establishment and pension list were drastically cut back, while provisions for widows and orphans of public servants were improved.

During the first years of the reign, careful financial administration was combined with favorable economic conditions to return a healthy surplus to the treasury and pay off a good part of the inherited national debt. The restrictive trade policies of the regency were relaxed.[50] The government's conversion plan, put through the Riksdag of 1800 and later modified to meet changing circumstances, at last restabilized the national currency, largely ruined by Gustaf III's unrestrained issue of unbacked paper notes after 1789, at least until war imposed new burdens on the economy by 1808.[51] Minor but useful reforms affected aspects of civil law and defense. Canal building proceeded apace.

The government and the king himself encouraged charitable foundations and societies for economic improvement. A new school ordinance in 1807 brought modest but long-needed reforms in the curricula of the *gymnasia,* or secondary schools, to meet the practical needs of the times. Through local initiative, moreover, the number of parish schools devoted to the lower classes increased markedly during the last years of the reign. Even under Count Fersen's chancellorship, material conditions were improved, faculty salaries raised, certain practical curricular revisions made, while enrollment and the number of degrees conferred increased at Uppsala University.[52] Throughout the period there was a steady increase in the employment of commoners in state service and acquisition of noble lands by non-nobles, furthering transition from a society based on birth and estate to one deriving from achievement and wealth.[53]

These were no small accomplishments, yet all pale in comparison with the government's epoch-making agrarian reforms, above all the Enclosure Ordinances of 1803, 1804, and 1807, progressively encompassing all the kingdom except Dalarna, Norrland, and Finland. Advancing enclosures would continue to transform both agriculture and the very nature of the countryside for decades to come, long after the fall of the regime that had initiated them. The long-term results can scarcely be overestimated. Enclosures broke up most of the old villages, forcing the majority of their inhabitants out onto their new consolidated landholdings, there to adapt to an often very different way of life from that they had known since time immemorial.

Peasant landowners increased greatly in number, often too in wealth and social standing, yet the proportion of tenants and landless laborers grew more rapidly, bringing about a deepening cleavage between a new rural middle class and an agrarian proletariat. The total area under cultivation, according to one estimate, almost trebled between 1800 and 1860, though by this time it was taking in increasingly marginal areas. Already by the 1820s, Sweden began to produce an exportable grain surplus for the first time since the 1680s. Further stimulus to productivity came with improved methods and new crops and implements. By the end of the century, Sweden's population would more than double, going since 1800 from 2.3 to 5.1 million, thus providing manpower for industrialization and a growing migration into the cities; by that time too, close to a million Swedes had settled permanently in North America.

Meanwhile the enclosures should not obscure a number of minor yet useful reforms affecting such matters as the obligations of manorial tenants, terms of employment for agricultural laborers, or disposition of village forest lands, which likewise tended to liberalize the agrarian economy. In Sweden, as in neighboring Denmark in this same period, the way for the social and economic ascent of the peasant class—the fundamental precondition for Scandinavian democracy—was cleared, and could surely only have been cleared, by royal autocracy.[54]

It might finally be noted that the most prominent of the agricultural innovators, including Baron Rutger Maclean, the original instigator of the enclosures, and Counts Jacob De la Gardie and Eric Ruuth, were likewise leaders of the Gustavian faction in the Riksdag of 1809–10.[55]

The late Gustavian autocracy of Gustaf IV Adolf's reign was thus both more vigorous and more important to the emergence of modern Sweden than the traditional conception will allow. Early in the twentieth century, sincere efforts were made to revindicate Gustaf Adolf on the basis of his foreign policy, which, it was maintained, if ultimately unsuccessful was nonetheless the result of realistic and practical considerations throughout. This attempt at revision provided a healthy antidote to tenacious prejudices in Swedish historiography tracing back to 1809, yet it has not very successfully stood the test of time."[56] If an *Ehrenrettung* is to be made, particularly from the vantage point of twentieth-century Sweden, it must look above all to the domestic accomplishments of the reign, traditionally overshadowed by its external failures, as well as to the vigorous reactions against the revolution of 1809 and its results.

Sweden's history, it has been avowed, is the history of its kings. If this be so, then it cannot ultimately be denied that Gustaf IV Adolf's personal role was both limited and tragic. If history is viewed in primarily political terms—if it is in Sweden as in England the story of "Freedom" which "slowly broadens from precedent to precedent," as Lord Tennyson put it—then the "Whig" tradition in Sweden is right in calling 1809 the great landmark of the recent past, for in no country outside England is the parliamentary tradition stronger and more continuous. But where history may be taken to mean above all the social and economic evolution of a nation, it is the Act of Security of 1789 that must be taken as the point of departure and the late Gustavian period—most of which fell within Gustaf IV Adolf's reign—is of far greater significance than either Gustaf III's earlier years or the era of Carl Johan Bernadotte that followed.

It is meanwhile notable that in returning as much as possible to the tradition of bureaucratic rule and indeed a reliance on old Gustavian bureaucrats, a wary surveillance of public debate, and a renewed and more successful intervention against his former master, Napoleon, leading at last to the acquisition of Norway by 1814, Carl Johan, the old Jacobin, in large degree paid tacit homage to his deposed predecessor's regime.

In February 1790, at the very time he began contemplating a monarchical crusade against revolutionary France, Gustaf III candidly observed to one of his aristocratic bureaucrats, "I am myself a democrat."[57] As he had put through his Act of Security within the past year, his comment was more than facetious. The reign of his son, Gustaf IV Adolf, who was not given to paradoxical witticisms, reveals in concrete fashion the same underlying paradox, of import well beyond his poor and thinly populated kingdom on Europe's northern periphery. The whole question of the relative successes of revolutionary and conservative forces in that age raises a still more perplexing question: which were actually revolutionary, which conservative, in what respects, to what degree?

Notes

1. The "shimmer" is from an oft-quoted verse in Esaias Tegnér's "Vid Svenska akademiens femtiåra minneshögtid, den 5 april 1836."

2. See *Hedvig Elisabeth Charlottas dagbok*, ed. Carl Carlsson Bonde and Cecelia af Klercker, 9 vols. (Stockholm, 1902–42), 7:391–94; 8:11; Sten Carlsson, *Den svenska utrikespolitikens historia*, vol. 3, part 1, *1792–1810* (Stockholm, 1952), 106.

3. For the historiography on Gustav IV Adolf, see Sture Bolin, "Gustaf IV Adolf i svensk historisk opinion," *Svensk tidskrift* 28 (1941): 323–36; Sten Carlsson, *Gustaf IV Adolf. En biografi* (Stockholm, 1946), 348–55; Sven G. Svenson, *Gattjinatraktaten*

1799. Studier i Gustav IV Adolfs utrikespolitik 1796–1800 (Uppsala, 1952), 9–30. On the succession, see Birger Sjövall, *Georg Adlersparre och tronfrågan 1809* (Lund, 1917).

4. Cf. Michael Roberts, "On Aristocratic Constitutionalism in Swedish History," and "The Swedish Aristocracy in the Eighteenth Century," in his *Essays in Swedish History* (Minneapolis, 1967), 14–55, 269–85; Lolo Krusius-Ahrenberg, *Tyrannmördaren C. F. Ehrensvärd* (Helsingfors, 1947), chapts. 1–4; Olof Dixelius, *Den unge Järta. En studie över en litterär politiker* (Uppsala, 1953); Sture M. Waller, *Rutger Macklean och 1809–1810 års riksdag* (Lund, 1953), 31–58; Rolf Karlbom, *Bakgrunden till 1809 års regeringsform. Studier i svensk konstitutionell opinionsbildning 1790–1809* (Gothenburg, 1964); Stig Jägerskiöld, "Tyrannmord och motståndsrätt 1792–1809," *Scandia* 28 (1962): 113–66. Cf. my article "Gustav III of Sweden and the Enlightenment," in this volume, 34–35.

5. On the initial impact of the French Revolution upon Sweden, see Alma Söderhjelm, *Sverige och den franska revolutionen*, 2 vols. (Stockholm, 1920–24), 1.

6. Cf. esp. Krusius-Ahrenberg, *Tyrannmördaren*, chapts. 1–4.

7. On Uppsala radicalism in the 1790s, see esp. Söderhjelm, *Sverige*, 2:178–98; Dixelius, *Unge Järta*, chapts. 2–4; Sven G. Svenson, "Studentens klang- och jubeltid. Från Juntan till skandinavism," in *Uppsalastudenten genom tiderna* (Uppsala, 1950), 81–96.

8. Dixelius, *Unge Järta,* 194; Svenson, "Studentens klang- och jubeltid," 90.

9. On the Norrköping Riksdag, see Malte Hamnström, *Om realisationsfrågan vid riksdagen i Norrköping år 1800* (Härnösand, 1896); Sam Clason, "Några anmärkningar rörande riksdagen i Norrköping år 1800," *Historisk tidskrift* (1897): 1–31; Erik Elinder, "Adolf Ludvig Hamiltons minnesanteckningar från 1800 års riksdag," *Personhistorisk tidskrift* 52 (1954): 73–142.

10. Georg Adlersparre, "Hvad är Jacobinisme?" *Läsning i blandade ämnen*, no. 7–8 (1798): 65–69; Hans Järta, "Hvilke äro de sannskyldige Jacobinerne?" *Läsning i ett och annat*, no. 3 (1800): 3–26. Cf. Dixelius, *Unge Järta*, 195–207, 293–96; Gunnar Kjellin, "'Hvilke äro de sannskyldige Jacobinerne?'—sengustavianska opinioner och stämningar," *Historisk tidskrift* (1963): 188–96.

11. Jöran Wibling, *Opinioner och stämningar i Sverige 1809–1810* (Uppsala, 1954), 87–88; *Excellensen A. F. Skjöldebrands memoarer*, ed. H. Schück, 5 vols. (Stockholm, 1903–4), 2:130–31.

12. Karlbom, *Bakgrunden*, 287–88, 297–98; H. G. Trolle-Wachtmeister, *Anteckningar och minnen*, ed. E. Tegnér (Elof Tegnér, *Valda skrifter*, 4, Stockholm, 1905), 184.

13. Nils Stjernquist, "Regeringsformens tillkomst," in *Kring 1809*, ed. Stefan Björklund (Stockholm, 1965), 42.

14. Krusius-Ahrenberg, *Tyrranmördaren*, chapts. 1–4, passim.; Dixelius, *Unge Järta*, 38–43, 61; my article "Gustav III and the Enlightenment," 35. On Gustav III's destruction of noble privileges in 1789, see Sten Carlsson, *Ståndssamhälle och ståndspersoner 1700–1865* (Lund, 1949), esp. 254–55, 259.

15. Bernhard von Beskow, *Lefnadsminnen* (Stockholm, 1870), 103–5; Sigfrid Andgren, *Konung och ständer 1809–1812* (Lund, 1933), 48, 93; Wibling, *Opinioner*, 234–35.

Foreign ideological influences on the Swedish revolution and constitution of 1809, though now generally recognized, have been much debated. See Fredrik Lagerroth, "Montesquieu och Sveriges grundlagar," in Björklund, Kring 1809, 104–19, which strongly discounts such influences. Gunnar Brusewitz in "Regeringsformens förut-sättningar. Författningskompromissen," Gunnar Heckscher in "Nationell och inter-nationell författningsdebatt 1809 och tidigare," in Björklund, Kring 1809, 55–103, 120–31, and especially Karlbom in Bakgrunden vigorously reaffirm them.

16. Anonymous, "Essai d'un récit historique des événements arrivés à Stockholm pendant l'année 1810," F MID Kantselyariya, 1810-g. D 10815, fol. 42, Central Archive, Moscow, in Ryska filmsamlingen 2, roll 41 (microfilm), Riksarkivet, Stockholm; my "Swedish Succession Crises of 1809 and 1810 and the Question of Scandinavian Union," in this volume, 142–43. Scævola [K. A. Strömbäck], Utländska diplomaters minnen från svenska hofvet (Stockholm, 1885), 22.

17. Trolle-Wachtmeister, Anteckningar och minnen, 6.

18. Ragnar Svanström and C. F. Palmstierna, A Short History of Sweden (Oxford, 1934), 318. See also Dixelius, Unge Järta, 414–27.

19. Sten Carlsson, Gustaf IV Adolfs fall (Lund, 1944), 365–80; Carlsson, Gustaf IV Adolf, 205; E. Ingers and Sten Carlsson, Bonden i svensk historia, 3 vols. (Stockholm, 1943–56), 2 (Ingers): 500–501; Karlbom, Bakgrunden, 301. Cf. Beskow, Lefnadsminnen, 226–27.

20. Michael Roberts, "On Swedish History in General," in his Essays in Swedish History, 5.

21. See my article "Russia and the Problem of Sweden-Finland, 1721–1809," East European Quarterly 5 (1972): 434–35, 440–41.

22. Ibid., 446–50.

23. On Gustav III's anti-aristocratic agitation, see Nils Staf, Polisväsendet i Stock-holm 1776–1850 (Uppsala, 1950), 151–52, 165–69, 328–29. On the Edict on the Rights and Liberties of the Peasantry [Allmogens fri- och rättigheter], see Eli F. Heckscher, Sveriges ekonomiska historia från Gustav Vasa, 4 vols. (Stockholm, 1935–49), 2:272–3, 280, 282; Ingers and Carlsson, Bonden, 2 (Ingers):84–85, 375–92.

24. Cf. Söderhjelm, Sverige och franska revolutionen, 2:109, 133–39, 204–5, 214–15. Söderhjelm seems indirectly to point toward such an interpretation, though she does not articulate it. Karlbom, in Bakgrunden, stresses the progressive ralliément of most of the aristocratic opposition, including its originally more "Jacobin" elements, around a socially conservative anglophile political philosophy, inspired by Montesquieu and Delolme, in response to the excesses and later corruption of the French Revolution, followed by Bonaparte's dictatorship.

25. Söderhjelm, Sverige och franska revolutionen, 2:110–17, 150–53, 157–63, 165; Dixelius, Unge Järta, 328.

26. Rutger Fredrik Hochschilds memoarer, ed. H. Schück, 3 vols. (Stockholm, 1908–9), 3:43; Richard Nordin, "En österrikisk diplomat om Sveriges inre förhållanden år 1797," Historisk tidskrift (1911): 49–50; Svenson, Gattjinatraktaten, 97–98, 334–35; R. Peyre, "Sympathies des états scandinaves pour la Révolution française et pour Na-poléon," Revue des études napoléoniennes 1 (1912): 335–48.

27. *Axel von Fersens dagbok*, ed. Alma Söderhjelm, 4 vols. (Stockholm, 1925–36), 4:65, 84–85; Hochschild, *Memoarer*, 3:327; Svenson, *Gattjinatraktaten*, 336–40. Cf. Dixelius, *Unge Järta*, 66. On the Peasant Estate at the Riksdag of 1800, see esp. Ingers and Carlsson, *Bonden*, 2 (Ingers):464–70.

28. Carlsson, *Gustaf IV Adolfs fall*, 380; *Hedvig Elisabeth Charlottas dagbok*, 8:113–14, 337; Sjövall, *Adlersparre*, 69–74; Scævola, *Utländska diplomaters minnen*, 23, 29–30, 34, 39–42.

29. Carlsson, *Gustaf IV Adolf*, 220.

30. On the emergence of the opposition in the Riksdag of 1809–10, see Andgren, *Konung och ständer*, 1–48; Waller, *Döbeln*, 9. Significantly, the only member of the Riksdag to seek openly to oppose deposition of the Vasa dynasty was the peasant, Peter Svartengren. See Ingers and Carlsson, *Bonden*, 3 (Carlsson): 238.

31. *Hedvig Elisabeth Charlottas dagbok*, 8:446–47, 477, 508–10, 514–16.

32. Wibling, *Opinioner och stämningar*, 105–19, esp. 112–13. See also Jöran Wibling, "Striden kring privilegierna och representationen 1809–1810," in Björklund, *Kring 1809*, 182–93. Concerning the probable socially conservative features of an English-style bicameralism at this point, see Karlbom, *Bakgrunden*, 313–14.

33. Wibling, *Opinioner och stämningar*, 82–104, esp. 82–83; Ingers and Carlsson, *Bonden*, 2 (Ingers):381–82, 3:235–51; Trolle-Wachtmeister, *Anteckningar och minnen*, 190–92. In actuality, through quasi-legal devises, commoners had already gained control of about fifteen percent of the immediate manorial land by 1809 (Carlsson, *Ståndssamhälle*, 153–54, 178). See also Waller, *Döbeln*, 105n.

34. Wibling, *Opinioner och stämningar*, 263–64n. The Finnish peasantry similarly fiercely resisted the Russian invasion in 1808–9, fearing that an autonomous Finland under Russian overlordship would become an "aristocratic republic," in which they themselves would be reduced to serfdom. Cf. my article "Russia and the Problem of Sweden-Finland," 454. See also *Statsrådet Johan Albert Ehrenströms efterlemnade historiska anteckningar*, ed. S. J. Boëthius, 2 vols. (Stockholm, 1883), 2:603.

35. Bernhard von Schinkel, *Minnen ur Sveriges nyare historia*, ed. C. W. Bergman, 10 vols. (Stockholm, 1852–68), 5:137, 144–45; *Bihang till Minnen ur Sveriges nyare historia*, ed. S. J. Boëthius, 3 vols. (Stockholm, 1880–83), 2:157; *För hundra år sen*, ed. Sam Clason and Carl af Petersens, 2 vols. (Stockholm, 1909–10), 72–75.

36. Despite considerable documentation, no real study of De la Gardie and his faction has been made. See, however, Ingers and Carlsson, *Bonden*, 3 (Carlsson):244, 249; Waller, *Döbeln*, 99–127.

37. See Einar Forssberg, *Karl August, gustavianerna och 1809 års män* (Hälsingborg, 1942).

38. Gerhard Hafström, "Mordet på Axel Fersen," *Svenskt biografiskt lexikon*, 15 (Stockholm, 1956), 733–43. Cf. H. R. Trevor-Roper, *The Gentry, 1540–1640*, Economic History Review Supplements, 1 (London, 1953).

39. Wibling, *Opinioner och stämningar*, chapts. 9–11, esp. 283–85; "Essai," Ryska filmsamlingen 2, fol. 41 (italics mine) ; *Handlingar ur Brinkman'ska arkivet på Trolle-Ljungby*, ed. G. Andersson, 2 vols. (Örebro, 1859–65), 2:365; A. Ahnfelt, *Två krönta rivaler*, 2 vols. (Stockholm, 1887), 1:107–8; *Utdrag ur danska diplomaters meddelanden*

från Stockholm 1807–1808, 1810 och 1812–13, ed. C. J. Anker (Stockholm, 1898), 72–73; Jöns Person Häggman, Anteckningar 180816, unpublished MS, D. 1048 a., Kungliga biblioteket, Stockholm, p. 29; Rune Hedman, "Massan vid det s.k. fersenska upploppet," *Historisk tidskrift* (1969): 2–71; Erik Lönnroth, "Revolution för en dag," *Dagens nyheter* (19 June 1960).

40. See Wibling, *Opinioner och stämningar*, 299–307; quotation by C. G. Brinkman, in Trolle-Wachtmeister, *Anteckningar och minnen*, 216.

41. Svanström and Palmstierna, *Short History of Sweden*, 298; Great Britain. Historical Manuscripts Commission, *The Manuscripts of J. B. Fortescue Preserved at Dropmore*, 10 vols. (London, 1892–1927), 6:65; Beskow, *Lefnadsminnen*, 226–27.

42. Cf. Sten Carlsson, "Det gustavianska tidevarvet," in his *Grupper och gestalter* (Stockholm, 1964), 91–97.

43. Svenson, *Gattjinatraktaten*, 95.

44. Hamnström, "Realisationsfrågan," 21; Fersen, *Dagbok*, 2:212–13.

45. Axel Linvald, "Comment le despotisme éclairé s'est présenté dans l'histoire du Danemark," *Bulletin of the International Committee of Historical Studies* 20 (1933): 715.

46. Sten Carlsson, *Bonde—präst—ämbetsman* (Stockholm, 1962), 67–68; Ingers and Carlsson, *Bonden*, 2 (Ingers):474–75; Wibling, *Opinioner och stämningar*, p. 94.

47. Trolle-Wachtmeister, *Anteckningar och minnen*, 57, 100–101, 115, 128–29, 132–33.

48. See Lars Dalgren, *Sverige och Pommern 1792–1806. Statskuppen 1806 och dess förhistoria* (Uppsala, 1914; in German translation in *Pommerische Jahrbücher*, 7).

49. On the concepts of "enlightened government" or "enlightened bureaucracy" versus "enlightened despotism" in later-eighteenth-century Europe, see Thad E. Hall, "Thought and Practice of Enlightened Government in French Corsica," *American Historical Review* (1969): 880–84; Helen P. Liebel, *Enlightened Bureaucracy versus Enlightened Despotism in Baden, 1750–1792* (Philadelphia, 1965), esp. 5–6, 11–14.

50. On Gustav IV Adolf's reforms in general, see Sten Carlsson, *Svensk historia*, 2 (Stockholm, 1961), 41–43, 263–71, 290–91; Ludvig Stavenow, *Den gustavianska tiden 1772–1809* (Stockholm, 1925), 276–77, 284–94, 322–42. On administrative reform, see also A. Forsell, "Utrikesförvaltningens historia 1721–1809," in Sven Tunberg et al., *Den svenska utrikesförvaltningens historia* (Uppsala, 1935), 261–98.

51. See esp. Hamnström, *Realisationsfrågan*.

52. See O. T. Sjöfors, *Kanslärsgillet och 1807 års skolordning* (Lund, 1919); for popular education, cf. my article "Popular Education in Eighteenth-Century Sweden: Theory and Practice," in *Facets of Education in the Eighteenth Century*, ed. James A. Leith, Studies in Voltaire and the Eighteenth Century, 167 (Oxford, 1977), 523–41. My findings on Uppsala University derive from research for my *Count Fersen Hans Axel von Fersen: Aristocrat in an Age of Revolution* (Boston, 1975).

53. See, above all, Carlsson, *Ståndssamhälle*, passim.

54. On the agrarian reforms, see esp. Heckscher, *Sveriges ekonomiska historia*, vol. 2, part 1, 257–83; Ingers and Carlsson, *Bonden*, 2 (Ingers):461–502; Gustav Sundbärg, *Emigrationsutredningen. Betänkande* (Stockholm, 1913), 91; Sten Carlsson, "Bondeståndet i Norden under senare delen av 1700-talet," *Scandia* 19 (1948–49): 196–213, reprinted without notes in Carlsson, *Grupper och gestalter*, 42–53.

55. Ingers-Carlsson, *Bonden*, 2 (Ingers):435 ff., 452–55, 477–78; Waller, *Döbeln*, 47, 109, 115–27.

56. See esp. Sam Clason, *Gustaf IV Adolf och den europeiska krisen under Napoleon* (Stockholm, 1913).

57. Beth Hennings, *Gustav III*, 2nd ed. (Stockholm, 1967), 284.

The Swedish Succession Crises of 1809 and 1810 and the Question of Scandinavian Union

Gustaf IV Adolf's involvement of Sweden in the War of the Third Co-alition in 1805 ultimately proved his undoing. In Pomerania during the summer of 1807, as his fitful campaigning against Napoleon neared its ignominious end, there already appeared the beginnings of a plot to depose him within the angry and disillusioned Swedish officer corps.[1] This fact did not remain unknown outside the beleaguered walls of Stralsund. As early as 22 June, Duke Frederik Christian of Schleswig-Holstein-Son-derburg-Augustenburg—brother-in-law to the crown prince–regent of Denmark who the following year became King Frederik VI—wrote to Count Joachim Bernstorff concerning Napoleon's latest successes. There-upon he continued:

> What will happen to our neighbor is of still greater importance to us. It is said that discontent in Sweden has manifested itself in the high-est degree and that it may be expected to break forth from one mo-ment to the next. The imagination loses itself in conjectures over the consequences of a revolution in Sweden. If it occurs at the moment when Europe is given a new form, it could stimulate grand projects in the mind of the universal master which could place us in a most embarrassing position. A great empire in the North alongside Rus-sia and England surely plays a large part in his thinking, and since

the King of Sweden leaves no choice between the two ruling houses, it could happen that he might bestow upon our Crown Prince the Swedish crown in recompense for his consistent neutrality. At any other time it would be completely ridiculous to consider such ideas. In the times we live in, the matter is not only possible but its execution would not be very difficult if the proper forms are observed. . . . But what should be done in such an event? It is almost infamous to accept the spoils of one's closest relatives and to put oneself in the same league as the brigands who are masters of the world; it would [however] be the greatest danger to refuse.[2]

A few days later, France and Russia concluded both peace and an alliance at Tilsit, in consequence of which Russia invaded Finland on 21 February 1808 and Denmark, as the ally of Russia and France, declared war on Sweden on 14 March. Within a year Gustaf IV Adolf's position had reached the point Duke Frederik Christian had foreseen: on 13 March 1809, the king of Sweden was deposed by a revolution, thereby opening up prospects during the year and a half that followed for the union of the Scandinavian lands.

The idea was a very old one and had indeed been tried with the Union of Kalmar, which lasted from 1397 until 1520, when Sweden (including Finland) broke away to form an independent kingdom, leaving Denmark and Norway united dynastically. As late as the War of Kalmar of 1611–13, Christian IV of Denmark sought to reestablish the Kalmar Union by force of arms. Thereafter, when Sweden emerged as the greatest Baltic power, Carl X Gustaf sought in 1660 to incorporate all of Denmark and Norway into Sweden as he had just done with the Scanian provinces.[3]

During the eighteenth century, new precedents were set. Carl XII, instead of aspiring to the union of all three Nordic kingdoms, considered by 1718 the idea of a peninsular state, including Norway, in compensation for the loss of territories across the Baltic, but not including Denmark. In 1743, when Sweden, again at war with Russia, was faced with a crisis over the selection of a successor, the Danish court advanced the candidacy of Crown Prince Frederik, later Frederik V, which gained much support, especially among the peasantry, but which was quashed by Russian opposition.[4]

During the 1780s, Gustaf III developed ambitious plans for the conquest for Norway. When, largely because of such adventurous ideas Gustaf aroused dangerous internal opposition, the court of Copenhagen was ready to profit from the situation and intimated to the Swedish chargé d'affaires, Gustaf d'Albedyhl, in July 1785 the desirability of a union between Denmark and Sweden. Already, it would appear, the candidacy of Crown Prince Frederik, later Frederik VI, was under consideration.[5] Gustaf IV Adolf meanwhile followed his father in seeking constantly for the opportunity to seize Norway.[6]

The earliest ideological background to the concept of Scandinavian unity must be sought far back in the Middle Ages. During the wars of the sixteenth and seventeenth centuries, Swedes and Danes came to regard each other as hereditary foes. Only with the emergence of Russia as the dominant power in the Baltic did this ill will begin to diminish, as shown by the Danish candidature for the Swedish succession in 1743.[7]

From the middle of the eighteenth century onward, there are signs of a growing Nordic sentiment in literature, especially from the Danish side, stimulated by the reaction to growing German cultural influence in Denmark, the awakening of interest in Nordic antiquity, and the influence of Montesquieu's theory of climate, which seemed to verify the existence of certain common Nordic virtues.[8] During the later part of the eighteenth century the expressions "Skandinavien" and "Norden," in an exclusively Scandinavian sense, become current.[9] In the spring of 1792, the Dane Frederik Sneedorf spoke to a group in London that called itself *Det Skandinaviske Selskab* (The Scandinavian Society) on the importance of the union of the three Nordic kingdoms. In his speech he asked that "we united Swedes, Norwegians, and Danes consider ourselves as belonging to only one fatherland, Scandinavia."[10]

Practical considerations on occasion required a common policy for Denmark and Sweden, as in the case of the Armed Neutralities of 1780 and 1794, but while the first of these revealed the depth of mistrust that still persisted between them, the second aroused considerable enthusiasm on both sides of the Sound as a portent of growing friendship and cooperation.[11] The effect was heightened by the envious admiration of many Swedish radicals during the repressive regency that followed the assassination of Gustaf III in 1792 for the model enlightened despotism in Denmark, and by the sympathy of Danish liberals for their Swedish brethren. The Scandinavianism of the 1790s was characterized by its affinity for radical social and political ideals, and its cosmopolitan view of membership in a larger Nordic community as a step toward the greater goal of world citizenship.[12] The high point in its development came in 1796 with the establishment in Copenhagen of *Det Skandinaviske Litteraturselskab* (The Scandinavian Literary Society).[13]

Enthusiasm for the Scandinavian ideal was however always stronger in Denmark than in Sweden, and interested Danes in the later 1790s suffered some disillusionment in this regard. After the brave effort of the Danish fleet to defend armed neutrality single-handedly against the British in Copenhagen Roads in 1801, there was a further tendency for Scandinavian sentiments to cool.[14]

The outbreak of war between Denmark and Sweden in 1808, however, offered new opportunities to both parties. Gustaf IV Adolf sought to foment rebellion among the Norwegians.[15] Frederik VI hoped to recoup the damage suffered through the second British attack on his fleet and capital in 1807. But ambitious plans for the campaign of 1808 failed to materialize.

Frederik's commander in southern Norway, Prince Christian August of Augustenburg, younger brother to the aforementioned Duke Frederik Christian, meanwhile speculated over the possibilities of revolution in Sweden.[16] The Danish government had neither sought nor desired the war with Sweden forced upon it by its French and Russian alliances. Yet it clearly perceived that if Sweden lost Finland to Russia, it would soon seek Norway in compensation, thereby threatening Denmark's very existence. The Danish minister to St. Petersburg, Baron Otto Blome, therefore pressed for a Russian guarantee to Denmark of a considerable part of southern Sweden to assure future communications with Norway, including not only the Scanian provinces—the old "East Denmark" lost a century and a half before—but enough hinterland to make them defensible. Alexander I, however, by then having taken Finland, was prepared to agree with Napoleon at Erfurt in September 1808 that the Danes might keep only what they themselves could conquer.[17]

Already in the summer of 1808, however, an exiled Swede in Copenhagen, Count Carl Fredrik Ehrensvärd—one of the regicides in Gustaf III's assassination—commenced work on a proclamation which revealed that in some official quarters at least there was an even greater ambition. Between January and March 1809, copies of this document were sent across the Sound by means of balloons, urging that Sweden's only salvation lay in offering the "crown of Scandinavia" to "Nordens Frederik." This and other propaganda was also disseminated from Norway, where both armies had long since tired of a war they regarded as both futile and unnatural.[18]

That Gustaf IV Adolf was successfully deposed by the revolution of 13 March 1809 was in large part thanks to Prince Christian August in Norway, who was understood to have concluded on his own an unofficial, private armistice with Lieutenant-Colonel Georg Adlersparre, permitting the latter to withdraw his troops from the front and march on Stockholm.

Christian August was aware that he was himself considered a prospect for the Swedish throne, but already on 10 March, he wrote his brother, Duke Frederik Christian, that he hoped to "perform a brilliant service for our king and fatherland," the details of which he wrote on 6 April. The "close union of the three Nordic realms under one scepter" would be the only means to save the Danish-Norwegian Dual Monarchy from "dissolution." Its basis should be a common, moderate constitution, drafted by delegates from all three kingdoms in consultation with the king. "This revolution" would have to come about "from above," which would require the sacrifice of unlimited sovereignty by the monarch, though the latter should remain powerful enough to assure "the felicity and security of the land."[19]

On March 11, Christian August reported to Frederik VI on his arrangement with Adlersparre; he foresaw, he wrote, a "civil war, which will bring the completely devastated Sweden to Your Majesty's feet." A week later, he was more specific: he hoped to persuade the Swedes to offer their crown voluntarily to Frederik, thereby assuring "the independence of the North." Thereafter, he repeatedly proposed to employ such indirect means as he could to secure the union. Although on 24 March, he suggested the Scandinavian kingdoms should eventually be "amalgamated," he refrained from proposing to Frederik the common, liberal constitution he had discussed with his brother. He was meanwhile seconded in his efforts by the influential Norwegian Count Herman Wedel Jarlsberg, who preferred a separate constitution and considerable autonomy for each of the three kingdoms.[20]

In Denmark, the revolution across the Sound caused much excitement. Frederik VI, then in Kiel, seems to have been taken by surprise and to have found it not entirely to his liking. Whatever it had meant to certain of his ministers, he had apparently regarded the "Balloon Proclamation" simply as propaganda, and indeed he showed remarkably little inclination toward the idea of union with Sweden.[21] Or, if it must come about, he evidently preferred that it be on his own terms, through force. He was at that very time preparing to land an army in Skåne while his Russian allies advanced into the Åland Islands and northern Sweden. His first reaction to the news from Christian August was thus to instruct him to watch for Swedish treachery and to seek to secure Danish occupation of Gothenburg (Göteborg) and other west coast ports as a pledge of the revolutionaries' good faith.[22]

Some of the latter in Sweden, meanwhile, had already considered union with Denmark. Count Carl Löwenhielm departed for Copenhagen, officially to announce the establishment of a regency under Gustaf IV Adolf's uncle, Duke Carl of Södermanland, but apparently also to sound out the possibilities for union under Frederik.[23]

Circumstances now prevented the Danish descent on Skåne, and the Russian offensive ground to a halt.[24] Frederik faltered. He was tempted to heed the urgings of Christian August and on 5 April wrote him that he approved fully of all he had done. It was better for the prince to act in his behalf, he added, than for him to take direct measures himself. Yet in the same letter, he recounted how he had impressed upon Count Löwenhielm his repugnance at dealing with "insurgents." Löwenhielm and his compatriots were deeply offended. When Christian August tactfully pointed this out to the king, he replied stiffly that he had spoken just as he should, since he could not countenance the dethroning of a sovereign monarch and besides could not act without his allies. But the slight was not forgotten in Sweden.[25]

Still, once back in Copenhagen, Frederik apparently fell under the influence of counselors warmly enthusiastic for the union idea.[26] Union with Sweden, he wrote Christian August on April 5, was "the great goal we are both working for," and added a few days later that it was the only means to save the Danish state and assure the future of the North. He was, however, much concerned over the constitutional problem involved. He balked at the thought of conceding to the Swedes more than "the appearance of freedom" and was determined to maintain his absolute sovereignty in Denmark and Norway.[27] Christian August warned that Sweden would not "subjugate itself unconditionally" and repeatedly urged avoidance of measures that might repel the Swedes from voluntary union. Its essential condition, he held, would be a liberal constitution, and on his own initiative he intimated to his contacts in Sweden that Frederik would be prepared to concede one. If necessary, he wrote the king on May 7, the constitution could eventually be modified.[28]

Frederik meanwhile feared losing the confidence of his Russian allies and continued to speculate over a military solution that could establish a union on terms more to his taste. "I am convinced," he wrote Christian August on 25 April, "when the Swedes once become frightened that if we do not get the whole of Sweden, at least some provinces, Skåne, Halland, and Blekinge, will be allotted to us and that they must then either elect me or receive a king from Russia, they will certainly prefer to choose me."[29] Nevertheless, he gradually became convinced that union was so essential to Denmark that he would accept a liberal constitution in Sweden, if need be.[30]

The Danish court naturally hoped for the support of Napoleon for the project.[31] "Can the French government hide from itself," Foreign Minister

Christian Bernstorff wrote to the Danish minister in Paris, K. V. Dreyer, on 5 April, that

> when Sweden loses Finland, it can no longer maintain its position as an independent state; it will then find itself dependent upon Russia's superior force; and can not Napoleon see that this [nation], having extended its power across the Gulf of Bothnia, will eventually expand to the Elbe? Thus, it is only by increasing and consolidating Denmark's power and by conceiving of Denmark's interests as coinciding with its own that France can find the means to maintain balance in the North.[32]

The emperor, however, then engaged in a difficult struggle with Austria and on uncertain terms with the Russian tsar, scrupulously avoided involvement in the Swedish succession problem. In May, the Swedish Riksdag barred Gustaf IV Adolf and his descendants from the throne. Without Napoleon's support for Frederik VI, it seemed certain the Swedes would now elect Duke Carl king. On 22 May, Christian August urged prompt and determined action to secure for Frederik the succession following the duke, who was old and childless, and in so doing revealed to the king his own ideal for a union: Frederik VI should appeal directly to the Swedish government and offer "a modified and uniform constitution for the whole of Scandinavia." This was more than Frederik could stomach. In June, the duke-regent was elected King Carl XIII. Christian August in Norway was deeply disappointed by the Swedes' short-sightedness but still hoped to work for his king's eventual succession.[33]

Frederik reacted strongly. He believed the Swedes had intentionally duped both Christian August and himself. "They give all hope for their throne," he complained bitterly on 5 June, "but dispose of it according to their own whims." He inveighed against their "deceitfulness," their "despicable and low behavior."[34]

Ever suspicious of the Swedes, whom he considered an unruly and unreliable people, Frederik particularly disliked the Swedish nobility. Enlightened despot in the best Danish tradition, emancipator of his peasantry, and agrarian reformer, he had neither sympathy nor understanding for the proud Swedish heritage of aristocratic constitutionalism. Behind the overthrow of the autocratic Gustaf IV Adolf he discerned the specter of aristocratic resurgence, the reimposition of a "system of oppression" upon the common man. With Carl XIII's election as king he saw "aristocracy at its height." Both his ministers and Danish liberals shared this attitude, and the "Balloon Proclamation," the work of the renegade Swedish nobleman

Ehrensvärd, had sought to arouse support for a union among disaffected elements of the Swedish bourgeoisie.[35]

Christian August too put his confidence in "the lower classes, that is, the greater part of the nation," expected little enthusiasm for union among the "privileged," and repeatedly urged on Frederik VI a constitution for Sweden that would confer "equal rights without regard to estate."[36]

The king now hoped to profit from the anticipated Russian summer campaign against Sweden and from France's successful termination of its Austrian war. He was alarmed over suspicions aroused in St. Petersburg by Christian August's ambivalent behavior and fearful lest Russia conclude a separate peace with Sweden. He thus returned resolutely to an aggressive policy. On May 28 he ordered Christian August to occupy Gothenburg and its environs immediately upon word of a Russian advance. Denmark, he added a week later, would now have to "force" the Swedes or to "work through Napoleon" to achieve a "favorable outcome." On 28 June, he wrote Christian August:

> It is deplorable that what the Swedes could have done voluntarily to their own advantage, circumstances will compel them to do; and when Finland goes to Russia and part of southern Sweden falls to Denmark, Carl XIII's kingdom will become very small and scarcely possible for him to sustain in the long run.[37]

Christian August now found himself in a difficult quandary. He was already deeply involved in secret negotiations with the Swedes. He feared Russia as a threat to the entire North. Rather than join in a war of conquest that would reduce Sweden to a "Russian province," he wrote the king, he would rather resign. "God forbid such a war, which would doubtless sooner or later bring Norway's subjugation under that barbaric yoke and thus the dissolution of the fatherland as a result." Salvation, he maintained, lay only in a strong Scandinavian union, "which can, in its time, shake the throne of Russia."[38]

Frederik, however, now put all his hopes in his allies and with increasing impatience ordered Christian August to break off all negotiations and attack as soon as the Russians did so.[39] In reply, Christian August proposed in such an event to advance into Sweden as rapidly as possible in secret cooperation with the Swedes themselves, supported by Swedish supplies and reinforcements, to save as much of the country as possible from Russian occupation. "Fear of the Russians, internal dissention, dissatisfaction with the nobility," he felt, would then drive the Swedes into the arms of the king of Denmark.[40] Frederik remained adamant: Christian August must advance in conjunction with the Russians, not the Swedes, "for that would involve an inconsistency, since they are our enemies."[41]

On July 18, the Swedish Riksdag elected as crown prince not Frederik VI but Christian August himself. Behind the choice lay in large part the secret desire of Adlersparre and the revolutionary party of capitalizing on the prince's popularity in Norway to foment an insurrection there against Denmark, to bring about union with Sweden. This program had by now gained the covert support of the Norwegian Count Wedel Jarlsberg, disillusioned by Frederik's refusal to abandon absolutism in his hereditary lands. Norway and Sweden could unite, in the latter's view, each with its own liberal constitution; perhaps Denmark might in time join them on the same terms.[42] Christian August agreed provisionally to come to Sweden once peace was concluded, if Frederik would permit, but loyally refused to hear of any insurrectionary schemes concerning Norway.[43]

Christian August was meanwhile saved from the painful necessity of attacking Sweden when the anticipated Russian offensive failed to materialize. Russia had already secured Finland and understandably lost confidence in Denmark. Having failed to unify Scandinavia, Copenhagen pressed more vigorously than ever for a Russian guarantee for Denmark's annexation of most of southern Sweden; it was ultimately a question, Baron Blome told the Russian foreign minister, of whether it was to be Denmark or Sweden that should continue to exist. But Russia would guarantee only what Denmark herself could conquer.[44]

With the British commanding the seas, Frederik's only resource remained the weak Norwegian army. On July 14, he commanded Christian August to advance and occupy the Gothenburg region without waiting any longer for the Russians. When he learned of the offer to Christian August of the Swedish succession, he promoted him to statholder of Norway and assigned actual command of the troops there to Prince Frederik of Hesse. Christian August meanwhile argued repeatedly that an offensive from Norway was physically impossible, and before long the new commander was forced to agree.[45]

On 17 September, the Russians concluded a separate peace with Sweden at Fredrikshamn, where they not only failed to guarantee Denmark's possession of Norway but even hinted that Sweden might there find compensation for the loss of Finland.[46] Already by August, the Danish cabinet dropped its demands and offered Sweden peace negotiations on the basis of status quo ante bellum. Adlersparre and his friends speculated over raising an insurrection in Norway if the war with Denmark could be prolonged. But their hopes proved exaggerated and peace was at length concluded at

Jönköping on December 10, 1809.[47] In January, Sweden also finally made peace with France.

As early as 7 April, Frederik VI's sister, Duchess Louise Augusta, wrote her husband, Duke Frederik Christian, that she suspected the Swedes wished to offer Christian August their crown, which he would accept "only to place it on the head of another." When he first informed Frederik on 28 May of the rumor that the Swedes might offer him the succession, Christian August assured him that he would accept only with his permission and as "a preparation for union." Thus, he did so only when it was clear the Swedes would not elect Frederik and he henceforward regarded himself as a kind of interim successor.

His plan, he revealed to his brother, would be sometime in the future, when circumstances permitted, to propose to Frederik VI or his successor a liberal constitution for all of Scandinavia, and if this were adopted, to abdicate in favor of his Danish kinsman, thereby bringing about the union.[48] Christian August suspected already in April that Adlersparre and his friends did not really wish union with at least the Danish mainland, which indeed they regarded as strategically exposed. But at least until Carl XIII's election as king he regarded them as "the most enlightened and respected men in Sweden." It seems evident that they, together with the Norwegian Wedel Jarlsberg, encouraged his hopes to induce him to accept the Swedish succession; later they sought to impress upon him the obstacles to a union including Denmark.[49]

Still, when Christian August met with Adlersparre at Kongsvinger on 15 December, he stated that he regarded Sweden as "destined by Providence to be the point of departure for the Scandinavian idea." The Nordic peoples had "the same language and interests, the same climate and national character, the same customs and faults; everything speaks for a common goal."[50]

Frederik VI and most Danes accepted the election of Christian August with fairly good grace.[51] Yet even the prince's opponents considered Scandinavianist solutions as well. In August, the president of the Danish Chancellery, F. C. Kaas, discussed secretly with Baron G. M. Armfelt in Gothenburg the project of replacing Christian August as Swedish crown prince with Frederik VI, on condition that the latter adopt as his own heir the son of the deposed Gustaf IV Adolf, Prince Gustaf, who in turn should be betrothed to Frederik's daughter, Princess Caroline, and whom Kaas believed could be raised to be more Danish than Swedish. The Danish princess apparently also interested the Swedish ministry as a prospective bride for the bachelor Christian August, and in the spring of 1810, Napoleon himself proposed such a match, though both the Danish king and the Swedish crown prince rejected the idea.[52]

Frederik meanwhile remained hopeful that Christian August might eventually bring about the union. In the spring of 1810, he sent Count Niels Rosenkrantz to Paris to congratulate Napoleon on his marriage to

Crown Prince Carl August, by Niclas Lafrensen, the younger. The former Prince Christian August of Augustenburg served as Danish viceroy and military commander in Norway during the war with Sweden in 1808–9 but was elected successor to Sweden's Carl XIII after Gustaf IV Adolf's deposition. He was the central figure in ambitious schemes to create a union of the Nordic crowns, prefiguring nineteenth-century Scandinavianism, until his sudden death in June 1810, a few months after arriving in Sweden. (Courtesy of Svenskt Porträttarkiv, Stockholm.)

Marie Louise, meanwhile to suggest the common interest of France and Denmark in a powerful Nordic state that could counterbalance Russia in the North, provided its sovereign possessed sufficient powers. Paris appeared not uninterested.[53]

In January 1810, the new crown prince arrived in Sweden, where he changed his name from Christian to Carl August, more congenial to Swedish ears.

Although he became immensely popular in Sweden as he had been in Norway, the new crown prince soon came to feel that Swedish opinion gave little hope for a Scandinavian union. "How could a durable [union] be formed from such heterogeneous parts without arousing great ferment, indeed anarchy?" he wrote to Frederik Christian on 6 March. "The favorable moment has been lost through stupidity." In the same letter, he spoke of the possibility of eventually adopting Prince Gustaf as his own heir, thereby reestablishing the Vasa house on its throne, a second alternative he had considered since the previous fall.[54] Only when he realized what great opposition this would arouse did he resign himself to the prospect of marrying and founding his own dynasty.[55]

It was evidently sometime in the spring of 1810 that the new Danish minister to Stockholm, Count Magnus von Dernath, wrote his government in an undated memorandum that he believed the prince could well have achieved a union had he immediately after his arrival sought with more vigor and less scruple to gain the support of influential circles in Sweden. Unfortunately, he complained, Providence had not marked Carl August with the stamp of greatness. Though Denmark might still seek to gain a union by stirring up anti-aristocratic passions against the regime in Sweden, such a course would be risky and Dernath concluded that Denmark must now put confidence in the crown prince's goodwill to assure against threats from Sweden.[56]

Meanwhile, as Carl August's hopes for a greater Scandinavia faded before his eyes, Swedish diplomacy sought unsuccessfully to gain Napoleon's support for the acquisition of Norway against suitable compensation for Denmark in Germany.[57] The question of Scandinavian unity thus seemed closed when Carl August suddenly died on May 28, immediately bringing the matter once again to the forefront.

The death of the crown prince made it necessary for a new Riksdag to elect another. The choice of the Adlersparre party fell on the brother of the deceased, Duke Frederik Christian of Augustenburg.[58] The Danish minister in Stockholm, Count Dernath, immediately saw the possibility of advancing Frederik VI's candidacy.[59] The Swedish and Danish governments quickly sought Napoleon's views concerning, respectively, Duke Frederik Christian and King Frederik. On 17 June, an article appeared in the French semiofficial *Journal de l'Empire*, expressing approval of a Scandinavian union under Frederik VI. On the same day, Napoleon spoke in favorable though noncommittal terms on the subject to the departing Danish envoy, Count Rosenkrantz.[60]

Shortly thereafter, however, Napoleon received a letter from Carl XIII, which he answered on June 24, unbeknown to Copenhagen, indicating— once again in noncommittal terms—favor toward the Augustenburg candidature. Later that same day, Napoleon learned from Marshal Jean-Baptiste Bernadotte that the latter had been proposed for successor by certain elements in Sweden.[61]

The emperor's apparently inconsistent behavior is explained by his position at that time. He was above all concerned with applying the Continental Blockade as effectively as possible against Great Britain throughout Europe and with improving his strategic position for an eventual war with Russia. For both reasons therefore, he desired a strong Scandinavia, closely allied if not united, and bound to the French system. At the same time, he did not wish to hasten a break with Russia by providing provocation. Carl August had fitted this pattern well and had been acceptable to St. Petersburg. Frederik VI might unite Scandinavia, but for France to support him would antagonize Russia. The choice of Frederik Christian seemed most likely to duplicate that of his brother, but Napoleon, while showing no great enthusiasm for it, did not oppose the candidature of his marshal, Bernadotte.[62]

Although there was much excitement in leading Copenhagen circles at the renewed prospect for Scandinavian union, Frederik IV himself, following his experience of the previous year, seems at first to have faced it with some reluctance. He evidently gave no further instructions to Rosenkrantz or his minister, Dreyer, in Paris, while Dernath in Stockholm was ordered to refrain from active measures since Frederik only wished to accept the Swedish succession if Napoleon would take the initiative. Thus virtually nothing was done until the beginning of July, with the return from Paris of Rosenkrantz, who now became foreign minister.

Believing Napoleon's goodwill assured, and supported most notably by his fellow ministers, Counts Ernst Schimmelmann and Frederik Moltke, Rosenkrantz initiated a period of vigorous activity to secure his king's election as Swedish crown prince.[63] Doubtless the most interesting aspect of this episode was the effort made by the pro-Scandinavianist literati in

Denmark to propagandize in favor of a union. Both Moltke and Schimmelmann, as well as Jens Kragh Høst, A. C. Gierlew, N. F. S. Grundtvig, the German C. F. Rühs, and one or two anonymous persons wrote pamphlets, pointing out to the Swedes the importance of a Scandinavian union to their future security, prosperity, and happiness.[64] Their arguments on the whole followed those given in Ehrensvärd's Balloon Proclamation of 1809 and anticipated almost all of the traditional Scandinavianist arguments of the nineteenth century.[65]

At last on 18 July, Frederik VI wrote personally to Carl XIII, formally proposing his candidature. After much discussion, the Danish government meanwhile instructed Dernath in Stockholm that it would accept in effect the Swedish constitution of 1809 for Sweden, though not for Denmark or Norway, and that the preferred order of candidates was first Frederik VI; second, his cousin and heir, Prince Christian Frederik; and third Duke Frederik Christian of Augustenburg.[66]

Dernath did his best to gain support for his master and on 24–25 July visited Örebro, where the Riksdag had convened, to deliver Frederik VI's letter to the Swedish king. There he met with members of the State Council, including the foreign minister, Lars von Engeström, who revealed some cautious interest in a union.[67] The pro-Danish French chargé d'affaires, J. J. Desaugiers, lacking positive instructions from Paris—for which he vainly implored—took the article in the *Journal de l'Empire* at face value and actively campaigned for the Danish candidature, going so far as to intimate that "the Kingdom of Scandinavia" might win back Finland and even include St. Petersburg if France should go to war with Russia, which brought him a sharp reprimand from his government.[68]

In St. Petersburg, Baron Blome strove to gain Russian support for the union.[69] Captain Louis Tuxen and a court functionary, H. R. Eppinger, were dispatched to sound opinion in Skåne, and in mid-July, Baron Charles Selby was sent to win over influential members of the Swedish nobility.[70] At the same time, Jens Kragh Høst and *Etatsraad* G. H. Olsen, important members of *Det Skandinaviske Litteraturselskab*, went to Sweden to exploit their widespread contacts in literary and academic circles. Others, including Ehrensvärd, wrote to friends and relatives in Sweden.[71]

Reactions in Sweden were, however, mainly negative or indifferent. The Swedes had bitter memories of the Kalmar Union, mistrusted Danish absolutism, and feared economic and cultural domination by the smaller Denmark, as well as the eclipse of Stockholm by Copenhagen. The recent war had revived old prejudices against the "Jute," while Danish and Norwegian privateers continued to prey on Swedish vessels seeking to run the Continental Blockade. Though union with Norway would clearly strengthen Sweden, there were fears that Denmark, especially Jutland and the Duchies, would be a strategic liability.[72]

Since the previous year in particular, the person of Frederik VI had become distasteful to most Swedes. A way around this stumbling block was soon discussed in Stockholm: the election of Frederik's heir, the twenty-four-year-old Prince Christian Frederik, who, it was hoped, could be to some extent "swedified" before ascending the throne. General Charles de Suremain, a French émigré in Swedish service, in particular espoused this solution. As Carl XIII cooled toward the rather colorless duke of Augustenburg, he had Suremain sound Desaugiers on the French attitude toward Prince Christian Frederik. The chargé d'affaires proved enthusiastic and warmly recommended the prince to Paris.[73]

On two occasions in particular, Carl XIII and his ministers seem seriously to have considered a Danish candidature: first, before receiving Napoleon's letter of June 24 with its vague approval for Duke Frederik Christian, and secondly, during the first flurry of excitement over Marshal Bernadotte. Dernath was at first optimistic that the marshal would eliminate the duke from the contest, in which case the king of Denmark could not but win; certain Swedes indeed suspected Napoleon of pushing Bernadotte to the fore as a backhanded means of securing union under Frederik.[74] All parties, meanwhile, were convinced that Napoleon's clear-cut endorsement of any candidate would immediately decide the matter, but despite the harried Desaugiers' constant entreaties, the emperor maintained an inscrutable silence.[75]

The arrival of Georg Adlersparre at the Örebro Riksdag at the beginning of August rallied the wavering supporters of the duke of Augustenburg, whom the Secret Committee, charged with nominating a successor, endorsed on 10 August.[76] Yet Duke Frederik Christian himself showed interest in a greater Scandinavia, though he was on strained terms with the Danish king and his heir, and made references to a union along the lines conceived by his brother, the late crown prince, endowed with a common, liberal constitution.

The rivalry over the Swedish succession between the duke, a subject of the king of Denmark, and his brother-in-law, the king himself, created much tension. Frederik Christian declined Carl XIII's direct invitation to present himself as a candidate to the Riksdag *if* this should stand in the way of Frederik's election; as this last seemed unlikely, the Swedish government took this conditional refusal as an indirect acceptance. The duke pointedly told Frederik VI he saw little chance of the king's election and that he himself would not refuse the Swedish crown if placed on his head by "a higher hand."[77]

Frederik became increasingly exasperated, seeing in the duke the principal obstacle to his own election and the achievement of Nordic unity, and in August sent a military detachment and a flotilla of gunboats to the duke's residence on the island of Als to "protect" the latter from being "abducted" to Sweden by the Adlersparre faction. Relations between the Danish royal house and the Augustenburg family henceforward remained irreconcilably embittered.[78]

Influential Swedes meanwhile made every effort to prevent Frederik VI's election. The Swedish minister in Copenhagen, Baron C. G. Oxenstierna, sent evidently misleading reports on the apathy of the Danish public toward union with Sweden.[79] More influential still were surely the dispatches of the bitterly danophobic minister to Paris, Baron Gustaf Lagerbjelke, who strongly intimated that although Napoleon declined to intervene directly in the Swedish succession, he had given indirect but clear signs that he supported Bernadotte. Lagerbjelke even claimed that he had himself turned Napoleon against Frederik VI and warned that the emperor would never forgive Sweden "for not having understood his intentions or having pretended not to understand him in such a vital moment as this."[80]

On 10 August, the same day the Secret Committee endorsed the duke of Augustenburg, Bernadotte's personal emissary J. A. Fournier, arrived in Örebro hinting at official French support, which in fact he did not possess, and bearing arguments and promises that turned the current of opinion in the Riksdag in favor of the marshal. On 14 August, the Secret Committee again voted, this time endorsing Bernadotte, who a week later, on August 21, was unanimously elected crown prince by the Riksdag. "No one thought of the king of Denmark," noted Foreign Minister von Engeström.[81]

As if to add insult to injury, there appeared in the Swedish journal *Allmänna Opinionens Organ* for 22 August an anonymous article calling for a close alliance with Napoleon and the annexation and complete assimilation by Sweden of both Norway and the Danish islands, which could best be achieved by the election of Bernadotte, a possibility the Swedish State Council had in fact considered on August 17.[82] In Denmark there was much alarm over Bernadotte's election, especially concerning the future of Norway, and in St. Petersburg Baron Blome on his own initiative proposed a revival of the traditional eighteenth-century Russian-Danish policy of weakening Sweden by fomenting internal dissension.[83]

Prince Christian Frederik, aroused at seeing Denmark faced with "the great fight for life or death," proposed grandiose plans for invading Sweden

and creating a union through force.[84] There were thereafter some speculations that Bernadotte's time in Sweden would not be long and that union
might yet somehow come about. During the Eidsvold constitutional convention in Norway in 1814, Christian Magnus Falsen published an impassioned appeal against union with Sweden under a "true French military
despotism" and for a free and honorable union under the Nordic Prince
Christian Frederik.[85] But in fact, the episode was over.

Thus there failed a number of possible schemes for uniting the Nordic
kingdoms: a union imposed by force of arms on dictated terms; the election
of Frederik VI or of Prince Christian Frederik as king or as crown prince
of Sweden in 1809 or in 1810; the abdication either of Carl August after his
election or possibly of his brother, Frederik Christian, if elected, in favor
of one of the former; the marriage of the Danish Princess Caroline to Carl
August or to Prince Gustaf; the voluntary adherence of Denmark to a fed-
erative union of Norway and Sweden under liberal constitutions. Count H.
G. Trolle-Wachtmeister in his memoirs suggested another possibility: that
Frederik VI himself offer Carl XIII the crowns of Denmark and Norway
in return for the succession to all three thrones upon the latter's death, a
temptation the Count felt Carl could not have resisted.[86]

Instead, a French soldier was unanimously elected Swedish crown prince.
On 31 August, the Swedish unionist C. U. Broocman wrote to his Danish friend Rasmus Nyerup, "All the Scandinavian voices did not prevail
against a single Gallic one. We are now considered quite fortunate. God
grant that this be so!"[87]

Whether he was basically antipathetic toward the idea of acquiring
the Swedish crown, as C. T. Sørensen maintained, or was genuinely eager
to attain it, as Edvard Holm held, Frederik VI must bear much of the
responsibility for the failure to create a Nordic union. His behavior was
not decisive, consistent, or tactful. He offended the Swedes with his stiff-
necked disapproval of their revolution in the spring of 1809, then during
the following summer put his hopes in an illusory policy of conquest that
his commander in Norway neither could nor would implement and that
his allies would not support.

After Carl August's death in May 1810, Frederik lost nearly two months
before acting openly to secure the Swedish succession, then persisted in
seeking it for himself when it became evident that union could best be
achieved through his heir, Prince Christian Frederik.[88] An honest but
routine-minded administrator, he possessed neither Carl August's breadth
of vision nor Bernadotte's strong-willed opportunism.

Carl XIV Johan, by Emil Mascré (1843). The former French field marshal Jean-Baptiste Bernadotte was elected as Sweden's crown prince, after Carl August's death in 1810, and ascended the throne in 1818. As crown prince he led Sweden into the Fourth Coalition against his former master, Napoleon, and in the process acquired Norway from Denmark as a separate kingdom in dynastic union with Sweden. In his later years the old Jacobin grew increasingly reactionary. (Courtesy of Svenskt Porträttarkiv, Stockholm.)

There seems little doubt that notwithstanding Frederik's shortcomings, had Napoleon so willed, a Scandinavian union could have been formed that would likely have been among his more durable creations, with far-reaching implications for Scandinavian and European history. Even Carl XIII's personal endorsement could probably have turned the scales.[89] To be sure, the idea was actively supported by only minorities in each country, while influential elements in Sweden, particularly, opposed it. There still seems reason to believe, however, that support for the idea was greater in Sweden both in 1809 and in 1810 than has been evident to hindsight, and that much of the opposition to it was lukewarm at best.[90] Only small groups were politically active in any of the Scandinavian lands; in Sweden, the revolution of 1809, the new constitution of that year, and the elections of Carl August and of Bernadotte were all the work of determined minorities. The ultimate durability of a Scandinavian union might at that time have been no more questionable than the survival of any of these innovations.

Thus there failed the greatest chance there has been for the reuniting of Scandinavia since the end of the Kalmar Union. The advocates of the traditional Swedish ambition of a purely peninsular union with Norway, excluding Denmark, had their way by 1814 over those who felt that Scandinavians belonged to but a single fatherland, whose ideal was now bequeathed to the generations that followed.

Notes

1. *Handlingar till kronprins Carl Augusts historia*, ed. Sam Clason, *Historiska Handlingar* 27, no. 2 (Stockholm, 1925; hereafter abbreviated Clason, *Handlingar*), 33.

2. Hans Schulz, *Aus dem Briefwechsel des Herzogs Friedrich Christian zu Schleswig-Holstein* (Stuttgart, 1913), 230.

3. Jerker Rosén and Sten Carlsson, *Svensk historia*, 2 vol. (Stockholm, 1961–62), 1:438, 586–88.

4. Ibid., 1:699–700, 2:136–38.

5. Julius Clausen, *Skandinavismen historisk fremstillet* (Copenhagen, 1900), 3–7.

6. Sten Carlsson, *Den svenska utrikespolitikens historia*, 3:1 (Stockholm, 1954), 83, 116.

7. Cf. Hans Lennert Lundh, *Skandinavism i Sverige* (Stockholm, 1951), 5–14.

8. Clausen, *Skandinavismen*, 1–3; Lolo Krusius-Ahrenberg, *Tyrannmördaren C. F. Ehrensvärd* (Helsingfors and Stockholm, 1947), 319–25, 400–1; Anton Blanck, *Den nordiska renässansen i sjuttonhundratalets litteratur* (Stockholm, 1911) ; Pierre van Tieghem, *Le préromanticisme*, 3 vol. (Paris, 1929–48), 1.

9. Bruno Lesch, "Två hyllningsdikter tillägnade Gustaf v. Paykull. Ett litet bidrag till skandinavismens förhistoria,"*Ord och bild* 45 (1945): 277; Bruno Lesch, "Ett skandinavismens förebud i Danmark. J. W. Sprengtportens sista färd," *Nordisk tidskrift*, ny ser. 21 (1945): 238.

10. The speech was titled "Vigtigheden af de tre Nordiske Rigers Forening"; Clausen, *Skandinavismen*, 7–8; Lesch, "Ett skandinavismens förebud," 238.

11. On Scandinavia and the Armed Neutrality of 1780, see P. Fauchille, *La diplomatie française et la ligue des neutres de 1780 (1776–1783)* (Paris, 1893), as well as my own article, "Sweden and the War of American Independence," in this volume, 59–60. On the ideological effects of the Armed Neutrality of 1794, see Clausen, *Skandinavismen*, 8–10; Krusius-Ahrenberg, *Tyrannmördaren*, 231, 400.

12. Krusius-Ahrenberg, *Tyrannmördaren*, 299–310, 326–30, 395, 401–3, 405; Blanck, *Nordiska renässansen*, 421; Clausen, *Skandinavismen*, 11–19.

13. Clausen, *Skandinavismen*, 19; Krusius-Ahrenberg, *Tyrannmördaren*, 402–3.

14. Clausen, *Skandinavismen*, 16–18; Krusius-Ahrenberg, *Tyrannmördaren*, 401, 403.

15. See "Upprop till norrmännen af Landshöfding J. L. Belfrage, Göteborg d. 5 Jan. 1809," in Clason, *Handlingar*, 9–10; Birger Sjövall, *Georg Adlersparre och tronfrågan 1809* (Lund, 1917), 9–10; Yngvar Nielsen, *Lensgreve Johan Caspar Herman Wedel Jarlsberg*, 3 vol. (Christiania, 1901–2), 1:174, 176; Aage Friis, "Frederik den Sjette og det andet svenske Tronfølgervalg 1810," *Historisk Tidsskrift* (Copenhagen), series 7, vol. 1 (1897–99): 243; Clausen, *Skandinavismen*, 20; Sjövall, *Adlersparre*, 2–8; C. T. Sørensen, *Bernadotte i Norden: eller Norges Adskillelse fra Danmark og Forening med Sverig*, 3 vol. (Copenhagen, 1903–4), Edvard Holm, *Danmark-Norges Historie fra den Store nordiske Krigs Slutning til Rigernes Adskillelse 1720–1814*, 7 vols. (Copenhagen, 1891–1912), 7: part 1: *Den udenrigske Historie 1807–1814*, 113–14, 119–24, 143–4.

16. Friis, "Frederik den Sjette," 243; Clausen, *Skandinavismen*, 20; Sjövall, *Adlersparre*, 2–8; Sørensen, *Bernadotte i Norden*, 1:113–14, 119–24, 143–4.

17. Holm, *Danmark-Norge*, 7:2: 97–100, 111; Sørensen, *Bernadotte i Norden*, 1:131.

18. The "Balloon Proclamation" is given in *DeLaGardiska arkivet*, ed. P. Wieselgren, 20 vols. (Lund, 1843), 20:242–56. Cf. Krusius-Ahrenberg, *Tyrannmördaren*, 404–11; Sjövall, *Adlersparre*, 10–14.

19. Clason, *Handlingar*, 33, 36, 44–5, 66, 70–3, 301; Schulz, *Briefwechsel*, 243–46. Cf. Hans Schulz, *Friedrich Christian Herzog zu Schleswig-Holstein. Ein Lebenslauf* (Leipzig, 1910), 318–19; Sjövall, *Adlersparre*, 92, 100–3; Einar Forssberg, *Karl August, gustavianerna och 1809 års män* (Hälsingborg, 1942), 10–11. See also Leland B. Sather, "The Prince of Scandinavia: A Biography of Prince Christian August of Schleswig-Holstein-Sonderburg-Augustenburg, 1768–1810" (Unpublished Ph.D. dissertation, University of California–Santa Barbara, 1975) and "Border War and Border Peace: The Norwegian-Swedish War of 1808 and the Swedish Revolution of 1809," in *Scandinavians in Old and New Lands: Essays in Honor of H. Arnold Barton*, ed. Philip J. Anderson, Dag Blanck, and Byron J. Nordstrom (Chicago, 2004), 53–70.

20. *Meddelelser, fra Krigsarkiverne. Udgivne af Generalstaben* (hereafter *Meddelelser*), vol.4, ed. C. T. Sørensen (Copenhagen, 1890), 209–12, 214–17, 220–21. Frederik VI's correspondence with Christian August and other officials in Norway in 1809 is also published in *Frederik den Sjettes fortroelige Brevvexling med Norge i Aaret 1809*, ed. C. T. Sørensen (Copenhagen, 1889), which is excerpted from the above. See also Nielsen, *Wedel Jarlsberg*, 1:193–9; Holm, *Danmark-Norge*, 7:2: 128–33.

21. This is the contention of Sørensen, *Bernadotte i Norden*, 1:179–83, who holds that Frederik VI was basically satisfied with the existing Dual Monarchy. Axel Linvald, in *Kong Christian VIII. Den unge Prins 1786–1813* (Copenhagen, 1943), 254n., criticizes Sørensen's treatment without entering into specifics.

22. Cf. Friis, "Frederik den Sjette," 243–5; Sjövall, *Adlersparre*, 114–15; *Meddelelser*, 4:212–13.

23. Sørensen, *Bernadotte i Norden*, 1:156–57, 165, 180–81. Sjövall, *Adlersparre*, 116, points out that there is no definite proof that Löwenhielm was instructed to, or did, discuss the prospect of a union in Copenhagen. Frederik's indignation in late May over what he considered Swedish trickery, however, seems to support this contention. See below.

24. It is generally held that the failure of the Sound to freeze solidly enough for the Danes to cross on the ice before the British navy could interfere caused the projected invasion to fail. See Holm, *Danmark-Norge*, 7:2: 113–14; Friis, "Frederik den Sjette," 244. Sørensen, *Bernadotte i Norden*, 1:150–5, however, claims conditions were highly favorable and blames Frederik VI's indecisiveness. Cf. also Sjövall, *Adlersparre*, 114.

25. *Meddelelser*, 4:218, 233, 237–38. Cf. S. J. Boëthius, *Bihang till Minnen ur Sveriges nyare historia*, 3 vols. (Stockholm, 1880–83), 2:99; Sjövall, *Adlersparre*, 115–16.

26. Sørensen, *Bernadotte i Norden*, 1:180–81.

27. *Meddelelser*, 4:218, 221–22, 228; Holm, *Danmark-Norge*, 7:2:133–34.

28. *Meddelelser*, 4:229–30, 234, 236, 239n., 240, 244–45; Clason, *Handlingar*, 71. *Meddelelser*, 4:231–32. Cf. ibid., 282; Sjövall, *Adlersparre*, 114.

29. *Meddelelser*, 4:231–32. Cf. ibid., 282; Sjövall, *Adlersparre*, 114.

30. *Meddelelser*, 4:246, 249.

31. Ibid., 231, 241, 246, 249, 258; Holm, *Danmark-Norge*, 7:2:192; Sjövall, *Adlersparre*, 131–33.

32. Holm, *Danmark-Norge*, 7:2:125.

33. Sjövall, *Adlersparre*, 131–33; *Meddelelser*, 4:253–55, 257–59; Clason, *Handlingar*, 85–87, 92–94, 100.

34. *Meddelelser*, 4:255, 261–62, 306n. It is difficult to accept the view of Sørensen, *Bernadotte i Norden*, 1:193–94, that Frederik was relieved at this point to give up the idea of union.

35. *Meddelelser*, 4:221–22, 248, 256, 261; *DeLaGardiska arkivet*, 20:253–54.

36. *Meddelelser*, 4:230, 234, 236, 268, 327; Clason, *Handlingar*, 301. Swedish aristocrats were themselves fearful of lower-class support for union under a Danish monarch. Cf. Boëthius, *Bihang*, 2:120–21.

37. *Meddelelser*, 4:256, 261, 282; Holm, *Danmark-Norge*, 7:2:146–50.

38. *Meddelelser*, 4:251–52, 260, 263, 272; Clason, *Handlingar*, 89–92. Cf. Holm, *Danmark-Norge*, 7:2:138–39, 151–53.

39. *Meddelelser*, 4:256–57, 261–62, 264–65, 267, 274–75, 281.

40. Ibid., 263, 266, 269, 272, 282–83, 287–89, 309.

41. Ibid., 267.

42. Clason, *Handlingar*, 102–3, 110–11; Sjövall, *Adlersparre*, 122–25, 216, 274–75, 366–67; Nielsen, *Wedel Jarlsberg*, 1:195, 198, 215–23, 253–60, 298–99, 317; Boëthius,

Bihang, 2:97; Sørensen, *Bernadotte i Norden*, 1:210, 248–49; Holm, *Danmark-Norge*, 7:2:129, 132–34.

43. *Meddelelser*, 4:302, 305. Older Danish scholarship tended to brand Christian August as a traitor for his acceptance of the Swedish succession. See especially C. F. Wegener, *Actmæssige Bidrag til Danmarks Historie i det nittende Aarhundrede*, in *Antislesvigholstenske Fragmenter* 15/16, ed. A. F. Krieger (Copenhagen, 1851), 97–127, passim., and more recently, Linvald, *Kong Christian VIII*, 1:177–78. The consensus of more recent historians is that Christian August, though loyal and well-meaning, became in spite of himself involved in a highly compromising situation. See Johan Forchhammer, "Christian August, Prinds af Augustenborg," parts 1–4, *Dansk Maanedsskrift*, ed. M. G. G. Steenstrup (1868), passim., esp. 1:1–10, 2:316–17, 3:417, 441–42, 4:356–57; Sørensen, *Bernadotte i Norden*, 1:187–89, 201, 208, 211–12, 215–16; Holm, *Danmark-Norge*, 7:2:145, 161, 200; Sjövall, *Adlersparre*, xx–xxii, 131, 287–90, 403; Forssberg, *Karl August*, 23–27; Nielsen, *Wedel Jarlsberg*, 1:221–23, 233–34, 262–63, 279–80, 329–32, 341–42. This view evidently agrees with that of Frederik VI and of Christian August himself. See *Meddelelser*, 4:421; Clason, *Handlingar*, 140.

44. *Meddelelser*, 4:238, 241, 292, 295–96; Holm, *Danmark-Norge*, 7:2:147–49, 155–58, 179; Sørensen, *Bernadotte i Norden*, 1:197–98, 203–4; Sjövall, *Adlersparre*, 325.

45. *Meddelelser*, 4:iv, 283, 296, 298–301, 308–11, 313–17, 321–24, 335–37; Holm, *Danmark-Norge*, 7:2:154–55, 159–60; Sørensen, *Bernadotte i Norden*, 1:201–2; Nielsen, *Wedel Jarlsberg*, 1:242–43.

46. Sjövall, *Adlersparre*, 325–26; Holm, *Danmark-Norge*, 7:2:179–80; Sørensen, *Bernadotte i Norden*, 1:203–5.

47. Sjövall, *Adlersparre*, 275–78, 285–86, 292–93, 337–39, 366–69, 393; Sørensen, *Bernadotte i Norden*, 1:12.

48. Schulz, *Briefwechsel*, 246; *Meddelelser*, 4:260, 264, 302, 325, 327, 412, 436–37; Clason, *Handlingar*, 149, 152, 158–59, 174, 209–11, 243; Sjövall, *Adlersparre*, 287–28n., 395–96.

49. *Meddelelser*, 4:217, 220, 234, 236, 261, 285, 306n., 322–23; Boëthius, *Bihang*, 2:97; Clason, *Handlingar*, 84–87, 92–94, 100, 110–11, 122, 301; Sjövall, *Adlersparre*, 104–10, 209–10, 287–90, 366–69; Nielsen, *Wedel Jarlsberg*, 1:214–23.

50. C. A. Adlersparre, *1809 och 1810. Tidstaflor*, 2 vols. (Stockholm, 1850), 1:225–26. Cf. *Meddelelser*, 4:471, 473; Clason, *Handlingar*, 197–99.

51. *Meddelelser*, 4:305, 327–28, 338, 433, 467, 472; Holm, *Danmark-Norge*, 7:2:168–70, 184. The allegations of Danish perfidy toward the prince made by C. A. Adlersparre in *1809 och 1810*, passim., cannot be taken at face value.

52. *Meddelelser*, 4:247–48, 422, 425–26, 433; Linvald, *Kong Christian VIII*, 1:182–83; Boëthius, *Bihang*, 2:201–2; Clason, *Handlingar*, 240.

53. Sørensen, *Bernadotte i Norden*, 2:221–22, 228–32; Holm, *Danmark-Norge*, 7:2:216.

54. Clason, *Handlingar*, 243.

55. Ibid., 248, 251–52, 259–60, 272, 276, 277–78; Schulz, *Friedrich Christian*, 329.

56. Sørensen, *Bernadotte i Norden*, 5:45–48.

57. Nielsen, *Wedel Jarlsberg*, 1:336–38; Friis, "Frederik den Sjette," 251.

58. Oscar Alin, *Tronföljarvalet 1810* (Stockholm, 1899), 1–4; Schulz, *Friedrich Christian*, 334–35; Sørensen, *Bernadotte i Norden*, 1:335–36.

59. *Utdrag ur danska diplomaters meddelanden från Stockholm 1807–1808, 1810 och 1812–1813*, ed. C. J. Anker and F. U. Wrangel (Stockholm, 1897), 61–62; Scævola [K. A. Strömbäck], *Utländska diplomaters minnen från svenska hofvet* (Stockholm, 1885), 484–86. Cf. *Meddelelser*, 5:6–7, 48–50.

60. Scævola, *Utländska diplomaters minnen*, 493–4; Clason, *Handlingar*, 288; Friis, "Frederik den Sjette,"270–73, 277.

61. Friis, "Frederik den Sjette," 274–75, 279, 281; Alin, *Tronföljarvalet 1810*, 5–7; *Correspondence de Napoléon I*, 32 vols. (Paris, 1858–70), 20:430–31.

62. Holm, *Danmark-Norge*, 7:1:212–13, 223–25, 237; Friis, "Frederik den Sjette," 271–74, 281–83; Albert Vandal, *Napoléon et Alexandre I*, 3 vols. (Paris, 1893–1908), 2:445–59; Boëthius, *Bihang*, 2:227–29, 251; [Charles de Suremain], *Mémoires du Lieutenant-Général de Suremain (1794–1815)* (Paris, 1902), 211.

63. Sørensen, *Bernadotte i Norden*, 1:234–37, 247–51; Holm, *Danmark-Norge*, 7:2:205–6, 210; Friis, "Frederik den Sjette," 258–61, 287–91.

64. [Frederik Moltke], *Aux suédois par un habitant d'Altona*; [Ernst Schimmelmann], *Ueber die Vereinigung der drei nordischen Reiche*; [J. K. Høst], *En Verdenborgers Stemme i et stort Anliggende*; [A. C. Gierlew], *Nordens Gjenforening*; N. F. S. Grundtvig, *Er Nordens Forening Ønskelig?*; [C. F. Rühs], *Til Skandinaverne af Literatus Christensen* [trans. R. Nyerup]; [anonymous], *Noget om Ørebro Rigsdag Julius 1810*; and *En dansk Mands velmente Opfordring til det svenske Folk*. Only Grundtvig did not use a pseudonym or anonymity. Cf. also Friis, "Frederik den sjette," 267, 312–32; Clausen, *Skandinavismen*, 20–24; Krusius-Ahrenberg, *Tyrannmördaren*, 421; Holm, *Danmark-Norge*, 7:2:231–34.

65. Friis, "Frederik den Sjette," 316. Cf. the anonymous Norwegian pamphlet titled *En Normands venskablige Sendebud till den Svenske Nation, skrevet i Marts Maaned 1809*, in Clason, *Handlingar*, 65–66.

66. Alin, *Tronföljarvalet 1810*, 119–20; Holm, *Danmark-Norge*, 7:2:216–17, 225–27; Sørensen, *Bernadotte i Norden*, 1:247, 249–56; Friis, "Frederik den sjette," 291–307.

67. Anker, *Utdrag*, 61–68, 71–80; Scævola, *Utländska diplomaters minnen*, 502–4; Friis, "Frederik den Sjette," 262–70, 307–10, 356, 362–72, 386–88; Lars von Engeström, *Minnen och anteckningar*, ed. Elof Tegnér, 2 vols. (Stockholm, 1876), 2:165–66, 335–38.

68. Scævola, *Utländska diplomaters minnen*, 484–86, 493–96, 503–7; Anker, *Utdrag*, 71–72, 75–76; Boëthius, *Bihang*, 2:251; Vandal, *Napoléon et Alexandre I*, 2:461–63.

69. Friis, "Frederik den Sjette," 406–7.

70. Ibid., 256–57, 291, 309–10, 326, 353–58, 362–68, 386–87.

71. Ibid., 320–21, 324, 356–59; "Jens Kragh Høst," in *Dansk Biografisk Leksikon*, 11 (Copenhagen, 1937), 152–54; Clausen, *Skandinavismen*, 25; Krusius-Ahrenberg, *Tyrannmördaren*, 423–27. Cf. Jens Kragh Høst, *Erindringer om mig og mine samtidige* (Copenhagen, 1835), 83–90; Rasmus Nyerup, *Rejser til Stockholm i Aarene 1810 og 1812* (Copenhagen, 1816), passim.

72. Anker, *Utdrag*, 65, 67, 76; *För hundra år sen*, ed. Sam Clason and Carl af Petersens, 2 vols. (Stockholm, 1909–10), 2:114, 147; Friis, "Frederik den Sjette," 265–66, 277–79, 299–304, 357–58; Clausen, *Skandinavismen*, 24–26; Holm, *Danmark-Norge*, 7:2:235–36; Sørensen, *Bernadotte i Norden*, 1:252–53, 256–57.

73. Anker, *Utdrag*, 67–68, 74–76 ; Scævola, *Utländska diplomaters minnen*, 495, 498, 502, 511; Suremain, *Mémoires*, 197, 207–13, 217–19; *Kong Christian VIII.s breve 1796–1813*, ed. Axel Linvald, 2 vols. (Copenhagen, 1965), 1:338–39; Linvald, *Kong Christian VIII*, 1:191–92; Friis, "Frederik den Sjette," 247, 268–69, 284–86, 357–58; Nielsen, *Wedel Jarlsberg*, 1:170; Sørensen, *Bernadotte i Norden*, 1:248–49, 253–54. Certain Swedes had already considered Prince Christian Frederik before the revolution of March 1809. See Sørensen, *Bernadotte i Norden*, 1:156–57.

74. Anker, *Utdrag*, 77–78; Scævola, *Utländska diplomaters minnen*, 505–8; Boëthius, *Bihang*, 2:255; Friis, "Frederik den Sjette," 276, 279–80, 284–85, 362–77; Vandal, *Napoléon et Alexandre I*, 2:464–66; Linvald, *Kong Christian VIII*, 1:188, 191.

75. Anker, *Utdrag*, 65–66, 75–79; Scævola, *Utländska diplomaters minnen*, 499, 505, 507, 512, 514; Friis, "Frederik den Sjette," 279, 307, 368, 393; Sørensen, *Bernadotte i Norden*, 1:236–37.

76. Scævola, *Utländska diplomaters minnen*, 507; Suremain, *Mémoires*, 219 ; Alin, *Tronföljarvalet 1810*, 180–85.

77. Clason, *Handlingar*, 243, 288; Schulz, *Friedrich Christian*, 337, 341–42; Schulz, *Briefwechsel*, 270–71; Hans Schulz, *Briefwechsel des Herzogs Friedrich Christian zu Schleswig-Holstein-Sonderburg-Augustenburg mit König Friedrich VI. von Dänemark und dem Thronfolger Prinsen Christian Friedrich* (Leipzig, 1908), 372–76, 511–29; Friis, "Frederik den Sjette," 322–23, 344–45.

78. Friis, "Frederik den Sjette," 377–93; Holm, *Danmark-Norge*, 7:2:228–30, 245–46; Clason, *För hundra år sen*, 2:116, 148; Linvald, *Christian VIII.s breve*, 1:338; *Meddelelser*, 5:7–8. The behavior and motives of Duke Frederik Christian in the second Swedish succession crisis of 1810 has given rise to much polemical dispute, largely inspired and obscured by the later involvement of the Augustenburgs in the Schleswig-Holstein conflict. Wegener, *Actmæssige Bidrag*, 127–67, passim., for instance, regards the duke as treasonable toward Frederik VI in 1810. More recent scholarship has tended on the whole to revindicate the duke. See Julius Clausen, *Frederik Christian, Hertug af Augustenborg (1765–1814). En monogrfisk skildring* (Copenhagen, 1896), 120–39; Schulz, *Friedrich Christian*, 333–56; H. Hjelholt, "Frederik Christians Stilling til det andet svenske Tronfølgervalg," *Historisk Tidsskrift* (Copenhagen), series 8 (1915), esp. 415, 419–21; also Holm, *Danmark-Norge;* Friis, "Frederik den Sjette."

79. Holm, *Danmark-Norge*, 7:2:248–50; Friis, "Frederik den Sjette," 324–27.

80. Boëthius, 2:222, 227–29, 239–42, 251, 259–65, 274–76, 281; Clason, *För hundra år sen*, 2:124.

81. Friis, "Frederik den Sjette," 383–84, 390–93 ; Sørensen, *Bernadotte i Norden*, 1:238, 257, 266–73 ; Schulz, *Friedrich Christian*, 349–54; Alin, *Tronföljarvalet 1810*, 290–91, 297, 299; Krusius-Ahrenberg, *Tyrannmördaren*, 428–31; Clausen, *Skandinavismen*, 24–25; Engeström, *Minnen och anteckningar*, 2:168.

82. [Anonymous], *Hwilket är det bästa wal af thronföljare, som nu kan göras?* (n. p., n. d.). Cf. Friis, "Frederik den Sjette," 395–97; Alin, *Tronföljarvalet 1810,* 221–46.

83. Holm, *Danmark-Norge,* 7:2:246–47; Friis, "Frederik den Sjette," 398–409; my *Scandinavia in the Revolutionary Era* (Minneapolis, 1986), 349.

84. Linvald, *Kong Christian VIII,* 192–93; Linvald, *Christian VIII.s breve,* 1:55–63. Cf. *Meddelelser,* 5:50–53.

85. Holm, *Danmark-Norge,* 7:2:183–85, 205–6; Linvald, *Kong Christian VIII,* 1:192; Linvald, *Christian VIII.s breve,* 1:58; Nielsen, *Wedel Jarlsberg,* 1:208; Friis, "Frederik den Sjette," 244–45, 247, 259, 305–7, 324. Sørensen, *Bernadotte i Norden,* 2:234–38, 252–57, is particularly critical of Frederik VI, claiming that all of Denmark's ills from that time derived from his failure to follow "the country's natural policy," as advised by all his counselors. See also my *Scandinavia in the Revolutionary Era,* 349.

86. Hans Gabriel Trolle-Wachtmeister, *Anteckningar och minnen,* ed. Elof Tegner, 2 vols. (Stockholm, 1889), 1:255–56.

87. Karl Warburg, "Rasmus Nyerups svenska brefväxling," *Samlaren* 15 (1894): 99n.

88. Holm, *Danmark-Norge,* 7:2:183–85, 205–6; Linvald, *Kong Christian VIII,* 1:192; Linvald, *Christian VIII.s breve,* 1:58; Nielsen, *Wedel Jarlsberg,* 1:208; Friis, "Frederik den sjette," 244–45, 247, 259, 305–7, 324. Sørensen, *Bernadotte i Norden,* 2:234–38, 252–57.

89. Anker, *Utdrag,* 77; Scævola, *Utländska diplomaters minnen,* 299, 505–7, 512, 514–15, 517; Clason, *För hundra år sen,* 2:116; Suremain, *Mémoires,* 211, 216. Cf. Suremain's speculations on the long-range implications of a union. Ibid., 211–13, 90.

90. Clausen and Friis, for example, represent the traditional view that support for a Scandinavian union was negligible in 1809 and 1810. For opinion in 1809, see Sjövall, *Adlersparre,* 284, 292–93. For 1810, Friis, "Frederik den Sjette," 259, 269–70, 278–79, 362, 370–74; Sørensen, *Bernadotte i Norden,* 1:234, 268; Holm, *Danmark-Norge,* 7:2:236, 249–50; *Meddelelser,* 5:50, 55; *Hedvig Elisabeth Charlottas dagbok,* ed. C. C. Bonde & C. af Klercker, 9 vols. (Stockholm, 1902–42), 8:573–74; Trolle-Wachtmeister, *Anteckningar och minnen,* 1:254–56; *Excellensen A. F. Sköldebrands memoarer,* ed. H. Schück, 5 vols. (Stockholm, 1903–4), 4:141–42; Jöran Wibling, *Opinioner och stämningar i Sverige 1809–10* (Uppsala, 1954), 276–79.

Scandinavianism, Fennomania, and the Crimean War

By October 1853, the "quarrel of monks" over the rights of the Latin and Greek churches in the Holy Land led, after tortuous diplomatic maneuvering, to war between Russia and the Ottoman Empire. In March 1854, Great Britain and France entered the conflict against Russia, backed by vociferously russophobic public opinion. The strategic question for the Western allies was where they might best attack Russia: either in the Black Sea, via the Straits, or in the Baltic against St. Petersburg itself, via the Sound. In the event, by the fall of 1854 they opted for the first alternative, concentrating their forces against the Crimea with its great Russian naval base at Sebastopol.

Nonetheless, the Baltic remained of great strategic interest. Sweden, if it joined Russia's enemies, might play an important role, both as a base of operations and as an ally in an assault against the Russian capital. This, in turn, would draw Finland into the fray. By 1855, after Sebastopol's fall, Sweden came close to entering the war but was forestalled when the Russians made peace in March 1856. Thus, the war itself was for Sweden a "nonevent" that failed to come about. Yet in a broader sense, it was a revealing episode that would have important long-term consequences for the North.

As Finland covered the approaches to St. Petersburg, it assumed particular strategic significance. But for Sweden there were deeper reasons for concern. Beginning in the twelfth century, Finland had been Christianized and incorporated as an integral part of the Swedish kingdom. Over six hundred years, its institutions, higher culture, and cultivated language had become Swedish. Strong ties united the two parts of the realm, and Finns had long played their prominent part in Sweden's government, military forces, economy, and cultural life.

In 1808–9, during the turmoil of the Napoleonic wars, the Russians invaded and occupied Finland. Tsar Alexander I claimed the territory as a province of the Russian empire in April 1808 and in June required the Finns to swear allegiance to him. In January 1809, however, he convened a Finnish *lantdag*, or diet, at Borgå (Porvoo), at which he declared Finland a grand duchy under his own suzerainty, promising to respect its existing constitution, laws, and religion. New central administrative institutions were established, while Swedish remained the official language. At Borgå, Alexander declared that he had placed Finland "in the rank of nations."[1] The Finnish forces had fiercely resisted the Russian invasion and indeed were still in the field while the Borgå diet was in session. Not until March 1809 did their last remnant capitulate in northern Sweden. By September Sweden was compelled to conclude the Peace of Fredrikshamn (Hamina), ceding Finland to the Russian emperor, thereby losing a third of its territory and a quarter of its population.

Even while the war lasted, the Swedish-speaking Finnish upper classes accepted this change of status with remarkable equanimity.[2] For this they were well prepared over the past century. Peter I's establishment of his new capital of St. Petersburg in 1703 and his decisive defeat of Carl XII's Swedish army at Poltava in 1709 during the Great Northern War (1700–1721) marked the end of Sweden's seventeenth-century "Era of Greatness" and its dominion over the Baltic region. Finland, while it remained under Swedish rule, however, posed a constant threat to the new Russian capital. It was twice invaded and occupied by the Russians, in 1709–21 and again after a rash Swedish attack against Russia in 1741–43. Although it was restored to Sweden both times, the Russians kept parts of southeastern Finland to guard the approaches to St. Petersburg.

The lessons of these wars were not lost on the Finns. It became increasingly evident that Sweden could not in the long run defend them against Russia. At the same time, the Russians no longer seemed as uncivilized as in the past. The cosmopolitan Enlightenment encouraged the utilitarian concept, *ubi bene, ibi patria*. During Sweden's "Era of Freedom," 1718–72, political factions frequently appealed to foreign powers, including Russia, for support. During the war of 1741–43, the empress Elizabeth, encouraged by disaffected Finns, issued a manifesto offering Finland autonomy under Russian overlordship, while demanding their oath of allegiance. When Gustaf III again declared war on Russia in 1788, a group of Finnish officers conspired with Catherine II to make Finland a Russian protectorate, although this time Finland escaped occupation and the loss of further territory. Still, the Russian threat remained, and autonomous status under Russia became ever more conceivable.

Gunnar Artéus has expressed the Finns' quandary: continued Swedish rule would assure participation in political power and a high degree of civic freedom, at the expense of security against repeated wars with Russia on Finnish soil; incorporation into the Russian empire would mean loss of guaranteed political and personal rights but a stable peace, protected by Russia's superior military strength. Alexander sought, as he wrote to his governor-general in 1810, to offer his new Finnish subjects "incomparably greater advantages than they would have had under Swedish dominion." The new regime provided real benefits to the Finnish elite, while reassuring the peasantry of their traditional rights.[3]

The transition was a soft one. Until 1812, Finns who wished to remain Swedish subjects could opt to depart for Sweden, while those in Sweden who chose to become subjects of the new grand duchy could relocate in Finland. There was considerable movement in both directions, even after the stipulated period. Émigrés were appointed to high positions on both sides. Until 1840, trade with Sweden continued unhindered and Swedish money circulated freely in Finland.[4]

If the Finns appeared to have come to terms with their new status, the loss of Finland was a shattering experience for the Swedes, leading to an outraged search for scapegoats and a wave of impassioned russophobia and lust for revenge. Blame for the debacle fell mainly upon King Gustaf IV Adolf for his inept leadership in the war. This, in large part, brought about his arrest in March 1808 by a junta of army officers and the calling of a diet (*riksdag*), which deposed him and his heirs, elected his elderly uncle King Carl XIII, and drafted a new constitution.[5]

Beyond that, it was widely believed that Finland was lost through weakness and treachery, particularly with the surrender, after only token resistance, of the great fortress and naval base at Sveaborg (Suomenlinna) in Helsingfors (Helsinki) Bay, by its commander, Admiral C. O. Cronstedt. It was too much for most Swedes to accept that they had been beaten by a better-led, -organized, -trained, -armed, and -supplied foe, with greater battlefield experience and higher morale, and they bitterly resented the

Finnish establishment's supine behavior toward the invaders. The Finns, for their part, blamed inept leadership and lack of reinforcement from Sweden during the war.[6]

For centuries, Swedes had regarded the Russians as their hereditary foes. The war brought an upsurge of russophobia, with the poet Esaias Tegnér in the van. "Like a thief in the night treacherously they crept / with hidden dagger./ Suddenly their banners flew / among a secure and peaceful folk," Tegnér wrote in 1808, "Our harvests they will scatter / our fathers' bones they will trample, / ravish our women's virtue. . . ." If only the Swedes were still the heroes of yesteryear, he lamented in 1811.[7]

The Swedes at first hoped that Finland might be regained, as it had been in 1721 and 1743. Alexander I's Tilsit alliance of 1807 with Napoleon was clearly breaking down. In a foreseeable war between them, Sweden, allied with France, might win back what it had lost. Largely in such hopes, the Riksdag elected the French field-marshal Jean-Baptiste Bernadotte, a commander of proven ability, as Crown Prince Carl Johan, successor to the childless Carl XIII, in August 1810.

Napoleon invaded Russia in June 1812. The new crown prince—by now the real ruler of Sweden—shared none of the Swedes' emotional attachment to Finland, regarding it as a potential liability if regained, and sought instead to acquire Norway from Denmark in compensation, thereby strengthening the security of the Scandinavian peninsula. Already in February 1812 he undertook to ally himself with Russia in the event of a French attack, in return for support in acquiring Norway. This alliance was confirmed in August by Alexander I and Carl Johan when they met in Åbo (Turku) in Finland. In a secret protocol, Sweden and Russia guaranteed the integrity of each other's existing domains. This meant that in return for Norway, Sweden formally renounced any future claim to Finland.[8]

Sweden joined the war against France in early 1813; in return, Russian troops reinforced Carl Johan's Swedish army in a brief campaign against Denmark in December 1813, forcing Frederik VI in January 1814 to relinquish Norway to the king of Sweden. After attempting to establish an independent kingdom, the Norwegians were compelled by November 1814 to join in a dynastic union with Sweden, although under their own constitution and government that limited the powers of the joint monarch. Many Swedes were disillusioned and considered Norway, under such terms, as scarcely an adequate exchange for Finland.[9]

With the general European peace in 1814–15, the Swedes seemed compelled to accept the new dispensation, however regretfully, and turned their interests toward their Scandinavian neighbors, Norway and Denmark, and proud memories of their shared Nordic antiquity. This became of the focus of the Gothic League (*Götiska Förbundet*), founded in 1810 among young intellectuals, most prominent among them the poets Esaias Tegnér and Erik Gustaf Geijer, who sought to inspire a national revival, based on rude virtues of the Saga age. This vision, which had eighteenth-century antecedents, inspired the idealistic Scandinavianist movement that found expression in periodic meetings of Swedish, Danish, and eventually Norwegian students, beginning in 1842.

Political motives were meanwhile not lacking behind this enthusiasm. The Danes felt increasingly threatened by separatism among the German population in Slesvig and Holstein. Scandinavian solidarity could not only strengthen national sentiment among the Danes in Slesvig but also ultimately provide allies against possible German aggression. This in turn reawakened concern for Finland. At the student meeting at Lund in 1843, the leading Danish Scandinavianist, Carl Plough, to stir enthusiasm among his Swedish companions, appealed to their sympathy for their Finnish brethren. The Russian government promptly summoned the Swedish minister to St. Petersburg to express its concern over the radical students, which it feared were the "obedient tools for revolutionary intriguers."[10]

To enthusiastic young Scandinavianists, it seemed altogether natural to regard the Finns, with their long common history, Swedish cultural heritage, and entirely Swedish-speaking educated elite, as fellow "Scandinavians," little concerned—or perhaps hardly aware—that the great majority of Finland's inhabitants spoke a Ural-Altaic vernacular totally unrelated to the Scandinavian languages.

Nationalism went hand in hand with liberalism in Metternich's Europe. The young Scandinavianists ardently sympathized with the various revolutions and national liberation and unification movements on the Continent: German *Burschenschaften*, Italian *Carbonari*, and Greek, Belgian, and French revolutionaries. Here traditional Swedish russophobia joined with the mounting detestation throughout the Western world for Russia as the heart and soul of the Holy Alliance. The infamous "Testament of Peter the Great," a French forgery probably from the late eighteenth century, held that it was Russia's ultimate ambition to dominate all of Europe. Anti-Russian passions rose to new heights in the West with Nicholas II's ruthless suppression of the Polish uprising of 1830–31 and especially his crushing of the Hungarian revolution on Austria's behalf in 1849.[11] In verse and song the Scandinavian students gave vent to their mounting russophobia, outrage over Finland's fate, and lust for revenge.

Particularly prominent in this regard was the Swede C. V. A. Strand-berg (pseud. "Talis Qualis"). In "Utmaning" (Challenge) from 1844, for instance, he summoned "the world's Goliath, the giant of the East" to a fair battle against the gallant Swedes. "What you took from us before / you did not take with the sword, but stole. . . . Slave! Thou shouldst be fired / by the thought alone of bleeding on soil that is free . . . / and to die among free men!" His "Vaticinium," declaimed at the student meeting at Lund in 1845, appealed, "*Finland!* So would I cry out / and from you all find an answer from the depths of your hearts." It foresaw how the stout-hearted students would embark for Finland, where the old love for Sweden needed only their encouragement to break forth. There they would "lay low the bloodied Cossack in the dust!"[12]

The example of the valiant Greeks in the Persian Wars against the co-lossus of their time cannot have been far from these classically educated students' minds. At the same time one may suspect that some in their excitement almost believed that brave toasts and rousing songs might alone suffice to put the craven Muscovite to flight! Moreover, if the oppressed Poles had risen up against the tsar in 1831, would not the Finns do likewise, with whole-hearted Scandinavian support?

The students reflected widespread liberal opinion in Sweden. By the 1830s there was rising discontent with the regime of Carl XIV Johan, who had come to the throne in 1818 and had become increasingly reactionary. Criticism came to focus largely upon the king's steadfast adherence to his Russian alliance of 1812. The king seemed the compliant tool of the Rus-sian autocrat in both foreign and domestic policy, which posed the greatest obstacle to progressive reform. The question arose why Carl Johan had not regained Finland in 1812 when there might have been a chance.[13]

In 1841, the aging Tegnér, in his poem "Kronbruden" (The Crown Bride) warned that "the Russian is the stereotype / of all force and oppression, the constant symbol of barbarism / . . . Away, away with the barbarian, enemy not to us alone, but to mankind!" The following year the Finnish-born Gustaf Henrik Melin's *Sveriges sista strid* (Sweden's Last Battle) gave a lurid fictional account of a future Sweden, invaded and occupied by an insatiably expansionist Russia, thanks to the treachery or indifference of "many of the noble caste." Melin paints a grim picture of the life that followed the invasion, clearly alluding to what was believed to exist in Finland. His particular villains were well-known, high-ranking Swedish reactionaries whom he portrayed as servile lackeys of the all-powerful tsar.[14]

The liberal opposition thus brought to the fore the question of Finland's actual status within the Russian empire, leading between 1838 and 1842 to a heated pamphlet war.[15] The first, preemptive blow was struck in 1838 by the prominent Uppsala professor of medicine Israel Hwasser, who after several years at Finland's university, first at Åbo, then at Helsingfors, had returned to his native Sweden in 1830. Hwasser was a staunch conservative and warm admirer not only of Carl XIV Johan but of Emperor Nicholas I as well.[16]

In an anonymous 109-page pamphlet Hwasser declared that while he recognized the deep sorrow in Sweden over the loss of Finland, the Finns themselves were now satisfied with their new situation and had no desire to return to Swedish rule. "The foster son does not wish to seem ungrateful to his foster father, but he wished to leave his house to seek his fortune on his own," he wrote. Reunion with Sweden would bring only war and would impede Finland's internal progress.

The heart of Hwasser's argument was meanwhile that even before Sweden renounced all claims to Finland at the Peace of Fredrikshamn, the Finns had "emancipated themselves from their former condition" and, at the Borgå Diet in March 1809, had concluded their own separate peace. The emperor of Russia thereupon made Finland "a state in its own right," guaranteeing its "own representative government, own constitution, and own laws." It was hardly to be expected that the Finns would willingly give up their new status. Taking a broader view, Hwasser considered that as Finland had received Western civilization from Sweden, it was its historic destiny to convey it to Russia, from whence it would in time spread eastward to the wild inhabitants of Asia. Sweden's wisest policy was to leave Finland alone and look instead to its morally justified union with Norway.[17] It seems not unlikely that Hwasser may have been secretly encouraged to write his tract by the king himself, who was adept at manipulating the press.

Hwasser's pamphlet promptly drew a sharp rebuttal from "Pekka Kuoharinen," pseudonym for the émigré Finn Adolf Ivar Arwidsson. At Åbo Arwidsson had been a leader in the early student movement for cultivation and use of the indigenous Finnish language. In 1821, after his appointment as a docent in history, he established a newspaper, *Åbo Morgonblad*, in which he sought to arouse civic spirit and criticized existing conditions. His activism caused anxiety among the Finnish authorities, and with the emperor's authority the newspaper was shut down after only nine months. Arwidsson was dismissed from his academic post. Failing to find other employment in Finland, he emigrated in 1823 to Sweden, where he devoted himself to literary pursuits and was eventually appointed royal librarian.[18]

In response to Hwasser, Arwidsson described Finland's guaranteed privileges within the Russian empire as a sham. In June 1808, Alexander I had proclaimed Finland annexed for all time as a "province of Russia," and this was what, step by step, it was becoming. The Finns had therefore not concluded a separate peace and renounced Swedish sovereignty of their own free will. At Borgå the emperor had allowed the diet no more than consultative functions. "This politically fictional house of cards thus collapses," Arwidsson declared. Finland lacked any firm guarantee against Russian encroachment. Moreover the diet had not been convened for the past thirty years, since Borgå.[19]

At the end of 1838, Erik Gustaf Geijer, now professor of history at Uppsala, brought out a survey of Swedish-Russian relations over the centuries, ending with a brief discussion of the dispute between Hwasser and Arwidsson. He agreed with Arwidsson that Finland was a Russian conquest and that its autonomy was illusory. Still, the illusion had its own reality for the Finns. He dismissed as unrealistic the idea that Sweden might have regained Finland in 1812. Even if recovered, it would prove impossible to hold. Geijer held that Sweden's union with Norway had, "like all sound policies, been determined by *true* conditions," and that the dual monarchy's present course was the best possible.

Arwidsson brought out an augmented version of his pamphlet in 1839–40. Hwasser countered with a new pamphlet on the Borgå Diet, offering detailed juridical arguments to demonstrate that it had possessed authority to act on behalf of Finland, guaranteed by its "contract" with the emperor. In Sweden he deplored the blind russophobia and exaggerated praise for "the Finland that had been," together with contempt for the new Finland. "They speak so much of threats from the East, but it actually seems as if they rather wish for them than believe in them." The real menace came from Sweden's own bitter internal conflicts. Hwasser urged the Swedes to forget the past and concentrate on their country's own development.[20]

Hwasser's new publication was followed in 1841 by a pamphlet by "Olli Kekäläinen." Its author was presumed to be Arwidsson, but this assumption has more recently given rise to controversy. The actual author appears to have been the Helsingfors law professor Johan Jacob Nordström, who left not long after for Stockholm, where in time he was appointed the royal archivist, and who here took a more cautious approach to avoid giving the Russians justification for further repression in Finland.

Kekäläinen's brochure undertook to reconcile the opposing views of Hwasser and Arwidsson. "Whoever closely follows this exchange will easily discover that Herr Hwasser confuses what *should be* with what *is*, and that Pekka Kuoharinen presents the situation as it *is*, without considering how it *should be*." They argued on different levels. Although Finland was a conquered land, Alexander I had concluded a "true contract" with its inhabitants, even though this had not been always been honored in letter or spirit. Unfortunately the exact nature of Finland's status had not been clearly set forth from the beginning. In theory, if one party did not live up to a contract, the other was no longer bound to it. But it would be unrealistic to expect that Russia would accept such an interpretation. Meanwhile, Finland was growing into its new role both economically and culturally. Thus a true friend of Finland could only urge it to live scrupulously up to its side of the bargain, to avoid any risk of losing the rights it presently enjoyed. Secret conspiracies or open resistance could only invite disaster, as the recent Polish uprising had proved.[21]

In 1842, the Finnish émigré Carl Fredrik von Burghausen, under the pseudonym "Paavo Suomalainen," responded to "Kekäläinen," depicting the latter's presentation as confused, inconsistent, and inconclusive. The Swedes knew little or nothing about present conditions in Finland, he wrote. But what did the Finns themselves know under heavy-handed censorship and with no chance of forming any kind of opposition? The conduct of their government was "an impenetrable secret." Finland's only real constitution was the emperor's will alone, which was often in violation of that supposedly guaranteed at Borgå—the former Swedish constitution of 1772, as amended in 1789. Von Burghausen thereupon detailed numerous ways in which, he held, this existing constitution had been violated. He concluded with attacks on various Finnish officials whom he regarded as the corrupt haiduks of the tsar.[22]

Thereafter Swedish opinion turned for the time being to other concerns. In 1844 Carl XIV Johan died and was followed on the throne by his son, Oscar I, in whom the liberals placed high hopes.

In his pamphlet from 1838, A. I. Arwidsson (Kuoharinen) had stopped short of urging Finland's reunification with Sweden. Since 1809, the Finns had begun to develop a "feeling of nationality of their own," finding inspiration in their "own inner folklife." Here he alluded to his own role while in Åbo as an early proponent of the Finnish language. Olli Kekäläinen likewise declared in 1841 that the Finns had begun to discover their own indigenous roots. "A people is not dead," he declared, "as long as it possesses its own language . . . for language is the distillate of the nation's whole antiquity, destiny, and history."[23]

For centuries language and status had gone together in Finland. Swedish had been the language of all official business and of higher culture, while Finnish—or rather various dialects of Finnish—remained the peasant vernacular, except in some coastal areas. To rise in social and occupational standing required a knowledge of Swedish and normally a Swedish name. Only by the later decades of the eighteenth century did interest in Finnish language and folklore begin to awaken in academic circles. After Finland's separation from Sweden, however, the Finns needed to find a new direction. "The emperor wants to make good Finns of us," wrote Baron Gustaf Mauritz Armfelt already in 1811, "and in God's name let us fulfill our destiny." The same idea soon recurred in a dictum customarily attributed to Arwidsson: "Swedes we are no longer, Russians we shall never be, therefore let us be Finns!"[24]

The one area in which the Finns were free to develop their own sense of nationality was the cultural. The young enthusiasts at the university, first in Åbo, then in Helsingfors after its transfer there in 1827, were inspired by German romanticism with its creed of one nation, one faith, one tongue. Like romantics elsewhere, the idealistic students were liberals. Although deriving from the Swedish-speaking elite, they aspired to unite their countrymen by promoting use of the indigenous language of the majority, would in time bridge the gap between the classes and the masses by bringing enlightenment to the peasantry. This change would require effort and sacrifice on the part of the educated classes, translation of literature into Finnish, and the establishment of Finnish schools.

In their idealistic combination of liberalism and cultural nationalism, the young "Fennomanes," as they came to be called, closely resembled the young Scandinavianists across the Baltic. As long as the movement remained focused upon language and culture alone, it found favor in St. Petersburg for loosening Finland's old ties to Sweden. The Russians welcomed and even supported the Finnish Literary Society (*Suomalaisen Kirjallisuuden Seura*) founded in 1831.

Enthusiasm for the uniquely Finnish was strongly reinforced by the publication of the epic *Kalevala* in 1835, based on the devoted research of Elias Lönnrot in Karelia, revealing a wealth of ancient lore still preserved there in folk memory. The expeditions of the philologist Mattias Alexander Castrén during the 1840s explored the Finns' linguistic relationship to the widely scattered Fenno-Ugric peoples of northern Russia and Siberia. Part 1 of *Fänrik Ståls sägner* (The Tales of Ensign Stål) by Johan Ludvig Runeberg, widely considered the most outstanding poet writing in Swedish during the mid-nineteenth century, described in 1848 Finland's heroic defense by its own forces in the war of 1808–9, powerfully strengthening Finnish pride. Runeberg's epic also became immensely popular in Sweden, where it could, however, be interpreted there in a different light. The stalwart loyalty of the Finnish soldiers could there be seen as proof of their devotion to Sweden, which seemed further confirmed by their Swedish names. In Finland it was clear that the fatherland they fought for was Finland itself.[25]

By the mid-1840s Johan Vilhelm Snellman emerged as the Fennomanes' leading ideologue, bringing a new doctrinaire stridency to the movement. In his Swedish-language journal, *Saima*, established in 1844, he spoke out forcefully against the continued Swedish cultural and linguistic hegemony in Finland. Not that Snellman did not appreciate Sweden. He was born in Stockholm of Finnish parents and spent his first seven years there. But he rejected its pale imitation in Finland. He forthrightly described the Swedish regime there as a "conquest" and "occupation" by an alien people for its own benefit, which had crippled the development of the native culture. While he appreciated that Sweden had brought Finland into the Western cultural orbit, he held that its debt had been amply paid in Finnish blood during Sweden's wars.

Snellman saw in the Finnish language the foundation of Finland's nationality and its bulwark against russification. He urged that it could and should supplant Swedish entirely, except as a tolerated local dialect on the coasts and islands. Finland's literature in Swedish, he held, lacked national character, which could find true expression only in the indigenous tongue. He accused Finland's Swedish-speaking upper classes of indifference to the needs of the people, when they should take the lead in unifying the nation.[26]

Together with most of the early Fennomanes, Snellman nonetheless wrote almost exclusively in Swedish, for the Swedish-speaking elite. Johannes Salminen has indeed described him as one of the great masters of *Swedish* prose in the nineteenth century. He never fully mastered Finnish. Still, as Salminen points out, enough of his followers would fennicize themselves that they would provide a unique example in Europe of a dominant linguistic minority that took the majority's needs to heart and acted accordingly.[27]

Snellman stoutly denied the argument that the day was still remote when Finnish could become an adequate vehicle for all official and cultural purposes and that to abandon Swedish would unfailingly lower the nation's cultural level. Still, it would take time and require devoted efforts, most notably by Pastor Gustaf Renvall and Elias Lönnrot, to combine the main regional dialects into a fully developed, standardized, and versatile language.[28]

Although Russian authorities initially favored the Fennomane movement, they became fearful, after the European revolutions in 1848–49, of the possible spread of radical ideas to the broader masses and beginning in 1850 they severely limited and censored publications in Finnish over the next four years. But there could be no turning back the national awakening.

Despite Fennomania, interest in Scandinavianism—above all its political liberalism—was meanwhile not lacking among the Finnish students. Indeed, at first the boundaries between the two movements were indistinct. Braving official disapproval, four Finnish students managed to attend the Scandinavian student meeting at Lund and Copenhagen in 1843, although one, a Fennomane, remained skeptical. All four were thereafter suspended from Helsingfors University.[29] How strong Scandinavian sentiment may have been in Finland at the time would be impossible to judge because of official censorship. But it cannot be discounted.

The coming of the Crimean War, beginning in the fall of 1853, brought all these forces into play.[30] In Sweden, it appeared that Finland's liberation and reunification with the old motherland lay within reach.

King Oscar I was of a cool, calculating, and secretive nature. In his youth he had confidentially expressed grave concern over Russia's power and ambitions, although up to now he had held to his father's "Policy of 1812."[31] He now played his cards carefully, knowing that the Baltic would be of great strategic importance. Already on 15 December 1853, anticipating war, Sweden-Norway and Denmark issued a joint declaration of neutrality, declaring their harbors, save only a few naval ports, open to the vessels of any belligerent power. The declaration clearly favored Britain and France, with their larger fleets, and it did not fail to draw protests from Russia.[32]

After their entry into the war in March 1854, Great Britain and especially Napoleon III's France showed a strong interest in a Baltic theater of operations and thus did their best to draw Sweden into the conflict. In secret negotiations they offered Oscar I the Åland Islands, where the newly constructed fortress at Bomarsund was Russia's advance base threateningly close to Stockholm. The king set as his conditions a guarantee of all of Finland, without which the Åland Islands would be untenable; Austria's participation in the war; and large subsidies. Even the siege and destruction of Bomarsund by the French in August 1854, which was clearly intended to force his hand, failed to move him. Already in early 1853, his foreign minister had told a Danish diplomat that if Sweden were to enter a war with Russia, it would do so as late as possible.[33]

The king privately busied himself with speculative war plans, while the liberal and radical press in Sweden called for intervention and the liberation of Finland. *Aftonbladet*, by far the most widely read Swedish newspaper, declared on 24 April 1854 that, as in the Thirty Years' War, the great powers of Europe now "draw the sword to defend a great and sacred principle" and that the Swedes now once again harkened to their heroic destiny. The radical *Folkets Röst* was particularly clamorous for intervention and inveighed against Sweden's "shameful" neutrality. It repeatedly proclaimed that "it would take no more than a word to call to our side all our Finnish brothers, poor in all but iron and heroism, to take up arms against the threatening colossus, who surely at our first appeal would rise

Oscar I, by K. T. Staaf (1858). At the onset of the Crimean War, Carl XIV Johan's son abandoned his father's close alliance with Russia and secretly planned for Sweden-Norway to intervene on the side of Britain and France when the time was right. Covertly he encouraged anti-Russian propaganda and agitation to regain Finland, seemingly oblivious of opinion there. (Courtesy of Svenskt Porträttarkiv, Stockholm.)

up as one man against Russian force and oppression," as it wrote on 13 May 1854. An anonymous pamphlet published in Gothenburg (Göteborg) in 1854 likewise declared:

It would be an eternal stain on the Swedish name were not every Swedish heart to pound with joy at the possibility of the liberation of Finland from the Russian yoke and were not the whole Swedish nation to rise up as one man if indeed they are called on to take part in the great struggle which our brothers on the other side of the Baltic are certain to wage against the "Northern giant."

Sven Eriksson has shown that Oscar I secretly encouraged and directed this agitation, not only in Sweden but abroad as well, clearly to prepare opinion for an intervention against Russia when the time was right. There was also enthusiasm for a war to revive Sweden's former military glory in conservative circles, most notably Crown Prince Carl (later Carl XV) and his coterie of young aristocratic "junkers."[34]

During that summer and the following one, the British and French carried on naval operations in the Baltic, using Swedish Fårösund as their main base and returning home during the winter months. They destroyed enemy shipping—almost all of it Finnish—and devastated points along the Finnish coast, most notably Brahestad (Raahe), Uleåborg (Oulu), and Lovisa (Loviisa), arousing bitter public indignation and spirited local resistance. Aside from the destruction of Bomarsund, they accomplished little directly, and by September 1854 the British and French began their main offensive against Russia in the Crimea. For the time being, activist ardor cooled in Sweden. The allies' Baltic operations nevertheless contributed significantly to their ultimate victory by tying down large Russian forces in the north that could otherwise have been sent to the Crimea.[35]

Piedmont-Sardinia joined the allies in January 1855, to gain a place at the eventual peace table. In February, the energetic Lord Palmerston became British prime minister, Emperor Nicholas I died, and was followed by his son, Alexander II. By September, the Russians, after a nearly yearlong siege, scuttled their Black Sea fleet and abandoned Sebastopol. The allies looked once again to the Baltic and to Sweden. Oscar I now felt the time was ripe.

Activist interest in Sweden revived as Russia's defeat seemed imminent. A. I. Ståhl (pseudonym for L. T. Öberg) came out with a belligerently russophobic collection of verse. "While the Britons over their dead / sweep their flag, proud and free, / and France (may heaven give its grace!) / is our hope and fate, / what do we?," demanded the fiery "Talis Qualis" in

1855. Meanwhile, the most passionate appeal for action now came from the Finn Emil von Qvanten, who after various adventures in the Far East and South Africa, had established himself in Sweden in 1853.[36]

Writing under the pseudonym "Peder Särkilax," von Qvanten brought out in 1855 a two-part tract titled *Skandinavism och Fennomani*—Scandinavianism and Fennomania—in which he sought to reconcile the two movements and direct them both toward the liberation of his homeland.[37] Like liberals throughout the West, von Qvanten saw the ongoing conflict as the unavoidable, fateful showdown between two totally incompatible worlds: Eastern barbarism, backwardness, and despotism versus Western freedom, enlightenment, and progress. Russia, with its unlimited lust for conquest, must be contained and expelled from its western outposts. No compromise was possible, for a lenient peace would uphold the "inner Russia" of reactionaries everywhere in Europe. Bordering on the Russian colossus, Sweden and Norway should be especially concerned. Should Sweden now join the Western alliance, or was it prepared to become a "Russian" province, like Finland?

The Finns, with their Western cultural heritage, were now joined to a people with completely alien values: "in Russia slavish despotism, an inheritance from Asia, in Finland free Germanic institutions, the centuries-old motherly gift from Sweden." Having seized Finland from Sweden by "treachery and force," the Russians slowly but surely sought to eradicate its Western traditions. After 1809 the Finns, abandoned by Sweden, had nowhere to turn but to their own roots. From the need to create national feeling and solidarity arose the Fennomane movement, since "five-sixths" of the nation spoke Finnish. Even under Sweden, Finns had shown distinctive characteristics. Von Qvanten disagreed with Snellman by maintaining that Finland's literature in Swedish was truly Finnish in the spirit revealed by the *Kalevala* and native folk poetry and song. If the Finns had shown little enthusiasm for Scandinavianism, this was not due only to Russian oppression but to their realization that they had their own path to follow.

Von Qvanten understood how Fennomania could cause confusion and alarm in Sweden, but he insisted that a national Finnish spirit was neither unnecessary nor ungrateful toward the Swedish cultural heritage. The movement was headed by idealistic Swedish speakers and thus demonstrated the strong sense of nationality shared by both language groups. Some of the extreme Fennomanes, von Qvanten admitted, had gone too far in questioning any further need for Swedish in Finland. He believed, however, that this extremism would be only a passing phase and saw no reason why Finland should not have two languages. Even so, he pointed out, the extreme Fennomanes sought no more than the uniformity in language that other countries—including Sweden since 1809—required.

Returning to the war, von Qvanten urged that it was vital that Sweden intervene. The union with Norway did not provide sufficient security. Sweden would be of decisive importance for an allied offensive in the Baltic, with its strategic coastline, its army of fifty thousand men, and not least its skerry fleet (*skärgårdsflotta*) of shallow-draft vessels for close inshore operations. Most important of all, Sweden's entry into the war would give heart to the oppressed Finns, long kept ignorant under strict censorship, and open their eyes to the true nature of the momentous struggle of West versus East. The British and French, after their wanton depredations, could never accomplish this.

Responding to those who believed the Finns were contented with their present status, von Qvanten held that only officially approved views could be freely expressed in Finland, whereas—for good reasons—his countrymen were far less satisfied than they showed. He did not deny that Finland had made some progress since 1809, but it could hardly compare in that regard with the West, including Sweden. A free Finland would have made far more.

But if Finland were liberated, what should become of it? Over the past half century the Finns had developed their own sense of nationhood and would never consent to returning to their old status as a Swedish "province." The Fennomanes would oppose a reunified state in which the Finnish-speaking element were submerged by a Swedish majority. The Finns' national feeling would not disappear. If they were to fight, it must be for their own independence. At the same time, von Qvanten rejected the idea of a completely independent Finnish state, too weak to resist Russian influence and eventual reconquest. The solution would thus be Finland as part of a freely concluded Nordic dynastic union, together with Norway and hopefully in time Denmark, strong enough to resist outside threats. Von Qvanten recognized the flaws in the existing Norwegian-Swedish union and proposed new ground rules for an all-Nordic union. Meanwhile, if decisively defeated and pushed back, the Russians should become disillusioned with their tsars' policy of conquest and demand civilization and freedom for themselves, after which they would carry these blessings into the interior of Asia.[38]

Von Qvanten's appeal gives evidence that there was now growing skepticism in Sweden toward intervention, largely due to resentments aroused by the Fennomanes, together with the thorny problem of the future of a liberated Finland. Kari Tarkiainen has pointed out that Swedish reactions to Fennomania still remain largely unexplored. Before the 1850s, he holds, most Swedes had hardly even been aware that most Finns spoke a different language. As ever more reports showed opposition in Finland to Swedish involvement, disillusionment set in among liberals and Scandinavianists. As early as 12 January 1855, *Aftonbladet* wrote indignantly that the Finns were welcome to their enthusiasm for Russia and that if their Fennomania should cause them to forget all their previous history and culture, acquired from Sweden, "we Swedes should not grieve too much over it." Even A. I. Arwidsson wrote to a friend early that year that he now wished only for peace, for Finland would be of no benefit to Sweden with its "petit-bour-geois Fennomane arrogance . . . filled with hostility toward Sweden."[39]

The most powerful reaction to von Qvanten's pamphlet came meanwhile from none other than August Sohlman, one of Sweden's most steadfast and prominent liberals and Scandinavianists, first anonymously in *Aftonbladet*, then as a pamphlet under his own name. "Peder Särkilax," he conceded, had given the most unbiased presentation thus far by a Finn. Still, it was one-sided and called for examination from a Swedish perspective. While Sohlman recognized the legitimacy of the Finnish movement per se, he took Särkilax to task for downplaying the extreme Fennomanes' manifest hostility toward the Swedish heritage and language. Swedes could hardly view with equanimity efforts to arouse among the Swedish element itself in Finland "antipathy toward everything Swedish and create an altogether false conception of the past relationship between Sweden and Finland."

Sohlman dismissed the ultra-Fennomanes' attempts to depict pre-Christian Finland as a highly developed society suppressed by the Swedish conquest. "Young Sweden," he wrote, had also heard "the powerful voice of nationality" and resented such accusations. Before the Swedes came, there was no Finland or Finnish nationality. Finland was "a creation of Swedish culture," even though Sweden had never sought to impede the development of the Finnish language. Finland's literature was, he claimed, essentially the work of authors of Swedish background writing in Swedish, and showing no distinctive Finnish characteristics. What had been writ-ten in Finnish since 1809 was of little value. To believe that "the Finnish nationality is capable alone of sustaining culture and social life in Finland," was a dangerous illusion.

Waxing hot, Sohlman declared that no people had shown itself so in-capable of an independent existence as the Finns, indeed as "the entire Tschudic race." If they were to cut themselves off from Swedish culture, they would revert to barbarism. The revered *Kalevala*, Sohlman claimed, was as nothing compared to the Scandinavian myths of gods and heroes.

Finnish poetry was weak and nebulous, revealing only a "monotonous melancholy," in stark contrast to the bold and enterprising Scandinavian spirit. While he hoped for Finland's liberation from the Russian yoke, Sohlman urged that it then be joined to Sweden as a self-government region, like Slesvig-Holstein under the Danish crown.[40]

Such a solution, Sohlman recognized, raised the question of reactions in Norway, Sweden's partner within the dual monarchy. He cited a recent article in *Norsk Maanedsskrift* by the foremost Norwegian historian of the time, Peter Andreas Munch, agreeing that the Finns, without Swedish culture and left to their own devices, would revert to "Tschudish" backwardness, that it was in the interest of all of Europe that Russia be weakened, and that Finland together with Sweden in an enlarged union would be no threat to Norway's position. Some Norwegians indeed believed that an independent Finland, together eventually with Denmark, would dilute Sweden's preponderance within a future union. Still, others feared that Norway's status would thereby be weakened.

In the balance, the Norwegians, who did not share the Swedes' nostalgic dreams of military glory or their traditional russophobia, were skeptical, if not hostile, toward a Swedish intervention against Russia in Finland's behalf. This difference in views stirred up Swedish resentments against the troublesome union partner. In Denmark, too, attitudes were notably cool toward a Swedish reconquest of Finland. Even in Sweden itself, there were growing misgivings in liberal circles that Finland, if reincorporated into Sweden, would bolster the forces of conservatism through an influx of "half-Russian barons" into the Noble Estate of the Riksdag.[41] Within less than two years the Scandinavianists' high hopes for Finland went up in smoke.

But what of opinion toward a Swedish intervention within Finland itself? It was as von Burghausen ("Suomalainen") wrote in 1842: what could the Swedes, or for that matter the Finns themselves, know about the true state of affairs there? It is nonetheless evident that sanguine expectations, both in Sweden and abroad, that the Finns would rise up in rebellion against their Russian masters at the first sight of the Swedish colors were overly—indeed wildly—optimistic.

Faint though they might be, any signs of opposition in Finland raised suspicion and alarm among the Finnish authorities and the Russian government. Only the émigrés in Sweden could express their views freely. To put Russian fears to rest, official reports protested the overwhelming loyalty of the Finns to the empire and their determined opposition to any

Swedish intervention. Even in the Swedish-speaking coastal districts, it was stated, the peasantry were determined to resist any Swedish attack and defend the benefits they now enjoyed.[42]

Behind Finnish imperial loyalism lay various motives. There was unquestionably a sincere attachment to the empire among much of the Swedish-speaking element, since Finland now enjoyed greater economic benefits than previously under Swedish rule. Aside from the Russian governor-general, only Finns of the Lutheran faith were permitted to hold official appointments in Finland, whereas they were eligible to serve throughout the Russian empire. There were far wider opportunities than before for official careers, both within Finland and beyond. More than three thousand Finns served as officers in the Russian military forces during the imperial period, including several generals and admirals, and two Finns even served as governors of Russian Alaska. There was a large Finnish colony in St. Petersburg. The Swedish-language poet Zacharias Topelius, a Fennomane and staunch loyalist, lauded the empire in verse, "from Åland's skerries to Sitka's—one realm alone." The great peasant majority had practical reasons for contentment under the present regime.

According to Juhani Paasivirta, the bitterness caused by the ravages of the British fleet during the war inspired a stronger imperial loyalism than had ever existed since 1809. Significantly their principal victims were Swedish-speaking inhabitants of the coasts and small seaports. Not least, although opinion in Sweden sought to downplay the Fennomane movement, its hostility toward a new Swedish domination was a potent factor.[43] In sum, most Finns believed they had little cause for complaint and were well aware that they enjoyed milder treatment than the Russians themselves, even though their special status remained vulnerable.

Above all it was a matter of sober realism for Finns to wish fervently that Sweden would refrain from intervention. War would bring devastation to the land. They would moreover find themselves confronted with a terrible dilemma: it seemed unthinkable to bear arms against their Swedish brethren, while to aid them would unfailingly bring retribution through the loss of Finland's autonomy and its complete incorporation as a Russian province. Even if Sweden might conceivably regain Finland, it would never be able to hold it in the long run and the result would be the same. To turn against Russia would be political suicide. As for the students at the Imperial Alexander University in Helsingfors, most of whom were preparing for official careers in church or state, no matter how liberal, Scandinavian, or apprehensive of Fennomane hostility some of them might feel, they were well advised to keep such views to themselves.

The loyalists were no less patriotic than the russophobe exiles in Sweden and their quiet sympathizers in Finland. Each group sought their nation's ultimate freedom but differed as to how it should be achieved. Realism, patriotism, and morality in such situations can be relative concepts, as Gunnar Artéus reminds us. The émigrés believed that Finland *could* be liberated by Sweden and the Western allies and thereafter remain secure within a strengthened Nordic union. The loyalists saw as the only realistic course unwavering loyalty to the empire in hopes of gaining ever greater autonomy, while fostering their nation's own cultural uniqueness. Finland, Topelius wrote—prophetically—to a friend in 1855, must above all be spared from direct incorporation into Russia and "await the day when the Russian colossus will collapse from within, for only then will its time have come." There can be little doubt in retrospect that the loyalists were justified in fearing a war that would have been ruinous for Finland, in both the short and long run.[44]

The bitterness aroused among the Fennomane loyalists by the attacks of their émigré countrymen would be forcefully expressed by J. V. Snellman in 1858, two years after the Crimean War ended. He branded as cowardly and unpatriotic the "pens—persons we can hardly call them—" who claimed to speak for "Young Finland." A. I. Arwidsson, who in Stockholm had largely inspired his own devotion to the Finnish national movement, Snellman treated with cautious respect, but for the rest he had only contempt. Seldom have émigrés served their countries well, he declared. "He who can compromise everything and everyone, protecting only himself, lacks the moral nerve that gives power to those who are capable of acting." Those of "manly character" recognized it as their duty "to remain where Providence has placed them, to endure what they must, and, whatever the circumstances may be, to find within them room for useful activity."[45]

The end of the Crimean War came as an anticlimax for Oscar I. In November 1855, Napoleon III sent General François Canrobert, the hero of Sebastopol, on a triumphal visit to Stockholm. Oscar I presented him with an ambitious war plan for a combined British-French-Swedish-Danish offensive against St. Petersburg the following year. Secret negotiations followed. As a preliminary step toward intervention, Sweden concluded the November Treaty with Britain and France, guaranteeing the dual monarchy of Sweden and Norway against territorial encroachment by Russia.

Unbeknown to the king, however, the French emperor was already seeking to end the war and had sent Canrobert to Stockholm to bring further pressure on Alexander II to come to terms. Now faced with the threat of intervention by both Sweden and Austria, Russia gave way and the Peace of Paris was concluded on 30 March 1856. Oscar was bitterly disappointed after unwittingly having helped to deprive himself of the opportunity he had eagerly awaited. The most he was able to gain in the peace settlement was the demilitarization of the Åland Islands.[46]

The Crimean War—the war that no responsible European statesman really wanted—had profound consequences for European international relations. It brought a definitive end to the Concert of Europe established at Vienna in 1814–15. Both Russia and Britain now largely isolated themselves from European affairs for a generation or more, clearing the way for the continental wars and national unifications of the 1860s and early 1870s, the period dominated by Napoleon III, Cavour, and Bismarck.[47]

Sweden's near-intervention meant the end of Carl XIV Johan's "Policy of 1812," but established neutrality ever more firmly as the bedrock of Swedish foreign policy. Thereafter, Swedish interest in Finland declined. As time passed, Alexander II's liberal regime in both Finland and Russia lessened Swedish anti-Russian prejudices. The Swedes became ever more concerned with their own internal questions and, turning westward once again with Scandinavian affairs.

The Finns turned eastward as Alexander II's regime offered new hope for increasing autonomy, including measures favoring the Finnish language. In attacking the Finnish émigrés in 1858, Snellman described them as belonging to the privileged Swedish-speaking element that looked down upon the Finnish-speaking masses and feared that they themselves would be overshadowed. There was nevertheless only one direction for the nation to go, Snellman proclaimed, and those who refused to recognize it would have to give way.[48]

Fennomania during its earlier phase had enjoyed broad support among the elite, even among those who, envisioning a bilingual Finland, made no effort to learn Finnish. Emil von Qvanten, for instance, regretted during the 1840s that he had not grown up in the Finnish wilderness with the Finnish language. But already by then a fissure appeared between the moderate and the extreme Fennomanes who rejected everything Swedish. The pamphlet debate during the 1840s and above all the stresses of the Crimean War exacerbated the split between Fennomane loyalism and Western-oriented liberalism. The Fennomanes accused the liberals of disloyalty and Scandinavianist sympathies. Mutual antipathy led by the 1860s to the "Suecomane" movement to protect Swedish language and culture in Finland. The conflict between the two linguistic camps would bedevil

Finnish internal politics down to World War II. But to this day Finland remains bilingual.[49]

The reaction of the Fennomanes against the Swedish element following the Crimean War raises the question of just how strong liberal Scandinavianism actually was in Finland at its height. To be sure, it appeared to fade after the war. Modern Finnish historians have generally dismissed it as relatively insignificant. But loyalist Fennomane and Russian reactions suggest that it may have been more widespread than it has since appeared. As Russia's defeat in the war appeared imminent, von Qvanten's ("Särkilax") Nordic vision of Finland's future aroused some ferment, not least among liberal Fennomanes, especially at the university in Helsingfors. Scandinavianism—or more properly Nordism—would leave its distinctive imprint upon Finnish liberalism, as it developed by the end of the century, language-neutral but most strongly represented among the Swedish-speaking elite. Political liberalism and linguistic nationalism, previously allied, parted company, at least down to the end of the century.[50] Looking ahead, it would be the Swedish element that would most resolutely resist Emperor Nicholas II's Russification policy in Finland after 1899, while most of the Fennomanes—the so-called "Old Finns"—still clung to their policy of loyalty and compliance.

During the second half of the nineteenth century Finland made considerable progress materially and intellectually. But it may be asked, *how* much progress? After the fall of the Soviet Union and the end of President Urho Kekkonen's policy of accommodation, this question has again come to the fore. Opposing Professor Matti Klinge's favorable treatment of Finland's imperial period, his colleague at Helsinki University, Docent Marti Häikiö—echoing Emil von Qvanten ("Särkilax") in 1855—has maintained that Finland's progress during that era had remained far more modest than in Sweden, Norway, or other Western countries, or than it would have been in an independent Finland. "For half a century," Häikiö wrote in 1999, "Finland descended into the same torpor as the eastern European countries after World War II." Klinge and Häikiö thereafter debated this point. A completely independent Finland was, however, virtually inconceivable in 1809, and it is doubtful whether its unique culture could ever have developed as vigorously as it did had it remained part of Sweden.[51]

There would be a brief sequel seven years after the Crimean War ended that showed that russophobia, together with dreams of both a Greater Scandinavia and of military glory had not yet entirely died out in Sweden. In 1863, the Poles rose up in a second rebellion against Russian rule and, confident of liberal sympathies in the West, looked abroad for help. In Sweden there was strong liberal opinion to intervene, based on the optimistic belief that Great Britain and France would do likewise. It was hoped, meanwhile, that the valiant Poles would arouse unrest in Finland as well, opening the way for its liberation. Once again, Finnish émigrés, above all Emil von Qvanten, agitated in Stockholm. King Carl XV was strongly tempted to act and secretly proposed a war plan to Napoleon III.

But the Riksdag and, in particular, the king's ministers were far more cautious and in the end issued only a only vague statement of sympathy. The British and French governments did no more. Russia, with support from Prussia, crushed the Polish uprising. Nonetheless, there was consternation and alarm in the Fennomane camp. J. V. Snellman feared that Sweden's willingness to intervene in the crisis would determine whether or not Finland would be invaded, which would bring sheer disaster. While harshly penalizing the rebellious Poles, Alexander II rewarded the Finns for their loyalty in 1863 by convening the Lantdag for the first time since 1809, after which it would continue to meet regularly. The same year, by imperial decree, Finnish was made the second official language in Finland, coequal with Swedish.[52]

The failure of Sweden-Norway to come to Denmark's aid in its German war in 1864, resulting in its loss of Slesvig-Holstein, is regarded as the deathblow of political Scandinavianism. As far as Finland was concerned, it was already moribund. No one could still seriously believe that the Finns longed to be reunited with Sweden and were prepared to rise up in rebellion to throw off the Russian yoke.

Still, the old bonds between Sweden and Finland would again be reaffirmed by the Swedish volunteers who joined the White forces in fighting for Finland's complete independence during the Finnish Civil War of 1918 and by those who served in Finland's defense against the Soviet Union during the Winter War of 1939–40. Since World War II, Finland, Sweden, and the other Scandinavian lands have been drawn ever closer together through Nordic Cooperation and more recently the European Union. There is now a freer flow of persons, products, and ideas across the Baltic than at any time since 1809.

Notes

1. See my *Scandinavia in the Revolutionary Era, 1760–1815* (Minneapolis, 1986), 300–301. In keeping with the usage of the time, I employ the Swedish names for Finnish towns. I also use the older spellings for monarchs' names, e.g., *Carl* for *Karl*, *Gustaf* for *Gustav*, etc.

2. See Carl von Bonsdorff, *Opinioner och stämningar i Finland 1804–1814* (Helsingfors, 1918); Päiviö Tommila, *La Finlande dans la politique européene dans 1809–1815* (Helsinki, 1962).

3. Bonsdorff, *Opinioner och stämningar*, 292–93; my *Scandinavia in the Revolutionary Era*, 302, 292–93, and "Russia and the Problem of Sweden-Finland," *East European Quarterly* 5 (1972): 431–55; Gunnar Artéus, "Realism, patriotism, moral. Den finska samhällseliten mellan Sverige och Ryssland 1713–1809," in Tapani Suominen and Anders Björnsson, eds., *Det hotade landet och det skyddade. Sverige och Finland från 1500-talet till våra dagar* (Stockholm, 1999), 113–14.

4. Kari Tarkiainen, "Svenska finlandsuppfattningar under tvåhundra år," in Suominen and Björnsson, *Det hotade landet*, 69.

5. See my *Scandinavia in the Revolutionary Era*, 278–79.

6. Wilhelm Odelberg, *Viceamiral Carl Olof Cronstedt* (Helsingfors, 1954); Max Engman, *Lejonet och dubbelörnen. Finlands imperiella decennier 1830–1890* (Stockholm, 2000), 9; Bo Hult, "Inledning," in Tapanani and Björnsson, *Det hotade landet*, 15–28; Tarkiainen, "Svenska finlandsuppfattningar," 17, 73–74.

7. Esaias Tegnér, *Samlade skrifter*, ed. Ewert Wrangel & Fredrik Böök, rev. ed. (Stockholm, 1919), 2:14–16, 35–38, 64–77.

8. My *Scandinavia in the Revolutionary Era*, 317–21.

9. Ibid., 348–53; my *Sweden and Visions of Norway: Politics and Culture, 1814–1905* (Carbondale, Ill., 2003), 28.

10. See Julius Clausen, *Skandinavismen historisk fremstillet* (Copenhagen, 1900), esp. p. 59; cf. my article "The Swedish Succession Crises of 1809 and 1810" in this volume, and *Sweden and Visions of Norway*, 59–61; Åke Holmberg, *Skandinavismen i Sverige vid 1800-talets mitt* (Gothenburg, 1946), 66–68, 75–76.

11. See, for ex., John Howes Gleason, *The Genesis of Russophobia in Great Britain: A Study of the Interaction of Policy and Opinion* (Cambridge, Mass., 1950); Kingsley Martin, *The Triumph of Lord Palmerston: A Study of Public Opinion in England before the Crimean War*, 2nd. ed. (London, 1963); Sven Eriksson, *Svensk diplomati och tidningspress under Krimkriget* (Stockholm, 1939), 4–6.

12. *Finland in Sveriges diktning*, ed. Ruben G:son Berg (Stockholm, 1903), vi, 103–12. Cf. Tarkiainen, "Svenska finlandsuppfattningar," 67.

13. See esp. Holmberg, *Skandinavismen i Sverige*, 66–68.

14. Kent Zetterberg, "Sverige och drömmen om Finland och Norden under 1800-talet. Reflexioner om skandinavismen, det nationalla uppvaknandet i Finland och Sveriges relationer till Finland och Ryssland," in Suominen & Björnsson, *Det hotade landet*, 102–3; Matti Klinge, "Rysshatet," in his *Från lojalism till Rysshat* (Helsingfors, 1988), 256; Tegnér, *Samlade skrifter*, 9:149; Gustaf Henrik Mellin, *Sveriges sista strid. Fantastiskt nattstycke* (Stockholm, 1840). Cf. Tarkiainen, "Svenska finlandsuppfattningar," 72–74.

15. This polemic battle is well summarized by Matti Klinge's "Nordens säkerhet och Finlands framtid," in his *Från lojalism till rysshat*, 154–67. See also Tarkiainen, "Svenska finlandsuppfattningar," 74–77. The pamphlets themselves (except for "Paavo

Suomalainen's," see below), are bound together in a single volume at the Royal Library in Stockholm, under Hwasser's title *Om Allians-Tragtaten* (See note 17, below). They were also published in German as *Finnlands Gegenwart und Zukunft*, trans. R. Adolf Regnér (Stockholm, 1842), also at the Royal Library.

16. Tarkiainen, "Svenska finlandsuppfattningar," 72; Carl Michael Runeberg, *Finland under Orientaliska kriget* (Helsingfors, 1962), 216–17.

17. [Israel Hwasser,] *Om Allians-Tragtaten emellan Sverige och Ryssland År 1812. Politisk betraktelse öfver Nordens nuvarande ställning* (Stockholm, 1838), esp. 15–21, 29, 38–40, 76–77, 83–90, 99–105. Cf. Klinge, "Nordens säkerhet," 154–57.

18. *Finsk biografisk handbok*, ed. Tor Carpelan, 2 (Helsingfors, 1903), 123–26. Cf. Liisa Castrén, *Adolf Ivar Arwidsson isänmaalisena herättäjänä* (Helsinki, 1951), German summary, 430–41; Eirik Hornborg, *Finlands hävder*, 4 (Helsingfors, 1933), 101–2; John H. Wuorinen, *Nationalism in Modern Finland* (New York, 1931), 47–55; Eino Jutikkala, *A History of Finland* (London, 1962), 201–2, 203.

19. Pekka Kuoharinen [A. I. Arwidsson], *Finland och dess framtid. I anledning av skriften: Om Allians-Tractaten emellen Sverige och Ryssland År 1812* (Stockholm, 1838), esp. 9–23, 26, 36–41, 61–64. Cf. Klinge, "Nordens säkerhet," 157.

20. Erik Gustaf Geijer, *Samlade skrifter*, ed. John Landquist, new ed., 8 (Stockholm, 1928), esp. 310–25, 600; Israel Hwasser, *Om Borgå Landtdag och Finlands Ställning 1812* (Uppsala, 1839), esp. 3, 35, 54–58. Cf. Klinge, "Nordens säkerhet," 160–61.

21. [Olli Kekäläinen,] *Finlands nuvarande Stats-Författning* (Stockholm, 1841), esp. 25–28, 35, 40–43, 47–48; Klinge, "Nordens säkerhet," 161–63.

22. Paavo Suomalainen, *Ett och annat om Finland* (Stockholm, 1842), esp. 3–10. Cf. Klinge, "Nordens säkerhet," 163–65; "Adolf Ivar Arwidsson eller Johan Jacob Nordström?," *Historiska och litteraturhistoriska studier*, 43 (1968): 55–86; "Diskussion: Kring Adolf Iwar Arwidsson och Johan Jakob Nordström," *Historisk tidskrift för Finland* 69 (1984): 18–52, 110–13.

23. Kuoharinen, *Finland och dess framtid*, 36–37, 61–64; Kekäläinen, *Finlands nuvarande ställning*, 47–49. Overall, on the rise of the ethnolinguistic movement, see Wuorinen, *Nationalism*.

24. Bonsdorff, *Opinioner och stämningar*, 224; Matti Klinge, *Kejsartiden*, Finlands historia, 3 (Helsingfors, 1996), 38; on the Finnish elite, Kaarlo Wirilander, *Herrskapsfolk. Ståndspersoner i Finland 1721–1870* (Stockholm, 1982).

25. See Berg, *Finland i Sveriges diktning*, iii; Tarkiainen, "Svenska finlandsuppfattningar," 72–73, 78–79. It was common practice at that time for the Swedish-speaking officers to assign Swedish names to their soldiers, even if they spoke no Swedish. On the critical role of the university and its students in Finland's cultural and political development, see Matti Klinge et al., *Kejserliga Alexanders universitet 1808–1917*, Helsingfors universitet, 2 (Helsingfors, 1989).

26. A useful anthology of Snellman's writings, well introduced, is *Snellman i urval*, ed. and introd. Johannes Salminen (Helsingfors, 1981), esp. 7–30, 70–75, 79, 81–91. His collected writings during this period are found in Johan Vilhelm Snellman, *Samlade arbeten*, ed. Kari Selén, 12 vols. (Helsingfors, 1992–98), 4 (1844–45) and 5 (1846–47).

Cf. Hornborg, *Finlands hävder*, 4:124–33; Wuorinen, *Nationalism*, 87–94; Jutikkala, *History of Finland*, 202–6.

27. Salminen, *Snellman i urval*, 5:11–12.

28. Ibid., 86–91; Klinge, *Kejsartiden*, 40–41.

29. Hugo Pipping, "Finlands ställning till skandinavismen," Svenska Litteratur-sälskapet i Finland, *Förhandlingar och uppsatser* 34 (Helsingfors, 1920): 130–95; Runar Johansson, "Skandinavismen i Finland," *Skrifter utgivna av svenska litteratursällskapet i Finland*, 214: *Historiska och litteraturhistoriska studier* 6 (Helsingfors, 1930): 217–333, esp. 222–33; Mikko Juva, "Skandinavismens inverkan på de politiska strömningarna i Finland," *Historisk tidskrift* (Swedish) 77 (1957): 330–37.

30. On the war in general, see, for ex., Trevor Royle, *Crimea: The Great Crimean War, 1854–1856* (New York, 2000); for a good, brief summary, see Agatha Ramm, "The Crimean War," in *New Cambridge Modern History*, 10: *The Zenith of European Power, 1830–70* (Cambridge, 1960), 468–92.

31. See Alma Söderhjelm and C. F. Palmstierna, *Oscar I* (Stockholm, 1944), 185–87; Eriksson, *Svensk diplomati*, pp. 15–17; Allan Jansson, *1844–1872*, Den svenska utrikes-politikens historia, 3:3 (Stockholm, 1961), 86–89; Carl Hallendorff, *Oscar I och Karl XV* (Stockholm, 1923), esp. 73–91, 115–35.

32. Jansson, *1844–1872*, 78–79, 92–93. Cf. Emanuel Halicz, *Danish Neutrality during the Crimean War* (Odense, 1977).

33. Jansson, *1844–1872*, 89. The best brief accounts of the Crimean War in the North are Edgar Anderson, "The Scandinavian Area and the Crimean War in the Baltic," *Scandinavian Studies* 41 (1969): 263–75, and "The Crimean War in the Baltic Area," *Journal of Baltic Studies* 5 (1974): 339–61, based on an evidently book-length manuscript that was never published. See also Juhani Paasivirta, *Finland and Europe: International Crises in the Period of Autonomy, 1808–1914* (Minneapolis, 1981), 87–96.

34. Jussi T. Lappalainen, "Oscar I:s planer 1854–56," *Militärhistorisk tidskrift* (1984): 5–19; Eriksson, *Svensk diplomati*, 30–60; Basil Greenhill and Ann Giffard, *The British Assault on Finland, 1854–1855: A Forgotten Naval War* (London, 1988), 148–49; [Fredrik Theodor Blomstrand,] *Kriget i Finska Viken År 1854* (Götheborg, 1854), 26–27; Carl Michael Runeberg, *Finland under Orientaliska kriget* (Helsingfors, 1962), 316–18; Holmberg, *Skandinavismen i Sverige*, 50–52, 232–33; Johansson, "Skandinavismen i Finland," 235; Jansson, *1844–1872*, 90–91. See also, for ex., *Aftonbladet*, 6 Mar., 4, 5 Apr. 1854; *Folkets Röst*, 1 Feb., 8, 11 Mar., 22 Apr., 6, 13 May 1854.

35. See Hornborg, *Finlands hävder*, 4:139–45; Paasivirta, *Finland and Europe*, 96–97; Klinge, *Kejsartiden*, 170–73, 176–79. Cf. Greenhill and Giffard, *British Assault on Finland*; M. Borodkin, *Kriget vid Finlands kuster 1854–1855* (Helsingfors, 1905; Russian original, *Voina 1854–1855 gg. na finskom poberezh'e*, St. Petersburg, 1904). In his novel, *Regnbågen* (Helsingfors, 1916), the Finnish-Swedish author Runar Schildt gave a fictional account of the burning of Lovisa.

36. Berg, *Finland i Sveriges diktning*, vi, 106–7; A. I. Ståhl, *Svensk och rysk* (Stockholm, 1855).

37. Peder Särkilax [Emil von Qvanten,] *Fennomani och Skandinavism*, 2 parts

(Stockholm, 1855). Cf. Cecilia Bååth-Holmberg, "Emil von Qvanten. En lefnadsskild-ring," *Svensk tidskrift* 3 (1893): 161–80, 207–44, 278–99.

38. Särkilax, *Fennomani och Skandiavismen*, esp. part 1:5–6, 15, 17–24, 32–34, 41–45, 54, part 2:3–4, 6, 8, 10, 12, 15–17, 21–23, 26–36, 60–61. Cf. Jansson, *1844–1872*, 66; Johans-son, "Skandinavismen i Finland," 149–51.

39. Johansson, "Skandinavismen i Finland," 253–56; Runeberg, *Finland under Orientaliska kriget*, 321–22, 327–28; Tarkiainen, "Svenska finlandsuppfattningar," 79; Zetterberg, "Sverige och drömmen om Finland och Norden," 104; Söderhjelm and Palmstierna, *Oscar I*, 397–403.

40. *Aftonbladet*, 5, 23 May 1855; August Sohlman, *Det unge Finland. En kultur-historisk betraktelse* (Stockholm, 1855), esp. 9–26, 32–43, 55–58. Cf. Johansson, "Skan-dinavismen i Finland," 252; Runeberg, *Finland under Orientaliska kriget*, 324; Juva, "Skandinavismens inverkan," 337–38.

41. Sohlman, *Det unga Finland*, 55–60. Cf. Johansson, "Skandinavismen i Finland," 236; Runeberg, *Finland under Orientaliska kriget*, 335–47.

42. Jansson, *1844–1872*, 97; Holmberg, *Skandinavismen i Sverige*, 233, 216–20, 240–42, 310–12; Johansson, "Skandinavismen i Finland," 237–48.

43. Engman, *Lejonet och dubbelörnen*, esp. 24, 26; Matti Klinge, *Krig, kvinnor, konst* (Helsingfors, 1997) and *Den politiske Runeberg* (Stockholm, 2004); Johansson, "Skandinavismen i Finland," 247–48, 252–53, 271, 332–33; Runeberg, *Finland under Orientaliska kriget*, 207–28, 314.

44. Artéus, "Realism, patriotism, moral," 118–19; Hornborg, *Finlands hävder*, 4:146–47; Johansson, "Skandinavismen i Finland," 247; Runeberg, *Finland under Orientaliska kriget*, 318–19, 331–33; Paasivirta, *Finland and Europe*, 96–101. On Topelius, cf. Matti Klinge, *Idyll och hot. Zacharias Topelius—hans politik och idéer* (Helsingfors and Stockholm, 2000).

45. J. V. Snellman, "Finska emigrationen i Sverige," in Salminen, *Snellman i urval*, 123–39, esp. 124–25, 127, 133, 138–39. Cf. Juva, "Skandinavismens inverkan," 338–39.

46. Jansson, *1844–1872*, 104–9; Söderhjelm and Palmstierna, *Oscar I*, 384–89; Lap-palainen, "Oscar I:s planer."

47. On the overall impact of the war for Europe, see, for ex., Gordon Craig, "The System of Alliances and the Balance of Power," in *New Cambridge Modern History*, 10, esp. 267–73.

48. Snellman, "Finska emigrationen i Sverige," 139.

49. Johansson, "Skandinavismen i Finland," 222, 228, 272; Bååth-Holmberg, "Emil von Qvanten," 219; Paasivirta, *Finland and Europe*, 99, 102–3. Cf. Pekka Kalevi Hä-mäläinen, *Nationalitetskampen och språkstriden i Finland 1917–1939* (Helsingfors, 1968).

50. See, for ex., Klinge, *Från lojalism till rysshat*, 262, and *Kejsartiden*, 180–81; Bååth-Holmberg, "Emil von Qvanten," 225–26; Hornborg, *Finlands hävder*, 4:152–53; Pipping, "Finlands ställning till skandiavismen," esp. 195; Johansson, "Skandinavis-men i Finland," 222–25, 273–74, 33; Juva, "Skandinavismens inverkan," 329–41, esp. 337–41; Wuorinen, *Nationalism*, 109–10; Paasivirta, *Finland and Europe*, 99, 102–3.

51. Martti Häikiö, "En förändrad syn på Finlands historia efter kalla krigets slut," in Suominen and Björnsson, *Det hotade landet*, 226–31. Cf. Klinge, *Kejsartiden;* Särkilax, *Fennomani och skandinavism*, 17–18; Engman, *Lejonet och dubbelörnen*, 18–21.

52. Jansson, *1844–1872*, 80–88; J. V. Snellman, "Krig eller fred för Finland," in Salminen, *Snellman i urval*, 144–58.

The Danish Agrarian Reforms, 1784–1814, and the Historians

In 1888, Edvard Holm brought out his still much-cited book, *Kampen om Landboreformerne i Danmark*.[1] By his title, the "conflict over the agrarian reforms," Holm meant the clash of opinion that preceded and contributed to the reforms initiated under Crown Prince Frederik's de facto regency, beginning in 1784. But the debate begun by Danish landowners, officials, and opinion makers did not end with the reform era itself. It was continued by Danish historians, who have pursued it with remarkable intensity and no small passion down to the present day.

In so doing, they have cultivated the field of agrarian history to an extent unequaled in the other Nordic countries and probably unsurpassed anywhere. That this should be so surely derives from the central place of the peasant question in Denmark's history. It has weighed heavily on the Danish historical conscience that in Denmark—alone among the Nordic lands—the peasantry had by the eighteenth century long since lost that ancient freedom which was the pride of their brethren elsewhere in the North and a model for enlightened Europe as a whole.

"In Denmark the freedom of the people existed in the widest sense in times of yore," the historian C.F. Allen wrote nostalgically in 1840. "The free-born peasants, at that time the only estate in the land, made law in free assembly and themselves resolved their own disputes."[2] This was the vision of a veritable Golden Age, seen against the background of the servitude into which the Danish peasants had fallen, first under the late-medieval *vornedskab* in the Sjælland (Zealand) island group, abolished in 1702, then under the *stavnsbånd* decreed, ostensibly for military reasons, in 1733 for the entire kingdom (except Bornholm and Amager). By the mid-eighteenth century, moreover, only about three percent of them remained freeholders.

By the same token, the abolition of the *stavnsbånd*, decreed in 1788, and the accompanying efforts of the crown to raise the peasants' social, economic, and cultural standing have naturally stood out as one of Denmark's proudest accomplishments and the symbol of its values as an emerging modern society.

In view of the sheer mass of the literature that has come out on the reform period, it might appear that only a foolhardy foreigner would rush in where Danish angels might fear to tread, and seek to describe this multifarious and never-ending debate. Be that as it may, it would appear to me that from its beginnings in the mid-eighteenth century, the "conflict over the agrarian reforms" has concerned itself above all with three fundamental questions. First, how bad were the "bad old days" before the reforms of 1784 to 1814? Secondly, what were the guiding motives of the reformers and of their opponents? And thirdly, how great a role did the actions of the government play in the amelioration of conditions among the peasantry?

The answers given to these questions through the nineteenth and twentieth centuries have reflected changing national concerns and sociopolitical ideologies, as well as shifting concepts of the potentialities and proper tasks of historical scholarship. What follows is a broad overview of the main trends and the most influential contributors.[3]

The main outlines of the debate were set already in the clash of opinion preceding and during the reform era itself. Advocates of peasant emancipation held an optimistic view of human nature and hence emphasized the juridical freedom of the *individual* as not only his or her natural right but as the essential basis for personal dignity and motivation for self-improvement, from which would derive benefits to both society and state. Their adversaries were pessimistic about the potentialities of human nature, at least when it came to the broader masses, and thus maintained that the *collective* good of state and society required that the peasantry remain subject to discipline, subordination, and compulsion under the paternalistic authority of their landlords, not least for their own welfare. As conservatives are wont to do, they regarded the proponents of emancipation as impractical dreamers, out of touch with actual conditions in the countryside.

The circle of individualism versus collectivism was completed by a significant cleavage within the pro-emancipation group, between those favoring a laissez-faire liberalism, who sought to counterbalance the freeing of the peasant from the *stavnsbånd* with the freeing of the landlord from any restraints on the disposition of his property, and those—most notably Count Christian Ditlev Reventlow and Christian Colbjørnsen—who managed to retain and extend controls over the landlord's property rights to preserve, by and large, peasant lands in peasant hands, either as freeholds or as protected leaseholds.[4]

The following century, from 1814 to the outbreak of World War I in 1914, may be broadly characterized as the Liberal Era. Early liberalism, as presented for instance by Gregers Begtrup, author of a seven-volume description of the state of agriculture in Denmark published between 1803 and 1812, or by A. S. Ørsted's memoirs, stressed the blessings of both peasant emancipation and increased agricultural productivity through the benevolent reforms of an enlightened absolutism, although on economic grounds it opposed the limitations the reforms had placed upon the landlord's property rights. English agriculture, based on free contracts between landlord and tenant, represented the ideal of Professor Begtrup and his friends in the Royal Danish Agricultural Society.[5]

During the 1830s and 1840s, three historians above all established the national-romantic tradition of the Great Reforms, which they set against a somber backdrop of misery and oppression before 1784. In 1837, Adolf Frederik Bergsøe came out with his ambitious, two-volume biography of Count Christian Ditlev Reventlow, which presented the most detailed account of the government's reforms between 1784 and 1814 to appear up to that time—and still one of the fullest to date—while extolling Reventlow as the very embodiment of those noble and generous ideals that had motivated them.[6]

Carl Ferdinand Allen published his history of Denmark in 1840, which likewise stressed how "the nation's noblest and best men" placed themselves at the head of the peasant cause to restore the lost golden age of "the freedom of the people," overcoming the "prejudice and blind egotism" of the "party of the high and mighty."[7]

Caspar Frederik Wegener addressed himself in 1843 to the increasingly literate Danish peasantry itself with a "little tale" glorifying the memory of Frederik VI (crown prince–regent until 1808), who had recently died in 1839.

If now Danish peasants throughout the kingdom, [he wrote,] when they gather on quiet winter evenings with children and housefolk around the hearth in the busy spinning room, read or hear a chapter of this little book, and enlighten it with observations and experiences, which they themselves, each within his own circle, must have had, then will love and gratitude toward King Frederik soften hearts and open eyes to the happiness he created for them, and awaken desire and determination to go forward along the way he has shown them; and Denmark will be strong through its peasantry, the peasantry contented with its fatherland.[8]

To these early-nineteenth-century romantic historians, the work of reform seemed self-contained and essentially complete by 1814. According to A. F. Bergsøe, Count Reventlow could at the end of his life feel deep contentment at the prospect before him:

The peasant was no longer the landed magnate's thrall-bound servant, who had only duties but no rights. . . . He was as free as the freest citizen of the state; his obligations and rights, as well as his relationship to the landlord, had been determined according to the principles of justice, and so fortified by the law that he was not in danger, through ignorance or inexperience, of losing those goods which were to be assured him. The fragmentation of landholdings, which everywhere had obstructed agricultural improvement, had practically disappeared, and where formerly the eye had descried only barren common lands, poorly cultivated fields, and dilapidated huts, it now constantly fell upon neat farmsteads on consolidated holdings and profitable fields. . . . The cotters [husmændene], that class of citizens as important for the farmers as for the national defense, whose condition had formerly been so miserable, had almost all been provided with land, and thus enjoyed a significant improvement in their circumstances, while many thousand tønder of previously untilled land had thereby come under the plow.[9]

The peasantry itself was on the whole less convinced that its circumstances were altogether to its liking, and it became politically activated within the framework of the consultive stænderforsamlinger, or local assemblies, established by Frederik VI in 1834. The end of royal absolutism and the establishment of a constitutional regime in Denmark in 1848–49 opened the way for a coalition of farmers, the Bondevenner, and the National Liberals to carry out what were by then some much-needed reforms to improve the

lot of both the remaining manorial tenants—at that time still amounting
to around one-third of the farmers—and the large and growing *husmand*,
or cotter, class. By implication, these later measures called into question
the nature and effectiveness of the earlier reforms of 1784 to 1814. For some,
Frederik VI and even C. D. Reventlow no longer appeared in so idealized a
light, a tendency already apparent, for instance, in Allen's history.[10]

The cross-currents stirred up within the liberal camp by midcentury
agrarian questions became further complicated by the debacle of National
Liberalism through Denmark's defeat by Prussia and Austria, and the loss
of Slesvig-Holstein, in 1864. The following decades saw the rise of a new
conservatism, culminating in the long ministry of J. B. S. Estrup between
1876 and 1894. Thus the next wave of writing on the reform era, stimulated
by the centennial of the abolition of the *stavnsbånd* in 1888—the so-called
"Jubilee literature"—represented, for the first time since the reform period
itself, a wide and finely differentiated spectrum of opinion.

In a brief survey brought out in 1888 by the Student Association in Copenhagen, J. R. Fridericia presented a sober and factual account of the
oppressed condition of the Danish peasantry and of the movement leading
to its emancipation, building upon a document collection he was then editing for publication. Although, in his view, the peasantry had reached the
nadir of its existence by the mid-eighteenth century, it had still not lost its
spirit and traditions of freedom. Yet it required the leadership of generous
and disinterested men of the educated classes, inspired by "that spirit of
renewal, which seized all of Europe in the eighteenth century," and fore-
sighted enough to recognize that the existing, outmoded system obstructed
the economic advancement of all classes, to break the peasant's bonds.

> They sought [he wrote] to bring to bear hitherto unharnessed forces,
> they sought to break old prejudices, burst old restraints, defy the
> survivals of the past; they wished for society to include the entire
> nation, to create freedom for all talents, enlightenment and happi-
> ness for as many as possible.

Fridericia's concluding words capture much of the bittersweet spirit
surrounding the Jubilee of 1888:

> Denmark's history in recent centuries has enough to tell of misfor-
> tunes, of loss of folk and land, of ineptitude, of conflict and dissen-
> tion, of disappointments and humiliations. But few are the political
> deeds the nation can look back upon with joy and pride. To these
> belongs first and foremost the liberation of the peasant estate.[11]

The same year saw the publication of Edvard Holm's study of the public debate over agrarian reform preceding the emancipation, alluded to at the beginning of this article. While he held that there could not be "the shadow of a doubt that those who saw deepest and most correctly were the friends of reform," he sought conscientiously to present both sides of the controversy with fairness and understanding. Although they naturally had personal interests to protect, those who sought to retain the *stavns-bånd* were convinced it was needed to uphold agricultural productivity, hence the economic security and well-being of all. "When we discuss the struggle over the reforms," Holm later wrote, "we have no right to pass judgement on hearts." Like Fridericia, he looked to the "spirit of the times for the essential motivation underlying the reforms of the later eighteenth century": its "belief in Man's right to personal and civic freedom and in the significance of this freedom for the good of society."[12]

Together with his various other monographs and articles, Holm's 1888 study helped to clear the ground for his monumental seven-volume history of the Danish-Norwegian monarchy from 1720 to 1814, the first part of which appeared in 1891. In the sections of this work on agrarian conditions and reforms, Holm presented an evenhanded, detailed factual narrative, while the basic assumptions remained basically those he had set forth in 1888. Characteristically he continued to give much attention to public opinion and debate.

Holm was well enough aware of rural Denmark's most pressing problem by his own day, that of a large and growing class of mainly landless cotters, subject to the exploitation of both farmers and estate owners. Yet he defended the well-intended efforts of the reformers of the late eighteenth century to provide rural laborers with their own plots of land. Altogether, he concluded, the great reforms had opened the way to constant, ongoing progress in the Danish countryside. "It was, in this sense, a moral rebirth which the great friends of the peasant from the end of the eighteenth century had given the Danish peasantry."[13]

During 1888–89, Vigand Andreas Falbe-Hansen published a major study of the eighteenth-century agrarian question. Like his predecessors and contemporaries, he too gave prominence to the cosmopolitan ideals of the Enlightenment. At that time, he proudly declared, it was Denmark that took the lead and showed the world how modern, liberal ideas could be realized through peaceful reforms for the good and happiness of the people, and for the strength of the state. Denmark became the model of peaceful liberalism.[14]

Falbe-Hansen was an economist and statistician, rather than a historian as such, and his truly original contribution was meanwhile his placing eighteenth-century political and social developments into the context of the overall economic trends (*konjunkturer*) of the period. Thus, for instance, both the establishment and the abolition of the *stavnsbånd*—the main concern of his work, as his title indicates—reflected changing economic circumstances. Although he worked in haste and his data was sometimes scanty, he set the course for much future research, as will be seen. The legal emancipation of the peasantry in 1788 cut the Gordian knot: from this Falbe-Hansen maintained that all the subsequent improvement in the peasants' condition would have followed of its own accord, even without further governmental reforms, which in Denmark served to protect the peasant farmer.[15]

Yet at the same time Falbe-Hansen was disturbed by the problem of the cotter class. For the first time in the literature on the subject, he showed a clear awareness that in solving its most urgent problems, the eighteenth century had bequeathed to the nineteenth its own greatest dilemma. The reformers, he came to feel, had concerned themselves too exclusively with the economic, rather than the social side of the agrarian question. It has been said that Falbe-Hansen began as a classical Manchester liberal and ended as a disciple of John Stuart Mill.[16]

The medievalist Johannes Steenstrup made an excursion into the eighteenth century with his contribution to the Jubilee, in which he clearly revealed the conservatism of the Estrup era. He held that the Danish peasant was not at all so badly off before emancipation, indeed that he enjoyed greater "civic freedom" under the law than the juridically free peasant in England. His arguments recall those of various landlords opposed to emancipation in the eighteenth century. Yet Steenstrup raises some serious questions, rightly recalling, as he does, that other factors were as essential to the peasant's overall well-being as his personal freedom. He meanwhile emphasized the positive and benevolent role of royal absolutism in bringing the peasant into the mainstream of Danish society earlier, more smoothly, and more fully than elsewhere in Europe.[17]

One of the less-noted contributions to the Jubilee literature, representing a political philosophy diametrically opposed to Steenstrup's, also questioned whether the destruction of the old Danish rural society had been an unmixed blessing. H. V. Lund was evidently the first to examine the reform era from a Marxian perspective. While it improved conditions for some members of the peasantry, it led to "results that in many respects ceded nothing to the age of landed magnates in terms of oppression and devastation, [that is,] to Capitalism."

This nonetheless represented a "great step forward," for "Capitalism is a necessary stage on the way to Socialism." Marx and Engels had become fascinated with the old Russian *obshchina* as a primitive form of communal landholding that might lead directly to communist common ownership; Lund stressed the historic significance of the traditional Danish *fælleskab*, or village commune, as a basis for peasant solidarity under long oppression. "The *stavnsbånd* without *fælleskab*," he wrote, "would have extinguished the last sparks of independence." The inexorable advance of capitalism into the countryside at the expense of both the individual farmer and the growing rural proletariat would necessarily lead in the end to the abolition of private property in land and the establishment of a new and more complete *fælleskab*.[18]

Niels Rasmussen Søkilde described himself as a "farmer from Fyn." As such, he deserves his place in this survey as a particularly notable example of the many self-taught laymen who have contributed so greatly to Danish agrarian history down to the present, especially on the local level. His brief history of the reform period, which also came out in 1888, is unpretentious yet clear, well organized, and solidly grounded in practical experience of farming and rural life. It contains a remarkable amount of detailed information and numerous quotations from sources not easily accessible elsewhere. Although he considered conditions hard for the peasantry in Denmark before 1784, Rasmussen Søkilde stressed that they were even worse in much of Europe, and he took pride in the idea that the movement for liberation (*frigørelse*) that led to violent revolution in France could be realized peacefully in Denmark, thanks to its enlightened leadership.[19]

Christen Christensen (Hørsholm), in the uncompleted second part of his ambitious study of Denmark's agrarian history, published in 1891, revealed the strong peasant-liberal, thus anti-absolutistic, traditions of his own background. Thus, while he painted a dark picture of peasant conditions before emancipation, he stressed the efforts of the peasants themselves in improving their lot, as opposed to reforms from above that left important problems, such as manorial labor obligations (*hoveri*), poorly resolved from the peasant viewpoint, and created new and no less pressing ones, above all that of the cotter class. To Christensen, the insatiable demands of the state under royal absolutism had both created the original evils and had stood in the way of their successful resolution, a position anticipated three years earlier by Falbe-Hansen.[20]

Together, the historians of the years around 1888 raised the study of the agrarian reforms of 1784–1814 to a high level of scholarly sophistication and set the principal themes that have occupied their numerous successors over the next hundred years, down to the present.

Little that was new was added to the debate for the next several decades, despite the appearance of various monographs, local studies, and multivolume histories of Denmark. A noteworthy exception would be the third volume of the military historian K. C. Rockstroh's study of the Danish army during the seventeenth and eighteenth centuries, which showed how the amalgamation of the rural militia with regular units, commenced for reasons of military expediency in the later 1760s, played an important part in undermining the traditional authority of manorial proprietors over their peasant tenants on the eve of the reform period.[21]

World War I, the Russian Revolution, the Great Depression, and the rise of the new Communist and Fascist totalitarianisms by the 1930s meanwhile all tended to stimulate a new *étatisme* in political thought and practice, which opened new perspectives on the eighteenth-century agrarian reforms. The outstanding representative of this trend was Hans Jensen, a brilliant but erratic scholar of peasant origins, whose earlier studies had persuaded him of the indispensable role of Danish royal absolutism in preparing the way for a democratic society.

To Jensen, in the first volume of his study of Danish land policy from 1757 to 1919, which came out in 1936, the crux of the eighteenth-century agrarian problem was not the peasant's lack of personal freedom but rather the virtual monopoly of landownership by manorial proprietors—of which the *stavnsbånd* was the symptom, rather than the cause—hence the danger that if emancipated, the Danish peasantry might be reduced to a landless rural proletariat, as was the case in much of central and eastern Europe. He therefore placed his main emphasis upon the government's positive program to secure and improve the peasant farmer's economic independence and well-being.

Earlier historians had seen the "conflict over the agrarian reforms" as a struggle between the "friends" and "enemies" of reform—meaning thereby essentially opponents and proponents of the *stavnsbånd*. To Jensen, the confrontation was not between "reaction" and "progress," but rather between "the various elements which sought progress or change, each in its own way." The real issue, in his view, was the extent of the landlord's property rights, specifically over his tenant farms. He thus recognized the importance of early government reformers, in particular Henrik Stampe in the later 1760s, who saw that the peasant's economic security must be assured before he became legally free.

His particular heroes were Christian Ditlev Reventlow—of whom he wrote a biography published in 1938—and Christian Colbjørnsen, the champions of what Jensen considered a specifically "Danish" social policy of "peasant protection" that he purported to trace back to the early sixteenth century. Against them were ranged reform-minded landowners who, inspired by French physiocracy and English practice, sought to acquire full disposition over their land. While both Falbe-Hansen and Holm had earlier been aware of the government's concern to protect the peasant farmer, this concept was central to Jensen's interpretation.[22]

In 1786, Christian Albrecht Fabricius had warned that unrestricted *laissez-faire* on the land would result in a "far more powerful aristocracy than the state has ever known in the past," a situation which should be intolerable to an absolute monarchy.[23] To Hans Jensen, the still undeveloped state of the administrative machinery had kept it so dependent upon the unpaid services of the manorial proprietors at the grass-roots level that in the mid-eighteenth century Denmark was subjected to a "well-developed practical feudalism under a formally absolute form of government." In the completion of its reform program, Jensen saw both the liberation of Danish absolutism from dependence upon the landlord class and the final fulfillment of its historic mission of leveling the vestiges of "feudalism." The "modern state" now came into its own, capable of realizing its own aims and ideas. This process amounted to a "real, even if bloodless, revolution" from above, parallel with and in contrast to the violent French Revolution from below.[24]

Hans Jensen provided the first really integrated interpretation of the agrarian reforms of 1784–1814, and he made a compelling and plausible case. But he did not escape criticism, at the time or since. He had not closely defined the benevolent social motives that he perceived behind the government's actions. A younger scholar, Fridlev Skrubbeltrang, took him to task in a lengthy review in *Historisk Tidsskrift* for studying the government's decrees and proclamations in isolation, without due attention either to actual conditions in the countryside before the reforms, as contained in the voluminous local reports upon which the various royal commissions based their proposals, or to the actual effects of the resulting decrees in practical life.

In 1939, Albert Olsen, who had just recently competed successfully against Jensen for a professorship at the University of Copenhagen, rejected Jensen's thesis that social considerations had motivated the reforms, in an illuminating study of eighteenth-century attitudes toward the peasant question expressed in both official sources and in literature. For Olsen, the needs of the national economy had been the determining factor. He furthermore pointed to various developments elsewhere in Europe to refute Jensen's concept of a uniquely Danish concern for protecting the peasant cultivator.[25]

World War II and the German occupation of Denmark meanwhile dampened enthusiasm for *étatiste* philosophies as such. It was perhaps a mercy of providence that Hans Jensen, an intense and restless idealist whose yearning for an integrated national community based on a healthy and protected rural society had led him to sympathize with German National Socialism, died in January 1945, shortly before the Liberation.[26]

Much of the postwar Danish work in agrarian history is, in effect, a reckoning with Jensen's interpretations. Activity in the field has never been more intense, stimulated by the education "explosion" in Denmark since the 1960s, neo-Marxian radicalisms, the so-called New Social History, and more recently developed technologies for the analysis of mass data.

Already by 1940, Fridlev Skrubbeltrang set new and exacting standards for detailed monographic research in agrarian history—in contrast to Hans Jensen's often somewhat undisciplined use of sources—in his great study of the rural proletariat on Sjælland, a penetrating analysis that largely anticipated the influence on postwar Danish scholarship of the French *Annales* school. At the same time he revealed how much primary research remained to be done in Danish rural history—a point Skrubbeltrang never ceased to make. There have been numerous followers in this genre, whose combined efforts have provided far greater concretization than was ever possible in the earlier, broadly interpretive, and schematized accounts of the reform era.[27]

Questions concerning the basic motives behind the reforms of 1784–1814 and the conflicts they engendered within Danish society have continued to receive much attention. The role of ideas, which had been central to Hans Jensen's interpretation, received further support through a major study by Johannes Hvidtfeldt, published in 1963, of the Danish government's agrarian reforms in the duchies of Slesvig and Holstein. In this context, Hvidtfeldt emphasized the significance of German cameralist thought, with its stress upon the protection of small-scale peasant farming, as opposed to French physiocracy and English agronomy, which favored large-scale, rational cultivation, both in the duchies and in Denmark proper. In an important work on Danish economic policy after 1784, the first part of which appeared in 1968, Hans Chr. Johansen argued that the government practiced a type of "late mercantilism" directed essentially toward social rather than state ends.[28]

Jens Holmgaard had meanwhile argued strongly in 1953 that the needs of the state treasury had provided the compelling motive for the agrarian reforms, based on a study of reforms on the crown domain in north Sjælland. His findings in this respect were questioned in 1975 by P. V. Christensen, but by this time Holmgaard was working toward new conclusions.[29]

Whatever their differences, interpretations of the reform era and its antecedents had assumed fundamental conflicts between the landed proprietors and their peasant tenants, and—once the reforms got under way—between the government and at least the majority of the proprietors. Yet in 1938 and again in 1946, Johannes Hvidtfeldt reached the new and disturbing conclusion that the tenant farmers shared an interest with their landlords in maintaining the *stavnsbånd*, to assure themselves of an adequate labor supply of cotters and other landless peasants. Although this view was criticized by Gunnar Olsen, it pointed the way to a growing trend to reexamine the conflicts of the reform era.[30]

By 1977, Jens Holmgaard expressed the view that the reforms represented the common interests of the government, the proprietors, and the farmers:

> The agrarian reforms were carried out for the government by an administration, in which the highest positions were held by landlords. . . . the reforms were essentially realized through cooperation between the state and the landowners, and in the well-understood interests of both—and undeniably also to the advantage of the farmers, but conversely, in its consequences, not for the cotter class. The explanation is that through the reforms, bound values, namely the resources of production that could not be developed under the old agrarian regime, were released.

In this process, moreover, it was above all the proprietors themselves who took the initiative on the local level in transforming the agrarian structure, while the role of the state was "simply to encourage and regulate." Holmgaard concluded that the reforms begun in the 1780s were the "necessary consequences" of economic trends since the 1730s: both the state and the proprietors sought greater profitability, while the state, for fiscal reasons, had to protect the peasant farmers. The price was paid by the rural proletariat."[31] While Holmgaard set forth these views in a tantalizingly brief article, he provided the best indication of the directions of research in the field over the past decade.

In an article in 1977, Jan Rågård, explicitly following Falbe-Hansen's and Holmgaard's "materialistic" views, as opposed to both Hans Jensen's "idealistic" interpretation and the "teleological" generalizations of certain Marxian commentators, sought to demonstrate how the desire of proprietors to rationalize production on manorial demesnes and thus to maximize profits determined a logical and interconnected sequence of changes to the Danish agrarian structure, beginning with land reallocation and consolidation. Once this process began, in his view, it had to follow the course it did, with relatively little guidance from above.[32]

Thorkild Kjærgaard, particularly in his important study of the problem of manorial labor obligations, followed up leads provided by Falbe-Hansen, Hvidtfeldt, and Holmgaard in stressing the role of long-term economic trends and the common benefits provided by the reforms to proprietors and peasant farmers at the expense of cotters and landless laborers. Rising prices and expanding markets in the decades preceding the reforms had already brought a significant improvement in conditions for peasant tenants, and this ultimately was more significant than the reforms themselves. In the end, moreover, the landlords acquired a freer disposition over their tenancies—at least in setting rents—resulting, in effect, in an agrarian system not so unlike that of England: a denial of Hans Jensen's view that the Danish model created by the reforms was diametrically opposed to English laissez-faire on the land. In Kjærgaard's view, too, government followed, rather than directed, the course of events in Denmark.[33]

Birgit Løgstrup, in her study of manorial functions in local administration, which came out in 1982, has emphasized the desire of the proprietorial class for reforms that would relieve it of an increasingly outmoded, onerous, and unprofitable burden of tax collection and military recruitment, especially once the reforms had been initiated.

Already in 1891, Christen Christensen had stressed the initiatives of the peasants themselves in improving their own conditions even before the reform era, not least through freehold purchases where possible, especially in Jylland (Jutland). This viewpoint has recently been forcefully reiterated by Claus Bjørn, who has shown that the peasants were active participants in the whole process of rural transformation, rather than—as traditionally assumed—merely passive objects of reform. In a monograph from 1979 on the opposition of a sizable group of Jutland proprietors to the reform program in 1790, Bjørn has meanwhile examined the role that program played in factional rivalry at court and stressed the government's tacit willingness to compromise to avoid damaging confrontations.[34]

Fridlev Skrubbeltrang's continued painstaking and pragmatic analysis of primary sources meanwhile naturally led away from the tendency of earlier historians to see the changes of 1784 to 1814 as a veritable revolution. In his great survey of Danish agrarian society from 1500 to 1800, published in 1978, he stressed long-term, "normal" evolutionary processes as opposed to short-term "revolutionary" changes. In the most original part of this work, for instance, he demonstrated how the actual dynamics of the landlord-tenant relationship resulted in a long and gradual improvement of the peasant tenant farmer's security and general well-being even before the public debate over agrarian reform got properly under way by the later 1750s. At the same time, he points to the compromises and shortcomings of the great reforms of 1784–1814, both for the remaining tenant farmers subject to manorial labor obligations and especially for the growing class of agricultural laborers.[35]

During the postwar period, too, certain historians, including Johannes Hvidtfeldt and H. V. Gregersen, concerned themselves with the impact of the French Revolution upon peasant attitudes during the reform period in Denmark and Slesvig-Holstein.[36]

What appears to be the new consensus was summarized by Ole Feldbæk in the fourth volume of Gyldendal's history of Denmark, which came out in 1982. Even so "central—and vastly simplified—a question as whether it was legislation that brought about social and economic changes, or vice versa," Feldbæk wrote, "can still only be answered with suppositions." In the end, he attributes these changes to "an interplay between the general economic and social development and Danish absolutism's attempts to guide society." It follows, too, that the tendency to demythologize the era of reforms has likewise tended to deheroize its great representative figures, such as C. D. Reventlow.[37]

The turn throughout the Western world toward a so-called new liberalism with its growing skepticism in recent decades concerning the effective role of the state in bringing about social change—even among intellectuals committed in principle to its ideals—seems apparent in this viewpoint.

It seems curious that no substantial study of the historiography of the reform era had appeared by the two-hundredth anniversary year of the abolition of the *stavnsbånd* in 1988. There were, however, some useful shorter treatments. Some of these were intended mainly as critical backdrops against which their authors present their own interpretations. Thus it was, for instance, with the introduction to Hans Jensen's seminal work in 1936; so too with Jan Rågård's article in 1977. Erik Helmer Pedersen briefly discussed the writing of Danish agricultural history from 1750 to 1973 in an article appearing in 1975.

Fridlev Skrubbeltrang meanwhile discussed the historiography on C. D. Reventlow in 1948 and in 1971 called attention to various traditional views concerning the reforms resting either on insufficient documentation or on tendentious reading of existing sources. Claus Bjørn provided a useful brief survey as part of an article, published in 1974, on the views on the reform era presented in its Danish schools. In 1979, Thorkild Kjærgaard called attention to the persistent liberal bias toward evaluating the reforms from the sole perspective of the "peasants"—that is, the peasant *farmers*, whether tenants or freeholders—to the relative neglect of the other elements of the rural population, the proprietors and the rural laborers. The annotated bibliography for the agrarian section of Ole Feldbæk's survey of Denmark's history between 1730 and 1814 offers useful insights.[38]

While the present article seeks, from the perspective of an outsider, to discern the main outlines of the historiography of this well-tilled field of scholarship, it must be recognized that a fully detailed study of this subject can only be the work of a Danish scholar with full and easy access to all the relevant materials.

As Denmark's history has remained the almost exclusive preserve of Danish historians, it is not surprising that they have not shown much awareness of work concerning their history done beyond their national frontiers. Yet some foreign scholars have made their contributions, to this field as to others.

Jan Rågård pointed in 1977 to the surprising lack of any "clearly Marxian treatment" of the reform era, despite the evident appeal of the topic to such an interpretation. It is not clear whether he took into account H. V. Lund's slender volume from 1888. He was in any event apparently unacquainted with the American Carol Gold's unpublished doctoral dissertation, "The Danish Reform Era, 1784–1800," at the University of Wisconsin, completed in 1975, after extensive research in Denmark. In it, she sought to demonstrate from a neo-Marxian perspective that the reforms were simply "adjustive concessions and diversionary mechanisms" through which the dominant landlord class managed to preserve its wealth and power during the age of the French Revolution.[39]

In Germany, Wolfgang Prange studied agricultural reform in Slesvig-Holstein, with some reference to its influence in Denmark proper. The

Swede Sten Carlsson and the Norwegian Kåre D. Tønnesson in significant articles placed Danish developments into the broader context of Scandinavian agrarian history in this period, as did the present author in a comparative history of the Nordic lands during the Revolutionary era, 1760–1815, published in 1986. The American Lawrence J. Baack, in a useful, brief survey, considered the Danish reforms from a comparative European perspective. In his study, *The End of the Old Order in Rural Europe,* published in 1978, the American economic historian Jerome Blum has placed Denmark (together with Slesvig-Holstein) into the wider context of what he calls Europe's "servile lands" before and during the era of emancipation. His study demonstrates how protean a task it is to compare and weigh the manifold factors that determined the overall condition of peasants in different lands and regions.[40]

The three basic questions of the *need, motivation,* and *efficacy* of the Danish reforms of 1784 to 1814 have been and will without doubt continue to be answered in widely varying ways. In retrospect, one sees some strange bedfellows along the way. The paternalistic arguments for preserving the *stavnsbånd* offered by conservative landlords before its abolition foreshadow Christian Colbjørnsen's demands for a state paternalism toward the peasantry during the reform years, as well as Hans Jensen's concept of a specifically "Danish" benevolent *étatisme* in the 1930s. The laissez-faire liberalism of many of the early patrician advocates of reform seems to reappear in Christen Christensen's, and later Claus Bjorn's, emphasis on peasant self-help, as opposed to formal legislation. The conservative Johannes Steenstrup seems paradoxically in agreement with the Marxist H. V. Lund regarding the survival of a doggedly independent spirit among the eighteenth-century Danish peasantry, while Steenstrup also anticipates both Fridlev Skrubbeltrang and Jerome Blum in his stress on the great variety of factors that determine the peasant's actual condition.

The two hundred years between the abolition of the *stavnsbånd* and its bicentennial in 1988 form a natural historiographical continuum, and I do not seek here to follow developments in the field beyond that point. Ole Feldbæk in his survey of Denmark's economic history between 1500 and 1800, published in 1993, provides an overview of the literature that came out around the time of the bicentennial. He well summarized the continuing trend to downplay the government's role. Recent research, he wrote, has "pried loose stone after stone from the foundation that bore up the tradition." Although they were not "negligible," the government's reforms came late, or even after the basic changes had taken place, and thus, he holds, the idea that Crown Prince Frederik and his enlightened ministers steered the process can no longer be upheld.[41]

The whole "conflict over the agrarian reforms"—to return to Edvard Holm's suggestive title from 1888—offers fascinating insights into a small and closely knit community of scholars, including many of its most revered historians, interacting with each other and with outside, cosmopolitan influences, in confronting a central episode in their national history.

Most significantly, however, this classic debate touches upon certain of the deepest concerns of the historian of any time or place: continuity versus change; free will versus determinism; the efficacy of state policy; the historian's own responsibility to his discipline and to the wider society of which he is a part.

Notes

1. Edvard Holm, *Kampen om Landboreformerne i Danmark i Slutningen af 18. Aarhundrede (1773–1791)* (Copenhagen, 1888).

2. C. F. Allen, *Haandbog i Fædrelandets Historie med stadigt Henblik paa Folkets og Statens indre Udvikling*, 3rd ed. (Copenhagen, 1845), 625.

3. The present study is based upon research for my *Scandinavia in the Revolutionary Era, 1760–1815* (Minneapolis, 1986),

4. For those unable to read Danish, my *Scandinavia in the Revolutionary Era* provides an introduction both to the contemporary debate and to the reforms themselves. See also L. J. Baack, *Agrarian Reform in Eighteenth-Century Denmark*, University of Nebraska Studies, new series, no. 56 (Lincoln, Nebr., 1977), 45 pp.; B. J. Hovde, *The Scandinavian Countries, 1720–1865: The Rise of the Middle Classes*, 2 vols. (Boston, 1943), vol. 1.

5. Gregers Begtrup, *Beskrivelse over Agerdyrkningens Tilstand i Danmark*, 7 vols. (Copenhagen, 1803–12); A. S. Ørsted, *Af mit Livs og min Tids Historie*, 4 vols. (Copenhagen, 1851–57). Concerning Begtrup and his contemporaries, see Hans Jensen, *Dansk Jordpolitik 1757–1919*, 2 vols. (Copenhagen, 1936, 1945), 2:3–14, 43.

6. A. F. Bergsøe, *Geheime-Statsminister Greve Christian Ditlev Frederik Reventlows Virksomhed som Kongens Embedsmand og Statens Borger*, 2 vols. (Copenhagen, 1837).

7. Allen, *Haandbog i Fædrelandets Historie*, 547, 601, 605.

8. C. F. Wegener, *Liden Krønike om Kong Frederik og den Danske Bonde* (Copenhagen, 1843), 3, 48.

9. Bergsøe, *Reventlov*, 2:299. One *tønder* of land equaled ca. 1.363 acres.

10. Cf. Fridlev Skrubbeltrang, "Christian D. F. Reventlow som danske Historikere har set ham," *Lolland-Falsters historiske Samfunds Årbog* 36 (1948): 383–400.

11. Fridericia, J. R., *Den danske Bondestands Undertrykkelse og Frigørelse i det 18de Aarhundrede. En skildring efter trykte og utrykte Kilder* (Copenhagen, 1888), 38, 95. Cf. *Aktstykker til Oplysning om Stavnsbaandets Historie*, ed. J. R. Fridericia (Copenhagen, 1888).

12. Holm, *Kampen om Landboreformerne*, 2, 6; Edvard Holm, *Danmark-Norges Historie fra den Store nordiske Krigs Slutning til Rigernes Adskillelse 1720–1814*, 7 vols. (Copenhagen, 1891–1912), vol. 6, part 1: 95.

13. Holm, *Danmark-Norges Historie 1720–1814*, vol. 6, part 1:344–45; part 2: 416–17.

14. V. A. Falbe-Hansen, *Stavnsbaands-Løsningen og Landboreformerne set fra Nationaløkonomiens Standpunkt*, 2 vols. (Copenhagen, 1888–89), 1:61.

15. Ibid., 1:63, 81, 147.

16. Ibid., 1:62, 2:154. Adolph Jensen in *Dansk Biografisk Leksikon*, 27 vols., ed. Povl Engelstoft and Svend Dahl (Copenhagen, 1933–34), 6:560.

17. Johannes Steenstrup, *Den danske Bonde og Friheden. Otte Foredrag over Bondestandens Fortid* (Copenhagen, 1888).

18. H. V. Lund, *Den danske Bondes Trældom og Frihed* (Copenhagen, 1888), 73, 127, 158. Cf. Karl Marx, and Friedrich Engels, *The Communist Manifesto*, ed. A. J. P. Taylor, (Harmondsworth, 1967), 56 (introd. to the Russian ed., 1882).

19. Rasmussen Søkilde, N., *Landboreformerne og den danske Bondestands Frigørelse før og efter 1788* (Copenhagen, 1888).

20. Christen Christensen (Hørsholm), *Agrarhistoriske Studier*, 2 vols. (Copenhagen, 1886) 2. Cf. Falbe-Hansen, *Stavnsbaands-Løsningen*, 1:16–19.

21. K. C. Rockstroh, *Udviklingen af den nationale Hær i Danmark i det 17. og 18. Aarhundrede*, 3 vols. (Copenhagen, 1909–26), 3, esp. 225–26, 250, 261.

22. Jensen, *Dansk Jordpolitik 1757–1919*, 2:445 (quotation). Cf. Falbe-Hansen, *Stavnsbaands-Løsningen*, 1:147–18; Holm, *Danmark-Norges Historie 1720–1814*, vol. 6, part 1:340–41.

23. Quoted in K. E. Svendsen, "Tyge Rothe og Chistian Albrecht Fabricius. En diskussion om den fremtidige produktionsmåde i Danmark," in *Danske økonomer. Festskrift i anledning af Socialøkonomisk Samfunds 75 års jubilæum* (Copenhagen, 1976), 102.

24. Jensen, *Dansk Jordpolitik 1757–1919*, 1:16, 232–33, 241. Cf. Hans Jensen, *Chr. D. Reventlows Liv og Gerning* (Copenhagen, 1939), 222–23 (passage translated in my *Scandinavia in the Revolutionary Era*, 380). Cf. Linvald, A., *Oplysningens Tidsalder*, Schultz Danmarkshistorie, ed. A. Friis et al., vol. 1, part 1 (Copenhagen, 1943), esp. 10, 150–51, 181, which closely follows Jensen's interpretation.

25. Fridlev Skrubbeltrang, in *Historisk Tidsskrift* 10, series 4 (1937): 134–40; Albert Olsen, "Samtidens Syn paa den danske stavnsbundne Bonde," *Scandia* 12 (1939): 99–139, esp. 114, 117–18, 133, 135.

26. See Povl Engelstoft's introduction to Jensen, *Dansk Jordpolitik 1757–1919*, 2: v–viii, and his biographical article on Jensen in *Dansk Biografisk Leksikon* 11 (1937), 425–26. Oral information from Professor Georg Nørregård, 1976.

27. Fridlev Skrubbeltrang, *Husmand og Inderste. Studier over sjællandske Landboforhold i Perioden 1600–1800* (Copenhagen, 1940). Later intensive studies in the same genre include, among others, Sigurd Jensen, *Fra patriarkalisme til pengeøkonomi* (Copenhagen, 1950); Gunnar Olsen, *Hovedgård og bondegård. Studier over stordriftens udvikling i Danmark i tiden 1525–1774* (Copenhagen, 1957), and *Træhesten, hundehullet*

og den spanske kappe (Copenhagen, 1960); Stig Jørgensen, *Udskiftningen af krongodset i Nordsjælland* (Hillerød, 1967); and Birgit Løgstrup, *Jorddrot og offentlig administrator. Godsejerstyret inden for skatte- og udskrivningsvæsendet i det 18. århundrede* (Copenhagen, 1983).

28. Johannes Hvidtfeldt, *Kampen om ophævelsen af livegenskabet i Slesvig og Holstein 1795–1805* (Aarhus, 1963). Cf. C. O. Bøggild-Andersen's review article in *Historisk Tidsskrift* 12, series 1 (1964): 350–81, which disputes Hvidtfeldt's emphasis on German influences. H. Chr. Johansen, *Dansk økonomisk politik i årene efer 1784*, 2 vols. (Copenhagen, 1968, 1980), 1; see also the same author's *En samfundsorganisation i opbrud 1700–1870* (Copenhagen, 1979).

29. Jens Holmgaard, "De nordsjællandske landboreformer og statsfinanserne," *Erhvervshistorisk årbog* 4 (1953): 59–78; P. V. Christensen,. "Den lille landbokommission og indførelsen af arvefæste på krongodset i Nordsjælland," *Fra Frederiksberg Amt* (1975), 27–71.

30. Johannes Hvidtfeldt, "Stavnsbåndet, dets Forudsætninger og Virkninger," *Vejle Amts Årbog* 1938, 4–49, and "Kvindestavnsbånd i 1750erne og 1760erne," in *Festskrift til Erik Arup* (Copenhagen, 1946), 250–65; Gunnar Olsen, "Stavnsbåndet og Tjenestekarlerne," *Jyske Samlinger*, ny række, 1 (1950): 197–218.

31. Jens Holmgaard, "De nordsjællandske landboreformerne—drivkræfter og motiver," *Fortid og Nutid* 27 (1977): 37–47, esp. 43–44.

32. Jan Rågård, "Landboreformerne i Danmark," *Kritiske historikere* (1977): 2–24. On the relative importance of the land reallocations, cf. Falbe-Hansen, *Stavnsbaands-Løsningen*, 1:77.

33. Thorkild Kjærgaard, *Konjunkturer og afgifter. C. D. Reventlows betænkning af 11. februar 1788 om hoveriet* (Copenhagen, 1980), esp. 35–38, 69–71. Cf. Kjærgaard's *Den danske revolution 1500–1800. En økohistorisk tolkning* (Copenhagen, 1991), in English, *The Danish Revolution, 1500–1800: An Ecohistorical Interpretation* (Cambridge, 1994), which stresses environment factors in the transformation of Danish agriculture, especially during the eighteenth century.

34. Løgstrup, *Jorddrot og offentlig administrator*; Claus Bjørn, "The Peasantry and Agrarian Reform in Denmark," *Scandinavian Economic History Review* 25 (1977): 117–37, *Bonde Herremand Konge. Bonden i 1740-tallets Danmark* (Copenhagen, 1981), "Bondeuro paa Fyn 1768–70," *Fynske Årbøger* (1978): 73–87, and "Den jyske proprietærfejde. En studie over godsejerpolitik og bondeholdninger omkring 1790," *Historie*, Jyske samlinger, new series, 13 (1979): 1–70.

35. Fridlev Skrubbeltrang, *Det danske landbosamfund 1500–1800* (Copenhagen, 1978), 429 (quotation). See also Skrubbeltrang's "Developments in Tenancy in Eighteenth-Century Denmark as a Move towards Peasant Proprietorship," *Scandinavian Economic History Review* 9 (1963): 165–75, which anticipates his findings concerning increasing security of tenure. In *M. H. Løvenskiolds hoveridagbog 1795–1797*, Bol og By. Meddelelser fra Landbohistorisk selskab 7 (Copenhagen, 1973), Skrubbeltrang stresses the shortcomings for peasant tenants of the reforms regarding manorial labor obligations. See esp. 7, 22–24. For a later, detailed microstudy in this tradition, see, for

ex., the ethnologist Palle Ove Christiansen's *A Manorial World: Lord, Peasants and Cultural Distinctions on a Danish Estate, 1750–1980* (Copenhagen, 1996).

36. Johannes Hvidtfeldt, "Social og politisk uro i Sønderjylland paa revolutionstiden," *Sønderjyske Årboger* (1945): 128–69; H. V. Gregersen, "Optøjerne i Åbenrå 1790," *Sønderjydske Årbøger* (1956): 209–14.

37. Ole Feldbæk, *Tiden 1730–1814*, Danmarks historie, ed. A. Christensen et al., vol. 4 (Copenhagen, 1982), 191, 311. For the changed attitude toward Reventlow, see, for instance, Kjærgaard, *Konjunkturer og afgifter*, 24, 69–70. Cf. Fridlev Skrubbeltrang, "Et ejendommeligt Reventlow-portræt," *Historisk tidsskrift* 81 (1981): 193–95.

38. E. H. Pedersen, "Dansk landborhistorie 1750–1973," *Erhvervshistorisk årbog* 26 (1975): 124–52, esp. 124–28; Friedlev Skrubbeltrang, "D. F. Reventlow, som danske historikere har set ham," and "Tradition og nyinstilling ved benyttelsen af kilder til dansk landbohistorie," *Fortid og Nutid* (1971): 230–42; Claus Bjørn, "Landboreformerne i den danske skoles historielærebøger," *Årbog for dansk skolehistorie* (1974): 46–68; Feldbæk, *Tiden 1730–1814*, 63–64, 188–94; Thorkild Kjærgaard, "Gårdmandslinien i dansk historieskrivning," *Fortid og Nutid* 28 (1979): 178–91. In a translated version of the above article, "The 'Farmer Interpretation' of Danish History," *Scandinavian Economic History Review* 10 (1985): 100n., Kjærgaard points out that the ambiguity about the meaning of *bonde* in Danish (and the other Scandinavian languages) may have contributed to some vagueness or even confusion in the whole discussion of the agrarian situation: it may refer either specifically to a farmer or to a member of the *bondestand*, or peasantry as a whole, including its unpropertied elements.

39. Rågård, "Landboreformerne i Danmark," 7; Carol Gold, "The Danish Reform Era, 1784–1800" (unpublished Ph.D. dissertation, University of Wisconsin, 1975), 14–16. Gold's model is provided by Harry Eckstein in his "On the Etiology of Internal Wars," in *Studies in the Philosophy of History*, ed. George H. Nadel (New York, 1951). Two recent Marxian studies dealing with Danish agrarian history are B. Scocozza, *Klassekamp i Danmarks historie*, vol.1 (Copenhagen, 1976), and M. Zerlang, *Bøndernes klassekamp i Danmark* (Copenhagen, 1976), but both concentrate on other periods.

40. Wolfgang Prange, *Die Anfänge der grossen Agrarreformen in Schleswig-Holstein bis um 1771* (Neumünster, 1971); Sten. Carlsson, "Bondeståndet i Norden under senare delen av 1700-talet," *Scandia* 19 (1948–49): 196–213; Kåre D. Tønnesson, "L'Absolutisme éclairé: le cas danois," *Annales historiques de la Révolution Française* (1979): 611–26, "Problèmes de la féodalité dans les Pays scandinaves," *Annales historiques de la Révolution Française* (1969): 331–42, and "Tenancy, Freehold, and Enclosure in Scandinavia from the Seventeenth to the Nineteenth Century," *Scandinavian Journal of History* 6 (1981): 191–206; my *Scandinavia in the Revolutionary Era*; Baack, *Agrarian Reforms in Eighteenth-Century Denmark*; Jerome Blum, *The End of the Old Order in Rural Europe* (Princeton, 1978).

41. Ole Feldbæk, *Danmarks økonomiske historie 1500–1800* (Herning, 1993), chapt. 4, esp. 153–55, and bibliography.

Finland and Norway, 1808–1917:
A Comparative Perspective

In 1800 there were two Scandinavian states, the Danish and Swedish monarchies. A decade and a half later there were four. As a result of Scandinavian involvement on opposite sides in the Napoleonic Wars and shifting alliances, both Finland and Norway emerged as new and separate national entities.

Finland, after more than six hundred years as an integral part of the Swedish realm, was conquered by Russia in 1808–9. Convening a Finnish *lantdag*, or diet, at Borgå (Porvoo), Tsar Alexander I proclaimed Finland an autonomous grand duchy under his rule, with its own constitution, administration, and laws, thereby elevating it "to the rank of nations."[1] In 1812, Alexander reincorporated the so-called Old Finland—the territories in the southeast that Sweden had been compelled to cede to Russia in 1721 and 1743—into his new grand duchy.

In late 1813, Crown Prince Carl Johan of Sweden (the former French Field Marshal Jean-Baptiste Bernadotte) attacked Napoleon's ally Denmark, forcing Frederik VI in the Treaty of Kiel to relinquish Norway to King Carl XIII of Sweden in January 1814. Norway was to comprise a separate kingdom in union with Sweden, after its having been in dynastic union under the Danish Crown for more than five centuries and in effect part of the Danish kingdom since 1536. The Norwegians made a determined attempt to establish their full independence, drafted a constitution, and elected a king of the Danish royal house. Carl Johan thereupon invaded Norway in July 1814, quickly demonstrating Sweden's military superiority. Nonetheless, through the Convention of Moss already in August, he accepted Norway's new, independently framed constitution, in return for dynastic union with Sweden. This settlement was confirmed by the new Norwegian *Storting*, or parliament, on 4 November 1814.

During the century that followed, Finland and Norway would face the same basic challenges of nation building, both political and cultural, within the limits set by their unions with more powerful neighboring states. Both would become fully independent around a century after these unions were formed: Norway in 1905, Finland in 1917. Similarities in developments in both these new Nordic states are evident. But there were marked differences as well. Both invite closer examination.[2]

By 1815, Finland and Norway had, *in principle*, become self-governing nations. In both, however, the union monarchs sought in various ways to reduce their autonomy. To be sure, the extent of their autonomy had not been altogether clearly defined from the start, which in time led to controversy in both cases.[3] But fundamental differences in the juridical status of the two lands become evident.

Finland received its autonomous status as an act of grace by the all-powerful Russian emperor—and there was no fast guarantee that what Alexander I granted he or his successors might not take away by imperial edict. The new grand duchy's position always remained precarious. In practice, Finland was essentially self-administered, but for more than half a century, not self-legislating.

Norway's status as a separate kingdom under the Swedish royal house was a negotiated agreement, beginning with the Convention of Moss, finally accepted by the Norwegian *Storting,* or parliament, in November 1814, and confirmed by the joint Act of Union in 1815. Norway's constitution of May 1814 was the most democratic of its time in Europe, far more so than Sweden's. In neither kingdom did the king hold absolute authority, but while he could exercise an absolute veto over legislation in Sweden, he possessed only a suspensive veto over two consecutive *Storting* sessions in Norway. Norway's status could not be changed by decree.

Carl XIV Johan, who ascended to the throne of the Dual Monarchy in 1818, made determined efforts between 1821 and 1836 to amend the Norwegian constitution to strengthen the crown's authority, but these moves were effectively blocked by the *Storting*, which automatically convened every three years. Thereafter, there were periodic attempts at bilateral negotiations to create a closer and more effective union. These ultimately came to naught, due to Norwegian opposition to anything that seemed to threaten an "amalgamation" with the more powerful Sweden, like that of the old Norwegian border provinces, Jämtland, Härjedalen, and Bohuslän, which Sweden had conquered in the seventeenth century.[4]

At Borgå in 1809, Alexander I declared that Finland's existing constitution remained in force, which was understood to mean Gustaf III's Swedish constitution of 1772, as amended in 1789. This stipulation well suited the emperor's purposes. The diet comprised the four medieval estates of the nobility, clergy, burghers, and landowning peasants (which would be abolished in Sweden in 1866). The old constitution furthermore specified that summoning the estates was the monarch's prerogative—which meant that no diet was called for more than fifty years. The ultimate authority in Finland lay with the emperor in St. Petersburg. Nonetheless, Finland's exact juridical status long seemed ambiguous enough to give rise to a heated pamphlet war in Stockholm's freer press between 1838 and 1842.[5]

Whereas the greatest efforts of the Swedish crown to amend Norway's constitution came during the first decades of the union, Russian efforts to "Russify" Finland came after 1899, during the final decades of its imperial period, and represented a far more serious threat to its autonomy due to its weaker powers of resistance.

The overall stability of the new dispensation in the North was meanwhile based from the beginning on agreement between Crown Prince Carl Johan of Sweden and Emperor Alexander I. At their meeting in Åbo (Turku) in Finland in September 1812, Carl Johan formally renounced any future Swedish claim to Finland in return for Russian help, which he received in 1813–14, in acquiring Norway for Sweden in compensation. Paradoxically, this "Policy of 1812" protected Norway against Carl Johan's periodic efforts to strengthen the crown's authority there. Russia had no desire to see a strong Scandinavia across the Baltic. Alexander I and Nicholas I repeatedly reminded Carl Johan of his commitment to the Norwegian constitution and cautioned him against any change in Norway's status. At the same time, confident that Finland was not threatened by Swedish interference, the Russians were content to leave Finnish affairs primarily in Finnish hands.[6] Both Sweden and Russia were above all concerned with their strategic security. In Norway and Finland, meanwhile, effective autonomy assured their peaceful internal evolution.

In the end, that Norway nonetheless enjoyed greater autonomy than Finland derived from the relative strength of their respective union partners. In this regard, there was a much closer balance between Sweden and Norway than between the vast Eurasian Romanov imperium and Finland, its small westernmost dependency. While Norway's population amounted to close to a third of Sweden's by 1814, Finland's was only around 2 percent of the Russian Empire's. The Finn Emil von Qvanten described his homeland in 1855 as "a little swallow's nest under the eaves of an immense buliding."[7] What might be conceivable in Norway seemed hardly thinkable in Finland.

Sweden offered the Norwegians only limited opportunities for trade or personal careers. Norway's commerce with other countries, especially Great Britain, including the services of its growing merchant marine, was always far greater than with Sweden. Few Norwegians migrated to Sweden; indeed a greater number of Swedes, mainly laborers, moved to Norway. Russia, meanwhile—above all nearby St. Petersburg—opened up a vast and lucrative market for Finnish products and wide opportunities for Finns throughout the empire. St. Petersburg was reckoned around 1870 as the world's largest Finnish city, with a Finnish-speaking population slightly greater than that of either Helsingfors (Helsinki) or Åbo. Many of the Finns there were skilled craftsmen, domestics, and mariners. It was largely via the cosmopolitan imperial capital that significant European cultural influences reached the grand duchy. Stockholm played no corresponding role for Norway. Numerous Finnish officers served in the Russian army and navy, as well as some in the imperial civil administration, while Russians, aside from the governor-general, were prohibited from holding corresponding positions in Finland.[8]

For both Norwegians and Finns, the rise of the liberal Scandinavianist movement during the mid-nineteenth century, which ultimately aspired to a union of all the Nordic nations, proved problematic for both political and cultural reasons. For Danes and Swedes there were underlying political goals. Against the threat of rising German nationalism in Slesvig-Holstein with strong backing within the Germanic Confederation, Danes sought support from their fellow Scandinavians. In Sweden, meanwhile, sentiment was strong for regaining Finland from Russia. Neither Norway nor Finland had political goals beyond their own internal development.

While there was much idealistic enthusiasm for the Scandinavianist ideal in Norway, there were serious apprehensions over what the country's relative significance might be in an all-Nordic union. In Finland, Scandinavianism seemed for a time attractive to a smaller circle consisting primarily of university students, above all for its political liberalism. But Russian might seemed unshakable and the growing Fennomane movement stressed the Finns' own unique origins, language, and culture, as distinct from both the Scandinavian and the Slavic. The political aspirations of the Swedish and Danish Scandinavianists came to naught in the Crimean and Danish-German Wars in the 1850s and 1860s.[9]

Nevertheless, given their limitations, there was a de facto increase in internal autonomy in both Norway and Finland during this period, to begin with under essentially progressive bureaucratic auspices. Before 1863 Finland had no parliamentary life at all, while in Norway, down to 1884, the bureaucratic class dominated both the administration and the Storting.[10] Bureaucratic reformers in both lands were particularly concerned with economic liberalization and abolished antiquated restrictions on free enterprise, which in the process led to greater civic equality. During the 1850s in particular they took the initiative in developing necessary economic infrastructures. In this regard, the construction of Norway's first railway, from Christiania (Oslo) to Eidsvold in 1854 parallels the opening of the Saima Canal, connecting Finland's vast interior lake system with the Baltic Sea, in 1856.

The dominant political line in Finland—as opposed to Norway—was unwavering loyalty to the emperor in hopes of preserving its special preferred status within the Russian empire. In recognition of their loyalty during the Crimean War and especially the second Polish Rebellion, Alexander II in 1863 at last convened their diet, the *Lantdag* or *Valtiopäivät*, for the first time since 1809. Thereafter it met regularly and gradually extended its powers. In 1906, after the first, unsuccessful Russian Revolution and serious agitation in Finland, the Finnish diet transformed itself from the most archaic to the world's most modern and democratic, replacing the medieval four estates with a unicameral legislature elected by universal suffrage, including women. The contrast was no less striking than that which had taken place in Norway in 1814. Still, under Russian overlordship, Finland's status clearly remained precarious, and by 1914 was again coming under growing threat.

Norway's great breakthrough occurred in 1884, when the *Storting* was able to establish the principle of ministerial responsibility, overriding the king's veto. This not only transferred the appointment and dismissal of state councilors from the king to the national legislature but it also in effect broke the political dominance of the bureaucracy. More significantly, it confirmed , once and for all, that the monarch's veto was suspensive only, even for constitutional amendments. Thereafter nothing could *legally* prevent the *Storting* from dissolving Norway's union with Sweden, even though it would survive for another quarter century. Democracy was further strengthened by the passage of universal male suffrage in 1898.

In the end, the existing unions broke up under very different conditions. In June 1905, the Norwegian *Storting* cut short a protracted conflict with Sweden over the management of foreign affairs by provoking a ministerial crisis and thereafter declaring the union dissolved when Oscar II was unable to appoint a new ministry. This maneuver aroused great indignation in Sweden. Military preparations, though largely, it might seem, of a symbolic nature, were undertaken on both sides. Nonetheless, a face-saving formula was found for dissolving the union through negotiation.[11] As public support for independence was overwhelming in 1905, dissolution left no lingering dissension in Norway.

Norway achieved its full independence under peaceful conditions. Finland ended its union with Russia amid the turmoil of the First World War and the breakdown of the Romanov empire during the Russian Revolution in 1917. It declared its independence in December that year. But it almost immediately faced an uprising early in 1918 of the radical socialist "Reds," many of whom aspired to a Finnish socialist republic within the new Soviet federation, which was defeated after bitter fighting by the Finnish "Whites," who with German support defended Finland's newly won, full independence.

Norway's and Finland's contrasting transitions to full nationhood were largely due to differing outside circumstances. There were, however, also striking differences in economic and social conditions. In Norway there were fewer contrasts between social classes, between wealth and poverty, between the elite and the masses—to say nothing of those between language groups—than in Finland, which at the same time had an Eastern Orthodox religious minority. While both lands underwent rapid industrialization and urbanization by the later nineteenth century, the resulting socioeconomic tensions were more drastic in Finland. Such conflicts as arose in Norway could be managed peacefully. In Finland the Civil War of 1918 was an ideological class war that would leave bitter memories and deep cleavages within Finnish society and politics over the coming decades.

By the early nineteenth century both Finland and Norway became in principle political nations. But they were not yet cultural nations. Norway still remained a cultural province of Denmark in both higher culture and the language of its upper classes, and looked to Copenhagen for cultural inspiration. Finland was still a cultural province of Sweden and looked to Stockholm. Both at first held closely to their older cultural traditions as a kind of moral defense against their new and stronger union partners.[12]

But in both lands, there were the beginnings of awareness of their own distinctiveness during the previous century. A Trondheim Scientific Society was founded in 1760, which, led by the historian Gerhard Schønning, devoted itself largely to the study of Norway's proud medieval past. A Norwegian Literary Society was founded in 1771—characteristically in Copenhagen. In Finland, Pastor Daniel Juslenius took up the study of indigenous Finnish vernacular during the early eighteenth century. This tradition was developed further by Henrik Gabriel Porthan and his disciples at Finland's university in Åbo (Turku) around 1800.[13]

In both countries, university students played a particularly important role in cultural nation-building, especially in Finland. The Royal Åbo Academy, established in 1640, which in 1827 was moved to the grand duchy's new capital, Helsingfors (Helsinki), and renamed the Imperial Alexander University, was throughout Finland's vital cultural center.[14] Norway's Royal Frederik University was established in Christiania (Oslo) only as late as 1811, and Norwegian cultural leadership always remained somewhat more diverse.

The assertion of a distinctive national identity provided a cultural barrier against amalgamation with respective union partners. When Count Gustaf Mauritz Armfelt wrote to a friend in 1811 that the emperor sought to make good Finns of his new subjects and urged that they should they fulfill their destiny, he was thinking in political terms. Soon after, the slogan became, "Swedes we are no longer, Russians we will never become, therefore let us be Finns," now expressing a cultural as well as a political dimension.[15]

Sentiments were much the same in Norway. While both Norwegians and Finns sought their distinctive roots in the past, they nonetheless looked primarily to different sources. Norway's proud, independent medieval past was well chronicled by the Icelandic skalds of the twelfth and thirteenth centuries, above all in Snorri Sturlason's epic *Heimskringla*, the chronicle of the Norwegian kings. Norwegians naturally looked in the first instance to their *history* in forming their national self-image. The nationalist school of historians, with Jacob Keyser and Peter Andreas Munch in the lead, held that the Norwegians were of distinct and purer Scandinavian origin than the Swedes or especially the Danes, and that the ancient *norrøna* culture of the *Eddas* and sagas was exclusively Norwegian (including Icelandic, which they considered Norwegian), rather than the common heritage of all Scandinavians. While they regarded Danish rule as a time of national decadence and degradation, historians later in the century, like both the conservative Yngvar Nielsen and the radical liberal Ernst Sars, recognized it as a significant period of preparation for eventual modern nationhood.[16]

Finland had never existed as an independent state and had no written history before the Swedes Christianized and incorporated the region into the Swedish kingdom, beginning in the mid-twelfth century. Its history had thereafter been essentially Sweden's. Zacharias Topelius indeed questioned in 1843 whether the Finns had any history of their own before 1809. Finns therefore looked above all to *language, ethnology,* and *folklore* as sources for their national revival. H. G. Porthan, followed by the young Åbo Romantics after 1809, collected old Finnish folklore. Elias Lönnrot created a sensation with the publication of the *Kalevala* in 1835–36, a vast folk epic from pre-Christian and pre-Swedish Finland, based mainly on preserved oral traditions that Lönnrot collected in neighboring Russian Karelia. Enthusiasts hailed it as a truly Homeric epic, and it has played a central role in the formation of the Finnish national identity down to the present. During the 1840s, meanwhile, the young linguist Mattias Alexander Castrén sought out folk groups throughout northern Russia whose languages were related to Finnish (and Estonian), to demonstrate the Finns' place in an ancient, widespread Fenno-Ugric family of peoples.

Norway, to be sure, had its folklorists, who played their significant role, not least in seeking out continuities with the country's medieval, pre-Danish past. Here Peter Christen Asbjørnsen and Jørgen Moe were of fundamental importance with their collections of Norwegian folk tales, which appeared during the 1840s and 1850s. Like the *Kalevala* in Finland, these collections would provide a rich source of inspiration for writers, artists, and musicians throughout the century and beyond.

Finland, meanwhile, strove to assert a history of its own, as distinct from Sweden's. The poet Johan Ludvig Runeberg created a new national epic with his *Fänrik Ståls sägner* (The Tales of Ensign Stål), part 1 of which came out in 1848, describing the Finns' valiant defense of their homeland in 1808–9, which had allowed them to accept their new status within the Russian empire on honorable terms. Later, historians such as Yrjö Sakari Yrjö-Koskinen and Johan Richard Danielson-Kalmari, who characterized the Swedes as conquerors and exploiters, sought out distinctive episodes in Finland's past. They, in turn, aroused opposition from Swedish-Finnish historians like Bernhard Estlander and Magnus Gottfrid Schybergson, who upheld Sweden's vital role in bringing Western civilization to Finland. These differing versions recall the historical debate in Norway over the significance of the country's Danish period. Still, there was a crucial difference: Norway was an "old-new" nation; Finland an entirely new one.[17]

In both countries, language played a central role in cultural nation building. In Finland, Swedish had for centuries been the language of administration and higher culture. Upward social mobility there required a knowledge of Swedish and adoption of a Swedish surname. By the 1820s, the "Åbo Romantics," including Eric Gustaf Ehrström, Carl Axel Gottlund, and Adolf Ivar Arwidsson, building on the tradition of H. G. Porthan and inspired by German romanticism, urged the cultivation of the indigenous Finnish language to bridge the gap between social classes, raise the cultural level of the peasantry, and create a true national identity.

What came to be called "Fennomania" entered a new radical phase by the 1840s, led by Johan Vilhelm Snellman, who called upon the educated classes—in Swedish—to abandon Swedish entirely and to make Finnish the sole official and cultural language of Finland. Many followed his lead out of national idealism, which often required great effort and sacrifice, since Fenno-Ugric Finnish is totally unrelated to the Scandinavian languages. Moreover, a standard literary Finnish, fully adequate for modern needs, was then still being developed, based mainly on the western form of the vernacular, thanks largely to the devoted efforts of Elias Lönnrot and Gustaf Renvall.[18]

In Norway, both literary Danish and the numerous Norwegian local dialects were all of related Scandinavian origins, but there too the question of language assumed great cultural significance. A gradual approach to linguistic distinctiveness was initiated in the 1830s by Henrik Wergeland, perhaps Norway's greatest lyric poet, who incorporated Norwegianisms into his Dano-Norwegian. This approach would later be systematically developed by the linguist Knud Knudsen. Meanwhile, a more radical solution was presented by Ivar Aasen, a self-educated scholar who during the 1840s synthesized a distinctive new Norwegian language, Landsmål, from several existing, largely West Norwegian, dialects.[19]

In both Finland and Norway, there was from the start a close association among language, class, and politics. Finnish and Landsmål appealed to the broader masses and to the radical intellectuals who sought to lead them toward a broader democracy. Cultural, conservatives staunchly defended Swedish in Finland and Dano-Norwegian in Norway.

There was meanwhile a contrast between language affiliation and union loyalism in the two countries. The Russian government favored the Fennomane movement as a welcome means to distance the Finns from their old Swedish sentiments. The Fennomanes were thus steadfastly loyal to the empire, whereas Swedish-speaking liberals took the lead in resisting any encroachments upon Finland's autonomy, especially during the "Russification" crisis from 1899 to 1906. In Norway, it was the advocates of Landsmål who most strongly supported the liberal party, Venstre, in its constant efforts to widen Norway's autonomy and eventually to dissolve the union with Sweden.

The loyal Fennomanes received their reward in 1863, when in addition to summoning the *Lantdag* Alexander II proclaimed Finnish coequal with Swedish in the grand duchy. The staunchly nationalist Norwegian *Venstre*, or party of the Left, then dominating the *Storting*, made *Landsmål* coequal with Dano-Norwegian in 1885.

Those who upheld the use of the traditional cultural languages argued that the exclusive use of Finnish or *Landsmål* would unfailingly lower their nation's cultural level and lead to cultural isolation from the other Scandinavian lands and the wider European world. Exponents of the new "national" languages, like Arne Garborg, Aasmund Vinje, and later the historian Halvdan Koht in Norway, or Snellman, Alexis Kivi, August Ahlqvist (Oksanen), Juhani Aho, Minna Canth, and the historian Y. S. Yrjö-Koskinen in Finland, gave impressive proof that that this was not so. For them, the "national" languages were the key to public enlightenment and national advancement. Arne Garborg in 1877 held that Norway would become truly Norwegian only when *Landsmål*, which alone could adequately express its cultural uniqueness, became its sole language. In this view he mirrors Johan Wilhelm Snellman's arguments for the exclusive use of Finnish beginning more than three decades earlier. Garborg indeed followed with keen interest the language struggle in Finland, which he saw as clearly analogous to Norway's, and applauded the increasing use of the indigenous Finnish tongue.[20]

It would meanwhile be a mistake simply to associate cultural and linguistic with political conservatism. In Finland, the situation was particularly complicated, since the small Swedish-speaking elite was a minority within the minority, far outnumbered by the Swedish-speaking farmers, fishermen, and seafarers living in their own districts on the coasts and islands. In Norway, the status of Danish as the sacrosanct language of religion led to indifference toward or resistance to the use of *Landsmål* among much of the peasantry. It is notable, for instance, that *Landsmål* never gained any significant following in northernmost Norway or among the Norwegian immigrant population in America. Liberal writers such as Bjørnstjerne Bjørnson, Alexander Kielland, Jonas Lie, and the more apolitical Henrik Ibsen held firmly to Dano-Norwegian. The leaders of the progressive liberal party in Finland, such as Carl Gustaf Estlander and Leo Mechelin, were mainly Swedish-speakers. There was meanwhile a notable similarity in the agrarian idealism of the *Landsmål* movement in Norway and of the Old Fennomanes in Finland, with their apprehensions of unbridled capitalism, industrialism, and urbanization, and puritanical disdain for upper-class ostentation and frivolity.[21]

Ultimately, what was at issue was the conflict between localism and cosmopolitanism, or as the Norwegian historian Anne-Lise Seip has expressed it, between "tradition" and "civilization." More than that, language conflict was bound up with the whole question of *what* and *who* could be considered truly "national." More specifically, where did the elite classes fit in? Could only what was entirely indigenous be acceptable? How receptive to outside influences could the nation be and still preserve its integrity?

Beginning already by the 1830s, contrasts were drawn, particularly by Runeberg, between Finland's inland and coastal populations. By the later nineteenth century these came to be attributed to racial differences between Germanic Swedes and Fenno-Ugric Finns, giving rise to growing dissension. There was meanwhile heated debate over the "Two Norways," beginning with the historian Ernst Sars and Arne Garborg in the mid-1870s. While they and their followers stressed a distinction between an elite of allegedly foreign descent and the genuine Norwegian peasant stock, Social Darwinist racial argument was not lacking in Norway either, with Andreas M. Hansen's *Norse folkepsykologi* in 1899, which sought to distinguish there between a superior Aryan "Nor-Folk" and a "Gor-Folk" of remote "Mongolian" origins.[22]

National identity in both Norway and Finland was powerfully reinforced by creativity in the visual arts, architecture, and music. One thinks immediately of the Norwegian painters Johan Christian Dahl in Dresden, followed by Adolf Tidemand, Hans Gude, and their followers among the Norwegians of the Düsseldorf School, Erik Werenskiold, Gerhand Munthe, and a host of others; of the architect Holm Munthe and the "Dragon style" of architecture; of the musicians Ole Bull, Halfdan Kjerulf, and Edvard Grieg. In Finland their worthy counterparts were, for instance, the painters Albert Edelfelt, Eero Järnefelt, and Akseli Gallen-Kallela; the architects of the national-romantic Hvitträsk School, Herman Geselius, Armas Lindgren, and Eliel Saarinen; the composers Jean Sibelius and Armas Järnefelt. In this regard, the illustrations by Werenskiold, Gerhard Munthe, and others for Gustaf Storm's translation of Snorri's *Heimskringla* (1899) provide a striking counterpart to Gallen-Kallela's paintings of motifs from the *Kalevala* and Edelfelt's illustrations for Runeberg's *Fänrik Ståls sägner* from around the same time, all of them classics of national iconography. Perhaps, too, it might seem characteristic that whereas Edvard Grieg could look to history for inspiration in, for instance, his "Sigurd Jorsalfar" and "Holberg" suites, Sibelius would invoke the myths of the *Kalevala* in "Leminkäinen's Death" and "The Swan of Tuonela."

While Norwegian and Finnish artists, architects, and musicians, like the literati Bjørnson, Ibsen, and Jonas Lie, or Runeberg, Zacharias Topelius, and Albert Edelfelt, played vital roles in the creation of their national identities, as individuals they were sophisticated and cosmopolitan Europeans, many of whom spent good parts of their lives abroad.

The endless discussion of differences between the "two nations"—and even the "two races"—in both Norway and Finland could be, and all too often were, greatly overblown. Finland, the historian Matti Klinge has more recently asserted, had essentially "one culture in two languages."[23] The same would be no less true of Norway, despite the lingering cleavage between *Landsmål*, now called *Nynorsk*, and modified Dano-Norwegian, now known as *Riksmål*.

As Norway's and Finland's circumstances were so manifestly similar during the period of their respective unions, there naturally existed a mutual interest. The Norwegian historian P. A. Munch—like the disillusioned Swedish Scandinavianist August Sohlman—was deeply skeptical toward the anti-Scandinavian Fennomane movement in Finland in the mid-1850s, and indeed toward the independent creative capacity of the "Tschudic" race. He rejected any comparison between Norway as a historic nation and Finland, which had no such past, but which rather, in his view, was created by Sweden. The Norwegian art historian Lorenz Dietrichson, who visited Finland in 1861, 1873, and 1884, meanwhile warmly admired its cultural flowering and maintained close contacts there, particularly with Runeberg and his family. There he found a lively interest in Norway and its obvious similarities to Finland, its cultural life, and not least its language controversy.[24]

Some mutual influences between Finland and Norway are apparent as well, although this intriguing topic has scarcely been examined. During the 1880s, Norwegian literary realism, best represented by Ibsen, Bjørnson, Kielland, and Garborg, strongly influenced Finnish literature in both languages. It has been said that for a decade Finland became "a literary colony of Norway." Bodil Stenseth, referring to an exchange of ideas with Professor Matti Klinge in Helsinki, has recently given some tantalizing details regarding Finnish influences in Norway, most notably Finnish inspiration for nationally oriented popular enlightenment. She notes, for instance, the long correspondence on this and related subjects between Zacharias Topelius and Nordahl Rolfsen, and the notable similarity between the former's *Finland i det 19:de seklet* from 1893 and the latter's *Norge i det nittende aarhundre* from 1900, both of them vastly influential in fostering national identities.[25]

There was naturally much sympathy in Norway for Finland during its "Russification" crisis from 1899 to 1906, not least in the light of Norway's own conflict with Sweden preceding the dissolution of their union, as notably exemplified, for instance, by Bjørnstjerne Bjørnson, whose pro-Finnish pronouncements were warmly appreciated by the Finnish resistance.[26]

Similarly, the Norwegian-Swedish union crisis in 1905 was naturally followed with keen interest in Finland. It nonetheless aroused mixed reactions there. Finns could look with admiration and envy at the Norwegians' national solidarity and success. But their defense of their own precarious autonomy was firmly based on the argument of the binding legal guarantee of their rights within the Russian empire, which, they held, *neither* side could violate. This principle was called into question by the *Storting*'s unilateral deposition of King Oscar II and dissolution of the Dual Monarchy.[27]

By the early twentieth century, Norway and Finland had matured as nations, politically and culturally, to the point that full sovereignty had become both a possibility—given the right conditions—and a necessity for their ongoing progress.

Nonetheless, the manner of their separation from their respective union partners differed drastically. In Norway independence came about peacefully, with the virtually unanimous backing of the entire nation. In Finland, the establishment and defense of full independence was violent and tragic, involving bitter internal conflict between deeply divided factions.

This difference reflected the ways in which the two unions had first come about. Finland was conquered and occupied by the Russians, and its Lantdag at Borgå in 1809 served as little more that an appropriate audience for Alexander I's declaration of its new theoretical nationhood. While the *Lantdag,* or *Valtiopäivät*, played an increasing political role after its reconvening in 1863, it always remained fettered by the emperor's overriding authority. There was on the whole little opposition to the regime as such, which nevertheless tended, when it arose, toward conspiracy at home and agitation by political émigrés abroad. After 1899 there were assassinations, mass demonstrations, and Cossacks in the streets. Following independence through fortuitous circumstances in 1917 and its determined defense in 1918, the Finns had to start anew and frame their own, fully national constitution—which nonetheless preserved significant "Gustavian" features as late as 2000.

Although realistically they had little choice by mid-1814 but to enter into a union with Sweden, the Norwegians already had their own constitution, which Crown Prince Carl Johan formally accepted on the king of Sweden's behalf. The specific terms of the union were negotiated, after hard bargaining on both sides, by November. Although disputes arose between Norway and Sweden over the following 91 years, these were largely symbolic in nature. With the resolution of the constitutional crisis of 1884, the Norwegian-Swedish union became in actuality what it had been in theory from its beginning: a truly voluntary association—which could be abrogated by the *Storting* at any time. In Norway there was no *kagal*, no assassinations, no blood in the streets, no foreign intervention. The Swedish historian Göran B. Nilsson has provocatively claimed that the only real change in Norway after 1905 was that it now had its own king and its own foreign minister. Otherwise there was no sharp break with the past. In 1905, Prince Carl of Denmark, elected king of Norway by the Storting, assumed the title Haakon VII, thereby reasserting the unbroken continuity of the Norwegian monarchy since the days of Harald Fairhair. Norway's constitution of 1814 still remains in effect today.[28]

The nature of the respective unions and the ways in which they were dissolved likewise affected Finland's and Norway's ongoing relations with their earlier and later union partners. In Finland, the Fennomane movement not only created internal dissension between the language groups but also led to serious tensions with Sweden, where there was deep resentment against its anti-Swedish position. Long pent-up frustrations with Russian constraints and encroachments before independence in 1917 and the internal struggle of Whites versus Reds resulted thereafter in virulent Russophobia in Finland and the severing of all normal relations with the new Soviet Union, at least down to the end of World War II. Nevertheless, the Swedish language and cultural heritage have remained alive and well in Finland down to the present, as have, in more modest degree, certain old Russian influences. Finnish-Swedish relations have now become closer and more cordial than at any time since 1809. Finland's relationship to Russia—in ways notably reminiscent of the imperial period—became increasingly cordial and profitable during the Paasikivi-Kekkonen era. These trends have continued since the fall of the Iron Curtain, after which, in 1995, Finland became part of a new partnership, the European Union.[29]

Having been separated from their old motherland by outside circumstances rather than by choice, the Norwegians maintained on the whole warm relations with Denmark and cultural exchange between the two nations has always remained lively and mutually enriching. Despite aroused emotions on both sides when the union with Sweden was dissolved through Norwegian initiative in 1905, amicable relations were soon restored between the former union partners. Indeed, since then Norway and Sweden have become closer than they ever were, or could have been, under the problematic union of 1814. It furthermore seems apparent that the Norwegians from the start tried harder than the Swedes to rebuild bridges after 1905.[30]

In the cultural sphere, both Finns and Norwegians at first held fast to their cultural ties with Sweden and Denmark, respectively, as well as to cosmopolitan classicism, as a moral defense against domination by their new, more powerful union partners. This period was followed in both cases by exuberant, self-assertive national romanticism by midcentury. Anne-Lise Seip has described a kind of golden age of national consensus in Norway during the 1840s, before linguistic and class conflict set in.[31] The same would seem to be no less true in Finland before the beginning of serious internal schisms after that time. Both cultures meanwhile underwent similar realist, naturalist, and neoromantic phases in art and literature during later decades.

Still, both cultural and political expression tended in Finland to be more extreme in reaction to more oppressive and insecure conditions, compared with Norway, with its firm democratic constitution and its independent legislature, which possessed wider powers than its Swedish counterpart.[32] Finland was moreover in close contact with various radical political and cultural movements in Russia during its later decades within the empire.

Ultimately, the greatest similarity between Norway and Finland during the "long nineteenth century" lay in their high level of creativity in both the political and cultural spheres—characteristically closely intertwined in both cases—showing the fresh energies of new nations striving toward full national self-realization.

Notes

1. Päiviö Tommila, *La Finlande dans la politique européene dans 1809–1815* (Helsinki, 1962), 33–34; Matti Klinge, *Kejsartiden*, Finlands historie 3 (Helsingfors, 1996), 24–25.

2. For the events described above, see my *Scandinavia in the Revolutionary Era, 1760–1815* (Minneapolis, 1986). Cf. Tommila, *La Finlande*; Torvald Höjer, *Carl XIV Johan*, 3 vols. (Stockholm, 1939–60), vol. 2; Sverre Steen, *Det frie Norge*, 1: *1814* (Oslo, 1951); Jörgen Weibull, *Johan och Norge 1810–1814* (Gothenburg, 1957).

3. On the overall history of Norway between 1814 and 1905, see esp. *Norges historie*, ed. Knut Mykland, 12 vols. (Oslo, 1976–79), vols. 10–12; T. K. Derry, *A History of Modern Norway, 1814–1972* (Oxford, 1973); Øystein Sørensen, "Det nye Norge i det nye Norden 1814–1850," *Norden efter Napoleon. Rapport till det Nordiska historikermötet 2004*, ed. Max Engman and Åke Sandström, Stockholm Studies in History, 73 (Stockholm,

2004), 55–78; For Finland, 1809–1917, esp. Klinge, *Kejsartiden*; Eino Jutikkala, *A History of Finland* (London, 1962); John H. Wuorinen, *A History of Finland* (New York, 1965); Max Engman, "Storfurstendömet Finland—nationalstat och imperiedel," in Engman and Sandström, *Norden efter Napoleon*, 150–86.

4. See Höjer, *Carl XIV Johan*, vol. 2; Raymond E. Lindgren, *Norway-Sweden: Union, Disunion, and Scandinavian Integration* (Princeton, 1959); my *Sweden and Visions of Norway: Politics and Culture, 1814–1905* (Carbondale, Ill., 2003), chapts. 2, 3.

5. Tommila, *La Finlande*; Klinge, *Kejsartiden*. For the pamphlet war in 1838–42, see Matti Klinge, "Nordens säkerhet och Finlands framtid," in his *Från lojalism till rysshat* (Helsingfors, 1988), 154–67; also my "Scandinavianism, Fennomania, and the Crimean War," in this volume.

6. See Alf Kaartvedt, "1814–1905. Unionen med Sverige," in Narve Bjørgo, Øystein Sørensen, and Alf Kaartvedt, *Selvstendighet og union. Fra middelalderen til 1905*, Norsk utenrikspolitikks historie, 1 (Oslo, 1995), 246–47; Torkel Jansson, "Två stater—en kultur. 1812 års politik och den svensk-finländska samhällsutvecklingen efter skilsmässan," in *Sverige i fred. Statsmannakonst eller opportunism?* ed. Tapani Suominen (Stockholm, 2002), 153–54, 160–61.

7. See my *Scandinavia*, 367; Engman, "Storfurstendömet," 151; Peder Särkilax [Emil von Qvanten], *Fennomani och Skandinavism*, 2 parts (Stockholm, 1855), 1:16.

8. Sten Carlsson, "Norrmän i Sverige," in his *Grupper och gestalter* (Stockholm, 1964); Jan Eivind Myhre, "Kajsa, Sven og hundre tusen svensker—invandring fra Sverige til Norge på 1800-tallet," in *Goda grannar eller morska motståndare: Sverige och Norge från 1814 till idag*, ed. Torbjörn Nilsson and Øyvind Sørensen (Stockholm, 2005), 89–104; Max Engman, *Lejonet och dubbelörnen. Finlands imperiella decennier 1830–1890* (Stockholm, 2000), *Peterburgska vägar* (Helsingfors, 1995), esp. 282–83, and "Storfurstendömet Finland," 165–72; Klinge, *Kejsartiden*.

9. See Julius Clausen, *Skandinavismen historisk fremstillet* (Copenhagen, 1900); Ruth Hemstad, "Nordisk samklang med politiske dissonanser. Skandinavisme og skandinavisk samarbeid på 1800-tallet," in Engman and Sandström, *Norden efter Napoleon*, 187–227; Theodore Jorgensen, *Norway's Relation to Scandinavian Unionism, 1815–1871* (Northfield, Minn., 1935); Mikko Juva, "Skandinavismens inverkan på de politiska strömningarna i Finland," *Historisk tidskrift* [Swedish] 77 (1957): 330–37; my "Scandinavianism, Fennomania, and the Crimean War."

10. See Klinge, *Kejsartiden*, 197–200; Max Engman, "Storfurstendömet Finland"; Øyvind Sørensen, "Det nye Norge i det nye Norden."

11. See esp. Lindgren, *Norway-Sweden*. There is a considerable literature, much of it polemic, on the dissolution of the Norwegian-Swedish union.

12. See Knut Nygaard, *Nordmenns syn på Danmark og danskene i 1814 og de første selvstendighetsår* (Oslo, 1960); Carl Schnitler, *Slægten fra 1814. Studier over norsk embedsmandskultur i klassicismens tidsalder 1814–1840* (Kristiania, 1911); Klinge, *Kejsartiden*.

13. Andreas Elviken, "The Genesis of Norwegian Nationalism," *Journal of Modern History* 3 (1931): 365–91; Oscar J. Falnes, *National Romanticism in Norway* (New York,

1933); Øystein Sørensen, *Kampen om Norges sjel*, Norsk idéhistorie, ed. Trond Berg Eriksen and Øystein Sørensen, 3 (Oslo, 2001), 23–51; Klinge, *Kejsartiden*; John H. Wuorinen, *Nationalism in Modern Finland* (New York, 1931).

14. Cf. Matti Klinge et al., *Kejserliga Alexanders universitet 1808–1917*, Helsingfors universitet 2 (Helsingfors, 1989).

15. Carl von Bonsdorff, *Opinioner och stämningar i Finland 1804–1814* (Helsingfors, 1918), 224; Tommila, *La Finlande*, 267; Klinge, *Kejsartiden*, 38.

16. See esp. Ottar Dahl, *Norsk historieforskning i 19. og 20. århundre* (Oslo, 1970); Falnes, *National Romanticism in Norway*; Anne-Lise Seip, "Nation-Building within the Union: Class and Culture in the Norwegian Nation-State in the Nineteenth Century," *Scandinavian Journal of History* 20 (1995): 35–50; *Jakten på det norske. Perspektiver på utviklingen av en norsk nasjonal identitet på 1800-tallet*, ed. Øyvind Sørensen (Oslo, 1998), esp. chapts. 13 and 14.

17. See esp. Wuorinen, *Nationalism in Modern Finland*; William A. Wilson, *Folklore and Nationalism in Modern Finland* (Bloomington, Ind., 1976); Engman, "Storfurstendömet Finland," 151–52, 173, 177, and "National Conceptions of History in Finland," in *Conceptions of National Identity,* ed. Erik Lönnroth et al. (Berlin and New York, 1994), 49–63; Juoko Nurmiainen, "Frågan om 'etnisk nationalism,' nationell självbild och 1700-talets historia," *Historisk tidskrift för Finland* (2003), 257–75. Cf. Elias Lönnrot, *Vandraren. Berättelser från Karelen 1828–1842*, ed. Rainer Knapas (Helsingfors, 2002).

18. Wuorinen, *Nationalism in Modern Finland*; *Snellman i urval*, ed. Johannes Salminen (Helsingfors, 1981); Klinge, *Kejsartiden*, 40–41, and "Vårt land på finska—och på estniska," in his *Från lojalism till rysshat*, 114–19.

19. Falnes, *National Romanticism in Norway*; Oddmund Hoel, *Nasjonalisme i norsk målstrid 1848–1865* (Oslo, 1996) and "Ivar Aasen som opposisjonell nasjonalist," in Sørensen, *Jakten på det norske*, 303–20; Anne-Lise Seip, "Det norske 'vi'—Kulturnasjonalisme i Norge," in Sørensen, *Jakten på det norske*, 107.

20. See Sørensen, *Kampen om Norges sjel*, 345–49; Seip, "Det norske 'vi,'" 103–4, 107; Arne Garborg, *Det ny-norske Sprog- och Nationalitetsbevægelse* (Kristiania, 1877), esp. 156–58 on Finland.

21. See Bodil Stenseth, *En norsk elite. Nasjonsbyggene på Lysaker 1890–1940* (Oslo, 1993), 50, 142; Dag Thorkildsen, "En nasjonal og moderne utdanning," in Sørensen, *Jakten på det norske*, 265–84; Arne Sunde, "A Minority within a Minority: The Promotion of Nynorsk in the United States, 1900–1920," *Norwegian-American Studies*, 34 (Northfield, Minn., 1995), 171–200, esp. 191–94; Klinge, *Kejsartiden*, 230–31, 280–81, 303, 390.

22. Ernst Sars, *Udsigt over den norske Historie*, 4 vols. (Kristiania, 1873–91), esp. 2:16, 400, 4:350–52; Garborg, *Den ny-norske Sprog- og Nationalitetsbevægelse*; Seip, "Det norske 'vi,'" 103–4, 107; Øystein Sørensen, *Kampen om Norges sjel*, 343–77; Stenseth, *En norsk elite*, 50, 141; Andreas M. Hansen, *Norsk folkepsykologi med politisk kart over Skandinavien* (Kristiania, 1899); Sten Högnäs, *Kustens och skogarnas folk: Om synen på svenskt och finskt lynne* (Stockholm, 1995).

23. Sørensen, *Kampen om Norges sjel*, 345–49; Matti Klinge, "Alla finnar är svenskar," in his *Runebergs två fosterland* (Helsingfors, 1983), 220–32, and *Let Us Be Finns: Essays on History* (Helsinki, 1990), 121 (quote). See also Max Engman, "Är Finland ett nordiskt land?" in his *Peterburgska vägar*, 275–98; Jansson, "Två stater—en kultur."

24. August Sohlman, *Det unge Finland* (Stockholm, 1855), esp. 55–60 on Munch; Högnäs, *Kustens och skogarnas folk*, 104–5; Sørensen, *Kampen om Norges sjel*, 222–23; Lorenz Dietrichson, *Svundne Tider. Af en Forfatteres Ungdoms-Erindringer*, 4 vols. (Kristiania, 1896–1917), 2:297–333.

25. Högnäs, *Kustens och skogarnas folk*, 32; Stenseth, *En norsk elite*, 106–7, 114–15; Cf. *Finland i det 19:e seklet*, ed. Zacharias Topelius (Helsingfors, 1893), and before that, *Boken om vårt land* (Helsingfors, 1875); Nordahl Rolfsen, *Norge i det nittende aarhundre* (Kristiania, 1900). Also Matti Klinge, "Zachris Topelius och boken om vårt land," in his *Från lojalism till rysshat*, 168–78.

26. Per Amdam and Aldo Keel, *Bjørnstjerne Bjørnson*, 2 vols. (1993, 1999), 2:369–71. Cf. Dietrichson, *Svundne Tider*, vol. 2, esp. 333.

27. Sune Jungar, "Finländska opinioner kring en union i upplösning," in *1905—unionsupplösningens år*, ed. Torbjörn Nilsson and Øystein Sørensen (Stockholm, 2005), 81–90.

28. Evert Vedung, "Varför ledde Norges succession 1905 inte till krig?" *Scandia* 66 (2000): 251–68; Göran B. Nilsson, "Edvard Grieg och den svensk-norska unionens underliga historia," *Nyt norsk tidsskrift* 13 (1994): 31.

29. My "Scandinavianism, Fennomania, and the Crimean War"; Sohlman, *Det unga Finland*; Matti Klinge, "Rysshatet," in his *Från lojalism till rysshat*, 235–88; Max Engman, "Finland som arvtagarstat," in his *Peterburgska vägar*, 87–125.

30. See my *Sweden and Visions of Norway*, 160–61. Cf. *Fra arvefiende til samboer*, ed. Grete Værnø (Oslo and Stockholm, 1990); Ruth Hemstad, "Skandinavismen og 1905: Fra Indian Summer til nordisk vinter," *Nordisk Tidskrift* 1 (2005): 1–16.

31. Seip, "Det norske 'vi,'" 102–3.

32. See Magne Malmanger, "Betryggende modernitet," in *Tradisjon og fornyelse. Norge kring århundreskiftet* [ed. Tone Skedsmo] (Oslo, 1994), 32.

The Discovery of Norway Abroad, 1760–1905

The Nordic lands were long almost terra incognita in the European consciousness, where they were vaguely pictured as a cold, Hyperborean wilderness. Occasional diplomats, soldiers, and merchants might have reason to visit Copenhagen or Stockholm, but few found their way to Norway before the latter part of the eighteenth century.[1]

Nevertheless, interest in the Nordic lands grew markedly during the eighteenth century. For this there were several reasons. Sweden's imperial "Era of Greatness" during the preceding century and, not least, the exploits of Carl XII had made a powerful impression. Northern commodities, including Norwegian timber and Swedish iron, became increasingly important on the European market. The philosophers of the Enlightenment, especially Voltaire and Montesquieu, looked to Scandinavia for edifying examples in their writings. It was moreover during the eighteenth century that Scandinavia itself began to contribute significantly to cosmopolitan European culture.

Both cultural and political developments in Europe during the later eighteenth century directed attention toward the North. The travel account became an increasingly popular literary genre, and those who wrote them were ever seeking out new and exciting destinations for the armchair traveler. In the past there had been few travelers to far distant places without practical business to conduct. Some had written accounts of their experiences, but these were essentially by-products. By the later eighteenth century, however, a growing number traveled for the sake of travel itself and—not least—to gather material for published accounts. Charles L. Batten has aptly described the ideal of travel writing during that period as "pleasurable instruction."[2]

The Pre-Romantic vogue meanwhile glorified wild, untamed nature in all its grandeur and idealized the sturdy virtues of the simple peasantry, in reaction against the overrefinement and corruption of the cities and luxury-loving elite. Romantic souls, following Jean-Jacques Rousseau, at first found their new unspoiled Arcadia in the mountains of Switzerland.

After 1789, revolution and war closed much of Europe off to peaceful travelers. Switzerland was overrun and reorganized as a French satellite republic. Scandinavia became the last haven of peace—the new Switzerland, the new Arcadia—at least until it, too, was drawn into the maelstrom of the Napoleonic Wars after 1805. The numbers of travelers and of travel accounts from the region first peaked by the later 1790s. According to Peter Fjågesund and Ruth A. Symes in their recent study of British perceptions of Norway during the nineteenth century, Romanticism underwent a "broad shift from south to north."[3] *"Kennst du das Land wo die Zitronen blühn?"* (Knowest thou the land where the lemon trees bloom?), wrote Goethe—yet he too was fascinated by the mythical North, the antithesis of the classical Mediterranean world.

Following the general peace in 1815, foreign travel resumed on a growing scale. While patrician "travelers" of the older type long continued to make their own arrangements and had the means to do so, there now began to emerge a new type, the middle-class "tourist," as entrepreneurs, particularly in Britain, undertook to handle the practical details. In 1851 the Englishman Thomas Bennett opened his agency in Christiania (now Oslo). Tourism was meanwhile promoted, particularly in Norway, by the growing use of steam vessels in coastal traffic from the 1830s and in the North Sea traffic from the 1850s on. For European tourists, Norway was an exciting destination—and it was close at hand.

The visitors to the North were of varying nationality. The British clearly predominated. Throughout the nineteenth century nearly two hundred travel accounts of Norway were published in Britain alone, considerably more than of the other Nordic lands. There also came sizable numbers of Germans, French, and others. Accounts of Norway were written even in such languages as Russian, Polish, Hungarian, and Greek. Some of the more interesting visitors came from the New World. The impact of such writings was of course greatly enhanced by romantic pictorial representations of Norway, book illustrations, separately sold prints, and at times the work of foreign painters.

The pattern for foreign reactions to Scandinavia, especially Norway, were set already during the first wave of travelers in the latter part of the eighteenth century. At first, like William Coxe, who visited Norway briefly in 1779, visitors were mainly interested in the region's exploitable resources, reflecting the rationalism and utilitarianism of the Enlightenment. This aspect would still be staunchly represented by the Prussian geologist Leopold von Buch, who was in Norway as late as 1806 to 1808.[4]

Meanwhile a more romantic vision of Scandinavia presented itself: that of the cradle of European "liberty." According to this view, the fierce and hardy "Goths" had freed Europe from Roman tyranny. Although it could in part be traced back to Tacitus and Jordanes, the idea received its classic formulation in Montesquieu's *L'Ésprit des Lois* in 1748, which described the North as "the factory of those instruments that broke the shackles forged in the South." This concept was popularized by the Swiss Paul Henri Mallet in his largely mythical history of Nordic antiquity and by his English translator Thomas Percy in the 1750s, giving rise to a Pre-Romantic "Gothic" cult in European literature, notably represented by such figures as Thomas Gray, William Haley, Thomas Southey, and Friedrich Gottlieb Klopstock.

Both Britons and continental Anglophiles now looked with pride to Scandinavia as their ancestral home. Glorification of rude "Gothic" virtues meanwhile expressed contemporary apprehensions of the degenerate and enervating effects of an overrefined and luxury-loving civilization, what James Thomson had already in 1729 called "the soft penetrating plague." In Norway, E. D. Clarke wrote in 1799, Englishmen could discover the ways of their stalwart ancestors. Even the Latin American Francisco de Miranda, mindful of Spain's Visigothic past, proudly referred to the Scandinavians as "our forefathers."[5]

By the 1780s, Pre-Romanticism became increasingly evident in travel accounts. Among the growing number who now visited Norway, the South American Miranda in 1787, the Saxon Carl Gottlob Küttner, the French émigré Jacques-Louis de Bourgrenet de La Tocnaye in 1798, and the Englishmen Thomas Malthus and Edward Daniel Clarke in 1799, were transitional types, reflecting both the Enlightenment and Pre-Romanticism. Mary Wollstonecraft, who in 1795 spent some months in Norway, most strongly represents the Pre-Romantic temper.[6] Already before 1800, foreign interest in Scandinavia heightened interest within the Nordic lands themselves in their own societies and legendary past.[7]

It is clear that through the following century the *Romantic* vision of Norway, well established before 1800, predominated. No greater contrast could be found within Europe to the more developed and progressive nations of the West, above all industrial and imperial Great Britain. Norway provided a fascinating attraction of opposites.

The Romantic view has at least three main aspects: *Majestic Norway, Norway the Land of Heroes,* and *Picturesque Norway.* The country contains some of Europe's most truly magnificent scenery, surpassing in that regard even its Scandinavian neighbors. The travel literature from at least the 1790s on is filled with rapturous descriptions of towering, snow-capped mountains, sparkling glaciers, narrow, winding fjords between steep, overhanging cliffs, rushing rivers and plunging waterfalls, the storm-blown Lofoton Islands, and the mysterious, remote North Cape. Characteristically, the Swede Peter August Gödecke in 1873 saw in the Jotunheimen massif "a temple in which God himself preached through his mighty work's vastness and beauty."[8]

This austere and awe-inspiring land was furthermore revered as the *home of the heroes of the Viking Age,* with whom northern Europeans by now enthusiastically identified. Few travel accounts failed to allude to this aspect. At a time when the English increasingly prided themselves on their Germanic origins, they identified the Norwegian strain in their ancestry as the source of their love of freedom, adventure, and enterprise. Rather than looking back to the Danelaw or Norse Northumbria, they tended specifically to seek their Viking strain in the Norman blood that ran in the veins of Britain's aristocratic empire builders. It was, William Howitt wrote in 1852, "The Scandinavian spirit of the brine / That set us forth to conquest, plunder, fame." "For an American," Charles Loring Brace wrote in 1857, "a visit to the home of the old Northmen is a visit back to his forefather's house. A thousand signs tell him he is at the cradle of the race which leads to modern enterprise, and whose Viking power in both hemispheres has not ceased to be felt." Brace indeed felt that the Viking spirit was now more strongly represented in the Western, rather than the Eastern, hemisphere.[9] That the latter-day Vikings had not lost their manly spirit would later be proven, for instance, by Fridtiof Nansen, who became a veritable cult figure before the end of the century.

The legendary world of the Norsemen likewise held a special fascination for Germany, ever since the days of Herder, Tieck, and the brothers Grimm, in its search for a lost, Teutonic mythical identity. There the *Edda* and Icelandic sagas were eagerly studied in the light of the epic *Niebelungen* and other surviving fragments of German mythology. Scandinavia,

Sulitelma and Lake, the wilds of Norway as portrayed in one of the most colorful widely read travel accounts of the nineteenth century. Sulitelma, in the far North, is Norway's highest peak. (Engraving from Paul Du Chaillu, *Land of the Midnight Sun: Summer and Winter Journeys through Sweden, Norway, Lapland and Northern Finland*, New York, 1881, vol. 1.)

and particularly Norway, appeared in a nostalgic light as the Germanic *Urheim*. Its impact upon the music dramas of Richard Wagner is well known, and partly through their influence, upon German *"völkisch"* racial theory—which did not bode well for the following century. German tourism to Norway, already sizable, became especially fashionable by the 1890s, thanks to Kaiser Wilhelm II, who almost annually, between 1889 and 1914, cruised the Norwegian coast aboard the imperial yacht *Hohenzollern* and who in 1913 erected a colossal statue of the Viking Fritiof at Vagnsnes in Sognfjord.[10] Throughout the nineteenth century the Germans were not far behind the British in writing travel accounts of Norway.

Against the backdrop of Majestic Norway lay *Picturesque Norway*, the land of proud, timbered farmsteads dating back to Viking times and tiny crofts on steep, rocky mountainsides, of simple *sæters* on high-lying pastures with rosy-cheeked milkmaids who sang as they went about their chores, of ancient stave churches, of colorful local folk dress, elaborate peasant weddings, athletic dances, and Hardanger fiddles. And in the remote far North lay the austere land of the nomadic Lapps, Europe's only indigenous nomads, with their wandering herds of reindeer.

Borgund Stave Church, engraved by Johan Christian Dahl. This twelfth-century wooden church reveals much of the romance of Old Norway, with its decorative elements from the Viking Age and its majestic mountainous setting. (From J. C. Dahl, *Denkmalen einer sehr ausgebildeten Holzbaukunst aus den frühesten Jahrhunderten in den innern Landschaften Norwegens*, Christiania, 1836–37).

Norway was fondly envisioned as the land of simple living and primitive innocence. While Mary Wollstonecraft in 1795 did not venture beyond the Vestfold coast, the descriptions she received of the interior, north of Christiania, "carried me back," she wrote, "to the fables of the golden age: independence and virtue; affluence without vice; cultivation of the mind, without depravity of heart; with 'ever smiling liberty,' the nymph of the mountain. . . ."[11] Nostalgia for the lost innocence that had long since disappeared in the visitors' homelands was seldom far below the surface in the travelers' accounts.

A new aspect of Romantic Norway became prominent particularly with the onset of tourism by the mid-nineteenth century: *Sporting Norway*, a paradise for prime fishing, hunting, foot-wandering, and mountain climbing. Englishmen in particular gloried in roughing it in the wilds. "The English have fairly occupied Norway for sporting," wrote the American Charles Loring Brace in 1857. His compatriot Bayard Taylor the same year admired the hardy young Britons he encountered and wished that "the spindle-shanked youths who polk and flirt" at the American summer resorts at Newport and Saratoga had "enough manliness for such undertakings."[12] A large part of the travel literature of Norway in the nineteenth century consists of high-spirited and often burlesque accounts, above all British, of exploits with rod and reel, rifle, alpenstock, and often sketchbook.

Alongside the image of Romantic Norway, there arose—seemingly in contrast—that of *Progressive Norway* during the nineteenth century. This is particularly evident in Sweden, Norway's partner in the Dual Monarchy of 1814, where Norway's Eidsvoll constitution—the most liberal and democratic of its time beside America's—became the guiding light of Swedish liberals and radicals seeking to reform their antique system of parliamentary representation from the 1830s on. Numerous voices were raised in the Swedish *Riksdag* and press in praise of Norway's progressive form of government.[13]

In Denmark, too, Norway gave powerful inspiration to the liberal constitution that at last marked the end of royal absolutism there in 1849. "The Norwegian constitution was the banner under which we in Denmark waged our struggle," wrote the Danish liberal leader Orla Lehmann in 1865.[14] The liberal Scandinavianist movement from the 1840s on added further luster to the Norwegian model throughout the North.

The Scotsman Samuel Laing gave the most influential support, outside Scandinavia itself, to the concept of progressive Norway in 1837. To him, Norway represented the fullest embodiment of the liberal ideal, surpassing even the United States. Liberty and equality, according to him, were based in Norway upon an essentially even distribution of property. "If there be a happy class of people in Europe," he wrote, "it is the Norwegian bonder [*bonde*]. He is the owner of his little estate, and has no feudal duty or feudal service to pay to any superior. He is the king of his own land, and landlord as well as king."[15] The Americans Brace and Taylor favorably compared Norway's liberal constitution with their own.[16]

Before the late nineteenth century, however, foreign accounts generally had little to say about Norway's towns and cities or about the life and culture of its upper classes. August Gödecke in the early 1870s, for example, wrote hardly a word about such things. They hardly seemed to fit the image of Romantic-Picturesque Norway or of its fondly imagined peasant democracy. Even those writers who gave some attention to the cosmopolitan urban scene, like Bayard Taylor in 1857 or the Franco-American Paul Du Chaillu in his immensely popular and widely translated *Land of the Midnight Sun* in 1881, seem to have done so out of a sense of obligation—and all too often what they had to say was condescending. Their hearts were clearly in the fjords and valleys.[17]

The foreigners' attitudes toward these aspects of Norwegian life reveal that while they were proud of progress at home, they were reluctant to see it in Norway, which they idealized as static and unchanging, an unspoiled refuge from the dislocations and conflicts of the "real" world beyond. "May no intruder," John Barrow Jr. wrote in 1834, "disturb your peaceful cottages with wild and pernicious theories, that lead only to confusion and ruin!" According to the American Robert Pritchett in 1879, "Our delight is to live out of our present century in fresh air and simplicity."[18]

The perspective widened with the dramatic flowering of Norwegian cultural creativity by the mid-nineteenth century. Again, its impact was felt first and most forcefully in neighboring Sweden and Denmark. Indeed, the Norwegian cultural breakthrough in Sweden, at a time of relative cultural stagnation there, was in some ways almost as remarkable as it was in Norway itself. It began with Ole Bull, the Norwegian Düsseldorf painters, and Bjørnstjerne Bjørnson's *Synnøve Solbakken* and other *fortællinger*, or peasant tales, in the 1850s, Henrik Ibsen's *Brand* in 1866, followed by Bjørnson's and particularly Ibsen's powerful contemporary Realist dramas, and the evocative music of Edvard Grieg. For decades, Norwegian culture inspired wide emulation in Sweden. August Strindberg wrote indignantly in 1886—when Swedish "Norvegomania" had reached its height—"Rome conquered Greece, but Greece conquered Rome. Sweden had taken Norway, but now Norway took Sweden."[19]

In Denmark, meanwhile, the critic Georg Brandes became the torchbearer for Ibsen's and Bjørnson's social realism, while Frederik Hegel of Gyldendals *Forlag* in Copenhagen was the publisher of most of the works of Norway's leading writers, in the common Danish-Norwegian literary language, during the later nineteenth century.

Before the 1860s, few visitors came to Norway from the other Scandinavian lands. Swedes and Danes preferred to travel elsewhere in Europe—or, increasingly, to America. Early book-length accounts of Norway, however, began to appear in Denmark by the later 1860s. Thereafter Danish visitors arrived in growing numbers. The Norwegian cultural vogue, the newly opened railway from Stockholm to Christiania, and August Gödecke's widely popular accounts from 1873 and 1875 now drew ever more Swedes to Norway.[20]

By the 1870s, Norwegian culture began to make conquests elsewhere in the Western world as well. A succession of Norwegian artists, beginning with Johan Christian Dahl in Dresden, Adolf Tidemand, Hans Gude and the other Norwegian Düsseldorf painters, and in time Edvard Munch, spent lengthy periods in Germany, as did Henrik Ibsen, who also lived there at times, and his Danish prophet Georg Brandes, all of whom received great acclaim and were widely influential.[21] British critics and translators, above all Sir Edmond Gosse, William Archer, and George Bernard Shaw, made Ibsen in particular a cult figure in the English-speaking cultural circles.[22] Halfdan Kjerulf's, Ole Bull's, and Edvard Grieg's music with its profoundly Norwegian character became renowned far beyond Scandinavia. In time Knut Hamsun and Sigrid Undset would become household names abroad. Norway became a revered contributor to Western culture. Moreover, a considerable amount of foreign verse and fiction came to deal with Norwegian motifs, often from the Viking Age, much of it popular and ephemeral, including much children's literature.[23]

Norwegian literature and the arts meanwhile conveyed a mixed message, reflecting conflicting views of the national identity within Norway itself tracing back at least to the controversy between Henrik Wergeland's "Patriot" and Johan Welhaven's "Intelligence" parties in the 1830s and 1840s. Bodil Stenseth has recently described the three-cornered conflict by the end of the century between the ultranationalist *Ungdomssrørsla*, or rural youth movement, which considered the peasantry the only true Norwegians and *landsmål* the only authentic national language; the "Lysaker Circle" around Fridtjof Nansen, Erik Werenskiold, and Gerhard Munthe, which sought to reconcile traditional Norway with the modern world; and the "Kristiania intelligensia," around Christian Krohg and his friends, with their cosmopolitan orientation and skepticism toward old traditions. Foreigners thus received cultural impulses from both the Romantic-Picturesque and from the Modern, Progressive traditions. Norway appeared at once a very old and a very new nation.[24]

This dilemma is evident in the presentation of Norway at the great international expositions of the later nineteenth and early twentieth centuries: whether to portray the Picturesque Norway the foreign public expected or to show Norway as an up-to-date, progressive nation. The result tended to be a national pavilion in the medieval "Dragon Style," filled with the products of modern industry.[25]

There were, as noted, variations in foreign perceptions of Norway, based in good part upon nationality and gender. Some contrast is apparent, for instance, between sporty Britons and more studious Germans. Before 1815, women travelers who left some account were extremely rare. Mary Wollstonecraft was the notable exception. But her particular concern with her own gender and with domestic life in general would be characteristic for the greater number that followed during the nineteenth century, a time, moreover, when Norway pioneered in the area of female emancipation.

Meanwhile, amid the general enthusiasm for Norway, some critical voices were heard. Poverty, filth, and backwardness were all too apparent in some of the more remote parts of the country. Von Buch in 1806 had little regard for the Norwegian fishermen in Finnmarken, regarding the Finns, or *kvener*, of the region, and even the Russians from the Murman coast as more sober and industrious. The Lapps, he felt, were destined for extinction, like the Indians of the Ohio Valley in America. Much as he admired the Norwegian peasants' frugality and simple way of life, August Gödecke, for example, believed that this consisted more of doing without than of working harder to acquire those things that would make life more pleasant. He was sharply critical of their suspicion of outside ideas, including more rational methods of farming. Norway, he was convinced, could be far more prosperous than it was.[26]

Sexual morality among the Norwegian peasantry was, especially for Anglo-Saxons, hard to understand during the Victorian age. While the Reverend Thomas Malthus in 1799 noted the high frequency of pregnancy before marriage, he tolerantly explained that this almost always led to marriage and indeed was socially accepted, Bayard Taylor was shocked by what he considered flagrant immorality, particularly in Gudbrandsdalen and Hedemarken.[27]

That all was not well in the land of the latter-day Vikings was shown by the growing numbers of Norwegians who emigrated, as noted especially by the Americans Brace and Taylor. Brace tells something of the reactions of emigrants, flamboyant in their American ways, who already in 1857 revisited their old homeland and were outspoken in their criticism of its backwardness and lack of enterprise. "Old Norway don't do beside the West, sir," one of them complained, ". . . We'd show 'em a thing or two if they'd come oute to Wisconsing!"[28]

A more frequent criticism was that of the corrupting influence of contact with the outside world. Mary Wollstonecraft was repelled by the mercenary character of the coastal population in Vestfold, contrasting it with what she imagined to be the simplicity and honesty of the peasantry in the interior. E. D. Clarke in 1799 remarked on the Norwegians' covetous and mercenary character, while La Tocnaye in 1801 considered that the avaricious inhabitants of Sunnadalen "must be the grandparents of our Normans." Among others who remarked on it, Bayard Taylor was especially exasperated by this characteristic.[29]

Many of the more serious travelers visited more than one Nordic land, which led to comparisons between them. The later eighteenth-century travelers found Norway—which for them generally meant Christiania, Øst- and Vestfold—more thriving and prosperous than neighboring Denmark or southern Sweden, and the Norwegians a livelier people. Samuel Laing strongly favored Norway over Sweden. By the mid-nineteenth century, Brace and Taylor praised Norway's democratic constitution in contrast to Sweden's antiquated system of government. But both, especially Taylor, and others as well, clearly preferred Sweden and the Swedes. Taylor was repelled not only by the avarice and chicanery he encountered in Norway but also by the Norwegians' "excessive national vanity," in contrast to the Swedes' scrupulous honesty and undue modesty.[30]

Perhaps the greater tendency of the Americans Brace and Taylor to be less tolerant than Europeans generally of the Norwegians' particular faults and failings may have had to do with their own sensitivity over coming from a country that had more than enough of primitive conditions, sharp dealing, and braggadocio. Similarly, the Swede, Gödecke, familiar at home with conditions basically similar to Norway's, was also critical of the Norwegians' hostility toward useful innovations.[31]

Despite such discordant notes, Norway during the later eighteenth and the "long nineteenth century" gained an enviable reputation throughout the Western world. This in turn brought its advantages, not least political.

Norway's great popularity in Great Britain contributed in no small measure to British support for the largely independent status it gained in its union with Sweden in 1814, as well as its successful dissolution of the union in 1905. It would also create a particular concern with Norway in Britain and the United States during World War II.[32]

Romantic-Picturesque Norway lives on in a sometimes uneasy union with modern, progressive, and prosperous Norway in the minds of the world beyond. It is a vision strongly supported abroad by *Norges Turistråd*, the Norwegian Tourism Council. It lives on even in Norway itself, where the national self-image could not but be affected by foreign perceptions of the land and its inhabitants. The themes first set already by the beginning of the nineteenth century have endured down to the present day.

Notes

This is an expanded version of a paper presented at "Norgebilleder" symposium at Schæffergården, Gentofte, Denmark, 2004.

1. The first part of this essay is based mainly on my *Northern Arcadia: Foreign Travelers in Scandinavia, 1765–1815* (Carbondale, Ill., 1998)., After I had begun working on this essay, I acquired Peter Fjågesund and Ruth A. Symes's just published *The Northern Utopia: British Perceptions of Norway in the Nineteenth Century* (Amsterdam and New York, 2003), which enriched my research on the topic for the later period. The most useful bibliography for travelers in Scandinavia as a whole is Samuel E. Bring, *Itineraria Svecana. Bibliotrafiska förteckning över resor i Sverige fram till 1950* (Stockholm, 1954), which is arranged chronologically and includes many accounts dealing in part with travel in the other Nordic countries. For Norway specifically, see Hjalmar Pettersen, *Utlændingers Reiser i Norge* (Kristiania, 1897), and esp. Eiler H. Schiøtz, *Itineraria Norvegica: A Bibliography on Foreigners' Travels in Norway until 1900*, 2 vols. (Oslo, 1970–86).

2. Charles L. Batten Jr., *Pleasurable Instruction: Form and Convention in Eighteenth-Century Travel Literature* (Berkeley, 1978).

3. Fjågesund and Symes, *Northern Utopia*, 33.

4. William Coxe, *Travels into Poland, Russia, Sweden, and Denmark*, 4th ed. (London, 1792), vols. 4 and 5; Leopold von Buch, *Travels through Norway and Lapland during the Years 1806, 1807, and 1808* (London, 1813).

5. Baron de La Brède et de Montesquieu [Charles-Louis de Secondat], *L'Ésprit des lois* (Paris, 1748), bk. 17, chapt. 2; Paul Henri Mallet, *Introduction à l'histoire de Dennemarc* (Copenhagen, 1755), and *Monumens de la mythologie et de la poésie des Celtes, et particulièrement des anciens Scandinaves* (Copenhagen, 1756); Thomas Percy, *Northern Antiquities* (London, 1770); Edward Daniel Clarke, *Travels in Various Countries of Europe, Asia, and Africa*, 6 vols. (London, 1810–23), 5:598, 620, 712–13; [Francisco de Miranda,] *Miranda i Danmark. Francisco de Miranda's danske rejsedagbog 1787–1788*, trans. and ed. Haarvarad Rostrup (Copenhagen, 1987), 146. Cf. Samuel M

Kliger, *The Goths in England: A Study in Seventeenth- and Eighteenth-Century Thought* (Cambridge, Mass., 1952); Margaret Omberg, *Scandinavian Themes in English Poetry, 1760–1800* (Uppsala, 1976); my *Northern Arcadia*, chapt. 6.

6. [Francisco de Miranda,] *Miranda i Sverige och Norge 1787. General Francisco de Mirandas dagbok från hans resa september-december 1787*, trans. and ed. Stig Rydén (Stockholm, 1950); Charles [Carl] Küttner, *Travels through Denmark, Sweden, Austria and Part of Italy in 1798 & 1799* (London, 1805); Jacques-Louis de Bourgrenet de La Tocnaye, *Promenade d'un français en Suède et en Norvège*, 2 vols. (Brunswick, 1801), in Norwegian, *En franskmann i Norge i 1799*, trans. Axel Amlie (Oslo, 1980), for the parts dealing with Norway; [Thomas Malthus,] *The Travel Diaries of Thomas Robert Malthus*, ed. Patricia James (Cambridge, 1966); Clarke, *Travels in Various Countries*; Mary Wollstonecraft, *Letters Written during a Short Residence in Sweden, Norway, and Denmark*, facsimile ed. (Fontwell, 1970).

7. See my *Northern Arcadia*, 176–77.

8. Peter August Gödecke, "En resa i Norge," *Land och folk. Tidskrift utgifven af Sällskapet för Nyttiga Kunskapers Spridande* (1873): 58. Cf. my "Peter August Gödecke, den svenska folkhögskolan och Norge," *Personhistorisk tidskrift* 98 (2002): 5–20.

9. William and Mary Howitt, *The Literature and Romance of Northern Europe*, 2 vols. (London, 1852), 2:33–34; Charles Loring Brace, *The Norse-Folk; or, a Visit to the Homes of Norway and Sweden* (New York, 1857), iii, 88. Cf. Paul B. Du Chaillu, *Land of the Midnight Sun: Summer and Winter Travels through Sweden, Norway, Lapland, and Northern Finland*, 2 vols. (New York, 1882), 1:3.

10. See Gerhard Martin and Walter Hubatsch, *Deutschland und Skandinavien im Wandel der Jahrhunderte*, 2nd. ed. (Darmstadt, 1977); Bernd Henningsen et al., *Skandinavien och Tyskland 1800–1914. Möten och vänskapsband* (Stockholm, 1997); Ivar Sagmo, "Norge—et forbilde eller et utviklingsland? Folk og land i første halvdel av 1800-tallet—set med tyske reisendets øyne," in *Jakten på det norske*, ed. Øystein Sørensen (Oslo, 1998), 74–91; Bo Grandien, *Rönndruvans glöd. Nygöticistiskt i tanke, konst och miljö under 1800-talet* (Stockholm, 1987), 121–30, and "'Det var ej dag, det var ej natt, det vägde emellan båda . . .' Refektioner kring Sognfjord," in *Myt och landskap. Unionsupplösning och kulturell gemenskap*, ed. Hans Henrik Brummer (Stockholm, 2005), 147–65. Also Paul Güszfeldt, *Kaiser Wilhelm II. Reisen nach Norwegen in den Jahren 1889 bis 1892* (Berlin, 1892); Birgit Marschall, *Reisen und Regierung. Die Nordlandsfahrten Kaisers Wilhelm II.* (Heidelberg, 1991).

11. Wollstonecraft, *Letters*, 167–68.

12. Brace, *Norse-Folk*, 142; Bayard Taylor, *Northern Travel: Summer and Winter Pictures. Sweden, Denmark, and Lapland* (New York, 1887), 317–18. Taylor's book was first published with the more accurate subtitle *Winter Pictures of Sweden, Lapland, and Norway* (New York, 1857).

13. See my *Sweden and Visions of Norway: Politics and Culture, 1814–1905* (Carbondale, Ill., 2003), esp. chapt. 2.

14. Orla Lehmann, *Norge og Nordmændene. Reiseerindringer fra 1836 og 1865* (Kjøbenhavn, 1865), preface (n. p.). Cf. Henrik Scharling, *En Sommer i Norge. Fra Christiania*

til Finnmarken (Kjøbenhavn, 1867), 23–29. See also Vagn Skovgaard-Petersen, *Tiden 1814–1864*, Danmarks historie, ed. H. P. Clausen and Søren Mørch, 5 (Copenhagen, 1985), 198; Claus Bjørn, *Fra reaktion til grundlov 1800–1850*, Gyldendals og Politikens Danmarkshistorie, ed. Olaf Olsen, 10 (Copenhagen, 1990), 255; *Dansk identitetshistorie*, 2: *Ett yndigt land 1789–1848*, ed. Ole Feldbæk (Copenhagen, 1991), 366.

15. Samuel Laing, *Journal of a Residence in Norway during the Years 1834, 1835, and 1836; Made with a View to Enquire into the Moral and Political Economy of that Country, and the Condition of Its Inhabitants* (London, 1837), esp. iii–iv, 120–22, 331, 333, 479–80. Cf. Laing's *A Tour of Sweden in 1836; Comprising Observations on the Moral, Political, and Economical State of the Swedish Nation* (London, 1839), which contrasts Norwegian with Swedish conditions.

16. Taylor, *Northern Travel*, 239–40, 328, 403; Brace, *Norse-Folk*, 54, 386–87.

17. Taylor, *Northern Travel*; Du Chaillu, *Land of the Midnight Sun*.

18. John Barrow Jr., *Excursions into the North of Europe* (London, 1834), 378; Robert Taylor Pritchett, *"Gamle Norge": Rambles and Scrambles in Norway* (London, 1879), 13. Cf. Sagmo, "Norge—et forebilde eller et utviklingsland?," 91; Fjågesund and Symes, *Northern Utopia*, 273–75.

19. See my *Sweden and Visions of Norway*, esp. chapt. 4; Arne Lidén, *Den norska strömnngen i svensk litteratur under 1800-talet* (Uppsala, 1926); Grandien, *Rönndruvans glöd*, esp. 130–40; August Strindberg, *Jäsningen*, in *Samlade skrifter*, ed. John Landquist, 55 vols. (Stockholm, 1912–19), 18:354–55, 358.

20. See, for ex., Lehman, *Norge og Nordmændene*; Scharling, *En Sommer i Norge*; Richard Kaufmann, *I Norge* (Kjøbenhavn, 1869); Gödecke, "En resa i Norge," 1–32, 193–231, 289–328, and *Turistbref från en resa i Norge sommaren 1875 af Finn* (Stockholm, 1876); my "Peter August Gödecke" and *Sweden and Visions of Norway*, 111–14; Grandien, "'Det var ej dag, det var ej natt,'" 139–42.

21. See esp. Henningsen et al., *Skandinavien och Tyskland*.

22. See esp. Ann Thwaite, *Edmund Gosse: A Literary Landscape* (London, 1984); Bernard Shaw, *Shaw and Ibsen: Shaw's "The Quintessence of Ibsenism," and Related Writings*, ed. and introd. J. L. Wiesenthal (Toronto, 1979).

23. See esp. Henningsen, *Skandinavien och Tyskland*; Michael Meyer, *Ibsen*, 3 vols. (London, 1967–71), vols. 2 and 3. I cannot agree with Fjågesund and Symes, *Northern Utopia* (31–32), that Norwegian cultural influence was a negligible factor in forming outside perceptions of Norway before the end of the nineteenth century. On British literature on Norwegian themes, see Fjågesund and Symes, ibid., 141–46.

24. Bodil Stenseth, *En norsk elite. Nasjonsbyggene på Lysaker 1880–1940* (Oslo, 1883); my *Sweden and Visions of Norway*, 174–75. Cf. Lidén, *Norska strömningar*, 292.

25. See, for ex., *Tradisjon og fornyelse. Norge kring århundreskiftet*, [ed. Tone Skedsmo] (Oslo, 1994), esp. 334–36; Brita Brenna, *Verden som ting og forestilling. Verdensutstillinger og den norske deltakelsen 1851–1900* (Oslo, 2001). In *Art, Culture, and National Identity in Fin-de-Siècle Europe*, ed. Michelle Facos and Sharon Hirsh (Cambridge and New York, 2003), several essays dealing, for ex., with Hungary, Russia, and Switzerland, reveal this same conflict between presentation of the traditional versus the modern at international exhibitions.

26. My *Northern Arcadia*, 125, 161–62, and "Peter August Gödecke," 15–16. Cf. Taylor, *Northern Travel*, 248.

27. Malthus, *Travel Diaries*, 153, 172. Cf. La Tocnaye, *Promenade*, 2:51–53, 195; my *Northern Arcadia*, 109–10; Brace, *Norse-Folk*, 33, 265; Taylor, *Northern Travel*, 285, 400. Fjågesund and Symes, *Northern Utopia*, has surprisingly little to say on this subject.

28. Brace, *Norse-Folk*, 97–99; Taylor, *Northern Travel*, 350.

29. Wollstonecraft, *Letters*, 172; Clarke, *Travels*, 5:599, 616–17; La Tocnaye, *Promenade*, 2:144; Brace, *Norse-Folk*, 57–58; Taylor, *Northern Travel*, 329, 346, 379–81, 405; Scharling, *En sommer i Norge*, 47–48; my *Northern Arcadia*, 114, 163.

30. Brace, *Norse-Folk*, 57, 99, 302, 386–87, 455–64; Taylor, *Northern Travel*, 239–40, 327–29, 379–80. Cf. Du Chaillu, *Land of the Midnight Sun*, 1:191.

31. Interestingly, Mark Davies has recently suggested a greater tendency among British travelers to criticize the slow pace of progress in Sweden than in Norway, in a manner similar to Gödecke's criticism of Norway. See his *A Perambulating Paradox: British Travel Literature and the Image of Sweden c. 1770–1865* (Lund, 2000).

32. See, for ex., Terje I. Leiren, "1814 and British Opinion," *Scandinavian Studies* 47 (1975): 364–82; Lars Tangeraas, "Castlereagh, Bernadotte and Norway," *Scandinavian Journal of History* 8 (1983): 193–223; my *Sweden and Visions of Norway*, 79. Cf. Fjågesund and Symes, *Northern Utopia*, 102–6.

The Silver Age of Swedish
National Romanticism, 1905–20

In reflecting on the past we are often struck by the disparity between the realities of a time and place, on the one hand, and the ideal picture of their society that contemporaries strove to create, on the other. How different a view of classic Greece in the fifth century B.C. do we not get from the *"edle Einfalt und stille Grösse"* (noble simplicity and quiet grandeur)—in J. J. Winckelmann's memorable description—of cool, white marble, and from reading Thucydides' account of the savagery of the Peloponnesian War? It is evident, moreover, that the ideal so often directly contradicts the reality in an obvious effort to counterbalance the evils of the times.

The problem of re-creating an objective picture of a past era is compounded by the contrasting approaches of scholars in different disciplines. Historians of literature and the arts typically concentrate upon avant-gardes and new directions, whereas general historians seeking to re-create life as it was actually experienced at the time look for what was most typical. Characteristically the prevailing cultural climate of an era is the work of yesterday's—rather than today's—avant-gardes.

A good example is the period between roughly 1905 and 1920 in Sweden. General historians reveal a society undergoing rapid and often traumatic change, fraught with social and industrial strife, and divided over fundamental conflicts of political principle. Historians of literature and the arts have sought above all to trace the origins of modernism during this period, as far back in time as possible. Yet in the experience of the great majority of Swedes there can be no doubt that these years saw the final culmination of the National Romanticism that had arisen in the 1890s. This seems particularly evident during the years 1914 to 1918 when Sweden, together with Denmark and Norway, maintained its precarious neutrality during World War I.[1]

This thought struck me with particular force when I was recently in Allhelgona Church, dedicated in 1918, built in wood, red-painted, and decorated in the style of a Dalarna country church, high on a wooded hill bordered by neoclassical apartment houses in chaste late Gustavian style, originally built for working-class families, only a stone's throw from bustling Götgatan in Stockholm.

The later impression of a generational shift in Swedish culture is created not only by the appearance of new faces and ideas after the beginning of the new century but also by the passing of many of the leading figures of the later nineteenth century from the scene. Artur Hazelius died in 1901, Oscar Levertin in 1906, Gustaf Fröding in 1911, August Strindberg in 1912.

Yet many of them lived on into the period and beyond. Indeed, some of their best work was accomplished during the second and third decades of the new century. Eugène Jansson died in 1915, Carl Larsson and Richard Bergh in 1919, Anders Zorn in 1920, Karl Nordström in 1923, Ellen Key in 1926, Erik Axel Karlfeldt in 1931. Meanwhile Selma Lagerlöf, Verner von Heidenstam, and Albert Engström lived on until 1940, Hjalmar Söderberg and Karl-Erik Forsslund until 1941, Wilhelm Peterson-Berger until 1942, and Prince Eugen until 1947.

Others who first achieved prominence around the turn of the century carried on, in their own ways, aspects of the National Romantic tradition: Bo Bergman, Henning Berger, Hjalmar Bergman, Anders Österling, Hugo Alfvén, Carl Wilhelmson, Carl Eldh. Meanwhile, influential critics, like Fredrik Böök, Klara Johansson, and Carl G. Laurin, held high the National Romantic banner. The academic historians, mainly political conservatives, such as Carl Hildebrand, Ludvig Stavenow, or Gottfrid Carlsson, concentrated on Sweden's past glories, while Carl Grimberg, Fabian Månsson, and others catered to a growing lay market for popularized history.

If the Pantheon of the 1890s continued to dominate the areas of literature, the fine arts, and music during this period, in architecture National Romanticism only fully came into its own after the turn of the century, particularly between 1905 and 1920 and for some years thereafter. The work of Carl Westman, Lars Israel Wahlman, Ragnar Östberg, Torben Grut, Ivar

Tengbom, and others expresses ideals already articulated by the writers, artists, composers, and folklorists. It is in this area that late National Romanticism has left its most impressive evidence. To take Stockholm and its surroundings alone, there are the Lawcourt building (*Rådhus*; 1909–15), Stadium (1910–12), City Hall (1911–23), Engelbrekt and Högalid Churches (1910–15, 1917–23, respectively), and the charming Diplomantstaden and Lärkstaden from the same period. The city and its suburbs abound with massive red-brick schools and other monumental public edifices, "bank palaces," and more modest but nonetheless imposing apartment buildings, for instance in Vasastaden or Råsunda, reflecting the sixteenth-century Vasa Renaissance or the Baroque or Caroline styles of Sweden's seventeenth-century era of greatness.[2]

Private villas in affluent suburbs like Djursholm, Saltsjöbaden, or parts of Bromma characteristically reflected peasant vernaculars—above from Dalarna. Increasingly, from around 1910, the Gustavian style of the late-eighteenth-century manor house provided a new source of inspiration for domestic architecture, at least down through the 1920s. The ideal was the old rural Sweden, as well described by the architect and designer Carl Malmsten in 1916:

> The classical calm, the peacefulness of the unbroken horizon, the gathered and monumental grouping of the buildings, are characteristics of the old Swedish building tradition. Simple farmsteads as well as manor houses, the white country churches, stately mansions and palaces from the Age of Greatness, Gothic as well as Classical buildings—all strive to achieve a unity without disturbing elements.[3]

In the introduction to a handbook for participants in the rural *egnahem*, or "own-home" movement, which got under way around the turn of the century, Adrian Molin called in 1909 for "simple, sound, inexpensive, and well-disposed dwellings *of a Swedish character*. No cheap imitations of foreign upper-class villas but Swedish homes like those our fathers built. For behind them lay *Swedish thoughts*, and it is Swedish thoughts we ought be to thinking."[4] National Romanticism is likewise reflected in the modest domestic architecture of the planned "own-home" suburbs for working-class families, such as Stockholm's Gamla Enskede.[5]

The building of numerous new churches, on both a monumental and a more modest scale, often through public subscriptions, in the larger cities, in working-class districts as well as in affluent suburbs, reflected the rejuvenation of the Church of Sweden from around the turn of the century in the face of urbanization, free-church evangelicalism, and indifferentism.

A private villa in Gävle, built around 1900. This fine example of late Swedish National Romanticism in domestic architecture combines graceful late-eighteenth-century classicism with details inspired by traditional peasant culture. (Courtesy of Eva Eriksson, Bromma.)

Best remembered in this regard is the "Young Church" movement associated with Einar Billing, Johan Alfred Eklund, Nathan Söderblom, and
Manfred Björkqvist, with its ideal of the historic "folk church," open to all,
as opposed to the free churches, which held out the prospect of salvation
exclusively for believers. It was in 1909 that Björkqvist and his band of
enthusiastic student comrades from Uppsala embarked upon their great
Christian crusade throughout the land. The same year saw the founding
of the movement's periodical, *Vår lösen*, and its publishing house. Its folk
high school and conference center, Sigtuna Stiftelsen, opened its doors in
1916. Eklund's once well-known hymn, "Fädernas kyrka i Sveriges land"
(Our Fathers' Church in Sweden's Land") from 1909 well expresses its ideal
of national unity and concord:

> Christian and free shall Sweden live,
> Alone shall it determine its fate.
> For this in manly and Christian faith,
> For this in strife or lawbound peace,
> King and folk unite.

Not surprisingly, given Sweden's increasingly multicultural population,
this hymn has since been omitted from the Swedish hymnal. The Young
Church movement was of course fervently patriotic, and it provided a sizable contribution to the building of the controversial armored warship,
the F-Boat, in 1912.[6]

Skansen, the national outdoor museum on Djurgården in Stockholm
and shrine of traditional Swedish peasant culture, was never more popular,
and it made some important new additions during these years, including
Älvrosgården (the Älvros farm) in 1915 and Seglora church in 1916. Skansen's powerful influence in turn was reflected in the thriving local folk-
culture, or *hembygd*, movement throughout the land with its numerous
hembygdsgårdar. Interest in traditional folk culture was characteristically
reinforced by the temperance societies, by the folk high schools (*folkhögskolor*), of which several first opened their doors during this period, and
by a growing number of adult study circles.[7]

The period between 1890 and 1920 saw intense efforts to rescue or re-create Sweden's fading folk culture, most notably among the urban bourgeoisie.
Old customs that had fallen out of use—even in places the traditional
Midsummer festivities—were revived, and a variety of new "folk" customs
were introduced. Folk dance and folk music groups, clad in revived (or
often re-created) folk dress, flourished—even among the far-off Swedish
element in America—whose repertory included many newly composed

dances and "dance games." Traditional handicrafts became the vogue and inspired new designs in, for instance, weaving, needlework, and furniture design.[8] The Swedish Tourist Society, *Svenska Turistföreningen* increasingly promoted popular tourism to historic cultural sites, as well as to Sweden's far northern wilderness.[9]

Children grew up with the idyllic vision of rural Sweden created, for instance, by Anna Maria Roos' *Sörgården* and *Från Onnemo* (both from 1912), the illustrated tales of Elsa Beskow and John Bauer, the songs of Alice Tegnér. In school they read Selma Lagerlöf's *Nils Holgerssons underbara äventyr* (The Wonderful Adventures of Nils) from 1906–7 and Heidenstam's *Svenskarna och deras hövdingar* (The Swedes and Their Chieftains) from 1908–9, which instilled national pride and traditional values.[10]

Already by the war years film was emerging as a significant new field of Swedish cultural activity. Its early products were often quintessentially National Romantic in motif and milieu. And what could be more thoroughly *gammelsvensk*, or old Swedish, in appearance than the studios in Råsunda of Svensk Filmindustri, established in 1919?[11]

The overall impression one gains from the cultural ambiance of the period is one of peace and social harmony, of common devotion to the fatherland, its nature, and the proud heritage of its past, of dedication to venerable, shared moral and cultural values. And this is particularly striking during the years of World War I, the Russian Revolution, and the Finnish Civil War, when Sweden struggled with severe material hardships and was rent by serious internal conflicts.

The contrast is heightened in retrospect by the advance, on a broad front, of cosmopolitan modernism during the 1920s. One must nevertheless hold with the literary historian E. N. Tigerstedt, that 1920, rather than 1910, marks the real divide (*"vattendelaren"*) in Sweden's modern literature, or—let us say—its culture in the wider sense. A more dramatic turning point, one might well argue, would be the Stockholm Exhibition of 1930 which heralded the breakthrough of Functionalism in architecture and design. The second decade of the twentieth century was at once the mature culmination and the swan song of creative Swedish National Romanticism.[12]

How is one to explain the final creative upsurge of National Romanticism during this period? The years prior to the outbreak of World War I were a time of considerable ferment and turmoil, beginning with Norway's unilateral dissolution of the Swedish-Norwegian union in June 1905. This came as a profound shock both to old-line nationalists, with their fond dreams of Sweden's past imperial greatness, and to liberal Scandinavianists, with their high ideal of Nordic brotherhood.

At the same time, the dissolution revitalized Swedish life in all areas: economic, social, political, and cultural. In renouncing the Norwegian throne Oscar II called upon his Swedish subjects to regain within what had been lost. Others looked more hopefully to the future. To a Norwegian journalist, Gerda Bergh wrote already in July 1905,

> What a tremendous gain it has been for Sweden that this dissolution has come about. It is like a dawning hope that the time will now come when we can vigorously devote ourselves to our internal development. Now we should be able to work toward great cultural goals and make Sweden strong.

Two years later Verner von Heidenstam wrote to Bjørnstjerne Bjørnson of a great national awakening extending far down into Swedish society. The "Young Right" (*Unghögern*), with Rudolf Kjellén in the van, envisioned a new Swedish "Age of Greatness" (*Storhetstid*) based on industry and technology.[13]

A greatly widened manhood suffrage went into effect in 1909, followed by the rapid breakthrough of the progressive Liberal party (*Liberala samlingspartiet*), soon to be followed by the Social Democrats, as Sweden's largest single political party. The General Strike of 1909 sent shock waves throughout society, causing many of the National Romantic artists and writers who had prided themselves on liberal or radical views to reexamine their political priorities. The country was rent by dissension over defense expenditures, against a background of mounting international tensions in Europe.

Then, in August 1914, came the Great War, which in horror and magnitude soon far exceeded anything civilized Europeans imagined possible in a rational and progressive world. Western society was shaken to its roots. Sweden succeeded in preserving its neutrality, but the war aroused profound fears over the security of the fatherland. A national moral mobilization, rising above internal divisions over class and material interests, seemed imperative. Such a *nationell samling* had long been the conservative nostrum in the face of Norwegian demands within the now defunct union, emigration, and labor disputes. The wartime emergency thus provided a welcome opportunity to rally Svea's sons and daughters around the blue-gold banner. It seems symptomatic, in this regard, that the National Society against Emigration (*Nationalföreningen mot emigrationen*), established in 1907, reached its highest membership in 1917, even though at that time emigration was practically impossible.[14]

During the early years of the war Sweden continued to enjoy the overall economic prosperity it had recently attained on the basis of profitable exports to the belligerent powers, above all Germany, as well as increased production to meet domestic needs. This provided the material means to support a thriving cultural life at least until 1917, when conditions became much bleaker until the end of the war.

That spring—following the February Revolution in Russia—growing shortages and rising prices led to demonstrations and rioting in Stockholm. Public measures on a large scale became necessary to relieve distress and stem popular discontent. As construction of architect-designed private villas largely ceased, lack of adequate workers' housing, high rents, and overcrowding led to the construction of entire blocks of apartment buildings for working-class families by communal housing authorities and co-operative housing associations. Although they were rationally planned and economically built, the aesthetic element was not overlooked in their construction, most often inspired by a restrained late Gustavian, neoclassical style. In addition, temporary urban housing was built of wood, characteristically painted red with white trim, in the style of the nineteenth-century farmsteads of central Sweden. Some indeed have been preserved, as in Stockholm's Vanadislunden, and have since become much-sought-after dwellings. Both types of housing during and after the war carried their ideological message of social conciliation and devotion to the fatherland and its cultural heritage.[15]

The war was followed by a general European economic recession lasting, in Sweden's case, until 1922. Shortages during the emergency increased reliance on Swedish agriculture, strengthening once again the ideal of the *bonde*, or farmer, as the backbone of the nation, culturally as well as materially. Since the turn of the century, confidence had been high in the economic feasibility of the small family farm, as opposed to large landed estate, given the rising costs and low productivity of hired labor. During the war years the rural "own-home" movement that encouraged and provided assistance for the establishment of independent small holdings rapidly gained ground. In the cities, the garden allotments (*kolonitr ädgårdar*), under municipal auspices, which had become popular before the war, gained new importance as a source of household food supplies, and the little cabins the *kolonister* were permitted to build, under strict controls, reflected in miniature the old rural *stugor*, or cottages, where so many of them had first seen the light of day.[16]

Largely isolated from the outside world in their dogged neutrality, Swedes tended during the war years to turn inward, to fall back upon their own cultural resources. In some ways, too, their inter-Nordic contacts increased, including cultural ties. To be sure there were tensions in Sweden between a small but influential group of "Activists," who urged intervention on the side of the Central Powers, and the majority that staunchly supported neutrality, as well as over reactions to the Russian revolutions of 1917. Still, on all sides the war aroused a strongly felt need to examine and reaffirm basic, traditional Swedish values, however these might be conceived. Beyond that, there was a manifest sense of Sweden's providential mission in preserving civilized values in a world gone mad. The founders of *Tidskrift för konstvetenskap*, for instance, hoped, as they wrote in their first number in 1916, that their journal would provide moral support in time of war, when it was especially important that "the neutral peoples maintain their culture, indeed strengthen and heighten it."[17]

What parallels may be drawn between national romanticisms in Sweden and elsewhere in the Western world during the conflict-ridden years leading up to the Great War and during the war itself? Everywhere internal and international conflict gave rise to appeals for national *ralliément*. Everywhere, too, it lent a new urgency to the search for heritage and fundamental values.[18] Developments were essentially similar in the other Nordic lands, with the tragic exception of Finland. Among the great powers nationalism assumed belligerently chauvinist forms, stressing heroism and sacrifice in the service of the fatherland. The proud isolationism and moralistic neutrality of the United States during the early war years show similarities to the Scandinavian countries, but the tone became bellicose and xenophobic after America itself entered the war in 1917. The examples of other neutral countries, such as Switzerland or The Netherlands during these years, would be instructive.

The long-term consequences of National Romanticism in Sweden were markedly disparate, for it could lend itself to varied interpretation. It could inspire the idealism of Swedish volunteers in Finland during its Civil War in 1918 or the Winter War in 1939–40—or conversely provide an ideological background for the little handful who joined the German SS during World War II. But for the great majority of Swedes, it inspired the vision of national community, where reason, justice, and humanity reigned, a haven of peace and beacon of hope for the wider world.

Those who have concerned themselves with the overall cultural impact of the First World War in the Western world have understandably stressed the shock, disorientation, and disillusionment it created at the time and after.[19] Swedish culture was by no means immune to such currents in the

postwar period. The Swedish example during the war years shows nonetheless how in a small neutral nation the storms without could inspire the
vision of a proud and ancient folk at peace with itself and the world.

In 1922, the Norwegian poet Nils Collett Vogt, whose wife was Swedish
and who spent much time in Sweden, wrote wistfully, "In Sweden since
1905 a new national life has blossomed forth. Can we Norwegians say the
same here?" In 1896, he recalled, Verner von Heidenstam had sternly taken
his Swedish compatriots to task for their lack of national feeling and exaggerated cosmopolitanism in his famous essay "Svenskarnes lynne" (The
Swedish Character). Now, Vogt declared, his own Norwegian countrymen
would do well to follow the Swedish example in reasserting their unique
cultural heritage.[20] The surging "national life" of which he wrote was the
final creative flowering of Swedish National Romanticism.

National Romanticism came to distill what, both for Swedes and for
outsiders, today seems the very essence of *svenskhet*. Indeed, one may
wonder to what extent Swedish National Romanticism ever really faded
away. To be sure, its creative phase is long past. No one today writes poetry
like Heidenstam's or Karlfeldt's, or novels like Lagerlöf's, or paints like
Carl Larsson or Prince Eugen. Yet what would Swedish culture be even
now without Skansen's venerable and lovingly preserved farm buildings,
folk dancers and Dalarna fiddlers in folk dress, the Midsummer pole, and
Christmas cards by Jenny Nyström and Aina Stenborg?

It was moreover during the period after 1905 that Swedish National Romanticism may be said to have become truly national, as the political
system took the last crucial steps toward democracy under the pressures
of the times. In 1907 the Riksdag passed a broad suffrage reform that went
into effect two years later, in 1909, as seen. Full parliamentarianism, with
the cabinet responsible to the legislature, became firmly established by
1917. Universal manhood suffrage came in 1919, followed in 1921 by voting
rights for women. As a result of these reforms the Social Democrats soon
emerged as the largest political party, with representation in the cabinet
by 1917, and in 1920 they formed their own first government with Hjalmar
Branting as premier. A series of welfare reforms, already largely initiated
earlier by the progressive Liberals, meanwhile provided greater security
for the working classes.[21]

With full democratic participation in national affairs, industrial workers—like rural farmers before them—could join wholeheartedly in a National Romantic culture that previously had seemed suspect as an essentially upper-class preserve. Commenting in 1895, on the contemporary

idealization of Swedish nature, Axel Danielsson had written ironically in the Social Democratic *Arbetaren*:

> Can a Social Democrat love . . . the wind's "mournful soughing in the dark forest," from which the logger's axe has put the forest nymph and other poetry to flight, love "the starry night," in which an army of exploited proletarians shiver in the cold, and the "summer light," in which they must labor in the sweat of their brow day and night? Can he love all of that? Yes, he can and should love it as the youth loves the maiden of his dreams, whom he first must conquer. . . .[22]

Both progressive liberals and moderate, reformist Social Democrats became increasingly concerned over what seemed a widening cleavage between "two nations" and strove to bridge the gap. In 1907, the Social Democratic leader Hjalmar Branting declared that while his party strove for a social revolution, it intended "by no means to destroy in blind hatred the cultural heritage of past generations," but rather to break the power of the plutocratic elite "to lay the broad material foundation on which may be built for the first time in history a true culture for all.[23] In 1912, the Liberal minister for Ecclesiastical Affairs, Fridtjuv Berg, carried out a broad democratic reform of the school system that cleared the way for the entire population to share in the national cultural heritage.[24]

The folk high schools (*folkhögskolor*) meanwhile played a particularly prominent role in seeking to integrate working-class youth into the national culture. Torsten Fogelqvist, rector of Brunnsvik Folk High School after 1912, saw this as their essential mission as the working class advanced toward political ascendancy. His colleague, Natanael Beskow, founder in 1912 of Birkagården Folk High School in Stockholm, urged that the individual be brought up to feel his solidarity with "our entire people in the past, present, and future."

By the 1920s the Social Democrats were proving their ability to guide the nation's peaceful development. By 1926 Nils Karleby, a leading Social Democratic ideologue, would declare it now more essential to foster national feeling than class consciousness in Sweden's working class. In a celebrated speech two years later, the party's leader, Per Albin Hansson, would set forth in essence the vision of the Swedish *Folkhem*, or "People's Home"—in many ways Ellen Key's earlier ideal of *det goda hemmet*, the "Good Home," writ large. The Social Democrats had, in effect, now successfully appropriated the conservative ideal of *nationell samling*—the patriotic rallying of the nation—and refashioned it on a truly national scale.[25]

It might be seen as a sign of changing times that *Landsorganisationen* (*LO*), the national federation of labor unions, in 1928 moved into and established itself in the architect Ferdinand Boberg's former Carlberg House, a building from 1899 with powerful National Romantic allusions to Sweden's seventeenth-century "Era of Greatness," located on Stockholm's Norra Bantorget—by then popularly known as "Red Square." Swedish workers might continue to march behind the red banner and sing the "Internationale" in the traditional May Day demonstration. But on *Kristi himmelfärdsdag*, Ascension Day, workingmen's choruses in traditional white visored caps could sing in *"Sköna maj"* of the glories of spring. And soon thereafter, at Midsummer, Swedish workers, too, could dance and sing with their children around the flower-clad maypole.

Notes

1. For Sweden's political and economic history during this period, see, for ex., Elis Håstad, *Sveriges historia under 1900-talet* (Stockholm, 1958); Franklin D. Scott, *Sweden: The Nation's History*, 2nd. ed. (Carbondale, Ill., 1988), chapt. 17; Rütger Essén, "Sverige under världskriget och kristiden," in *Svenska folket genom tiderna*, ed. Ewert Wrangel et al., 13 vols. (Malmö, 1938–40), 11:25–52.

2. See esp. Eva Eriksson, *Den moderna stadens födelse, Svensk arkitektur 1890–1920* (Stockholm, 1990), and *Den moderna staden tar form. Arkitektur och debatt 1910–1935* (Stockholm, 2001); [Jan Torsten Ahlstrand et al.,] *Konsten 1890–1915*, Signums svenska konsthistoria (Lund, 2001), esp. 27–55.

3. Elisabet Stavenow-Hidemark, *Villabebyggelse i Sverige 1900–1925* (Stockholm, 1971); *Stockholms förstäder och villasamhällen* (Stockholm, 1911); Gustaf Näsström, *Dalarna som svenskt ideal* (Stockholm, 1937); Carl Malmsten, "Om svensk karaktär inom konstkulturen," in his *Om svensk karaktär inom konstkulturen* (Stockholm, 1916), 19–20, 40.

4. *Svenska allmogehem*, ed. Gustaf Carlsson (Stockholm, 1909), 16. Italics in the original.

5. Eriksson, *Den moderna stadens födelse*, esp. 393–99.

6. Lars Ridderstedt, *100 kyrkor på hundra år. Kyrkfrämjandet och kyrkobyggandet i Stockholms- regionen 1890–1990* (Stockholm, 1993); Edvard Rohde, *Svenska kyrkan omkring sekelskiftet* (Lund, 1937); Hilding Pleijel, *Ungkyrkorörelsen i Sverige. En historisk konturteckning*. Skrifter i teologiska och kyrkliga ämnen, 4 (Lund, 1937); Scott, *Sweden*, 571–72; *Den svenska psalmboken* (Stockholm and Gothenburg, 1931), no. 533. Conversation with Pastor David Holm, Stockholm.

7. *Skansen under hundra år*, ed. Arne Biörnstad (Höganäs, 1991); *Skansens hus och gårdar* (Stockholm, 1980); H. Arnold Barton, "Skansen and the Swedish Americans," *Swedish-American Historical Quarterly* 48 (1997): 164–80; B. Walldén, "Hembygdsrörelsen," in *Svenska folket genom tiderna*, 11:315–34; Josef Rydén, "Hembygden för

framtiden," *Fataburen 1991. 90-talet* (Stockholm, 1991), 223–37; Göran Rosander et al., *Karl-Erik Forsslund: författaren, folkbildaren, hembygdsvårdaren* (Hedemora, 1991); Karl Hedlund, "Den svenska folkhögskolan under nittonhundratalet," in *Svensk folkhögskola under 75 år*, ed. Karl Hedlund (Stockholm, 1943), 156–215.

8. *Swedish Folk Art: All Tradition Is Change*, ed. Barbro Klein and Mats Widbom (New York, 1994); Nils-Arvid Bringéus, *Årets festseder* (Stockholm, 1876); H. Arnold Barton, "Cultural Interplay between Sweden and Swedish America," *Swedish-American Historical Quarterly* 43 (1992): 5–18. Cf. *The Invention of Tradition*, ed. E. J. Hobsbawm and Terrence Ranger, (Cambridge, 1981), esp. Hobsbawm's introduction.

9. *Svenska Turistföreningen 100 år*, Svenska Turistföreningens årsskrift 1986 (Stockholm, 1985).

10. See Herbert Tingsten, *Gud och fosterlandet. Studier i hundra års skolpropaganda*, 2nd. ed. (Stockholm, 1969).

11. See *Svensk filmografi*, ed. Lars Åhlander, vol. 1: *1897–1919* (Stockholm, 1986), and vol. 2: *1920–1929* (Stockholm, 1982).

12. E. N. Tigerstedt, *Svensk litteraturhistoria*, 3rd. ed. (Stockholm, 1967), 473.

13. Zeth Höglund, *Hjalmar Branting och hans livsgärning*, 2 vols. (Stockholm, 1928–29), 2:370; Birgitta Rapp, *Richard Bergh—konstnär och kulturpolitiker 1890–1915* (Stockholm, 1978), 68; *Bjørnstjerne Bjørnsons brevveksling med svenske 1858–61*, ed. Øyvind Anker, Francis Bull, and Örjan Lindberger, 3 vols. (Oslo, 1960–61), 3:257; Rudolf Kjéllen, *Nationell samling. Politiska och etiska fragment* (Stockholm, 1906), esp. 1–18, 28–29.

14. H. Arnold Barton, *A Folk Divided: Homeland Swedes and Swedish Americans, 1840–1940* (Carbondale, Ill., 1994), 265.

15. Eriksson, *Den moderna staden tar form*, 212–25. Cf. Rut Liegren, *Så bodde vi. Arbetarbostaden som typ- och tidsföreteelse* (Stockholm, 1961).

16. Nils Edling, *Det fosterländska hemmet. Egnahemspolitik, småbruk och hemideologi kring sekelskiftet 1900* (Stockholm, 1996); Olle Gellerman, *Staten och jordbruket* (Stockholm, 1958), 55–66; Elisabet Stavenow-Hidemark, "Småbruksrörelsen—idé och verklighet," *Fataburen 1967* (Stockholm, 1967), 65–80; Michael Shephard, "The Romantic, Rural Orientation of the National Society against Emigration," *Swedish Pioneer Historical Quarterly* 21 (1970): 69–83; John Toler, *Per Jönsson Rösiö: The Agrarian Prophet* (Stockholm, 1992); Magnus Bergquist, *En utopi i verkligheten. Kolonirörelsen och det nya samhället* (Gothenburg, 1996); Eriksson, *Den moderna stadens födelse*, 415–17.

17. Inga Lena Ångström-Grandien, *"Tidskrift för konstvetenskap, ett forum för konstforskning," Konsthistorisk Tidskrift* 70 (2001): 77.

18. See, for ex., George Dangerfield, *The Strange Death of Liberal England* (New York, 1935); Barbara Tuchman, *The Proud Tower* (New York, 1966).

19. Cf. Paul Fussell, *The Great War and Modern Memory* (New York, 1975); Robert Wohl, *The Generation of 1914* (Cambridge, Mass., 1979).

20. Nils Collett Vogt, "Svenskerne og vi," in his *Levende og døde. Smaa portrætter og skildringer* (Kristiania, 1922), 188–89. Cf. *Verner von Heidenstams samlade verk*, ed. Kate Bang and Fredrik Böök, 23 vols. (Stockholm, 1943–44), 9:10–30.

21. For the role of the Liberals in the early political and social welfare reforms, see esp. *Liberala pionjärer,* ed. Håkan Holmgren (Uppsala, 2002).

22. See, for ex., Staffan Björck, *Heidenstam och sekelskiftets Sverige* (Stockholm, 1946), 34–37, esp. 35 (quote).

23. Jan Larsson, *Hemmet vi ärvde. Om folkhemmet, identiteten och den gemensamma framtiden* (Stockholm, 1994), 89.

24. See Gunnar Richardson, "Fridtjuv Berg och den gemensamma skolan," in Holmberg, *Liberala pionjärer,* 97–109.

25. Larsson, *Hemmet vi ärvde,* 72, 76, 90–93, 108, 110–11. Cf. Ronny Ambjörnsson, "En skön ny värld. Ellen Keys visioner och en senare tids verklighet," *Fatuburen 1991. 90tal,* 260–78.

From Warfare to Welfare State:
Sweden's Search for a New Identity

It is often said that national feeling in Sweden is relatively weak, compared with that of its Nordic neighbors, Norway, Finland, Iceland, and even Denmark. The Russian-born Uppsala historian Alexander Kan has made this point by comparing the exuberant celebration of national holidays in Norway and Finland with the "practically inconspicuous" observance of such holidays in Sweden and Denmark.[1] This evident lack of patriotic fervor did not fail to arouse much indignant criticism in Sweden, particularly during the years around 1900, when the nation faced what seemed serious threats from emigration, from the conflict with Norway over its status within the Dual Monarchy, and from the internationalist Social Democratic and labor movements.

The poet Verner von Heidenstam deplored in 1896 his countrymen's excessive modesty in admiring all things foreign while attaching little value to what was their own. Swedish literature, he complained, was filled with self-criticism, which was always warmly received. Such self-doubt, appealing as it may appear, was to Heidenstam a sure sign of decline. According to Gustaf Sundbärg in 1911, nationalism, the great intellectual current of the nineteenth century, had passed Sweden by, just as Italy had been bypassed by the great sixteenth-century Reformation. Idealism in Sweden was characteristically cosmopolitan, he held, rather than national in orientation, so that there one need be no more idealistic than to become a *vegetarian*—to forget that one had a fatherland. In contrast,

Norway's history, as compared with Sweden's during the nineteenth century, is the history of a people filled with the most powerful national spirit, in contrast to a people lacking in any national instinct. . . . Herein lies the most important explanation for Norway's strength and for Sweden's weakness.

Sundbärg recalls Bjørnstjerne Bjørnson's observation in 1898 that the Swedes were an old people who doubted, while the Norwegians were a young people who believed. Even across the Atlantic in America, the Swedish visitor Paul Peter Waldenström noted wearily in 1902 that the Norwegians there were more Norwegian than the Swedes were Swedish. Similar complaints are not hard to find.[2]

It has been held that both the Swedes' and the Danes' lack of conspicuous patriotism derived from their long histories as established nations, with their own institutions, cultures, and languages. The Swedes could look back on a still not too distant past in the seventeenth century, when their country had been a great European military and imperial power. They could, that is, take for granted what the inhabitants of the newer Nordic nations, Norway and Finland, were still striving valiantly to create.

Moreover, Sweden has had the rare good fortune to remain at peace for nearly two hundred years, since 1814, whereas Norway, Denmark, and Finland during the same period have had to fight hard battles to preserve their territory and indeed their very independence. This factor can hardly be stressed too strongly.

After the end of the Napoleonic wars, Sweden was no longer confronted with any imminent threat to its security. In 1812, when Napoleon invaded Russia, Crown Prince Carl Johan—the former Napoleonic marshal Jean-Baptiste Bernadotte—concluded an alliance against France with Emperor Alexander I, through which Sweden renounced any future claims to Finland, which the Russians had conquered shortly before. In return Russia committed itself to helping Sweden acquire Norway from Denmark in compensation. By late 1814, after a brief attempt to establish its complete independence, Norway joined Sweden in a dynastic union as a self-governing kingdom. The menace from the East was eliminated at last, and the crown prince, who became King Carl XIV Johan in 1818, could henceforward rely on steadfast Russian backing.

The question has been much debated whether Carl Johan's "deal" with Alexander I in 1812 was intended already at the time to initiate a consistent policy of neutrality for Sweden or whether it was simply an opportunistic maneuver to profit from the immediate circumstances of the time.[3] With benefit of hindsight, it is nonetheless evident that Sweden has indeed succeeded in remaining neutral down to the present.

Sweden stands in contrast to both Finland and Norway, which despite themselves were transformed during the Napoleonic wars from parts of the centralized Swedish and Danish monarchies into new national entities, albeit in union with stronger neighboring powers, Russia and Sweden. The challenge for the Finns and Norwegians was to construct new nations where they had not existed before—in Norway's case at least not since the later Middle Ages. Both sought energetically throughout the nineteenth century and beyond to create new national institutions and distinctive cultural identities, backed by growing national feeling. Remote and thinly populated Iceland likewise strove toward greater political and cultural autonomy.

The case of Denmark was somewhat different. While it was an old, established kingdom, it faced a growing German threat on its southern border, which led to war in 1864 and the loss of Slesvig-Holstein. Hence national sentiment was strong there as well.[4]

Still, there was a deeper-lying reason for the apparent lack of national sentiment in Sweden: a fundamental conflict of views over what ought to be its proper focus.

Sweden from the end of the sixteenth century had been a great military power that dominated the Baltic region. But this "Era of Greatness" ("*Storhetstiden*") had ended in 1709 with Peter the Great's victory over Carl XII's Swedish army at Poltava. At the Peace of Nystad (Uusikaupunki) in 1721, Sweden lost its possessions in the eastern Baltic, except for most of Finland.

Throughout the eighteenth century views were thereafter divided in Sweden between those who were prepared to accept Sweden's more modest position in the European arena and cultivate good relations with Russia, the old archenemy, and those who sought revenge and the reconquest of lost territories. On two occasions, in 1743 and 1788, Sweden declared war on Russia in vain attempts to reestablish its great-power status.[5]

Then in 1809—a century after Poltava—Sweden was compelled to cede Finland to Russia, as seen above. The loss was a bitter one. The territories surrendered in 1721 had been relatively recent Swedish conquests. But Finland was an integral part of the Swedish kingdom for over six centuries, since the Middle Ages. It included a third of Sweden's territory and a quarter of its population. There were—and are still—innumerable ties across the Gulf of Bothnia. The Swedes now faced the same painful problem of adjustment as they had after 1721, in even harsher terms.

Again, reactions varied, even within the same individual. A notable example would be the poet Esaias Tegnér, whose poem "Svea" in 1811 breathed hatred for the barbarous Muscovites. But in revised form the following year, the poem resignedly appealed to his countrymen, "Weep, Svea, for what you have lost; but protect what you have. . . . within Sweden's borders win Finland once again."[6] Many Swedes, meanwhile, did not consider union with a self-governing Norway an adequate compensation for Finland.[7]

There were thus *two* competing forms of nationalism in Sweden throughout the nineteenth century, and even beyond. On the one hand, there was the old patriotism, staunchly monarchist, conservative, even reactionary, with its fond memories of Sweden's "*fornstora dar*" (past days of greatness) and its nostalgic dreams of—somehow, someday—regaining past imperial grandeur. This attitude surfaced at various points. It aroused powerful sentiments for revenge against Russia and the reconquest of Finland in alliance with Great Britain and France during the Crimean War of 1854–56. King Oscar I was on the verge of entering the conflict—just as it ended. It flared up again briefly during the second Polish uprising against Russian overlordship in 1863.[8] It was periodically riled by what it considered impudent demands by the Norwegians within the union, together with their unwillingness to bear what the Swedes considered a rightful share of the burden of their common defense.

The old militant patriotism is well symbolized by the fading battle flags hanging above the tombs of the great warrior kings in Stockholm's Riddarholm church and the portraits of grim martial ancestors in old manorial halls. It is even recognizable in formal Swedish social behavior, which unmistakably recalls a militarized society that long endured after Sweden ceased to be a great power.

The older Swedish patriotism was parodied in Henrik Ibsen's *Peer Gynt* by the aristocratic "Trompeterstråle," who at times in act 2 mutters about Swedish valor on battlegrounds of yore. In an expression widely used by their liberal opponents, both Norwegian and Swedish, Bjørnstjerne Bjørnson described those who cherished outworn dreams of Sweden's past imperial grandeur as "*stor-svensker*," or "Great-Swedes," and ridiculed them for brandishing "Carl XII's hat."[9]

The new "*fosterlandskärlek*," or love of native land, was pacifistic, tolerant, accepting of Sweden's new small-power role in Europe, idealistically pan-Scandinavianist in relation to its Nordic neighbors, sympathetic toward Norway—from which it drew great inspiration both politically and culturally—and supportive of the Norwegians' aspirations within the union. Its broader Scandinavian vision it shared with Bjørnson, who considered it an even higher ideal than state nationalism—provided there were full equality between the Nordic nations.[10] The new nationalism drew far less upon history than upon the quiet beauties of the Swedish landscape and Sweden's ancient folk culture.[11]

The new national sentiment gained ground—but only slowly. Nonetheless, the middle 1890s saw a resurgence of the old, traditional patriotism. Times were good, trade and industry were rapidly expanding, emigration was at a low level, at least for the time being, there was much new building in Stockholm's more fashionable quarters, and the Norwegians were forced to beat a humiliating retreat when they attempted to establish an independent consular service. The high point of this triumphant national wave was the Stockholm Industrial Exhibition of 1897, celebrating the twenty-fifth year of King Oscar II's reign.

The year before, Verner von Heidenstam brought out his celebrated essay "Om svenskarnes lynne" (On the Swedish Character), cited earlier, calling for a more robust assertion of national pride. This appeal was followed in 1897–98 by his two-part epic novel *Karolinerna*, which vividly describes the heroism and sufferings of Carl XII's armies in facing their many foes in the Great Northern War and thereby winning immortality in tragedy. These works, taken together, were a moving appeal for the traditional values of stoic devotion to duty and to the crown, to valor, discipline, loyal obedience to authority, and contentment in frugal circumstances. Largely in response, an enthusiastic cult of Carl XII reached its height within Swedish conservative circles, fittingly symbolized by the king's heroic statue at the foot of Stockholm's Kungsträdgården, pointing with brazen, gauntleted hand eastward, toward Russia.[12]

Heidenstam's appeal aroused fears within the intellectual Left of a new upsurge of chauvinistic nationalism, which led to a now largely forgotten debate with Ellen Key, the seeress of the Swedish liberals, that sets in striking relief the differences between the old and new nationalisms. "Sverige för svenskarna" (Sweden for the Swedes), Ellen Key wrote in 1897, was the new patriotic slogan that combined the currents of militarism, obscurantism, protectionism, and growing anti-Semitism. Key took Heidenstam to task for seeking inspiration for a national spirit in Sweden's past greatness rather than in its future promise. The essential thing, she held, was simply to *be* Swedish, rather than consciously to adopt certain prescribed attitudes. For her, true Swedish national sentiment was "the deep, shy, taciturn, modest love of [our] homeland, the earth-bound feeling for our own forest-scented home place, which—like any great love—is a passionate stillness, a humble pride, an aching bliss." By overvaluing oneself one became neither a good patriot nor a good citizen of the world.

The aristocratic Heidenstam looked to the upper-class, cosmopolitan elite for the nation's natural leadership. Ellen Key reminded him that the Swedish nation did not reside only at Stockholm's more fashionable addresses and in noble manor houses, and argued that the country's greatest weakness lay in the gap between its social classes. The true Swedish character, she held, was to be found among the common folk. From their midst, within a generation or two, the new cultivated party of the Left would emerge from red-painted cottages and attic rooms to lead Sweden into a better future. Heidenstam replied the following year, defending his view that effective national leadership could come only from above. There followed a lively debate on the nature of true love of fatherland, with contributions from a number of leading cultural personalities.[13]

The real test of strength between the two nationalisms arose over the growing conflict with Norway around the turn of the century, during which the liberals strongly supported the Norwegians' demands for full equality within the union while the conservatives staunchly upheld Sweden's primacy. During the tense early 1890s, Swedish liberals avidly petitioned their government to make concessions and warned it against attempting to use force against Norway. Hjalmar Branting, leader of the fledgling Social Democratic movement, went so far as to suggest darkly that perhaps someone from the broader masses might take judgment into his own hands and with a well-placed bullet at home prevent a fratricidal war, for which he was tried for incitement to violence. The liberal *Riksdag* member and historian Hans Forssell warned in the newspaper *Svenska dagbladet* in September 1895 that while the tactics of the Great-Swedes united Norway, they divided Sweden, since their true aim was Norway's subjugation.[14]

On the opposite side, the conservative historian and chancellor of Uppsala University Oscar Alin asked rhetorically in 1896 whether it was consistent with Sweden's honor that it simply relinquish what it had won through bloody sacrifice and in return for the loss of valuable provinces (i.e., Finland). In an article in the conservative *Göteborgs Aftonblad* in 1899, the political scientist Rudolf Kjellén saw in the conflict with Norway nothing less than the test of Sweden's moral fiber and willpower.[15]

The climax was reached when the Norwegian *Storting*, or parliament, unilaterally renounced the union in June 1905. Conservative ultranationalists in Sweden clamored for war to avenge the slight and put the impudent Norwegians in their place. The great majority of Swedes keenly resented what they saw as a serious affront to the aging and popular Oscar II. But it soon became evident that neither the monarch nor the majority of his Swedish subjects were prepared to use force to preserve the existing union. While there were numerous expressions of loyalty to the crown, widely circulated petitions and large demonstrations strongly opposed any resort to war. The entire liberal intellectual establishment rallied in support of peace and accommodation. The liberal leader Adolf Hedin—not to be confused with the archconservative *Sven* Hedin—appealed to the labor movement, going so far as to urge that its members refuse induction if called out to fight against their Norwegian brothers. In the end, a negotiated compromise settlement was reached with Norway, recognizing its complete independence.[16]

The dissolution of the Swedish-Norwegian union in 1905 appears to have been the decisive turning point in the emergence of the new Swedish nationalism. The older, militant patriotism did not, however, die out altogether. During World War I influential "activist" circles sought to ally Sweden with Germany against the old Russian archenemy, and Swedes eagerly volunteered to serve with the White forces in Finland during the civil war there in 1918. Swedes again served as volunteers in Finland's Winter War of 1939–40 against the Soviet Union under the slogan "Finland's cause is ours."

Still, looking back, Gustaf Sundbärg got to the heart of the matter when he wrote in 1911:

> National feeling in its true meaning, the dominating idea of our era, has been connected to all of the upward social movements of the time. Our Swedish patriotism—a phantom from the seventeenth century—has managed almost exclusively to look backward; it has not succeeded in arousing any enthusiasm for the ideas and challenges of our own times. . . . Thus Sweden is one of the few countries in which the liberal party has not been the patriotic party—which otherwise has been the rule throughout the world.[17]

With the end of the union with Norway in 1905, the last, tattered remnant of the time-worn Swedish imperial dream receded into the past. By then most Swedes were surely relieved to see it go. Once again, it was a matter of gaining within what had been lost without, as Esaias Tegnér had expressed it in similarly troubled times in 1812 and as Oscar II himself reiterated in 1905. Gerda, wife of the painter Richard Bergh, wrote to a Norwegian friend already in July 1905 that the dissolution of the union was a tremendous breakthrough for Sweden. In it she saw the dawning of a new day when her homeland could vigorously devote itself to its own internal development. A new and vital national spirit was now apparent throughout the land, as Verner von Heidenstam enthusiastically wrote to Bjørnstjerne Bjørnson two years later.[18]

Sweden turned with renewed energy to its own internal affairs. The feeling was in the air that a new, peaceful "Era of Greatness" was at hand, this time based on progress in science, industry, and the arts. With the end of the union with Norway, a lingering sentimental Scandinavianism gave way at last to a purely *Swedish* sense of nationality over the following decades.[19]

The new national identity, moreover, now became ever more inclusive. The old nationalism had identified the monarch, the aristocracy, the military, the bureaucracy, and the church as the Swedish state. The newer liberal national sentiment, beginning already by the later eighteenth century, had seen the propertied middle classes, including ever more prominently the land-owning peasantry, as the bone and sinew of the nation. The creative National Romanticism around the turn of the last century in particular idealized Sweden's ancient peasant culture.

This development, however, was regarded with deep skepticism by Sweden's new and growing industrial working class, which was then mobilizing under the labor and Social Democratic movements. They tended to brand it as a "bourgeois nationalist" smoke screen to distract from the nation's growing social ills. What could the long summer twilight or colorful Midsummer festivities mean to the oppressed laborer? The great General Strike in 1909 revealed an alarming rift between social classes.

Both progressive liberals and moderate reformist Social Democrats were concerned over the widening gap. In 1907, the Social Democratic leader Hjalmar Branting declared that while his movement strove to bring about a social revolution, this was in no way intended to destroy the cultural heritage of past generations. Rather, it was to clear the way for a society in which, for the first time in history, that heritage might be shared by all. This was the ideal held forth in his successor Per Albin Hansson's celebrated speech in 1928, in which he launched the concept of *Folkhemmet*—the People's Home—in which *all* might rightfully share in Sweden's bounty, both material and cultural. This ideal remains the basis of his party's program to the present day. The nation's cultural heritage at last became truly *national* in scope.[20]

Sweden's vital development after 1905 could not fail to impress foreign observers. Already in 1922, the Norwegian poet Nils Collett Vogt, who had a Swedish wife and spent much time in Sweden, wrote that in Sweden a new national life had blossomed forth since 1905 and wondered if the same could be said for Norway. A ninety-year period of weakness had passed, and now, with awakened national instincts, Sweden went forth to meet its future. The enthusiasm for the Swedish "People's Home" aroused by Marquis Childs's celebrated *Sweden, the Middle Way* after 1936 in the United States and beyond, is well known. Swedes nowadays indeed often like to refer affectionately to their country as *"lagomlandet"*—in essence, "The Land of the Middle Way."[21]

By now, as we enter the twenty-first century, the old nationalism is long dead and is indeed distasteful to most present-day Swedes. The transformation has led to a strangely ambivalent attitude toward the nation's past. The Finnish historian Max Engman maintained in 1994 that "it has been said that Swedish historical consciousness consists of having no historical consciousness, at least not a national historical one. Swedes see Sweden as a democratic, peace-loving, internationally inclined society. With such a self-image it is difficult to accept a past that includes an empire and one of the most efficient war machines in European history."[22] Compared with the other Nordic lands, for instance, history appears to be relatively neglected in school curricula and on bookstore shelves, in favor of current social studies. For peoples who have in more recent times had to fight to achieve or defend their independent nationhood, history is an indispensable part of their national identity.

Divided views over the true nature of the national identity and destiny were, of course, not unique to Sweden. In Norway there was hot debate over the question of whether the peasantry alone were "true" Norwegians, excluding the old merchant and official classes, which were originally of largely foreign origin. In Finland, there was dissension over the place of the Swedish-speaking element of the population. Yet faced with the challenges of nation building under the constraints of political unions with more powerful neighbors, both Norway and Finland naturally developed more demonstrative forms of nationalism than did Sweden.

Swedes are still not much inclined to boast to foreigners about their homeland. Indeed they are often at pains to point out to them that life in Sweden is not always as ideal as they may imagine. Heidenstam and his fellow social critics from around the turn of the last century would once again sadly shake their heads at such behavior. But among themselves, their deep, abiding love of Sweden's varied landscape and constant fascination with their own rich cultural heritage is unmistakable. One need only delve into such impressive publications as *Svenska turistföreningens årskrift*, *Kulturens värld*, or *Månadsjournalen* to be altogether convinced.

But there is more to it than that. What Swedish nationalism lacks in historical depth today, it makes up for in a strong sense of Sweden's providential mission in the world, a tradition extending well back in time. In the late seventeenth century, the Uppsala scholar Olof Rudbeck identified Sweden as the mythical lost Atlantis, the wellspring of civilization. The new "Atlantean" vision, as it has emerged during the twentieth century, is of Sweden as the peaceful, reasonable, and humane model for the ideal world of the future.[23] It is a vision that has a kind of imperial grandeur of its own. Be not deceived. However modest it may appear on the surface, self-confident Swedish national pride runs deep.

Old and new in Johanneshov. A lovingly preserved eighteenth- or early-nineteenth-century house located against a backdrop of high-rise apartment buildings from the 1950s in a Stockholm suburb. (Photograph by the author, 2007.)

Notes

1. Alexander Kan, "Scandinavian Conceptions of National History—A Model for Soviet Historians?" in *Conceptions of National History*, ed. Erik Lönnroth, Karl Molin, and Ragnar Björk (Berlin and New York, 1994), 214–25. See also Max Engman, "Commentary," ibid., 246.

2. Verner von Heidenstam, "Om svenskarnes lynne," in *Verner von Heidenstams samlade verk*, ed. Fredrik Böök and Kate Bang (Stockholm, 1943), 9:10–30; Gustaf Sundbärg, *Det svenska folklynnet*. Emigrationsutredning, Bilaga 16 (Stockholm, 1911), esp. 46, 59; Francis Bull, "Bjørnson og Sverige," in *Bjørnson-Studier*, ed. Gerhard Gran. Smaaskrifter fra det Litteraturhistoriske Seminar (Kristiania, 1911), 255–56; Paul Peter Waldenström, *Nya färder i Amerikas Förenta Stater* (Stockholm, 1902), 50.

3. *Sverige i fred: Statsmannakonst eller opportunism? En antologi om 1812 års politik*, ed. Tapani Suominen (Stockholm, 2002); Stig Ramel, "From Horn to Bernadotte: Sweden's Transformation from a European Great Power to a Nordic Small Power," in *Scandinavians in Old and New Lands*, ed. Philip J. Anderson, Dag Blanck, and Byron J. Nordstrom (Chicago, 2004), 1–16.

4. For excellent surveys of the beginnings of political and cultural nation building in Denmark, Norway, Iceland, and Finland, see Øystein Sørensen, "Det nye Norge i det nye Norden 1814–1850," Max Engman, "Storfurstendömet Finland—nationalstat och imperiedel," Anna Agnirsdóttir, "Iceland 1800–1850, New Beginnings," and Steen Bo Frandsen, "Det nye Norden efter Napoleon," in Max Engman and Åke Sandström, eds., *Det nya Norden efter Napoleon* (Stockholm, 2004), 19–54, 55–78, 79–118, 150–86. The literature on aspects of the subject for each country is of course voluminous.

5. See my "Russia and the Problem of Sweden-Finland," *East European Quarterly* 5 (1972): 431–55; Ramel, "From Horn to Bernadotte."

6. Esaias Tegnér, *Samlade skrifter*, Ny kritisk upplaga, ed. Ewert Wrangel and Fredrik Böök (Stockholm, 1919), 2:77.

7. See my *Sweden and Visions of Norway: Politics and Culture, 1814–1905* (Carbondale, Ill., 2003), 18, 28.

8. See my "Scandinavianism, Fennomania, and the Crimean War," in this volume.

9. Bull, "Bjørnson og Sverige," 185, 255–56; Bjørnstjerne Bjørnson, *Brevveksling med svenske 1858–1909*, ed. Øyvind Anker, Francis Bull, and Örjan Lindberger. 3 vols. (Oslo, 1961), 3:6.

10. Bjørnstjerne Bjørnson, *Artikler og Taler*, ed. C. Collin and H. Eitrem, 2 vols. (Kristiania and København, 1913), 2:400–401; Bull, "Bjørnson og Sverige," 266.

11. See my *Sweden and Visions*, chapt. 5.

12. Heidenstam, *Samlade verk*, 9: 10–39. Cf. Heidenstam's *Karolinerna* (Stockholm, 1897; in English, *The Charles Men*, New York, 1920.) Cf. Magnus Rodell, *Att gjuta en nation: Statyinvigningar och nationsformering i Sverige vid 1800-talets mitt* (Stockholm, 2002), esp. chapt. 4.

13. Heidenstam, "Om patriotism," "Inbillningens logik," and "Om det nationella," in *Samlade verk*, 9:22–31, 39–60, 102–11; Ellen Key, "Om patriotismen. Öppet bref till min vän Verner von Heidenstam," in her *Tankebilder*, 2 (Stockholm, 1898), esp. 3–6, 11,

18–19, 27–36. Much of this debate, together with other contributions to it, is included in the anthology *Svenska krusbär: En historiebok om Sverige och svenskarna*, ed. Björn Linnell and Mikael Löfgren (Stockholm, 1996). The above discussion is based largely on my *Sweden and Visions*, 152–58.

14. See my *Sweden and Visions*, 75–77.

15. Nils Elvander, *Harald Hjärne och konservatismen: Konservativ idédebatt i Sverige 1865–1922* (Stockholm, 1961), 200.

16. My *Sweden and Visions*, 79–83.

17. Sundbärg, *Svenska folklynnet*, 29.

18. Rapp, *Richard Bergh*, 68; Bjørnson, *Brevveksling med svenske*, 3:257.

19. See, for ex., Rudolf Kjellén, "Den konservativa åskådningen i svensk politik," in his *Nationell samling* (Stockholm, 1906), 28–29; Lennart Limberg, "Almost a Century of Work: Preserving Swedishness Outside of Sweden," in *Scandinavians in Old and New Lands*, 125–58, esp. 126–27; Ruth Hemstad, "Fra 'Indian Summer' til 'nordisk vinter'—nordisk samarbeid og 1905," in *Goda grannar eller morska motståndare? Sverige och Norge från 1814 till idag*, ed. Torbjörn Nilsson and Øystein Sørensen (Stockholm, 2005), 11–27.

20. My "The Silver Age of Swedish National Romanticism, 1905–1920," in this volume; Jan Larsson, *Hemmet vi ärvde: Om folkhemmet, identiteten och den gemensamma framtiden* (Stockholm, 1994).

21. Nils Collett Vogt, "Svenskerne og vi," in his *Levende og døde. Smaa portrætter og skildringer* (Kristiania, 1922), 188; my "The New Deal and the People's Home," in *Migration och mångfald: Essäer om kulturkontakt och minoritetsfrågor tillägnade Harald Runblom* (Uppsala, 1999), 201–17.

22. Kan, in *Conceptions*, 246; cf. Erik Lönnroth in ibid., 3.

23. Olof Rudbeck, *Atland eller Manheim*. 3 vols. (Uppsala, 1679–1702); cf. Ramel, "From Horn to Bernadotte," 14–15.

Acknowledgments

Writings by H. Arnold Barton on Scandinavian History

Index

Acknowledgments

The author wishes to express his thanks to the publications in which the essays in this volume first appeared for permission to reprint copyrighted material, as follows:

Eighteenth-Century Studies

"Gustaf III of Sweden and the Enlightenment," *Eighteenth-Century Studies* 6 (1972): 1–34.

Scandinavian Studies

"The Swedish Succession Crises of 1809 and 1810, and the Question of Scandinavian Union," *Scandinavian Studies* 42 (1970): 309–33.

"Late Gustavian Autocracy in Sweden: Gustaf IV Adolf and His Opponents, 1792–1809," *Scandinavian Studies* 46 (1974): 265–84.

"The Silver Age of Swedish National Romanticism, 1905–1920," *Scandinavian Studies* 74 (2002): 505–20.

"The Swedes and Their Eighteenth Century." *Scandinavian Studies* 76 (2004): 33–46.

"From Welfare to Warfare State: Sweden's Search for a New Identity." *Scandinavian Studies* 77 (2005): 315–26.

"The Discovery of Norway Abroad, 1760–1905." *Scandinavian Studies* 79 (2007): 25–40.

Taylor & Francis (UK) Journals (http://www.tandf.co.uk/journals)

"Gustaf III of Sweden and the East Baltic, 1771–1792," *Journal of Baltic Studies* 7 (1976): 13–30.

"The Danish Agrarian Reforms, 1784–1814, and the Historians." *Scandinavian Economic History Review* 36 (1988): 46–61.

"Scandinavianism, Fennomania, and the Crimean War," *Journal of Baltic Studies* 36 (2005): 131–56.

"Finland and Norway, 1808–1917: A Comparative Perspective." *Scandinavian Journal of History* 31 (2006): 221–36.

William & Mary Quarterly

"Sweden and the War of American Independence," *William & Mary Quarterly,* 3rd Series, 23 (1966): 408–430.

The following essay is copyrighted by the author:

"Gustaf III of Sweden and the French Revolution," *Personhistorisk tidskrift* [Uppsala, Sweden] 89 (1993): 81–101.

Writings by H. Arnold Barton
on Scandinavian History

Books

Count Hans Axel von Fersen: Aristocrat in an Age of Revolution. Boston: Twayne
Publishers, 1975. Pp. 530.

Canton vid Drottningholm. Ett mönstersamhälle för manufakturer från 1700-talet.
[Canton at Drottningholm: A Model Community for Manufactures from the
Eighteenth Century.] Stockholm: Bokförlaget Arena, 1985. Pp. 61.

Scandinavia in the Revolutionary Era, 1760–1815. Minneapolis: University of Min-
nesota Press, 1986. Pp. 447.

A Folk Divided: Homeland Swedes and Swedish Americans. Carbondale: Southern
Illinois University Press, 1994, and Uppsala [Sweden]: Studia Multiethnica Up-
saliensia, vol. 10, 1994. Pp. 448.

Northern Arcadia: Foreign Travelers in Scandinavia, 1765–1815. Carbondale: Southern
Illinois University Press, 1998. Pp. 224.

Sweden and Visions of Norway: Politics and Culture, 1814–1905. Carbondale: Southern
Illinois University Press, 2003. Pp. 227.

Articles and Essays

"Sweden and the War of American Independence," *William & Mary Quarterly,* 3rd
Series, 23 (1966): 408–30.

"The Swedish Succession Crises of 1809 and 1810, and the Question of Scandinavian
Union, *Scandinavian Studies* 42 (1970): 309–33.

"Russia and the Problem of Sweden-Finland, 1721–1809," *East European Quarterly* 5
(1972): 431–55.

"Gustav III of Sweden and the Enlightenment," *Eighteenth-Century Studies* 6 (1972):
1–34.

"Late Gustavian Autocracy in Sweden: Gustav IV Adolf and His Opponents, 1792–
1809," *Scandinavian Studies* 46 (1974): 265–84.

"Gustav III of Sweden and the East Baltic, 1771–1792," *Journal of Baltic Studies* 7
(1976): 13–30.

"Popular Education in Eighteenth-Century Sweden: Theory and Practice," in *Aspects of Education in the 18th Century, Studies in Voltaire and the Eighteenth
Century,* ed., James A. Leith, 167 (Oxford, 1977): 523–41.

"Canton at Drottningholm: A Model Manufacturing Community from the Mid-Eighteenth Century," *Scandinavian Studies* 49 (1977): 81–98.

"Scandinavia and the Atlantic Revolution," in Warren F. Spencer, ed., *The Consortium on Revolutionary Europe: Proceedings, 1982* (Athens, Georgia, 1983), 145–58.

"Canton vid Drottningholm på 1700-talets mitt" [Canton at Drottningholm in the Middle of the Eighteenth Century], in , *Brommaboken 1984 Bromma hembygdsförenings årskrift 55*, ed. Edward Bolin, (Bromma, Sweden 1984): 4–19.

"The Danish Agrarian Reforms, 1784–1814, and the Historians," *Scandinavian Economic History Review*, 36 (1988): 46–61.

"Gustav III of Sweden and the French Revolution," *Personhistorisk tidskrift* [Uppsala, Sweden] 89 (1993): 81–101.

"Uppkomsten av manufakturerna i Canton vid Drottningholm" [The Origins of the Manufactures in Canton at Drottningholm], in *Samfundet S:t Eriks Årsbok 1994: Yppighet och armod i 1700-talets Stockholm* (Stockholm, 1994), 42–54.

"*Iter Scandinavicum*: Foreign Travelers' Views of the Late Eighteenth-Century North," *Scandinavian Studies* 68 (1996): 1–18.

"The Further Reaches of the Baltic: Foreign Travelers' Impressions, 1760–1815," in *Mare Nostrum—Mare Balticum. Commentationes in Honorem Professoris Matti Klinge* (Helsinki: Raud, 2001), 211–36.

"Peter August Gödecke, den svenska folkhögskolan och Norge" [Peter August Gödecke, the Swedish Folk High School, and Norway], *Personhistorisk tidskrift* 98 (2002): 5–20.

"Kanton," in *De kungliga svenska slotten. Kina,* ed. Göran Alm (Stockholm: Byggförlaget, 2002), 306–27.

"The Silver Age of Swedish National Romanticism, 1905–1920," *Scandinavian Studies* 74 (2002): 505–20.

"Norska strömningar i Sverige. Politik och kultur 1814–1905" [Norwegian Currents in Sweden: Politics and Culture, 1814–1905], Kungl. Humanistiska Vetenskaps-Samfundet i Uppsala, *Årsbok 2001* (Uppsala, 2003), 5–20.

"The Swedes and Their Eighteenth Century," *Scandinavian Studies* 76 (2004): 33–46.

"Scandinavianism, Fennomania, and the Crimean War," *Journal of Baltic Studies* 36 (2005): 131–56.

"From Warfare to Welfare State: Sweden's Search for a New Identity." *Scandinavian Studies* 77 (2005): 315–26.

"The Discovery of Norway Abroad." *Scandinavian Studies* 79 (2006): 25–40.

My writings on Swedish-American history are listed in "Writings by H. Arnold Barton on Swedish-American History and Culture," in my book *The Old Country and the New: Essays on Swedes and America* (Carbondale: Southern Illinois University Press, 2007).

Index

Lesczynski, Stanislaus (king of Poland), 70
Levertin, Oscar, 7, 8, 10, 243
Lidner, Bengt, 63
Lie, Jonas, 218, 220
Liljencrantz, Johan, 25
Lilljehorn, Pehr Ulrik, 55
Lindgren, Armas, 219
Linné, Carl von (Linnæus), 5, 19
literature, foreign, 27, 227–37, 250
Livonia. *See* Baltic Provinces
Locke, John, 14, 15, 32, 35, 120
Løgstrup, Birgit, 201
London, 60, 138
Lönnrot, Elias, 170, 171, 216, 217
Louis XIV (king of France), 3, 14, 22, 37
Louis XVI (king of France), 24, 33, 38, 94, 96–98, 101–2, 104, 106, 110
Louise Augusta, Duchess, 145
Lovisa (Loviisa), 174, 186n35
Lovisa Ulrika (queen of Sweden), 5, 8, 14, 15, 25, 27, 31, 32
Löwenhielm, Count Carl, 140, 141, 156n23
Lucchesini, Marquis Jerome, 78–79
Lund, H. V., 195, 196, 203, 204; Pehr af, 50, 62
Lund, Sweden, 6, 165, 166, 172
Lysaker Circle, 235–36

Mably, Gabriel Bonnet de, Abbé de, 19, 24, 32
Maclean, Baron Rutger, 129
Maistre, Joseph de, 29
Mallet, Paul Henri, 19, 229
Mallet du Pan, Jacques, 79
Malmsten, Carl, 244
Malmström, Carl Gustaf, 7
Malthus, Thomas, 229, 236
Månsson, Fabian, 243
Marie Antoinette (queen of France), 6, 31, 54, 95, 99
Marie Louise (empress of the French), 147
Marmontel, Jean François, 17, 18, 23, 26, 37, 58

Marstrand, 50, 60
Marx, Karl, and Marxism, 195, 196, 199, 201, 203–4
Masreliez, Louis, 4
Maupeou, René Nicolas de, 20, 23, 24
Mechelin, Leo, 218
Melin, Gustaf Henrik, 166
Mendelsohn, Moses, 25
Mesmerism, 29
Metternich, Prince Klemens, 165
Mill, John Stuart, 195
Mirabeau, Honoré Gabriel de Riquetti, Conte de, 18, 23, 25, 26, 29
Miranda, Francisco de, 30, 229
modernism, 243, 247
Moe, Jørgen, 216
Molin, Adrian, 244
Moltke, Count Frederik, 148–49
Montesquieu, Charles de Secondat, Baron de, 16, 17, 19, 20, 22, 32, 37, 38, 92, 120, 138, 227, 229
Montgomery-Silfverstolpe, Malla, 100
Montmorency, Count Mathieu de, 124
Morellet, André, Abbé, 18
Mörner, Count A. G., 123
Moss, Convention of (1814), 210
Mounier, J. J., 120
Mozart, Wolfgand Amadeus, 4
Munch: Edvard, 235; Peter Andreas, 178, 215, 220
Munthe: Gerhard, 219, 235; Holm, 219

Nansen, Fridtjof, 230, 235
Napoleon I (Bonaparte, emperor of the French), 118, 130, 136, 139, 141–43, 146–48, 150–51, 154, 164, 209, 257. *See also* Wars, Revolutionary and Napoleonic
Napoleon III (emperor of the French), 172, 180, 181, 183
National Romanticism. *See* Romanticism
National Society against Emigration, Swedish, 248
nature: Norwegian, 230; Swedish, 1, 6–7, 128, 244, 247, 252, 260–61, 265

H. Arnold Barton, professor emeritus of history at Southern Illinois University Carbondale, is one of the nation's foremost scholars of Nordic and Swedish American studies. Among his books are *Letters from the Promised Land: Swedes in America, 1840–1914*; *The Search for Ancestors: A Swedish American Family Saga*; *Northern Arcadia: Foreign Travelers in Scandinavia, 1765–1815*; *A Folk Divided: Homeland Swedes and Swedish Americans, 1840–1940*; and *Sweden and Visions of Norway: Politics and Culture, 1814–1905*. He was named Swedish American of the Year in 1988 by the Royal Swedish Ministry of Foreign Affairs and the Vasa Order of America, received an honorary doctorate from Uppsala University in 1989, and was made a Knight-Commander of the Royal Swedish Order of the Polar Star in 2000 by King Carl XVI Gustaf of Sweden.